UNIX, POSIX, and Open Systems

The Open Standards Puzzle

John S. Quarterman
Texas Internet Consulting

Susanne Wilhelm
Windsound Consulting

 Addison-Wesley Publishing Company

Reading, Massachusetts • Menlo Park, California • New York
Don Mills, Ontario • Wokingham, England • Amsterdam • Bonn
Sydney • Singapore • Tokyo • Madrid • San Juan • Milan • Paris

This book is in the **Addison-Wesley UNIX and Open Systems Series**
Series Editors: Marshall Kirk McKusick and John S. Quarterman

Deborah R. Lafferty: Sponsoring Editor
Thomas Stone: Senior Editor
Patsy DuMoulin: Production Administrator
Denise Descoteaux: Marketing Manager
Roy E. Logan: Senior Manufacturing Manager
Marshall Henrichs: Cover Designer
Jaap Akkerhuis: Troff Macro Designer
Lyn Dupré: Copy Editor

UNIX is a registered trademark of UNIX System Laboratories in the United States and other countries. Many of the designations used by manufacturers and sellers to distinguish their products are claimed as trademarks. Where those designations appear in this book, and Addison-Wesley was aware of a trademark claim, the designations have been printed in initial caps or all caps.

The methods and procedures presented in this book have been included for their instructional value. They have been tested with care, but are not guaranteed for any particular purpose. The publisher does not offer any warranties or representations, nor does it accept any liabilities with respect to the methods or procedures.

Library of Congress Cataloging-in-Publication Data

Quarterman, John S.,
    UNIX, POSIX, and open systems : the open standards puzzle / John
S. Quarterman, Susanne Wilhelm.
        p.   cm
    Includes bibliographical references and index.
    ISBN 0-201-52772-3
    1. UNIX (Computer file)   2. Operating systems (Computers)–
Standards--United States.   I. Wilhelm, Susanne.   II. Title.
QA76.76.O63Q37   1993
005.4'3--dc20   92-19965
                                                              CIP

1 2 3 4 5 6 7 8 9 10–HA–95949392

To the open systems standards community

To my mother Doris S. Wilhelm

Series Foreword

Marshall Kirk McKusick
John S. Quarterman

Addison-Wesley is proud to publish the **UNIX and Open Systems Series.** The primary audience for the Series will be system designers, implementors, administrators, and their managers. The core of the series will consist of books detailing operating systems, standards, networking, and programming languages. The titles will interest specialists in these fields, as well as appeal more broadly to computer scientists and engineers who must deal with open-systems environments in their work. The Series comprises professional reference books and instructional texts.

Open systems allow users to move their applications between systems easily; thus, purchasing decisions can be made on the basis of cost-performance ratio and vendor support, rather than on which systems will run a user's application suite. Decreasing computer hardware prices have facilitated the widespread adoption of capable multiprocess, multiuser operating systems, UNIX being a prime example. Newer operating systems, such as Mach and Chorus, support additional services, such as lightweight processes. The Series illuminates the design and implementation of all such open systems. It teaches readers how to write applications programs to run on these systems, and gives advice on administration and use.

The Series treats as a unified whole the previously distinct fields of networking and operating systems. Networks permit open systems to share hardware and software resources, and allow people to communicate efficiently. The exponential growth of networks such as the Internet and the adoption of protocols such as TCP/IP in industry, government, and academia have made network and system administration critically important to many organizations. This Series will examine many aspects of network protocols, emphasizing the interaction with operating systems. It will focus on the evolution in computer environments and will assist professionals in the development and use of practical networking technologies.

Standards for programming interfaces, protocols, and languages are a key concern as networks of open systems expand within organizations and across the globe. Standards can be useful for system engineering, application programming, marketing, and procurement; but standards that are released too late, cover too little, or are too narrowly defined can be counterproductive. This series will encourage its readers to participate in the standards process by presenting material that details the use of specific standards to write application programs, and to build modern multiprocess, multiuser computing environments.

Newer operating systems are implemented in object-oriented languages, and network protocols use specialized languages to specify data formats and to compile protocol descriptions. As user interfaces become increasingly sophisticated, the level at which they are programmed continues to evolve upward, from system calls to remote procedure call compilers and generic description environments for graphical user interfaces. The effects of new languages on systems, programs, and users are explored in this series.

Foreword
Carl Cargill

The quest for *open systems* in the world of Information Technology has been lengthy, complex, and confusing. Much of the delay in achieving open systems can be traced back to the need by vendors to compete with one another and to innovate — to change things to achieve higher performance, lower price, or any of a myriad of other market factors, all based on technology. Users encouraged the competition, rewarding "fast" or "complex" or "large" by buying the offered systems.

In the late 1970s, however, a gentle revolution began. Computing became ubiquitous — and the advent of the personal computer showed that work done on a home computer could not be transferred to work done on an office machine. As interoperability became a necessity in the eyes of users, vendors leapt to the answer that they knew — more and faster technology. Over the past five years, however, this answer has proved to be not the one that the users sought. The users were looking for a different answer — because they had asked a different question. The question was, very simply, "How do I, as a user, ensure that anyone who needs information and knowledge has access to it at the right time and in the right format?"

This book provides a fascinating look at an industry in transition — an industry trying to move a ubiquitous operating system called UNIX into commercial acceptability, and the attempts of non-UNIX vendors to understand the siren song of UNIX. It shows, more accurately than any other document that I've found, how the standardization process changes an industry. It also shows the glacial power and speed (unfortunately) of standards — once set in motion, the compelling need that created POSIX could not be stopped. Modifications occurred, but almost always in response to an implicit or explicit user requirement. The book also shows how the user question of information interoperability, rather than equipment or data interoperability, is finally being addressed by the industry.

This book shows that the *market* — an often-abused term — does understand what it is doing, and does respond. It is compelling reading, and should be required for anyone who wants to understand how the Information Technology market works, both strategically and tactically.

Foreword

James Isaak

The world of UNIX standards started in 1981, when /usr/group (which is now Uni-Forum) started a committee on the subject. In 1984, the work of this group moved into an IEEE Computer Society project that was approved in 1983, and was joined by many new participants including NBS (which is now NIST). In 1985, AT&T Computer Systems (now NCR), which was responsible for marketing UNIX (which is now done by USL), published SVID. Also in 1984, a group of vendors called BISON in Europe (now known as X/Open) formed to create specifications for a "level playing field." BISON was originally composed of Bull (aka Honeywell-Bull), ICL (aka Fujitsu), Siemens, Olivetti, and Nixdorf (now Siemens-Nixdorf). By 1986, the first IEEE Standard was published as "POSCE" (called IEEEIX), now known as POSIX.

It is quite clear that some guide is needed to keep track of the relevant concepts in this moving mosaic. As the world of UNIX merges into the mainstream of information technology, and the full range of capability needed for complex applications needs to be described, we enter a cacophony of acronyms. In addition to traditional C, TCP/IP and FORTRAN, we find Ada, COBOL, OSI, X.400, SQL, ODIF, DME; from groups such as OSF, UI, JTC 1, X3, ANSI, all put into a coherent structure by organizations such as NIST, POSC, EWOS, and OIW.

While you might want to ignore this mumbo-jumbo, that could be bad for your ROI (return on investment). In a competitive world where changes in business and technology abound, the alphabet soup of standards offers one of the few paths to move forward into the future with confidence.

This book provides you with the secret decoder ring that will help to translate standards jargon into a practical approach to applications portability and interoperability of open systems.

Preface

UNIX, POSIX, and Open Systems: The Open Standards Puzzle is a guidebook to formal standards and industry specifications related to the historical UNIX operating system, particularly the POSIX (IEEE P1003 and ISO/IEC IS 9945) operating system interface and application environment standards.

Most standards and specifications are small when compared to the general distributed environments, including networks, that many users want. But users want environments that support portable and interoperable software. Some standards and specifications are profiles that show how to form such environments. If profiles are jigsaw puzzles and the standards and specifications are the pieces, the pictures on them show the environments that vendors should implement to support user applications.

More than one puzzle can often be constructed out of the same sets of pieces, by choosing different subsets of pieces, and by orienting them differently (with different parameters and options). Some profiles even reference other profiles, producing puzzles within puzzles that show large environments to be constructed from smaller environments. The specification of profiles to describe environments for particular classes of applications is called *profiling*. For profiling to work well, we also need an Open System Environment (OSE), described by a reference model that classifies the pieces according to general shapes and pictures, a taxonomy that says how to fit them together without their edges overlapping, and a guide that gives practical advice.

The Open Standards Puzzle explains how these standards, specifications, and profiles are related, how they are made, and how you can influence them. It will help you use them in building real systems.

The Market and the Puzzle

Standards are important to users as tools to provide more functions, and to increase choices and productivity. They are important to vendors and even nations as tools of competition. The economic and political importance of standards is based on their technical specification of interfaces that are important to distributed computing and open systems. Standards can promote these new paradigms of computing while easing the integration of older, legacy, systems. Single standards tend to be just pieces of the larger puzzles vendors and users need to solve. Cutting the pieces and fitting them together is best done with input from all affected parties.

Standards for Users. According to Senior Executives for Open Systems (SOS), who are ten very large companies that use computers but do not produce them as their main businesses,

> The creation of a computing environment based on widely implemented vendor neutral standards is essential to compete in the global marketplace of the '90s and beyond [SOS 1991].

Standards are becoming big business; sales can be won or lost on the basis of standards conformance alone. For example, many government contracts require conformance to specific standards, and the United States government constitutes a large part of the United States UNIX market, which is a large part of the POSIX and open systems markets. In the past few years, all major UNIX system vendors have committed to comply with the POSIX (IEEE 1003 and IS 9945) set of standards for operating system interfaces and application environments. Such commitments mean that standards will remain a major factor in these markets for years to come.

The Global Playing Field. Standards are seen by many as tools of competition:

> Happily, the U.S. retains one big advantage that lies outside the scope of a story about manufacturing: software. More and more of the value in big computer systems lies in the software that controls them. With English as the universal business language, the U.S. has a natural advantage setting world standards [Kupfer 1992].

Standards have even been called a national trust. Others hold that standardized software is commodity software, which some say gives the Japanese an advantage over the rest of the world. Such an argument would assume that software innovation was solely an American capability. This assumption would be incorrect:

> But here too Japan is coming on strong. Computer companies and consumer electronics companies, including Sony, have launched major drives to develop new operating systems [Kupfer 1992].

And there are more than two players of the global economic game:

> The biggest chill is blowing from Europe. When a truly unified market becomes a reality at the end of 1992, factories that sell electrical products in Europe will need to be certified as meeting a new set of

standards. These so-called ISO 9000 standards evaluate factories on every aspect of their operations, from training to manufacturing. U.S. exporters worry that the Europeans will wield the certification process as a nontariff trade barrier and shut them out [Kupfer 1992].

This is essentially the "level playing field" argument, which has also been heard regarding the OSI network protocols. Whether a particular playing field is level seems to depend on your point of view. Developers, sellers, buyers, users, and standards participants need to know the nature of the playing field and some of the rules of the game. Then they can better decide whether the playing field is level, and perhaps what to do about it.

The Computing Paradigm Shift. Unlike twenty years ago, computing now takes place on any desktop, not just on a few large machines isolated in special rooms. Computers come from a multitude of vendors, but must communicate with other machines in other rooms or on other continents. Users want to move programs among machines, and employers want to move users among machines. Vendors want to sell applications for a variety of platforms, and platforms for many applications. Some vendors use standards to open closed markets by getting industry consensus on specifications for interfaces that were formerly provided only by a single vendor's system. Everybody wants applications that can communicate and systems that can exchange data and information, whether by network, tape, or disk. Distributed computing is replacing timesharing, personal computing, and networked computing. Open systems that provide distributed computing are replacing proprietary systems with proprietary interfaces, because they can accomplish more and sometimes cost less.

Yet legacy systems, which are the older systems that represent large investments, must be taken into account. A single programming interface may be implemented across a wide range of systems, including legacy systems. Many vendors of older systems are implementing such interfaces. Legacy systems may also be made accessible by use of standard network protocols.

Distributed computing usually does not cost less overall. The real reasons for moving to distributed computing are increased capabilities, greater flexibility of incremental expansion, and choice of vendors.

Pieces and Puzzles. SOS wrote that "All Companies agreed that they had a common need to accelerate the commercial availability of Open Systems based on vendor neutral standards and enabling technologies in a proactive manner" [SOS 1991]. Specifications of interfaces and protocols are needed so interoperable and portable software can be written, sold, and bought. Specifications independent of any single vendor are best, because they can be used to build a vendor-independent computing environment. Such specifications are called *standards* when produced by an accredited standards body using a formal process. They are best produced with input from those who need to use them. Open processes are needed, so that the results will not be biased towards the specific concerns of any vendor or user, and will help solve real problems.

The specifications and standards needed to build real open systems are fractured like a jigsaw puzzle. Even standards that form whole pieces, like those for the C, Fortran, or Cobol programming languages, or the RS-232-C interface, are small compared to a whole puzzle. The box of open system puzzle pieces for application programming includes pieces named POSIX, the C programming language, and the X/Open Portability Guide, among others. The main pieces in the box for networking are labeled TCP/IP and OSI. But users need completed' puzzles, not boxes of pieces. When a user wants a new picture (environment), a puzzle (profile) must be constructed to specify the kinds of pieces that are wanted, and actual pieces must be selected from these (and perhaps other) boxes to solve the puzzle.

The pieces may be assembled to form many different puzzles, such as a file server, a turnkey realtime system, a batch processing environment, a traditional interactive timesharing system, or even a complete distributed computing system. These puzzles are called profiles. Profiles describe sets of standards and specifications, together with specified values for options and parameters. A profile is specified to support the requirements of a particular application, class of applications, or environment. A user who asks for MS-DOS plus QuickBasic has specified a profile, but in a vendor-specific manner. If every user, application writer, or system interface vendor assembled a different set of standards or specifications, even from the same larger set, there would be almost as much confusion as if there were no standards. Vendor-independent profiles are more generally useful, especially when written by independent bodies using open processes, as are formal standards. Many standards bodies and industry and user groups have constructed profiles and guides that define sets of standards for particular purposes, such as multiprocessing, transaction processing, and network login hosts.

A single standard or specification is usually focused around a technical, political, or marketing need, and is too small to form a whole puzzle. Each piece may be an international, regional, or national standard. It may be a formal standard or a de facto standard (a specification). New pieces (and puzzles) are being made all the time by working groups, technical advisory boards, and joint technical committees; others are made by marketing, market share, or free reference implementations. A standard may be rough cut by one group, polished by another, and painted by still another. Because some standards have to incorporate or at least not prohibit many divergent practices, the pieces may not fit well even when finished. The shape of a piece may change after it has already been used to solve a puzzle. In fact, squeezing a piece to fit is explicitly permitted, as long as the original shaper said where and how much you could squeeze. This is what the options and parameters used by profiles are for.

The Need for User Involvement. Continual involvement by users in the development of standards or profiles will help ensure that the final documents will address user needs [TSG-1 1991]. But the standards themselves do not describe the processes by which they are created. It is often difficult to determine which bodies are responsible for a standard, specification, or profile, even just for those related to UNIX or POSIX. Users want solutions, not puzzles or pieces.

The Book

UNIX, POSIX, and Open Systems: The Open Standards Puzzle is a handbook for use by programming, marketing and sales, or acquisition and procurement professionals to determine which standards puzzle pieces are useful and necessary for their tasks. It gives reasons for building, selling, buying, and using open systems and distributed computing. It describes the historical relations between the UNIX system and open systems. It tells why standards are needed. It discusses some of the advantages and drawbacks of particular standards and of standards in general. Wherever possible, it points out what you might expect but will not find in a standard.

The book contains a snapshot of many of the available standards related to POSIX. POSIX is the set of standards produced by the IEEE Computer Society (IEEE/CS) Technical Committee on Operating Systems Standards Subcommittee (TCOS-SS) P1003 working groups. It also includes ISO POSIX, which is the set of international standards produced by the ISO/IEC (International Organization for Standardization/International Electrotechnical Committee) JTC 1 (Joint Technical Committee One) SC22 (Subcommittee 22) WG15 (Working Group 15), such as the International Standard IS 9945-1, *Information Technology — Portable Operating System Interface (POSIX) — Part 1: System Application Program Interface (API) [C Language]*. The book also discusses related non-POSIX TCOS-SS working groups such as P1238, P1201, and P1224.

The book has extensive coverage of profiles. It discusses issues that affect many standards and profiles, such as language independence, conformance, and internationalization. Language independence permits applications to be written in several programming languages for the same system interfaces. Conformance to specifications is important both to application developers (so they will know their products will run) and to users (so they will know what products will meet their needs). Internationalization helps a variety of software products to reach international markets.

There are two traditional ways of looking at distributed computing: from the viewpoint of the network; and from the viewpoint of the operating system and its interfaces. This book takes the latter viewpoint. The book is about open systems, which are essentially operating systems. It treats networking as an issue that is relevant to many standards. The network viewpoint is otherwise left to another book [Carl-Mitchell & Quarterman 1993].

This book is mostly about standards for application program interfaces. The standards covered are those most directly related to open systems. Standards for databases, documentation, and electronic data interchange are not covered except in passing, for example. The book is also *not* an application portability programming tutorial. It does not cover point by point details of each standard, specific changes required for standards compliance, nor complete requirements for application portability. Instead, it tells who produces standards and how, what's in them and how they are related, and how to use them together and how to change them.

   Much of this book is about the context in which the standards evolve. Specific details of any given standard may not yet be finished, and may be interpreted and modified. We believe the reasons a standard is created, its intended purposes, and the profiles that reference it, are as important as the contents of the standard itself. This is a how-to book for understanding and using standards, and for affecting the processes that create them. It provides a foundation for further investigations by the reader.

Organization

The book contains fifteen chapters and is organized in four parts. Each part opener contains a brief introduction to that part. The parts are named from the puzzle metaphor: Part 1, **Context**; Part 2, **Cutters**; Part 3, **Pieces and Patterns**; and Part 4, **Puzzles**.

   Part 1, **Context**, gives the motivation for open systems, and tells how standards can be used to help build them. Part 2, **Cutters**, describes the bodies that produce the standards, that is, the groups that cut the puzzle pieces and define the puzzles they are supposed to fit into. Part 3, **Pieces and Patterns**, describes specific base standards and extensions, that is, the puzzle pieces themselves, and discusses issues such as networking and internationalization that color many pieces. Part 4, **Puzzles**, describes profiles, which are puzzles that can be made out of the pieces.

   In addition, there are three forewords, this preface, references at the end of each chapter, two appendices, a glossary, and an index.

• **Forewords**   In addition to the series foreword, there are forewords by Carl Cargill and James Isaak. Cargill is the author of *Information Technology Standardization*, a general work about standardization. Isaak is chair of the *TCOS-SS (IEEE Computer Society Technical Committee on Operating Systems Standards Subcommittee)*, which is the sponsor of the IEEE POSIX standards committees. He is also the convenor of the ISO POSIX working group. He was an early participant in the work that led to the /usr/group 1984 Standard, and he has been a major figure throughout the history of POSIX.

• **Part 1, Context**   Three chapters give the context needed to understand the rest of the book. People want to use distributed computing environments that provide many resources in a transparent manner. Open systems are needed for distributed computing, and the UNIX system has historically been used for this. Open standards are needed for open system interfaces, and the POSIX standards are the central ones. These chapters discuss these issues, and give terminology for fitting standards, specifications, and profiles together to solve the puzzles of open systems for distributed computing.

• **Part 2, Cutters**   The second part of the book contains a comprehensive list of standards bodies related to the UNIX operating system. The first chapter gives details of formal standards bodies. The second chapter describes industry groups that produce specifications and influence standards, and user groups that educate people and influence standards. The third chapter describes some examples of processes used by standards bodies. If standards are pieces of jigsaw puzzles, these are the processes used to cut pieces out of plywood or sheet goods.

• **Part 3, Pieces and Patterns**   The third part of the book is about standards and issues, that is, the puzzle pieces and the patterns that can be seen in them. The first chapter lists and describes all the TCOS committees and their projects, whether they have been completed or not. The rest of the third part is about issues. Networking may be the most important of them, and is treated first. The next chapter describes the issues surrounding programming language bindings, including some details of bindings of IEEE 1003.1 to C, Ada, and FORTRAN. Conformance testing and internationalization each have a chapter.

• **Part 4, Puzzles**   Standardization is time consuming, and standards bodies often focus individual base standards on narrow technological areas, so that they can be completed in a reasonable amount of time. Real systems cover wider technological areas, so it is necessary to specify several standards and options and parameters for them, in order to support a functional objective. The fourth part of the book describes these functional standards or profiles that select standards pieces to fit into puzzles. A chapter describing kinds of profiles and their relations to each other and to standards is followed by chapters on TCOS profiles, industry specifications and distributed management, and procurement profiles.

• **Appendices**   There are two appendices. The first gives access information for standards bodies and for publications about standards. The second is a standards puzzle acrostic challenge supplied by Jim Isaak that asks the reader to classify acronyms as standards, standards bodies, specifications, or companies. This approach reflects the humor of the current confusing situation, where users must locate usable specifications and put them together in a coherent way, without much guidance.

• **References, Glossary, and Index**   Numerous bibliographic citations occur in the text, and the actual references are gathered at the end of each chapter. The glossary defines major (and many minor) terms and acronyms. The index indicates where they are used in the text. Expansions of acronyms are given both in the glossary and in the index for easy reference.

Readers

This book is suitable for someone new to standards to learn what the central open systems standards are, how they fit together, how they are made, and where to find additional information about them. Familiarity with the UNIX operating system is useful, and some sections require familiarity with the C programming language. You don't even have to have a technical background to benefit from reading this book. But even if you are already intimately familiar with the technology, you will find useful information here about what is being done with it.

Since standards have been developed or are being developed in all areas of computation from system interface to graphical user interfaces, the list of people who need to be informed about them is long. The short list includes those in

1. application development

2. marketing and sales

3. acquisition, procurement, and purchasing

The long list includes system administrators, operating system developers, system programmers, system integrators, standards participants, and end users. These people all want to know how to build and use real systems and environments using standards, specifications, and profiles. Different people have different needs, and may want to read the book in different orders. We hope everyone will read the first three chapters, in Part 1, **Context**, which give the context for the rest of the book. Since the chapters on standards bodies and processes in Part 2, **Cutters**, describe the organizations that make the pieces and puzzles, reading them will make the rest of the book more comprehensible. The reader in a hurry may want to read Part 2, **Cutters**, to get an overview of standards bodies and to look up specific bodies, standards, or topics in the index when needed. Anyone who wants to affect the standards process should read Chapter 6, *Processes*, and perhaps also Chapter 8, *Protocols and Standards*. Further reading suggestions are given in the following subsections.

Because the book is mainly about context, it will be of interest to many computer professionals, including system programmers, operating system developers, sales engineers, system administrators, system integrators, standards participants, managers, consultants, and end users. All these can consult *The Open Standards Puzzle* to learn how standards are produced and how they fit together.

Application Development. A major reason cited for standards development is application portability, and an open systems standard directly related to UNIX and POSIX is usually an *Application Program Interface (API)* standard or an *Application Environment Profile (AEP)*. Application programs that conform with API and AEP standards can be ported to different platforms with less effort. An application that runs on more platforms has a wider market. Application developers will want to read the descriptions of specific standards and profiles in the chapters in Part 3, **Pieces and Patterns** and Part 4, **Puzzles**. Part 3 will also be useful in describing approaches to known issues that cross standards and platform components.

Some of these standards are not finished yet. Application developers may want to participate in the standards process to make sure the resulting standards meet their needs, for example, by accomodating new hardware technology. Lack of participation by application developers has been noted by many standards groups as a problem in producing adequate standards. All national standardization bodies have been requested to encourage the participation in standardization of people and organizations that use standards [Isaak 1991].

Marketing and Sales. It's been said that standards are marketing. That's not all they are, but it's certainly one thing. To reach a wider market, product marketing needs standards information. This can be used for making decisions about marketing strategies, assisting in the choice of standards that are important for their product, developing appropriate sales brochures, and training sales staff. Marketing personnel should find Part 4, **Puzzles**, of the most use, plus Chapter 10, *Conformance Testing*.

Sales personnel can use a good working knowledge of the standards world in telling their customers which standards a product complies with and what benefit such compliance will provide. Hardware vendors are constantly asked "will your hardware run the Whiz Bang software?" or "Will your hardware be able to communicate with brand Z hardware?" If both pieces of hardware conform with the same standard, there is a good chance that the answer to these questions is yes. Similar situations apply to software platforms such as operating systems. Chapter 10, *Conformance Testing*, and Part 4, **Puzzles**, should be of particular interest to sales personnel.

There is also a basic difference between the kinds of standards and conformance needed for interoperability and those needed for application portability. Portability requires standards for application platforms such as operating systems, and standards for applications, together with separate conformance testing for each. Interoperability involves peer entities (processes, programs, computers, networks) communicating with one another, with any pair of peer entities using the same standards. Conformance of a single implementation to a standard can sometimes be tested, but is not nearly as important as actual demonstrated interoperability in a network with many different implementations from many vendors. These issues are discussed in Chapter 8, *Protocols and Standards*.

Acquisition, Procurement, and Purchasing. It would be nice if customers knew what vendors knew. However, time is limited, and emphases differ. Customers may be more interested in fitting together pieces from many vendors to form an integrated working environment.

Acquisition may include specifying procurement requirements, determining products that fit, and buying products. People specifying procurement requirements need to know standards, so they can say which standards and specifications products must conform to. Those using such requirements to make actual purchases don't need to know as much about standards, but the more they know, the better they can determine what products match the requirements.

Informed use of standards can help a user become vendor independent and hardware independent, which can lead to lower costs and greater capabilities. Standards can permit multiple sources, and produce leverage with suppliers. But standards will not solve all problems, and care must be taken not to overestimate claims about them. Conformance to some networking standards doesn't necessarily mean the conforming systems will interoperate, for example; see Chapter 8, *Protocols and Standards* and Chapter 10, *Conformance Testing*.

More generally, Part 4, **Puzzles**, describes the larger environment specifications, and Part 2, **Cutters**, describes the bodies and processes that produce them.

When an implementation of a particular standard is being chosen, its description in Part 3, **Pieces and Patterns**, can be useful. When a thorny issue such as internationalization (I18N) comes up, the discussion of it in Part 3, should help.

System Administrators. People who keep systems running have all the problems of application developers, system integrators, and end users, plus more. Carefully selected standards can help simplify these problems. The standards of most interest will be those for system administration, distributed management environments, and distributed computing, but all those involve other standards, as well. Chapter 14, *Industry Profiles*, should be of particular interest, probably in combination with the rest of the chapters in Part 4, **Puzzles**.

Operating System Developers and System Programmers. People who develop platforms for other professionals to use have an even larger set of concerns. System programmers need to know how to implement standard interfaces, and they also need to stay abreast of the standards situation so they can adapt their implementation to future changes in standards. If your system doesn't have memory management, for example, you may want to be sure basic interface standards don't require that facility. Part 3, **Pieces and Patterns**, describes specific interfaces, and Part 2, **Cutters**, discusses the bodies and processes that produce them.

System Integrators. Standards can make system integration easier, if the system integrator knows which standards will make each system fit with another system. Part 4, **Puzzles**, and Part 3, **Pieces and Patterns**, are of particular interest. It is important not to put together systems by simply checking a list of standards and ensuring implementation of all parts of all of them. It may seem obvious that options are by definition optional, but some procurement specifications require specific values for options. Procurement specifications should leave some options optional. For example, a requirement for all of 1003.1 includes a requirement for the *mmap* facility, that is, for user-accessible memory mapping. Some computers, such as those made by Cray, do not have memory management hardware, so requiring all of 1003.1 would inadvertently exclude such computers from consideration. Avoiding checklist specification is a good idea. Profiles are often useful in tailoring a system or a procurement to a particular application. For example, IEEE 1003.10 is for supercomputing environments, and 1003.15 is for batch processing.

Standards Participants. Let's not forget those who spend large numbers of their working hours producing standards and specifications. Careful attention to the technical details of a single standard can leave little time for understanding the processes by which it is standardized. Participating in one working group leaves little time to learn about other working groups, their documents, and their processes. This book provides concise information on a range of related standards, in Part 3, **Pieces and Patterns**, information on how they are related, in Part 4, **Puzzles** and throughout. It also describes the bodies and processes that produce those standards, in Part 2, **Cutters**.

Standards processes are not fast by nature, since they must carefully balance technical considerations, and most of the processes used for the standards in this book require consensus or decision by large majority. Yet the economic and political pressures on these processes are enormous, and the main goal behind those pressures is more speed in the processes. Standards participants need to be aware of this, so they can balance speed against good standards. In some cases, technical mechanisms, such as the use of computer networks in the standards process, may permit greater speed while maintaining technical content. In other cases, standards participants may need to resist hurrying, so they can preserve consensus. More comments on these subjects may be found in Chapter 6, *Processes* and Chapter 8, *Protocols and Standards*.

Participants in one standards process under one standards body need to be aware of other bodies working in related areas with different processes. Often, an industry consortium or workshop will attempt to produce specifications faster or across a broader technical area than a formal standards body can. These emphases have their advantages. They also usually require cooperation among the groups concerned, to avoid duplication of effort or lessened consensus or technical content. Bodies and processes are discussed in Part 2, **Cutters**. Particularly thorny cross-component issues are discussed in Part 3, **Pieces and Patterns**.

People concentrating on standardizing a particular interface may want to keep their noses to the grindstone and to ignore where the interface will fit. But one of the biggest problems of formal standards groups historically has been the fragmentation of their standards into technology-driven pieces that don't fit together well, and that don't add up to produce a complete puzzle with a picture users want to see. Progress has been made recently in standards architecture. Taxonomies, frameworks, and guides are in progress or finished, as described in Part 4, **Puzzles**. Participants need to ensure their standards will fit into the new architecture. Cross-component issues such as language independence, security, conformance testing, internationalization, and, of course, networking have been identified and organized approaches have been constructed, as discussed in Part 3, **Pieces and Patterns**. Standards participants need to be aware of these issues, and incorporate them into standards from the outset, so the standards don't have to be modified later.

End Users. End users need to be able to sort out the sales mumbo jumbo. This involves answering such questions as "Will brand X hardware run brand Q software?" "Will brand X hardware communicate with my current installation of brand Y hardware?" "Will I have to learn a new set of commands or procedures?" "Will I have to modify my existing applications?" By being familiar with the standards that govern these areas, the end user can be prepared to ask the vendor the required questions. Also, if a vendor attempts to talk up compliance with a standard that is not necessary to the user, the informed user can ignore such hype. Much of this can be left to acquisitions personnel, but they need guidance from the end user.

Another fine point is distinguishing a claim from a vendor that "X is *the* standard for the industry" from "X conforms to the ABC industry standard." The former can be true (X can be a de facto standard), but is often a matter of opinion of the vendor of X. The latter is more specific, and often more meaningful. Telling the difference between access to new technology and sales hype can be difficult; this book should help. Chapter 3, *POSIX and Open Standards* and Chapter 10, *Conformance Testing* are especially relevant.

Throughout the book, but especially in Part 1, **Context**, we also try to describe the outside forces at work on standardization. Many people and organizations see standards as the key to open systems and distributed computing, which are seen as necessary to company, national, or regional economic competitiveness. Economic considerations this pervasive are also political issues. End users include voters and captains of industry. They should be aware that standards are useful, but will not magically solve all problems. Standards are technical tools. They can be used in helping to solve economic and political problems, but too much pressure on the standards processes can ruin the technical content of the standards, and their utility with it.

The lack of standards is hurting the computer industry, which paradoxically means that fewer resources are available to produce standards. Many people believe standards are by their nature a hindrance to innovation and that resources spent on standardization are wasted and should have been spent on research. Bad standards certainly can get in the way of innovation, yet standards have to take existing technology into account. Balancing these conflicting needs in a standardization process is difficult. Yet it is necessary, since, good or bad, ready or not, standards have a strong effect on one of the most productive industries in the world.

Decisions of this magnitude should not be made just by computer vendors, or just by standards bodies. They should be made with input from all of those affected, most of whom are end users. For this to happen, end users must have some understanding of standards processes and architecture. We hope this book, particularly Chapter 6, *Processes* and Chapter 12, *Frameworks*, will bring some of that understanding to people who do not have the time to read a standard or attend a meeting. We also hope it will encourage some who otherwise would not participate in standardization processes, or in decisions about them, to do so.

Finally, standards are developed in response to needs. While most early standards related to the UNIX system used to be produced according to vendors' needs, a large and increasing number of them now are profiles that are intended to address users' needs. Users need to tell standards bodies what they need.

Terminology

This book is not a standard, and it is not written as one. We do not expect claims or testing of conformance to the book, and we prefer readability over pedantic precision. Where possible, we use plain American English, with care to avoid idioms that would be unclear in other forms of English. Where plain Anglo-Saxon will do as well as a Latinate verbosity, we stick with the short words. We do not think that to accomplish something is better than to just do it.

We are not limited to solely technical material, and we make a point of including opinions, sometimes including several viewpoints on the same subject. Undue precision of language is avoided in such cases where it might give an unwarranted impression of certainty. Why and how are often more ambiguous than what, and we do not pretend otherwise, nor do we pretend to know all the answers, nor even all the facts.

We try to be precise whenever and we can and wherever it is appropriate to do so. We avoid weasel-wording, even when discussing a standard in which it appears. If we know why a standard tries so carefully not to say something, we usually spell out the reason.

Where necessary, we use specialized standardization terminology. We try to define such jargon when first used. Some words, such as "open," don't look like jargon, but have acquired various specialized meanings in different contexts. For some of these, there are multiple definitions in the text. We try to point these out where they occur. We provide a glossary and an index for quick reference. In some cases, such as the conformance testing terms in Chapter 10, this book may include the first complete explanation of all the basic terms and their relations to one another.

In a few cases, we have invented terms, or have added slightly new usages for them. We have done this mostly where there are several existing names. The most common occurence is in our usage of "POSIX System Interface Standard" or, where it is obvious by context that POSIX is meant, just "System Interface Standard" to refer to both IEEE Std 1003.1-1990 and IS 9945-1:1990 from ISO/IEC JTC 1 SC22 WG15. We use this term in preference to the more approved short form, "POSIX.1," as being more transparent to the reader not already familiar with the jargon. Occasionally we refer to one of these two documents separately, such as when discussing the process by which it was produced, and then we use the more specific name, IEEE Std 1003.1-1990 or IS 9945-1:1990. Another example of a generic term we use is "POSIX Shell and Utilities Standard," instead of "POSIX.2," for IEEE Std 1003.2-1992 or IS 9945-2:1992. And we use "POSIX Test Methods Standard" for IEEE Std 1003.3-1991.

Wherever possible, we use the names for standards preferred by the TCOS-SS Profile Steering Committee (PSC) in their Standing Document 22 [Nielsen 1991].

Acknowledgments

We thank the standards community in general for assisting in the creation of this book. Many people have been very generous with their time and expertise, and the book would not exist in its present form without them.

Certain people have made particularly remarkable contributions to the project. We thank Michelle Aden, Anna Maria Alvaré, Jaap Akkerhuis, Helene Armitage, Ralph Barker, Rich Bergman, Linda Branagan, Smoot Carl-Mitchell, Vint Cerf, Lyman Chapin, Bill Cox, Steve Coya, Dave Crocker, Steve Crocker, John Curran, Dominic Dunlop, Don Folland, Bob Gambrel, Michael Hannah,

John Hill, Randall Howard, Aya Imaizumi (Sakamoto), Jim Isaak, Hal Jespersen,
Lorraine Kevra, Martin Kirk, Kevin Lewis, Roger Martin, Shane McCarron, Gary
Miller, Yasushi Nakahara, Martha Nalebuff, Mary Lynne Nielsen, Craig Partridge,
Erik van der Poel, Paul Rabin, Marc Rochkind, Keld Jrn Simonsen, Paul Smith,
Henry Spencer, Capt. Sandra L. Swearingen, Amanda Walker, Stephen Walli,
Bruce Weiner, Jason Zions, and *MKS (Mortice-Kern Systems)* for use of their
toolkit that implements much of IEEE P1003.2 under MS-DOS, and Heinz Lyck-
lama, Wally Wedel, Kirk McKusick, and Michel Gien for believing that user
groups have a role to play in standardization. We also thank any others whom we
may have forgotten to mention.

References

Carl-Mitchell & Quarterman 1993.   Carl-Mitchell, Smoot, & Quarterman, John
    S., *Practical Internetworking with TCP/IP and UNIX,* Addison-Wesley,
    Reading, MA (1993).
Isaak 1991.   Isaak, Jim, "WG15 resolutions related to profile work," WG15,
    Rotterdam (29 May 1991).
Kupfer 1992.   Kupfer, Andrew, "How American Industry Stacks Up," *Fortune,*
    pp. 30–46, Time, Inc. (9 March 1992).
Nielsen 1991.   Nielsen, Mary Lynne, "Profiles references list; PSC SD-022,"
    Standing Document (PSC SD-022), Profile Steering Commitee (22 Novem-
    ber 1991).
SOS 1991.   SOS, "User Requirements Letter," Senior Executives for Open Sys-
    tems, also known as the Group of Ten: American Airlines, Du Pont, General
    Motors, Kodak, McDonnell Douglas, Merck, Motorola, 3M, Northrop, and
    Unilever, Washington, DC (27 June 1991).
TSG-1 1991.   TSG-1, "Standards Necessary for Interfaces for Application
    Portability," ISO/IEC JTC 1 TSG-1, Tokyo (1991).

Contents

Part 2   Cutters   73

Part 3   Pieces and Patterns   141

Appendix A   Resources 343

Appendix B   Puzzle Challenge 365

Glossary 371

Index 399

PART 1

Context

This first part of the book discusses what users want from computing and how standards can help provide it. Distributed computing requires open systems, which have historically been related to the UNIX timesharing system, which was originally developed by AT&T. Other operating systems, such as MS-DOS, have been important in developing user expectations for open systems, but this book focuses on relatives of the UNIX system. Divergent variants of this system led to the production of interface standards, such as POSIX. POSIX and related standards are the collective subject of this book. The chapters in this part provide the context to understand how distributed computing, open systems, and standards are related, and what they have to do with UNIX and POSIX. This is *The Open Standards Puzzle* .

Computing Models

This part begins in Chapter 1 by describing how and why users want access to resources, and how various computing models have been constructed to get those resources to the users. Various traditional models, such as batch computing, timesharing, personal computing, and networked computing, are examined. The more recent and more general model of distributed computing comes from elements of all of these previous models. In these models, we can also see part of the evolution of the term *open,* which has come to have more shades of meaning even than *network* or *system.* We will follow the definitions and development of this term, alone and as an adjective, in this and later chapters.

UNIX and Open Systems

The heart of distributed computing is open systems, which are operating systems with certain properties. Open systems are described in Chapter 2.

The traditional operating system most often used as an open system is the UNIX timesharing system. Chapter 2 explores the historical development of this system and its relations to the distributed computing model. Networking is an important facet of these relations. Increasingly divergent and numerous variants of UNIX led to a desire for related interface standards.

POSIX and Open Standards

Standards for open systems are examined in Chapter 3. The historical relations of the POSIX standards to UNIX and open systems are discussed. The chapter includes a brief introduction to standards terminology.

CHAPTER 1

Computing Models

Modern computing environments use networks and a variety of computer hardware and software to provide convenient computing services to users. This is called distributed computing. Software for such diverse environments must fit together, which requires a model of the kinds of pieces needed and how they should interact.

This chapter provides a tour through some current and historical computing models in order to show what they have to do with open systems and open standards. By "model," we mean an approach to computing, involving such features as centralization or decentralization. We will use a more specialized definition of the word "model" later. Here, we use the word as a convenient term to refer to stages in the history of computing.

A quick look at some current industry models shows that they are all trying to cover similar areas with slightly different software and approaches. A survey of historical computing models clarifies the motivations behind distributed computing, and what it has to do with timesharing, networked computing, and personal computing.

Each computer used to provide key resources in distributed computing should be an open system, and the main characteristics of open systems are directly related to those of distributed computing. Open systems need open specifications, preferably standards. Systems with open licensing of implementations of open specifications are usually open systems.

Note that open specifications as well as open licensing are needed: this excludes proprietary systems such as MS-DOS and MacOS. Closed licensing of implementations is one of the historical motivations for open specifications. Open systems can be used to build distributed computing, especially in conjunction with recent industry computing models.

1.1   Models

The average computer user wants the monitor screen to be a set of transparent windows, so that the user can see applications and other people through them. But the user often gets a stack of glass pieces of assorted sizes: some are lenses, some mirrors, some stained glass. It's more like a kaleidoscope than a window. The desired information often isn't visible until some of the pieces are shifted to bring it into focus. It's not even shattered and refitted window glass that might fit back together like a jigsaw puzzle; then the user could see through it, although with obstructions. But the pieces of most current computing environments didn't come from the same sheet of glass in the first place, so there are gaps, and overlaps, and distortions in the user's view.

Most of this book is about how to fit small pieces together into usable shapes. This chapter is about some large shapes and some large classes of pieces that can be used to compose them. These shapes and classes are computing models. Let's consider some general features of these models, then look at some real examples, and talk about how they can be useful.

Distributed Computing

Most computer users don't really want to use computers: they just want problems solved, or they want to communicate with people. That is, they want resources and services, and they have found they have to use computers to get them. Resources include databases, spreadsheets, and text processing software. Services include electronic mail or conferencing, to communicate with other people. Users may also want to communicate with a group of people while using resources to accomplish a joint task. They don't care whether there is one computer involved or two hundred; no network or a worldwide one.

Computing environments almost this transparent can sometimes be built. Computing experts know there are layers upon layers of software and hardware between the user and the other person or the application. This software and hardware often come from many different manufacturers, yet must all work together to provide resources for the users. The whole environment must be manageable by a few people, and it must be possible to add new pieces without disrupting service. A computing environment that is diverse, manageable, and extensible, and also transparent so that all this complexity is hidden from the user, implements *distributed computing*.

No matter how transparent it is, distributed computing is still built out of hardware and software. The software the user sees most directly provides a user interface and user applications. Underneath that are distributed services. These depend on networking protocols, and on operating system services. The hardware is under all that, as shown in Fig. 1.1. Some of the services, protocols, and hardware terms shown in Fig. 1.1 may be unfamiliar, but we will discuss them in this chapter, and they are listed in the index and defined in the glossary.

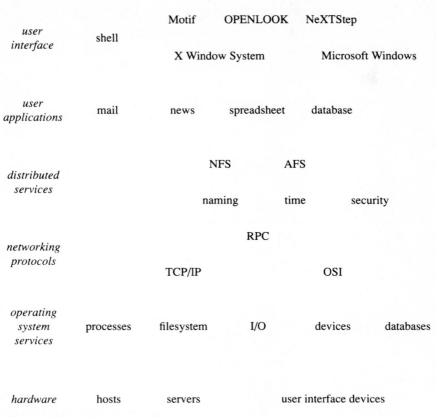

Figure 1.1 Distributed computing layers.

The layers in Fig. 1.1 are deliberately not exactly those of any well-known layering model. They are neither those of the ISO-OSI seven layer model, nor those of the Internet model, because those are network protocol layering models, not computing models, and they do not include all the layers we are interested in here. (We give an overview of the relevance of those layering models and protocol suites to open systems in Chapter 3, *POSIX and Open Standards*, and we discuss both of them in more detail in Chapter 8, *Protocols and Standards*.) The layers in Fig. 1.1 are not exactly the layers from any of the popular industry consortia models that we discuss in this book, because we want to avoid favoritism. We will discuss some of these industry models in more detail in Chapter 15.

Sometimes it is useful to group the hardware into user interface devices, hosts, and servers. User interface devices usually have screens and keyboards, and often have mice. Hosts have user login accounts. Servers have resources dedicated to providing services to other systems; for example, a file server probably has large disks. In addition, there is network hardware, such as cables and routers. For the discussion in this chapter, we can lump most hardware together.

Most of the software categories we've just named are also very inclusive. For example, networking protocols include whole protocol suites, such as TCP/IP or OSI [Malamud 1992].

Some Industry Models

Several popular industry models for distributed computing are shown in Fig. 1.2. These are *ONC (Open Network Computing)* from *SMI (Sun Microsystems, Inc.),* the *OSF DCE (Distributed Computing Environment),* from the *OSF (Open Software Foundation)* and *UI-ATLAS* from *UI (UNIX International).* There is a progression from smaller, earlier models, such as Sun's ONC [SMI 1990], through larger, later ones, such as OSF DCE [OSF 1991] and UI-ATLAS [UI 1991].

Figure 1.2 Some software models.

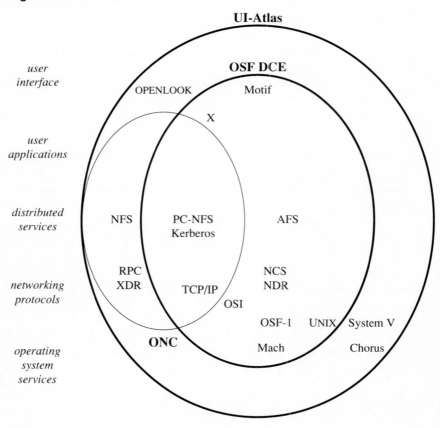

The figure shows some illustrative areas in which the models use the same or different software. ONC and OSF DCE use different distributed filesystems: ONC uses Sun's *NFS (Network File System)* while OSF uses the *Andrew File System (AFS)*. Yet both models use Sun's *PC-NFS* to provide distributed filesystem services to MS-DOS users. And both use *Kerberos* for authentication of users over networks. Similarly, both models use the TCP/IP protocol suite, but ONC includes Sun's *RPC (Remote Procedure Call)* and *XDR (External Data Representation)* protocols for remote procedure call support, while OSF DCE includes the *NCS (Network Computing System)* implementation of the *NCA (Network Computing Architecture) RPC (Remote Procedure Call)* and *NDR (Network Data Representation)* protocols.

The OSF DCE is larger than Sun's ONC, in that it addresses both operating system and user interface issues that ONC does not, and it has specific software associated with those layers. For example, OSF DCE includes the Motif *GUI (Graphical User Interface),* while Sun provides the OPENLOOK GUI (even though it is not properly part of Sun's ONC).

UI-ATLAS explicitly incorporates both the OSF DCE and Sun's ONC. Both NFS and AFS are acceptable, for example. However, the OSF DCE has the associated OSF-1 operating system, based on the Mach operating system. UI-ATLAS is built around UNIX System V Release 4.1, from *USL (UNIX System Laboratories).* In addition, USL has agreed to coordinate interfaces with the Chorus operating system from Chorus systèmes of Paris. It is not clear that the UI-ATLAS architecture extends to incorporating OSF-1, but it is shown that way in the figure anyway. We will come back to such details in a later chapter.

Two more models are shown in Fig. 1.3. These are *Solaris,* from SunSoft and *ACE (Advanced Computing Environment),* produced by a consortium. Solaris and ACE are intended to be complete software and hardware packages, not just software models, frameworks, or architectures. Other possibilities to examine might include MS-DOS from Microsoft for Intel processors, and MacOS from Apple for the Macintosh, but those, in addition to being single-vendor systems and being tied to specific hardware, are not designed to interoperate with other environments. That combination of constraints makes them less interesting in this discussion of distributed computing models.

Solaris includes Sun's ONC, plus the GUI OPENLOOK, the Deskset desktop environment, and the operating system SunOS. Although Solaris is being built to run on multiple hardware platforms, we show in Fig. 1.3 its initial platform, the SPARC hardware from *SMCC (Sun Microcomputer Corporation),* plus the Intel hardware. ACE runs on the Intel processors and the MIPS chip. ACE includes two very different operating systems: Microsoft NT from Microsoft, the vendor of MS-DOS; and the *Open Desktop Environment (ODT)* from the *Santa Cruz Operation (SCO),* with Motif as its window system, and based on OSF/1. SCO ODT, like SunOS, Chorus, Mach, and OSF-1, is a variant of the UNIX operating system invented at AT&T Bell Laboratories and currently licensed by USL. They all require UNIX licenses. UI, USL, and SCO have announced an intent to keep ODT and System V Release 4.1 compatible.

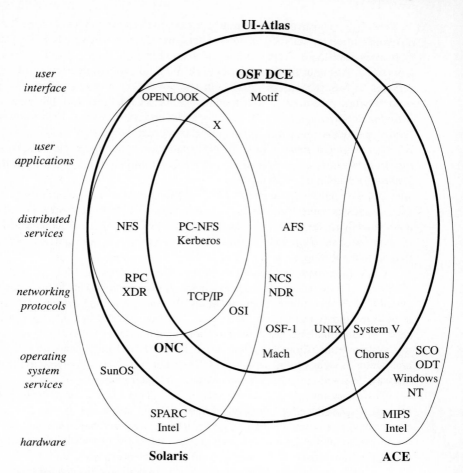

Figure 1.3 Some software models and product packages.

Meanwhile, SunSoft has acquired the part of *ISC (INTERACTIVE Systems Corporation)* that previously produced ports of UNIX System V for Intel hardware in cooperation with AT&T. Thus, the operating systems of ACE and Solaris are partly produced by historical competitors. When looking for an interface or a facility, it is good to remember that these models are, to some extent, marketing for the underlying software and hardware products associated with them. It is also worthwhile to remember that they are not even the same kinds of things, although the trade press often compares them as though they are. UI-ATLAS is a computing architecture, which is much like what we are calling a model here, but perhaps more general. OSF DCE is a set of software products, yet ones that fit together into an architecture. UI doesn't produce software, but USL does. OSF does produce software.

A model from a different kind of source was recently proposed by a group called *SOS (Senior Executives for Open Systems),* also known as the Group of Ten, and as the Standards for Open Systems group. These are Vice Presidents and other high-level executives of ten major companies: American Airlines, Du Pont, General Motors, Kodak, McDonnell Douglas, Merck, Motorola, 3M, Northrop, and Unilever. None of them are computer vendors, but all of them depend on computers. They agreed on "a common need to accelerate the commercial availability of Open Systems based on vendor neutral standards and enabling technologies in a proactive manner" [SOS 1991]. They informed their actual and potential computer vendors of this, by sending each of them a copy of a letter. The letter included a sketch of a very broad model for computing. It included all of the areas mentioned above, staying close to OSF's model in most of them. It also included other areas, such as office documentation and electronic data interchange. This letter, much like the morning newspaper hitting the windowpane, woke a lot of people up. It made many vendors much more conscious of a very strong desire on the part of real users for computing products that work together to accomplish the users' objectives.

What do all these intersecting yet divergent models mean to the end user? For one thing, they mean that someone else has to select and integrate technology to produce an environment to hide all this complexity. The models themselves are attempts to organize choices for such selection and integration. But they cannot do that job for you by themselves.

These models are like menus. You still have to choose the meal. Your users may want selections from several menus, and they may want home cooking for items on no menus. The differences in terminology in these models make selection somewhat like having to read several different languages, depending on the cuisine of the restaurant, when all you really want to do is order bread. This book is about recognizing bread when you see it, so you can order it, and about how to find the ingredients to bake it yourself if you can't order it.

1.2   History

People familiar with mainframes or personal computers may wonder why such complicated models are necessary. Mainframe environments are usually built with software and hardware mostly from a single vendor. Software for personal computers may come from many sources, but it is written to the same operating system and hardware platform. Both mainframes and personal computers traditionally provide all computing resources on one computer. But a group of interconnected computers can include specialized machines and software, so that the whole environment is more capable than any single machine could be. Large disks, fast CPUs, sophisticated display devices, printers, and other elements can be linked by networks. Such networked environments permit the development of transparent distributed computing.

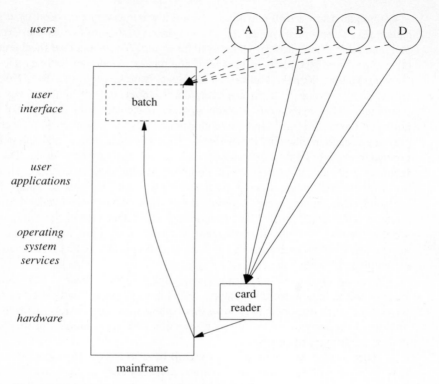

Figure 1.4 Batch computing model.

Capable and diverse interconnected environments usually have three characteristics that lead to the complications of these models:

- Multiple operating systems, which require application software *portability*

- Networking, which requires *interoperability* of applications and operating systems through interchange of data and information

- Users who need to use different computers without relearning everything; this is *user portability*

These three characteristics led historically to characteristics of open computing such as diversity, manageability, extensibility, and transparency. Let's look at some previous computing models to see how this happened. In the very early days of computing, real programmers soldered wires, and somewhat later they toggled in bits. But let's start our historical review after compilers were invented, that is, after there was software somewhat as we know it today. Let's start with batch computing, timesharing, and proprietary networking; take a side trip through standalone personal computing; and return through networking to the mainstream and distributed computing.

Batch Computing

Once upon a time, computers filled whole rooms and people accessed them by feeding punched cards into a card reader, as in Fig. 1.4. A set of cards made up a job. These jobs were batched together to be run when it was convenient for the computer. It was not convenient for the user, who had to wait in line behind other users. As can be seen in Fig. 1.4, the only user interface was the batch interface, and all services and resources were provided by the mainframe. There were no networking protocols or distributed services, because there was only one computer. Some batch systems, such as the IBM 360, did have limited portability across similar hardware.

Batch computing is still very useful for certain specialized environments, such as supercomputing. Batches tend to be submitted over general purpose networks these days, instead of from card readers, but the model is otherwise not much changed.

Centralized Timesharing

Timesharing systems are easier to use than batch systems, and that is why there aren't many batch systems left. Users can run jobs whenever they want to, and interactively. But early timesharing systems were generally still accessed directly through terminals connected by dedicated cables to the mainframe. The computer was still a monolithic singular entity, containing everything of use, as shown in Fig. 1.5.

UNIX became a timesharing system of this type in its early days, but didn't stay that way. It was ported to many different hardware platforms. This operating system portability was motivated by and promoted a desire for application portability across at least those same hardware platforms. This was usually done with source code, and is application portability at the source level. The presence of UNIX on many different platforms also led to a desire to network them.

When there is a need for data entry on character-based terminals, or any use for inexpensive interactive user access to computing facilities, a timesharing system may still be the best solution.

Proprietary Networks

Proprietary networks and dialup modems permitted distant access to computers, which made them popular. But distant terminals looked much like local ones. Each had a single window, with line-oriented commands. The basic access model in networking technology such as IBM's SNA (System Network Architecture), as shown in Fig. 1.6, is a star network with the mainframe at the center and all the terminals connected directly to it. This is not much different from the timesharing model. Other proprietary networking methods are more general, and are discussed later under distributed networking.

Large commercial conferencing and database systems still use essentially this model, with proprietary application protocols for use over dialup connections. Some of them even use proprietary data link and transport protocols, although

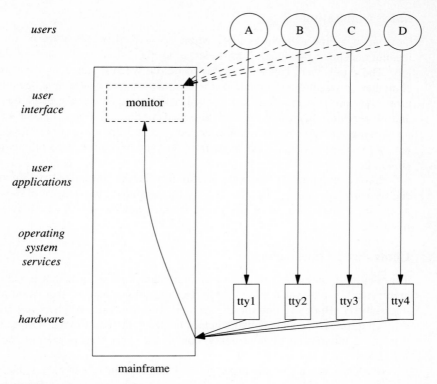

Figure 1.5 Timesharing model.

many will also use generally available protocols such as Kermit. The center of the star is still a mainframe or minicomputer. The points are usually personal computers, but they are used much like smart terminals. PC bulletin board systems also use essentially this model.

Personal Computing

Personal computing was once seen as the most desirable computing model by many. But it is more like the timesharing model than it might appear, and there are drawbacks, such as the lack of networking.

A personal computer provides dedicated computing resources to a single user. This is the greatest strength of personal computing. It is also related to the biggest problem of personal computers: they equate single-user computing with single-process computing. Early personal computer designers provided dedicated computing resources. Unfortunately, they did so with operating systems that permit only one task at a time. This turns out to be very unfortunate for distributed computing, as we will discuss later. PCs also often have no security, which means no protection against bugs or viruses in imported software; and personal computer

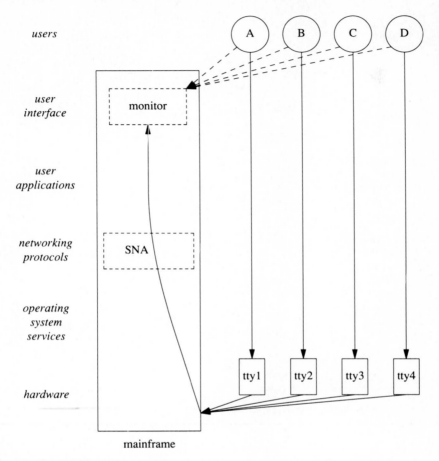

Figure 1.6 Proprietary networking.

applications can crash the system. Such applications often access the hardware directly at a very low level, making portability to other hardware platforms very difficult. Address space limitations of some popular PC hardware platforms make application programming in general difficult, and indirectly make portability more difficult. Except for such limitations, personal computing is much like mainframe timesharing, with a little mainframe for each user, as in Fig. 1.7. However, many personal computers, especially the Macintosh, also provide graphical user interfaces, unlike mainframes.

Personal computers are inexpensive, and they permitted many new people to use computers. A few operating systems, such as CP/M and MS-DOS, and common hardware platforms, such as the 8080 or i386 processors, used known hardware and software interfaces. These interfaces allowed organizations other than the computer vendor to supply software, permitting users to get many useful

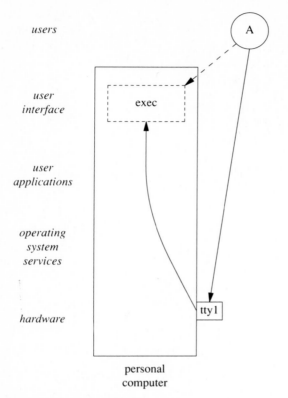

Figure 1.7 Personal computing.

products off the shelf. This is software portability, using an application binary interface (ABI). Users didn't have to wait for the hardware vendor to see a need, or to develop the software themselves, unlike in the early batch or timesharing environments.

Cost is also a major factor. For example, OS/360 on platforms by IBM, Amdahl, Fujitsu, and other vendors used a common ABI. PC ABIs are for hardware individuals can afford to own, which is an important addition to the other factors. These factors together created a mass market for commodity software.

It is relatively easy to copy data and information, including programs, from one PC to another, whether with floppy disks or by communication software using RS232-C ports. But software is often copy-protected, and these techniques are not as convenient as true networking. Information tends to deteriorate with copying in a personal computing environment. Each person makes a copy, modifies it slightly, and passes it on in an ad hoc manner. There is no guarantee that any pair of computers will communicate again, or that any copy of the information will be checked against any other copy. Networking has come to some personal computers, in the forms of Novell NetWare, Apple's AppleTalk, and even TCP/IP. But it comes late, and most PCs are still standalone.

Backups on a personal computer have to be done by the single user, often using dozens of floppies. So, unlike in a timesharing environment, which has support staff to back up a common shared machine, backups for personal computers often don't get done. A timesharing or networked environment often has several kinds of printers. If a personal computer user wants to use a different kind of printer, buying one may be the only solution. Similarly, everyone who wants a certain personal computer application has to get a copy on their own computer. This limits applications available according to the money and disk space available to each user.

Nonetheless, personal computing is a large and growing segment of computing, and standalone PCs are still hard to beat for many small scale and single user applications, such as small databases and spreadsheets.

Networked Computing

Distributed networking connects computers with distributed network protocols, as shown in Fig. 1.8. Unlike the early proprietary networking methods, no single central machine is used for communications. Instead, any machine may communicate directly with any other machine, and this is sometimes called peer-to-peer networking. Any given resource may be provided by one or more computers somewhere on the network. A machine providing a resource is a server for it, and the machine using the resource is a client for it. This is the client/server model of computing. This model, by any of these names, clearly distinguishes between resources and computers, unlike any of the previous models we have discussed.

Common resources include computer mediated communications protocols such as electronic mail (one-to-one) and news (many-to-many). Perhaps the most common resource sharing protocol is some form of distributed filesystem (dfs). Such a dfs involves the operating system, but a single operating system cannot do it alone.

When a computer can communicate with another across the network using common protocols, without special knowledge of the details of the other's implementation, that is interoperability. If the specifications for the protocols used are freely available, are implemented by a variety of vendors, and have an open input process, this is open networking as well as distributed networking. Open networking makes interoperability much easier, which permits many vendors to compete in providing network resources.

Open networks are often built from Ethernet and TCP/IP protocols. Ethernet was specified by Xerox, Digital, and Intel [Digital-Intel-XEROX 1982], and there is a related standard, IEEE 802.3 [IEEE 1985; IEEE 1988; IEEE 1992]. TCP/IP was originally produced by researchers on the ARPANET (the oldest packet switching network) and the Internet (the largest network in the world). Almost every computer vendor now implements it. The idea of open networking is also being pursued in the OSI (Open Systems Interconnection) protocol model and protocol suite, which are being specified by ISO (the International Organization for Standardization).

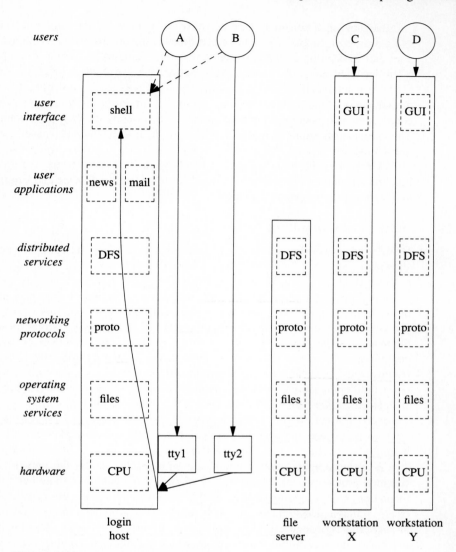

Figure 1.8 Networked computing.

Distributed proprietary network protocols such as Xerox Network Service (from Xerox) and DECNET (from Digital) were developed by several companies. But they did not spread into general use in networks with different kinds of machines, because their network protocol specifications were not freely available, and there were no open input processes into their specification. Personal computer networks using technology such as Novell NetWare or AppleTalk are similar [Akkerhuis *et al.* 1991]. In fact, Novell NetWare is based on XNS. But proprietary protocols do not directly address questions of communication with machines of other operating systems and sizes. And there are no open input processes for Netware or AppleTalk. There are signs that some proprietary network technologies are opening up. DECNET is now incoporating OSI. Novell has produced a portable implementation of NetWare that runs on various operating systems, including UNIX, and USL and Novell are collaborating in a joint venture called UniVell.

In an open distributed network, a user can access a file on another machine about as quickly as if it were local. But the user may still need to know where the file is. Some resources, particularly file systems, may be distributed across servers. But most resources are still specific to particular machines. The computers are still more visible than the resources, which makes the environment harder to use than many users would like.

Probably most large computer networks use peer-to-peer, client/server, distributed networking. Transparency is definitely an issue, but these networks have many users anyway.

Distributed Computing

Looking at distributed computing from the inside, that is, at the way it is provided, it doesn't look much different from networked computing. As shown in Fig. 1.9, there may be more different kinds of systems on the network. Some of them may not even provide local files. An X terminal, for example, is a computer dedicated to providing a graphical user interface on top of the X Window System. Such devices are typically less expensive than complete workstations. Many users will move off of dedicated character-cell terminals onto devices such as X terminals because the latter can be put anywhere on the network and can provide a graphical user interface on a high resolution screen. Other users may use personal computers that have been integrated into the network so that they function as workstations. This diversity of kinds of computers, together with diversity of vendors for them, is a major characteristic of distributed computing, but not one that users care about much.

If you look at distributed computing from the users's point of view, as in Fig. 1.10, it is very different. The network and all the accessible resources on it appear local to the user's system. The user sees a GUI, and some applications through it. Everything else is somewhere in the distributed computing environment, but the user doesn't know or care where. The user does not see distinctions between distributed or local resources. The location of remote resources is not relevant.

The distributed computing environment is a telescope, the GUI is the eyepiece, and the various protocols and hardware inside are the other optics. The user looks through the eyepiece and doesn't care what's inside, as long as the desired images appear.

In true distributed computing, a user can use a GUI to point at an icon and to drag a file across the network without even knowing there is a network. Resources on the network are more visible than the computers that provide them. Operating systems and network protocols have to know about details of location, routing, and access methods, but users don't care and don't have to know. This is

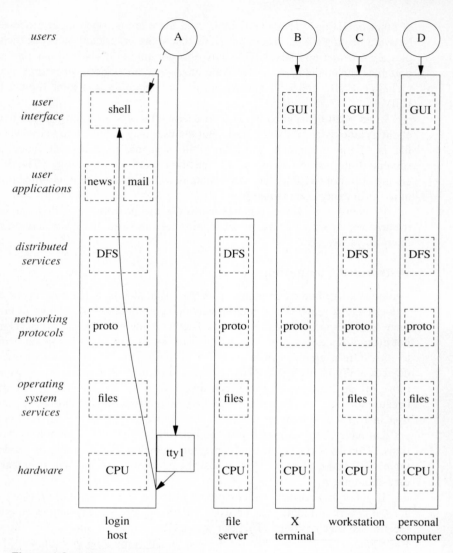

Figure 1.9 Distributed computing.

transparency. If a GUI with a similar look and feel is provided on different user interface devices across the network, there may even be user portability. The degree of similarity required of user interfaces on different platforms is a matter of some contention. Applications written for either Motif or OPENLOOK will generally run under the other, and users can probably move between them without too much difficulty. How much difficulty is too much is the question.

Distributed computing avoids duplication of data by permitting all users to have access to the data. It also makes communications among users easy. These

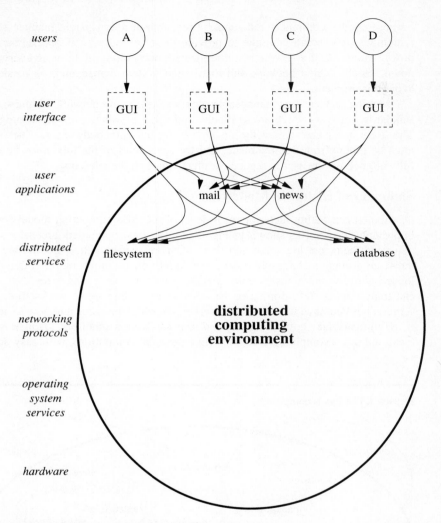

Figure 1.10 User view of distributed computing.

things promote work done by groups. Software that integrates these functions of resource sharing and computer mediated communications in order to promote group work is called groupware. There isn't much of it available for use across networks yet. This is partly due to the lack of adequate standards for services that such software could use.

Distributed computing is more fault-tolerant than batch processing, timesharing, or personal computing, because resources are dispersed across a network. It is usually easier to fix a machine on a network without taking the whole network down than to fix a device on a single machine without taking the machine down. Distributed computing is also more fault-tolerant than networked computing, because several computers can supply a resource in a transparent manner, so the remaining servers can continue to provide the resource even if one server goes down. However, if a service is not replicated, one failure might bring everything down. Sophisticated network and distributed system management is needed to avoid this problem.

Making services this manageable requires system and network administration standards, some of which are available, and some of which are still in progress. The users don't care where the resources are, but somebody must. The optics must be ground to a fine tolerance, and the mechanics of the tube must be carefully aligned for the user to see a clear image through the telescope.

Summary of Historical Models

Distributed computing incorporates aspects of previous computing models, while improving on them, as shown in Fig. 1.11. Personal computers are there when you need them, but are small and don't share resources well. Timesharing systems can provide manageable access to a variety of resources, but are often overloaded with too many tasks to do, making your job take a long time. Networks can transfer data and information between an extensible set of workstations and servers, but you have to know which server has which resource and how to access it. With distributed computing, the end user can have a small but adequate set of local dedicated computing resources (like personal computing), with easy access

Figure 1.11 Models compared.

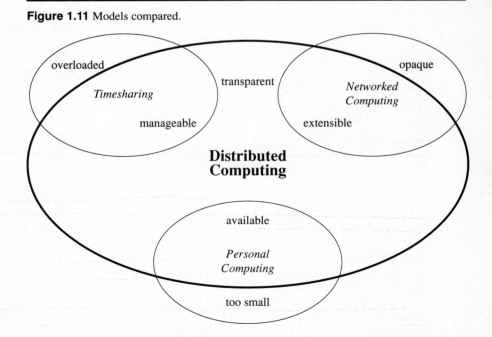

to a manageable variety of resources (like a timesharing system), yet with the resources distributed over an extensible network (as in the networked model).

All the previous models still have their uses, in certain domains of application. Distributed computing, by building on the good points of the previous models, should be more generally applicable than any of them. It is also more than the sum of these previous models, since it adds transparency: you don't have to know where a resource is to use it, and you don't need different access techniques for different resources.

1.3   Open Systems

All the old models still have their uses. But distributed computing is more general than any of them. Each computer used for distributed computing, or at least the computers used to provide key resources and services, should be an open system. An open system permits application portability and interoperability, and possibly also user portability.

- *Interoperability* is the ability to move data and information across networks.

- *Application portability* is the ability to move application programs from system to system.

- *User portability* is the ability of a user to move from one system to another without having to learn everything again.

For portability and interoperability to be possible across a wide range of different vendors' products, open systems must implement specifications that are widely available. Such specifications are usually better if both vendors and users participate in their development, that is, if they are produced by open processes. Portability, interoperability, and user portability have been found in several historical computing models. They are combined in open systems, which add open processes [POSIX.0 1991].

The UNIX timesharing system was one of the first portable operating systems. (Other contenders for first include UCSD/Pascal and one from Data General.) After its first ports, in 1978, this system quickly became available across a huge range of hardware, from microcomputers to supercomputers. Application portability, particularly portability of the source code for applications, became very important for UNIX. But UNIX systems tended to be too different for that to work generally. The basic UNIX programming interfaces were and are being specified and standardized by a variety of processes. Many of these interfaces are implemented by software that is not UNIX in any other traditional sense, so applications written for UNIX are now also portable in source form across a variety of software platforms.

As network protocols with freely available specifications, such as Ethernet and especially the TCP/IP protocol suite, became widely implemented and used,

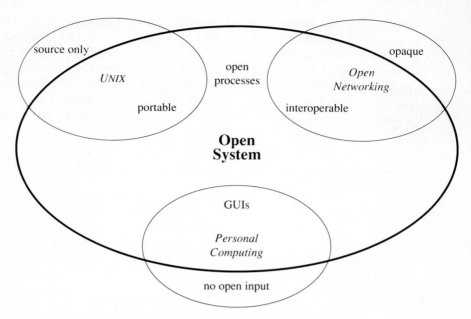

Figure 1.12 Historical systems and open systems.

interoperability became practical. The spread of such open networks inside universities, corporations, and other organizations, and the exponential growth of the worldwide TCP/IP Internet, made interoperability not only desirable, but indispensable. However, they lacked integration with the operating system, and transparency to the user.

Personal computing led to open licensing of PC operating systems such as MS-DOS, and to a large market in turnkey PC applications, such as Lotus 1-2-3, and Dbase-II. MS-DOS applications are portable to systems from many vendors. However, they are portable only across a limited variety of hardware platforms, and until recently only on top of MS-DOS. Although the *Application Binary Interface (ABI)* to the operating system is relatively distinct from the operating system implementation, there is no open process for input into the design of the MS-DOS ABI. PCs also often lack interoperability. Personal computers did not produce open systems, but they strongly influenced the concept. PC systems, especially the Macintosh, also made graphical user interfaces indispensable to many users, and made computers usable by many new users who find GUIs easier to use than command line interfaces.

The current idea of an open system is a result of a variety of influences, but especially of these three, as shown in Fig. 1.12: application portability from UNIX; interoperability from TCP/IP, OSI, and other open network protocols; and commodity software markets and graphical user interfaces from personal computing. The demand for these open system elements led to open processes. For example, the POSIX standards specify interfaces historically related to UNIX, but the specifications are developed using processes that allow input from a wide variety of people. Some other open system elements, such as the OSI protocols, have actually been designed by standards committees, instead of being derived from previous software. Still others, such as TCP/IP, have not used formal standards processes, but have taken input from many sources, and have insisted on practical interoperability testing of implementations.

This book is about these processes, the specifications and standards they produce, and how you can use them in building open systems. Two of the major forces behind open systems, application portability and interoperability, were strongly influenced by UNIX and related systems. The POSIX standards are based on these historical systems, and the TCP/IP protocols were largely developed on them. Many of the servers, login hosts, and workstations in real distributed computing environments are based on UNIX or conform with POSIX. This book focuses on POSIX and related standards, and how they can be used to build open systems.

1.4   Specifications and Interfaces

For open systems to work together in distributed computing, they need to use common interfaces and protocols, which means they must implement them from common specifications. Vendors of applications, operating systems, computers, and networks must agree on these specifications. This requires a process for all interested parties to help write the specifications: an open process. Open specifications that are used widely may produce commodity markets, which are good for building distributed computing environments, because they provide choices of facilities, vendors, and prices.

A user procuring a computer, operating system, or application may not want to require a particular vendor's make and model, because that would preclude any other vendor from offering a better deal. Instead, procurements usually describe specifications of interfaces, and how the interfaces should fit together into a desired environment, including additional requirements such as performance goals. So open specifications are good both for building open systems and for buying and selling them.

Specifications have implementations. Specifications may be for interfaces or protocols, or for related things like data formats. These are all used in building open systems and open environments. Interface specifications are the key to open systems. Some of them are shown in Fig. 1.13.

The ellipse in Fig. 1.13 is the operating system. Network protocol and distributed filesystem services are normally provided by the operating system and are shown inside the ellipse. In traditional systems, these services may be provided by the operating system kernel. In operating system implementations such as Mach or Chorus, the micro-kernel may provide only primitive facilities, such as message passing and synchronization, whereas higher level facilities, such as protocols and distributed filesystems, may be provided by kernel processes.

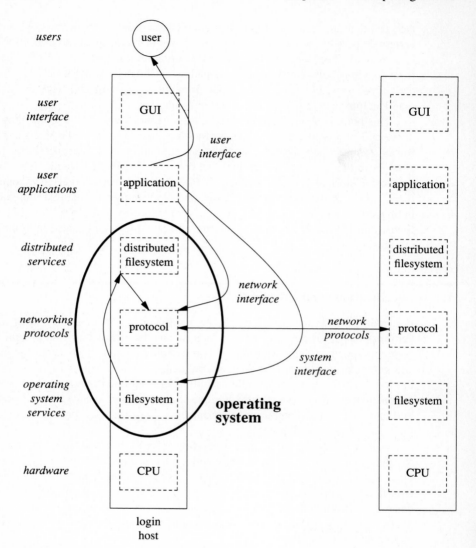

Figure 1.13 Interface specifications and protocols.

Implementation details such as these do not matter to the application, as long as the services are provided, and open interfaces to them are available.

The interfaces of interest for this book are as follows: those between the application and the user; and those visible to the application, that is, those that cross the elliptical boundary of the operating system in Fig. 1.13. That is, user interfaces, network interfaces, and system interfaces.

Specifications

A specification is a document that says what a piece of software or hardware does, and how it should be used. Such a specification may be nothing more than the vendor's documentation for a product. It may also include design documents that were used in producing the software or hardware; such design documents may be models in the general sense, intended to show how different pieces fit together. Each vendor will have different versions of such proprietary documents, so the documents are not very useful in selecting among different vendor's products. Instead, specifications written by third parties are often more useful. Such specifications need to be evolved and maintained using an open process that permits all interested parties to provide input, with provisions for updates for innovations in hardware and software. Specifications with all these features are called open specifications. An open specification produced by a formal standards body using a formal process is called a standard. An open specification may also be written by a vendor consortium or a user consortium. But a consortium specification is not a standard, because it is not produced by a formal standards process. The basic advantage of a formal standards process is widespread credibility, which is based on the standards body having used a known process. In addition, formal standards can be referenced by other formal standards. Some standards bodies have recently come to permit normative references to specifications that were not originally written by open processes [POSIX.0 1991]. The more important issue is control of the further development of the specification. We will examine these issues in more detail in Chapter 3, *POSIX and Open Standards*, and in Chapter 12, *Frameworks*. Examples may be found throughout the book.

Open specifications are clearly needed for network protocols, so that various vendors can produce products that will interoperate. They are also important for interfaces to those protocols, so application writers can write applications that will be portable to the vendors' systems. Open specifications for interfaces to basic operating system facilities are just as important for portability. User interfaces also require open specifications, if users are to be able to use more than one vendor's products. Open specifications are the key to distributed computing.

Implementations

A product that is written (software) or manufactured (hardware) according to a specification is an implementation of that specification. This is a matter of point of view: the product may have been designed and even written first and later adapted to match the specification, but from the point of view of conformance to the specification, the product is an implementation. Open systems are normally implementations of many open specifications. A real system usually needs to implement a range of open specifications to provide a sufficiently broad set of interfaces. Some implementations also implement several open specifications in the same general technical area, so that they can support more potential applications, or run on more platforms.

It is important to distinguish the implementation from the specification. Internal details of the implementation are normally beyond the scope of the specification. The implementation will usually provide facilities beyond the specification. Any real system must include such extensions to the specification, to account for local hardware, software, and administration requirements. Implementations are used in distributed computing, but they should not be the focus for distributed computing models or open systems, because they are specific products.

Interfaces

Clear interface specifications that keep the functions of the interface separate from the underlying implementation permit application software portability, both across existing hardware and software platforms, and to new generations of platforms. The more implementation details an interface specification includes, the more likely it will be hard to implement on some platform that doesn't work that way internally. Such overspecification can also limit the creativity of the implementor, and may make the use of innovative techniques difficult by making them nonstandard. So the most useful specifications mostly specify interfaces, not implementations. For example, IEEE Std 1003.1-1990 is called the System Interface Standard because it specifies an interface that includes functions such as *open*, *close*, *creat*, *read*, and *write*. It says that *creat* has to correspond exactly in behavior to that of *open* with certain options. But it does not say whether *creat* has to be implemented as a separate system call or perhaps as a library routine that calls some other system call.

The System Interface Standard specifies an application program interface. Specifications for other kinds of interfaces are also useful. Several kinds of interfaces can be seen in Fig. 1.13. They are shown from the point of view of an application program running in a login host. The application is written using a system interface specification, such as the System Interface Standard, for the interface with operating system services such as the filesystem. The application uses a network interface specification, in sending and receiving information using a networking protocol. It must know what functions to use to access that protocol. A specification for those functions, related data structures, and procedures for using them can make such programs more portable. The network interface specification may be the manual pages for the Berkeley socket construct or AT&T's *TLI (Transport Layer Interface)*, or it may be an actual standard, such as IEEE P1003.12 will be. Interface specifications also exist for data formats and for human interfaces, such as for graphical user interfaces. The user interface specification may be the documentation for the X Window System, or it may be something more formal. Interface specifications are the key to open systems, which are the heart of distributed computing.

This book is about certain kinds of interface specifications: those into the operating system and to the user. That is, those used by the application. In Fig. 1.13, there are more interfaces than we have discussed. For example, the application does not normally access the distributed filesystem directly. Instead, the application uses the normal operating system filesystem interface, and the operating system uses specific distributed filesystem procedures where necessary. The distributed filesystem implementation in turn uses network protocols. But these interfaces are not used directly by the application, and thus are not discussed much in this book. Protocol interfaces for user programs are of more interest.

Protocols

A network protocol is a specification for how to send, receive, and interpret information across a computer network. Protocols are usually specified in layers, and each protocol in each layer may only specify how to communicate with the layer below and the layer above. In this sense, network protocols are just more interface specifications. However, eventually information passed to network protocols travels over a network to reach another process or computer. The actual format of the data on the wire must be specified, so that each computer will interpret that format the same way. For this reason, network protocols are shown differently from interfaces in Fig. 1.13. Examples of network protocols include *TCP (Transmission Control Protocol),* and *IP (Internet Protocol),* which are part of a set of protocols called the TCP/IP protocol suite. Others include the *OSI (Open Systems Interconnection)* protocol suite, which includes protocols such as X.25 and TP4.

Environments

Single standards or specifications alone usually are not enough alone to determine whether a product or set of products is sufficient to support needed applications. Procurements are often really for environments to support classes of application interfaces. These environments often correspond more closely to actual implementations than do individual specifications or standards. The documents that specify them are called profiles, or functional standards. Protocols for general environments often include both interfaces for programs or users and network protocols. A profile that describes a very general environment may be called a guide, and an implementation of that environment may be an open system. The purpose of open systems is to support environments that provide resources users need.

This book concentrates on open system interface specifications that are related to the historical UNIX operating system. These are the industry specifications and formal standards related to the POSIX standards.

1.5 Summary

Many computing models have developed over time. Several of them are still competing, such as the centralized timesharing model against the networked model. Even within the same general model, such as distributed computing, there are many architectures and industry models that don't necessarily fit together.

Distributed computing is a good goal for local computing environments. Human expectations within a department or a company can be relatively uniform, and an environment to fit them is probably possible. Such an environment is probably not possible at a global scale, as long as there are different human languages and cultures. But internationalization helps.

The distributed computing goals of transparency, diversity, manageability, and extensibility are all desirable, regardless of whether true distributed computing can be attained. These goals all require interface specifications, as do the more basic goals of application portability, interoperability, and user portability. The best interface specifications to build open systems with these characteristics are often standards. This book is about interface standards and specifications that are related to UNIX and POSIX.

References

Akkerhuis et al. 1991.   Akkerhuis, Jaap, Seebass, Scott, & Stettner, Heidi, "Tying UNIX Systems and Macintoshes together," *Proceedings of the 1991 SUUG Conference* (Moscow, 22–28 September 1991), Soviet UNIX system Users Group (September 1991).

Digital-Intel-XEROX 1982.   Digital-Intel-XEROX, *Ethernet Local Area Network Specification Version 2.0,* Digital Equipment Corporation, Marlboro, MA (November 1982).

IEEE 1985.   IEEE, *Carrier Sense Multiple Access with Collision Detection,* IEEE, Piscataway, NJ (1985). ANSI/IEEE Std 802.3-1985; ISO/IEC DIS 8802/3:1985.

IEEE 1988.   IEEE, *Supplements to Carrier Sense Multiple Access with Collision Detection,* IEEE, Piscataway, NJ (1988). Includes thin Ethernet standard 10BASE2 and broadbase standard 10BROAD36.

IEEE 1992.   IEEE, *Carrier Sense Multiple Access with Collision Detection,* IEEE, Piscataway, NJ (1992). ANSI/IEEE Std 802.3-1992; ISO/IEC IS 8802/3:1992.

Malamud 1992.   Malamud, Carl, *Stacks,* Prentice-Hall, Englewood Cliffs, NJ (1992).

OSF 1991.   OSF, "Distributed Computing Environment: Overview," Open Software Foundation, Cambridge, MA (April 1991).

POSIX.0 1991.   POSIX.0, *Draft Guide to the POSIX Open Systems Environment,* IEEE, New York (September 1991). IEEE P1003.0/D13.

SMI 1990.   SMI, "Distributed Computing Road Map: The Future of Open Network Computing," Sun Microsystems, Mountain View, CA (May 1990).

SOS 1991.   SOS, "User Requirements Letter," Senior Executives for Open Systems, also known as the Group of Ten: American Airlines, Du Pont, General Motors, Kodak, McDonnell Douglas, Merck, Motorola, 3M, Northrop, and Unilever, Washington, DC (27 June 1991).

UI 1991.   UI, "UI-ATLAS Distributed Computing Architecture: A Technical Overview," UNIX International, Parsippany, NJ (September 1991).

CHAPTER 2

UNIX and Open Systems

Operating systems provide basic resources, such as processes, and basic services, such as access to hardware devices. In addition, they can provide distributed services, such as filesystems, and network protocols are implemented within them. Operating systems mediate between the user and the hardware, including the network. The operating system provides many of the services of distributed computing. General-purpose operating systems can be used to tie less-capable systems into a distributed computing environment. Operating systems are the basis of open systems, which are the basis of distributed computing.

The UNIX operating system was originally developed by AT&T, and is now a product of *USL (UNIX System Laboratories), which is partially owned by AT&T.* In this chapter, we discuss the UNIX system and various other systems that have evolved from it or are otherwise related to it. The UNIX system and its relatives have proved particularly useful in facilitating distributed computing. These systems have promoted application portability for a long time, and many of them are themselves portable across hardware platforms. Together they run on everything from laptops through workstations and multiprocessors to supercomputers. They have also been instrumental in the development of protocols for open systems interconnection, including both TCP/IP and OSI. These systems have even proved versatile enough to help glue other operating systems together into a distributed computing environment, because of their support for multiple processes, network protocols, and open interfaces. Finally, the UNIX system and its relatives have an unusual combination of open licensing and open input processes. These features of application and operating system portability, of availability of network protocols and specifications of interfaces for them, of basic operating system features, especially multiple processes, and of open interfaces to all of them, make systems related to UNIX highly competitive as open systems.

The early UNIX system was open in a very practical way: it came as a complete system, from device drivers to text formatters, with all the source code. This very openness led to many variants. This excess diversity in turn led to the current demand for standard interfaces, which all the variants (and even completely different underlying systems) can then implement.

UNIX itself is a specific manufacturer's trademarked, licensed, copyrighted, and trade secret product. Even though that vendor (AT&T and later USL) has been forthcoming with licenses to those who want them, a desire to make, sell, and buy systems without need for such a license is another strong force behind standardization of interfaces. So the flexibility and openness of the early UNIX system has led to a market demand for openness of a different kind, an openness of standardized interfaces.

An open system is an implementation of open interface specifications. But the openness of the interface standards does not require an implementation of them to be open. Open systems are proprietary implementations with open interfaces. AT&T and other vendors continue to sell proprietary implementations, but they also agree on some common interface standards.

2.1   The UNIX System

If application portability is good, being able to port a whole set of related applications at once should be even better. Applications usually run on top of an operating system. If you can port the operating system, it is easier to port applications that run on it.

The UNIX system was the first widely used portable operating system. Vendors liked this, because it meant they didn't have to write a whole new operating system for each new hardware architecture. The timing was also right, as the microprocessor revolution was just starting. UNIX traditionally comes with a set of related applications that its users expect, such as text editors and formatters, electronic mail facilities, and network protocols. And UNIX is a software development environment. It was written by programmers for programmers, and has many sophisticated programming tools. Writing new applications is well-supported, and the system supports applications of every kind.

UNIX was distributed with source code, which permitted users to fix bugs on the spot. Since it originally came without support or updates, "required" might be more accurate than "permitted." This also permitted many variants, which has led to much user confusion. But those variants allowed faster evolution than might otherwise have been possible. Many important features, such as virtual memory, multiple terminal support, and networking, were first added by organizations outside of AT&T.

Users and buyers of the UNIX system used to be found only in academia and government. Today, that is no longer true, because the business and manufacturing communities have discovered the advantages of the system. UNIX systems are now used worldwide. Along with the increased diversity of users comes an increase in the number of systems used in both the traditional (academic and governmental) and new (commercial and operational) areas. Continued growth is still predicted. But there is not just one UNIX system.

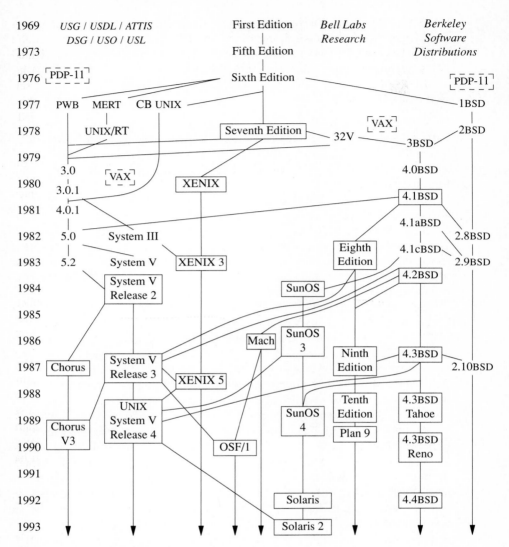

Figure 2.1 Selected UNIX operating system history.
Adapted from Leffler, et al., The Design and Implementation of the 4.3BSD UNIX Operating System, *Reading, MA: Addison-Wesley Publishing Company, Inc.* © *1989.*

Reprinted with permission.

UNIX Family Tree

Variants of the UNIX system proliferate, cross-pollinate, evolve, and merge, as shown in Fig. 2.1. They vary greatly in size, scope, and facilities provided. This family tree is quite a bit different from one for MS-DOS, which would be essentially a straight line. Comparatively, the UNIX world is much richer.

Significant changes have been made from the original AT&T Bell Laboratories design. Many variants still incorporate AT&T source code, and most require an AT&T license, for that or other reasons. Let's talk about the early Bell Laboratories systems first, and then about some of the variants.

Bell Labs Research

UNIX was invented in 1969 at Bell Laboratories, by two researchers, in an attic. Early versions (and all the research versions) were numbered after the current edition of the users' manual. First Edition UNIX through Seventh Edition UNIX were the early systems produced by the Bell Labs Computer Systems Research Group, from 1969 through 1978.

Sixth Edition, in 1976, was the first version of UNIX that was widely available outside Bell Labs. (It is also known as Version 6, or V6; but *not* as System 6.) It ran on the PDP-11, but was mostly written in a medium-level language, C. The system was distributed with the C source code, unlike most other contemporary operating systems. This was a big advantage, because bugs could be fixed where they were found, and new facilities could be added. But it also marked the beginning of divergent versions.

Seventh Edition, in 1978 (Version 7, or V7) was the last version distributed by the original Bell Labs Computer Systems Research Group. It ran on the PDP-11, but came with the *PCC (Portable C Compiler),* which facilitated porting the operating system itself. 32V, also in 1978, was the VAX version of V7. This was not the first port of UNIX. One had been done previously in Australia, and Bell Labs had previously ported Seventh Edition to Interdata machines. But it was the VAX port that established the reputation of UNIX as a portable operating system, perhaps due to the later popularity of the VAX hardware.

Eighth, Ninth, and Tenth Edition UNIX were produced from 1983 to 1990. Bell Labs Research systems continued to be influential, particularly with their innovation of streams, which were user-stackable protocol modules in the kernel. Streams were also used to implement the Remote File System (RFS), which was later distributed by AT&T. Various other facilities were first implemented on these systems, such as **/proc**, which allows accessing processes as files, and an early implementation of the C++ language, which was first available as a class preprocessor for the C language. Much work on user interfaces was done at Bell Labs, such as the BLIT bitmapped terminal, which offloaded some processing from the main system, but not as much as a workstation would.

Plan 9 came from Bell Labs in 1989. Many of the same people who produced Research UNIX continued working on Plan 9. It was partly derived from some of the Research UNIX work on user interfaces. This new system is built around intelligent terminals similar to the BLIT, file servers, and CPU servers. It is intended to provide transparent distributed computing much like UNIX with graphical user interfaces.

Bell Labs research systems occasionally have direct effects on standardization. We discuss one such case, involving Plan 9 and codesets, in Chapter 11, *Internationalization.*

Berkeley Software Distributions (BSD)

The Computer Systems Research Group (CSRG) at the University of California at Berkeley (UCB) has been very influential in the development of UNIX, particularly in networking. The BSD systems started as a set of addons to the Bell Labs Research systems. Early BSD releases were not complete operating systems; instead they were mostly application programs, such as vi, the first full-screen text editor written specifically for UNIX. These early software tapes were for the PDP-11, and were released in 1977 and 1978, as 1BSD and 2BSD. The main number 2 was retained for later PDP-11 releases, through at least 2.10BSD in 1987.

3BSD was an important piece of work that added demand paging of main memory to 32V, in 1978. This was the first implementation of virtual memory in UNIX.

4.1BSD, in 1980, was the next major BSD release. It had terminal independence, using the **termcap** facility. This was important at the time, since there were hundreds of different kinds of character cell terminals on the market, and bitmapped displays had not yet become common. 4.1BSD also had many new device drivers, and job control, modeled after TWENEX, the PDP-20 version of UNIX produced by BBN from TENEX, Digital's operating system for the PDP-10. Job control permits the user to stop a set of related processes (a job) and do something else. The user can put the job in the background and let it run as if it had been started with the shell ampersand (&) suffix. The user can restart a job, regardless of whether it has since been put in the background. Job control was partly intended as a stopgap until window systems could be implemented, but it is still often used with window systems.

4.2BSD, in 1983, was the most influential Berkeley release. It had a native implementation of the TCP/IP and Ethernet network protocols, a fast file system, and reliable signals. Its *socket* interface to the networking facilities became widely used. 4.2BSD was partly funded by DARPA, the same federal government agency that funded most of the early work on the ARPANET. DARPA wanted a UNIX system for use by DARPA researchers. One of the things they needed was a good implementation of the TCP/IP protocols. Because 4.2BSD was government funded, its implementation of TCP/IP was available to anyone for the cost of distribution. It became available just when inexpensive hardware permitted new and old computer vendors to incorporate it in workstations and other systems. So 4.2BSD provided a free reference implementation of the TCP/IP protocol suite. This saved vendors time, because they did not have to implement it themselves. It also made a vendor more likely to choose TCP/IP over, for example, the *XNS (Xerox Network System),* which was a proprietary protocol suite that was popular at the time, but did not have freely available specifications or a reference implementation.

4.3BSD [Leffler *et al.* 1989], in 1986, was faster and more reliable. It included an implementation of XNS, and had more network interfaces.

4.3BSD Tahoe, in 1988, was an intermediate release that supported the CCI Power Series in addition to the VAX. It had network bug fixes, revised bootstrapping, and disk format labels.

4.3BSD Reno, in 1990, was another intermediate release. It had POSIX compatibility, with 90 percent of the POSIX System Interface Standard implemented, and much of the then-current draft of 1003.2. It has a variety of filesystems, including Sun's *NFS (Network File System)* and a complete implementation of the GOSIP OSI network protocol stack. Most of this code does not require an AT&T license. It has already been ported to i386 processors, in addition to earlier platforms.

4.4BSD will probably be released some time in 1992. It will have a new virtual memory system, a merger of sockets with UNIX System V STREAMS, more OSI protocols, and support for more hardware architectures.

UNIX System V

While the Bell Labs Computer Systems Research Group was distributing Seventh Edition UNIX, various other versions were used inside AT&T. These included PWB, MERT (not really a UNIX system), CB UNIX, and UNIX/RT.

UNIX System III, in 1982, merged most of the internal systems, together with outside ideas, and was licensed to the public.

In 1983, the court-ordered divestiture of Regional Bell Operating Companies from AT&T permitted AT&T to sell computers.

UNIX System V [Bach 1987], in 1983, included semaphores, shared memory, and messages, all of which were new to UNIX, at least in a widely available version. Although this new system was lacking in some features already available in other systems such as 4.1BSD, most notably paging, it was well received by much of the market, and AT&T marketed it with the slogan "UNIX System V: Consider it Standard."

UNIX System V Release 2 Version 4, in 1984, added a new implementation of paging, with copy on write, plus quite a few previously missing device drivers, and many applications derived from BSD. This system narrowed the technical gap between UNIX System V and 4.2BSD.

UNIX System V Release 3, in 1987, included STREAMS. This is a reimplementation of the Eighth Edition streams package. The *TLI (Transport Layer Interface)* was added, and *RFS (Remote File System)* was made available using it.

UNIX System V Release 4, in 1990, merged many features from POSIX, BSD, XENIX, SunOS, and other systems. System V Release 4 was the result of a contract between AT&T and Sun. Almost all vendors of UNIX or similar systems now support programming interfaces like this system. Those interfaces are specified in the *System V Interface Definition (SVID)*, which we will come back to later.

AT&T System V source code is now developed by *USL (UNIX System Laboratories)*, which is an independent company, although AT&T has a large share in it. USL takes input from *UI (UNIX International)*, which has many industry vendors as members.

Another large vendor consortium, the *OSF (Open Software Foundation)*, produces a system, OSF/1, which has a kernel with little or no AT&T source code. However, the kernel was originally based on UNIX System V Release 3, and many of the utilities are derived from AT&T source code, so OSF/1 requires an AT&T license.

In general, almost any modern system related to UNIX will have a programming interface that conforms to the SVID (and perhaps to other interface specifications as well, particularly XPG and POSIX, in increasing order of number of conforming implementations).

XENIX

XENIX is a version of UNIX for PC-class machines. It was originated by Microsoft Corporation, but was made popular by the *SCO (Santa Cruz Operation)*. It was originally based on Seventh Edition, and later on UNIX System V. *ISC (INTERACTIVE Systems Corporation)*, under contract to AT&T and Microsoft, ported System V Release 3 Version 2 to the Intel hardware. But SCO has not picked up UNIX System V Release 4. The majority of UNIX systems are XENIX systems.

Ultrix, SunOS, HP-UX, and AIX

There are many proprietary systems related to or derived from UNIX and produced by many different companies. Knowing that we must omit many from our discussion, we choose to mention a few here, for various reasons.

Ultrix. The UNIX system has run on hardware from *Digital (Digital Equipment Corporation)* longer than on that of any other vendor. UNIX was invented on a PDP-7, and most early UNIX development was done using PDP-11s. Ultrix is Digital's product related to the UNIX system. It was originally a port of 4.2BSD, and later adopted many UNIX System V features. Digital maintains a strong position in the UNIX system market with Ultrix.

SunOS. *Sun Microsystems, Inc (SMI)* is a company that has always used UNIX systems exclusively on its hardware. Very early Sun hardware used a port of Seventh Edition UNIX. But SunOS evolved from a port of 4.1cBSD. It later adopted many UNIX System V features, and UNIX System V Release 4 is a merger of System V and SunOS, plus features from other systems. Sun has concentrated on workstations and fileservers, and has been instrumental in building the UNIX workstation market. See also Chapter 15.

In 1991, Sun partitioned itself into several smaller companies, one of which, SunSoft, is producing a portable version of SunOS that will run not only on Sun's SPARC hardware, but also on Intel and other platforms.

HP-UX. HP-UX is *HP (Hewlett-Packard)'s* system related to the UNIX system. HP-UX was originally based on 4.2BSD. It later adapted the interface of UNIX System V Release 2. Still later, it adopted many 4.3BSD features. HP has concentrated on workstations and interoperability. HP and HP-UX have one of the largest pieces of the UNIX system market.

AIX. *AIX (Advanced Interactive Executive)* from *IBM (International Business Machines, Inc.)* was originally a port of UNIX System V Release 2. It later incorporated many BSD features. It now conforms to the POSIX System Interface Standard. IBM has been active in funding test suites, as well.

AIX 3.2 is a worldwide system that permits a single binary to work in any country. Multiple languages may be supported simultaneously. That is, configuration for Japanese at installation does not prohibit use of French, German, or other languages on the same system. We will discuss this more in Chapter 11, *Internationalization*.

It appears that AIX started a shift in thinking inside IBM towards open systems and input, and perhaps towards embracing international and national standards.

Mach and Chorus

Mach and Chorus are micro-kernel based systems related to the UNIX system. Both use AT&T-licensed application programs derived from UNIX System V and 4.3BSD. The major differences are in the kernels, which have been completely reimplemented.

Mach was developed at *CMU (Carnegie Mellon University)* as a research project partly sponsored by DARPA, the same U.S. government agency that sponsored much of the BSD work. The Mach kernel was originally based on Sprite, another DARPA research project at Berkeley, but later was based on the 4.3BSD kernel. It has since been completely reimplemented as a micro-kernel that provides basic facilities, with much of rest being supplied by processes [Young *et al.* 1987; Accetta *et al.* 1986].

The *Chorus* system is produced by Chorus systèmes of Paris, France. It began with a project called SOL at the *French National Research Institute for Computer Science and Automation (INRIA)*, reimplementating Seventh Edition UNIX in Pascal. Chorus is not a reimplementation of the SOL project. It is a new development, and was originally implemented in C. It has since been reimplemented in C++, and involves a micro-kernel and associated processes [Rozier *et al.* 1988].

Other Influences

UNIX has always borrowed ideas from other systems (and other systems have increasingly borrowed from UNIX). The idea of the shell, which is a command language interpreter that can be replaced by the user, came from the MULTICS system [Organick 1975], as did the hierarchical organization of the filesystem. Much of the general emphasis on timesharing features came from the *MIT (Massachusetts Institute of Technology)* CTSS operating system. The *fork* operation for producing a new process with copies of the executable code and data space of an old one came from the Berkeley GENIE (SDS-940 or XDS-940) system. Berkeley's job control was modeled after similar facilities in TENEX and the MIT ITS system.

UNIX continues to absorb ideas from other operating systems, and other, completely different, kernels support UNIX (or POSIX) interfaces. Some related distributed systems include Mach, Chorus, and Amoeba. At least one of these, Chorus, is written in an object-oriented relative of C, called C++.

Networking and UNIX continue to be mutual strong influences. The implementation of TCP/IP in 4.2BSD permitted that protocol suite to become the most widely implemented in the world.

Graphical user interfaces are a current area of work. There are at least two competing ones. Some of their competition is occuring in the standards arena.

Standards have come to influence the systems that are available as strongly as those systems influence standards. Hardly any vendor will sell nor user will buy a system interface related to UNIX that is not conformant to at least the POSIX System Interface Standard (IEEE Std 1003.1-1990). Differences between rival versions are often worked out in standards committee meetings. In many cases, the resulting compromises have caused all the existing implementations to change. On one hand, standards make some changes to existing interfaces harder, and thus may impede innovation. On the other hand, standards help create a solid consensus base from which to build new facilities.

Since UNIX has become commercially viable in the past 5 years or so, the way it is distributed has changed. The printed manual and source code used to fit in a briefcase. The manual alone may now fill a shelf, it may not be available in paper at all, or may not be available online, depending on the vendor. Many vendors don't put everything that was included in a traditional UNIX distribution on their machines. Text processing, extra languages, and even the C compiler are often unbundled into separate packages that cost more. Much of this unbundling is done to address the mass market that personal computers currently occupy. The typical end user in that market has no desire to compile a program, and often wouldn't know how to write one. This kind of packaging makes the system more marketable in some new markets, but causes disgruntlement among many of its old supporters. What effect it will have on the ability of the system itself to evolve is yet to be seen.

Popularity of UNIX

Because UNIX has become popular, it is changing according to influences such as standards and marketing that its original proponents often do not like. Ironically, many of the things that made the system so widespread are now seen as problems in selling it.

UNIX became popular for many reasons. It was written in a high level language, with few machine-specific parts of the operating system. This, together with the availability of its source code, made bug fixes and modifications easy and portability plausible. It also made divergence possible, and the microcomputer revolution made them inevitable. This divergence made porting application programs among variants difficult, and led to the formation of the *usr/group Standards Committee,* which was the parent of many of the current standards committees, including IEEE P1003.1, P1003.4, P1003.6, and X3J11.

From its earliest days, UNIX has had the support of a user community. (These days there are several with different agendas.) It was first popular among researchers, which led to government support for versions such as BSD and Mach. Eventually, it became the system of choice for a number of government agencies. These agencies wanted a uniform system for procurements. This led to the *National Institute of Standards and Technology (NIST)* producing their own standards and trying hard to speed the progress of other standards such as POSIX.

The development of usable microprocessors and falling hardware prices brought UNIX out of academia and government and into business and other uses. That, combined with networking, particularly its widespread use on corporate networks and the growth of the TCP/IP Internet, started a phase of explosive growth. There are only so many researchers and academics. Eventually, as the pool of users increased, it had to consist mostly of other people. Most users are now just that: users, not developers. They want stability, not innovation; thus they want standards.

As already mentioned, UNIX has always had a tendency to absorb useful things from other systems (though not everything, e.g., ISAM). This tendency has recently brought not one, but two, major graphical user interfaces to UNIX, making the system usable by large numbers of people who did not like shell commands. Reconciling this diversity is another reason standards are needed. Some GUI users feel strongly about look-and-feel issues, and are strongly behind such standards. It is important to note that it is common for multiple standards to exist in the same technological area. Examples include the various bus standards, such as VME, Multibus, and EISA; the various data link layer networking protocols, such as IEEE 802.3, 802.4, 802.5, FDDI, and HIPPI; and a plethora of programming language standards, such as those for Pascal, Ada, and Modula 2. As we will discuss in Chapter 7, multiple POSIX-related GUI standards are now being constructed by IEEE P1201.1, P1295.1 (Motif), and P1295.2 (OPENLOOK). What standards bring to such competition is some clarity of choice, and the advantages of open processes.

Finally, the demand for open systems has brought commercial acceptance for UNIX, even as it remains a favorite of researchers and academics. A system that is as popular in the accounting department as in engineering needs to be a stable system. This is both bad and good. Innovation is what made UNIX and systems like it widespread in the first place. Large sales provide resources for further innovation, but marketing may prevent innovations from becoming available.

The Era of Consortia: X/Open; and OSF versus UI and USL

Most vendors of systems related to UNIX are members of one or more of three or more vendor consortia: X/Open, OSF, or UI, which are listed in Table 2.1. Vendor consortia are basically strategic alliances intended to gain market share for their members. To attain that goal, consortia whose members produce operating systems usually write interface specifications so that application programs can be portable to all their systems, and can interoperate among them. Consortia can also write profiles that specify values of options found in formal standards, so that

Table 2.1 Vendor Consortia.

Product	X/Open	OSF	UI/USL
specification	XPG	AES	SVID
operating system	—	OSF-1	UNIX System V
GUI	—	Motif	Open Look
distributed computing		DCE	UI-ATLAS
distributed management	XSM	DME	DOMM

everyone using the specification will choose the same values for the options. Since options in standards are sometimes produced by contention between two consortia, each consortium can just choose its favorite value in its own specification.

The earliest vendor consortium related to UNIX is the X/Open Company, Ltd, which was formed in 1984 under the name BISON. X/Open does not produce software; it produces specifications (and test suites). It publishes a book called the *X/Open Portability Guide (XPG)* that specifies a *Common Application Environment (CAE)*. This CAE covers a broad area, including things such as COBOL that are not addressed by any of the POSIX standards committees (although some popular language standards are identified in the IEEE P1003.0 POSIX Guide [POSIX.0 1991]). The XPG also specified many technological areas earlier than related formal standards bodies could. This is one of the major advantages of consortium specifications over formal standards: speed. X/Open has also provided a large amount of useful input to POSIX and other standards.

The *Open Software Foundation (OSF)* was formed in 1988 as a reaction to a business alliance between AT&T and Sun. It was originally called the Hamilton Group. OSF has been active in producing both specifications and software. Their first *Request for Technology (RFT)* was for a graphical user interface, including its look and feel. They settled on Motif, which has become widespread. They chose Mach as the basis of their OSF/1 operating system. The interfaces to OSF/1 and Motif are given in OSF's *Application Environment Specification (AES)* OSF has produced influential specifications for both a *Distributed Computing Environment (DCE)* and a *Distributed Management Environment (DME)*.

Partly as a reaction to OSF, AT&T formed *UNIX International (UI)* to collect corporate member input and provide direction for UNIX System V. UI was originally called the Archer Group. Actual software is now produced by *UNIX System Laboratories (USL)*, which was originally a subsidiary of AT&T, but is now a separate company, only partly owned by AT&T. The specifications for the system are in the *System V Interface Definition (SVID)* UI has chosen OPENLOOK as its GUI. They have also produced UI-ATLAS, which is an inclusive architecture for distributed computing and management. Chorus systèmes and USL have an agreement to keep Chorus and UNIX System V compatible.

X/Open has come to play somewhat the role of a neutral third party between UI and OSF. This does not necessarily mean that X/Open, even in conjunction with OSF and UI, can produce what many application writers and users would like: a single set of interfaces, merging 4.4BSD, Mach, OSF/1. System V, and all the other variants. Some users might like a single system with a single implementation even better, but X/Open clearly will not produce that, since X/Open writes specifications, not software.

History reminds us that, when the conflict between BSD and System V appeared to be resolved, the conflict between OSF and UI sprang up to take its place. Other players and alliances, such as SunSoft and ACE, keep springing up to challenge whatever pair of players seem to have a lock on the market. Some take up strategies that may be completely new, such as free software developed and given away by the *Free Software Foundation (FSF)* (including a good C compiler) and UCB CSRG, yet maintained for pay by Cygnus, Inc. and BSDI (Berkeley Software Design, Inc.).

Old players may come back with renewed force: 4.2BSD served as the basis for a lot of systems (and was the predecessor of Mach); 4.3BSD strongly influenced POSIX; 4.4BSD will not require an AT&T license, and has already been ported to a number of important hardware platforms. A pre-release has already been turned into a product by BSDI.

From competition comes innovation. It is quite likely that the forces of software and hardware innovation, combined with the desire of the market for variety, will keep the number of important systems from ever reducing to one. Given interface standards, the number of different implementations is not a problem. For example, there are many implementations of ANSI C. The more interesting question is how much interfaces will diverge.

Licensing

In almost every document about UNIX, no matter by whom, you will find a footnote that says "UNIX is a Registered Trademark of UNIX System Laboratories" (or the older "UNIX is a Registered Trademark of AT&T Bell Laboratories"). Not only is it a trademark, but AT&T and USL have been vigorous in advocating its proper application. For example, they insist that the word "UNIX" is an adjective, not a noun, and they have made several user groups change their names to add the word "system" after "UNIX."

Not only is the word trademarked, but the source code is licensed, copyrighted, and trade secret, all three at once. A license permits someone other than USL to use the source code, or a binary UNIX system, so it is the most interesting of those three forms of protection. A license implies control of modifications to both the implementation and the interface.

Academic institutions have traditionally gotten relatively inexpensive site licenses that permitted them to allow almost anyone who needed to to look at the source. Commercial licenses are more expensive.

Most UNIX systems sold today no longer come with source code. Such binary distributions can be cheaper, and are liked by vendors because the user can't modify them easily. Many traditional users dislike them for the same reason. Good or bad, source code licensing is one reason for binary distributions.

Many vendors base their operating systems on UNIX. That is, they take UNIX source code from AT&T and modify it to add proprietary or other features, or take UNIX features and add them to their own operating systems. Examples include Ultrix (from Digital), HP-UX (from HP), SunOS (from Sun), and AIX (from IBM). These systems all support interfaces like those of UNIX, plus various others, and are sometimes called UNIX, even though that really means UNIX System V from UNIX Systems Laboratories (USL).

Such vendors pay license fees to USL for use of the source code and for each system sold, whether with or without source. Yet the result is not UNIX, unless USL agrees to let the vendor call it that, as USL permitted SCO to do with XENIX. UNIX is one specific vendor's make of software.

Several other systems support the same programming interfaces as UNIX, but have completely different internal implementations. Such systems include Coherent, Whitesmith, Charles River Data Systems, Mach, and Chorus. They may use no AT&T licensed source code in their equivalents to the UNIX kernel, that is, in the code that supports the application programming interface, even though licensed UNIX applications are usually provided. One group, UCB CSRG, is working on a system completely free of AT&T code, and their next release, 4.4BSD, may be that. OSF/1 from the Open Software Foundation (OSF) is based on Mach. USL has recently made an agreement to coordinate Chorus and UNIX System V.

All these systems support the same general classes of services and interfaces. The boundaries between UNIX and not-UNIX are becoming sharper (licenses) and more blurred (interfaces) at the same time. The emphasis has changed from UNIX itself to interfaces that may be historically derived from UNIX or its relatives, but that are now available on a range of operating systems. These systems now run across the entire scale of hardware used by competing operating systems.

Since the divestiture agreement permitted AT&T to sell hardware, there has been a potential conflict of interest between that role for AT&T and the other role as sole supplier of the licensed software for UNIX to an entire industry. Whether AT&T sees this as a conflict is not clear, but some of the rest of the industry does see it that way.

Standards committees promise group consensus on common interfaces that can support multiple implementations. Such standardized interfaces can be implemented across a wider range of hardware than any single underlying implementation can. One of the often-unspoken goals of standardization related to UNIX is to have the interfaces for UNIX-related systems controlled by an open process, rather than by a single vendor.

Given open interfaces, the significance of licensing of a single implementation is lessened, because other vendors can still ensure that their implementations interoperate and provide portability. These interfaces, and the standards and specifications that define them, are what we want to examine in this book.

2.2   Networking

A computer with peripherals and other components from diverse manufacturers is not an open system by itself. Even if application programs written for it can be ported to different hardware or software platforms, it is not an open system according to the current usage of that term. No open system is complete without interoperability.

The term *open system* has come to include open networking. The best-known term for open networking is *OSI (Open Systems Interconnection),* which refers to the movement of data and information among systems on a network by means of well-known network protocols. This provides information portability. Major goals of open systems and of OSI are shown in Fig. 2.2.

The acronym *OSI* refers to a specific reference model and protocol suite specified by OSI. This OSI, also known as ISO-OSI, is not the only protocol suite that fits the definition of open systems interconnection, however. Others include several proprietary protocol suites, such as XNS and DECNET, and one open protocol suite, TCP/IP. OSI purists will assert that TCP/IP has nothing to do with OSI, because TCP/IP does not conform to the specific OSI Basic Reference Model [ISO 1992] that has been accepted by ISO and CCITT. In a literal sense this is so, but here we are discussing the goals of open systems. It is clear that TCP/IP has gone further than any other protocol suite in achieving them, simply because it is the most widely implemented protocol suite in the world, and it serves as the basis of the largest computer network in the world (the Internet), as well as supporting a large number of smaller distributed computing environments. Its history is also closely intertwined with that of UNIX.

Historically, OSI has been somewhat separate from open systems, which originally were more concerned with application portability than with interoperability. But easy transportation of information promotes portability of programs. Many open systems are part of networks; a modern operating system is incomplete

Figure 2.2 OSI and open systems.

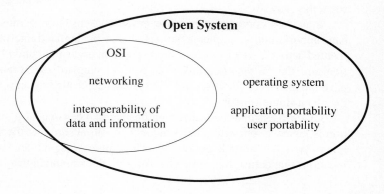

without networking. As we saw in Chapter 1, open systems these days are taken to include interoperability: open systems have absorbed OSI. OSI is now almost a proper subset of open systems, as shown in Fig. 2.2. We do not show OSI as entirely within open systems, because OSI could connect systems that are not open, for example, that lack open programming interfaces, even though they do communicate by open network protocols.

Much of the development of the TCP/IP protocols in the last decade or so has been done on UNIX or related systems. Even much of the recent development of the OSI protocols has been done on those same systems. So it is not surprising that many open network services are provided from these operating systems, which have become the mainstays of distributed computing.

OSI

Traditionally, the capitalized term *OSI (Open Systems Interconnection)* refers to a specific protocol model with the seven layers shown in Table 2.2, and a specific protocol model that fits that model. Example ISO-OSI protocols include X.25, TP0, and TP4. The protocol stack shown in Table 2.2 is a set of OSI protocols that are commonly used together, especially in Europe. There are other OSI protocol stacks; we will discuss some of them in Chapter 8.

TCP/IP

Many of the ideas of Open Systems Interconnection are also found in other protocol models and suites, including Digital's DECNET and IBM's *SNA (System Network Architecture),* and especially TCP/IP. Even though the Internet Model and the TCP/IP protocol suite have different layers (see Table 2.3) than the ISO-OSI model, many of the underlying ideas (such as decomposition of protocols into layers to reduce complexity) are the same; in fact, many of the ISO-OSI ideas were derived from the Internet Model and its predecessor. We will discuss layering issues more in Chapter 8.

Table 2.2 OSI layers.

	Layer	Examples
7	Application	VTM, FTAM, MHS
6	Presentation	IS 8822/X.216, IS 8823/X.226
5	Session	IS 8226/X.215, IS 8327/X.225
4	Transport	IS 8072/X.214 (TP0-TP4)
3	Network	X.25
2	Data Link	HDLC
1	Physical	X.21

Table 2.3 Internet protocol model.

Layer	Examples
Process/Applications	TELNET, FTP, SMTP
Transport	TCP
Internet	IP
Network	X.25, Ethernet, FDDI
Physical	various

The TCP/IP protocols are designed to interconnect networks so that they appear to the user as a single large network. That is, the protocols are used to build internets. TCP/IP has become so popular that the largest internet built from it, called simply the Internet, is the largest network of any kind in the world, except for the telephone network. Most of the computers on the Internet run UNIX or something like it.

Much of the early popularity of TCP/IP can be traced to the 4.2BSD implementation of those protocols, which was distributed at cost of distribution, and served as a reference implementation. Various other networking applications or facilities, such as NFS from Sun and the streams protocol facilities from AT&T, have kept UNIX at the forefront of networking technology.

The Client/Server Model

The client/server model is the basis of both the networked computing model and the distributed computing model. It is worth examining in some detail, because it is also the main reason that multiprocess operating systems such as UNIX are better as network servers than are single-process personal computer operating systems.

The TCP/IP File Transfer Protocol (FTP) is a traditional networked computing service. To retrieve a file, a user uses a client FTP program on the local machine to talk to a server FTP program on the machine with the file. The client and server FTP programs provide the file transfer service to the user. The server process may serve many client processes. This is the client/server model.

There are many different network services. For software to tell them apart, a *port* number is used. The client FTP knows that the server FTP process will be accepting connections on a well-known port (21), so the user doesn't have to tell it that. A local port is needed for the client end of the FTP control connection, but the operating system normally assigns that port automatically. A separate pair of ports is needed for each actual file transfer, but the client and server FTP implementations take care of that. Each end of each connection is normally handled by a separate process. The same server process may sometimes handle more than one client, but there is usually at least a separate server process for each active service. This is one reason a multiprocess operating system is desirable on a server system.

All the port assignments are done by the programs without the user having to know about them. However, FTP does not know where files are. The user has to tell the client FTP program which host to connect to. So FTP does not make the network transparent. In contrast, for distributed computing services such as transparent filesystem access (TFA), the user doesn't need or want to know which host a file is on. The distributed computing model needs to make the host level of connection addressing as transparent as the networked computing model has already made the process level of connection addressing. It does this by building on the client/server model.

The FTP protocol expects to send data back and forth for an extended period, so FTP is a connection-oriented service. The client and server record each other's address information for continued use, and the server will often create a separate process to handle each new connection. This is another reason a multiprocess operating system is desirable.

Not all services are connection oriented. A protocol that retrieves a single database entry, such as for contact information for a user, doesn't usually need an extended connection. The client process may send a single datagram and expect a single datagram back. A single server usually handles all service requests for its host. Some important distributed computing services, such as TFA, are sometimes implemented by connectionless services.

Many distributed applications are peer-to-peer in the sense that they are not constrained to a star configuration around a single hub machine, unlike terminals attached to a mainframe. But most distributed applications are not implemented so that every peer user process communicates directly with every other one. Instead, the client/server model is usually used. That is, each client user program communicates with the server, which coordinates communications among the clients. There may also be multiple servers, coordinating communications among themselves. This is a third reason that a multiprocess operating system, used to coordinate processes performing related tasks, is desirable for server systems.

Why UNIX for Networking

The popular single-user operating systems such as MS-DOS and MacOS do not have some of the capabilities of more general operating systems. In particular, they don't have multiple processes. This is changing. MacOS System 7 has limited multitasking and better support for peer-to-peer communications, for example. Novell NetWare provides many of the capabilities found under UNIX. And OS/2 was designed to have multiple processes. But UNIX systems are still the mainstays of many networks of diverse operating systems.

Many end-user applications are available for personal computer operating systems. An increasing number of PC clients for network services are becoming available. But PC operating systems are not well suited for running servers to provide network services to other machines. This is because PC operating systems are generally not only single-user, but also single-process. Recently introduced PC operating systems such as NT and OS/2 are changing that, but UNIX still has a lead. Most network services use the client/server model, which requires at least one server process on the server machine. For connection-oriented services, that model requires at least one server process per active client.

So open network server machines usually run multitasking operating systems. Quite a few such operating systems exist. Many of them are proprietary to particular vendors. Such vendors tend to have their own proprietary network protocols, and have concentrated on providing network services for them, more than for the open network protocol suites.

Starting in 1980, there was one multiprocess operating system that ran on a variety of vendor hardware and was intimately involved with networking: UNIX, particularly 4.3BSD, and later System V Release 4. It and its more recent relatives, such as Mach and Chorus, have become the glue that holds open networks together, because they provide the open network services that make such networks work.

Other Operating Systems

Many vendor-specific operating systems not related to UNIX, such as VMS from Digital or VM/CMS from IBM, support many of the same kinds of services, but with different interfaces. Where they support the same network application protocols, they can be used as hosts or servers like the UNIX relatives. Basically, if it can network, you can fit it in somehow. But these other operating systems often lack at least one basic feature of UNIX: portability of the operating system itself to different hardware. This portability permits UNIX users to use the same system on a very wide range of hardware. Many other operating systems do not permit as much portability of applications. And many of them are not as openly licensed.

Operating systems using open interfaces derived from UNIX are often preferable to vendor-specific operating systems for use as network servers for these reasons. Many operating systems cannot implement POSIX interfaces, but some can. Open interface specifications such as POSIX may even be implemented on completely non-UNIX operating systems, such as VMS or OS/2. Interface specifications have become more important than implementations.

2.3   Degrees of Openness

Open specifications and open licensing of implementations are two different things. Each comes in many degrees. One view of this is shown in Fig. 2.3, where input into the specification increases towards the right, and licensing of software implementations becomes easier towards the top. Proprietary systems are in the lower left, openly licensed systems with little outside input are towards the upper left, and open systems are on the top and towards the right. There are no examples in the lower right of the graph, presumably because people will not participate in an open process that produces specifications that can only be used by a single vendor. One suggestion that comes close to fitting in that lower right corner is AppleTalk.

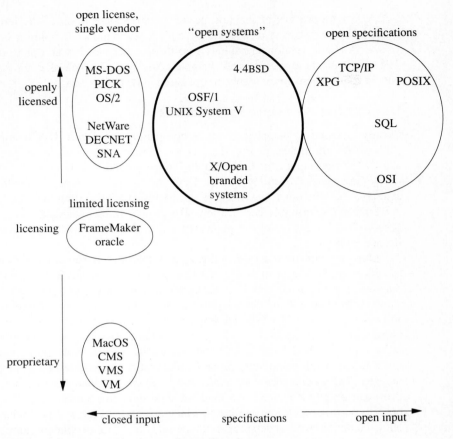

Figure 2.3 Open specifications and open licensing.

Closed Systems and Applications

Proprietary operating systems, such as VM, CMS, VMS, and MacOS, aren't normally licensed to other vendors, and users have little control over their specifications. These are found in the lower left corner of Fig. 2.3. They were the most common kinds of systems available when the batch and timesharing computing models were prevalent. There are exceptions. The Macintosh operating system is neither a batch nor a timesharing system, but it is proprietary. UNIX is a timesharing system, but it is not a proprietary system in this sense.

MS-DOS, PICK, and OS/2 have little input into their specifications from sources outside of the companies that produce them, but many vendors can and do license them. These and similar systems are found in the upper left corner of the graph. Most personal computer operating systems are found there.

SNA, DECNET, and Novell NetWare are network protocol suites with similar properties. They correspond to the proprietary network model.

A few proprietary application packages fit in the middle of the left of the graph. This software is distributed by only a few vendors for only a few platforms. A single vendor determines who those other vendors and platforms are. The Oracle database system is an example. Another is FrameMaker, the page layout package. There are probably no operating systems like this.

Open Systems and Open Specifications

Openly licensed systems with some open input into their specifications are towards the top middle of Fig. 2.3. These include UNIX with input from USL, and OSF/1 with input from OSF, and the X/Open branded systems that conform to the *XPG (X/Open Portability Guide)*. Here, the X/Open systems are shown as less available than the other two, because of the difficulty of getting the brand, which is a kind of conformance certification. We show 4.4BSD towards the upper right, because it conforms to several published and draft POSIX standards and has few license restrictions.

Open specifications go far to the right of the figure. The easier it is to get a specification, the closer to the top that specification is shown. Some specification documents are expensive and are packaged in many pieces, like OSI, so they are shown lower than others. Some specifications are free and are available over networks, like those for TCP/IP, so they are shown at the top. POSIX goes in the upper right of the graph. The OSI protocols have relatively open processes, but the amount of actual input is limited because much of the work takes place at the international level, where only properly constituted national delegations may participate. The specifications are public and there are no actual licenses, but getting them can be problematical, and there are few implementations. TCP/IP is very open to outside input, has public specifications, and is very widely implemented, but is lacking in well-understood input methods for those people not familiar with a great deal of history.

All the open specifications are shown to the right of all the open systems, because any real operating system requires facilities that will not be in any standard or open specification. New hardware and software technology may outpace standardization. Proprietary hardware can require extensions that should not be standardized, but may also fill a market niche.

The Market

The graph in Fig. 2.3 shows input and availability, not numbers of users, numbers of machines, or dollar values of sales. We could show some such usage measure as a third dimension. We'd see big hills over MS-DOS and TCP/IP, with a smaller but fast-growing one over the open systems. There used to be a large mountain over the proprietary systems, but it is eroding as more users turn to those other, newer hills. Open licensing and open input make systems more popular. Open input also encourages systems that run on different kinds of hardware, and that may be quite different outside of the areas of the open specifications. Open licensing of implementations of open specifications is characteristic of open systems.

Many systems with both open input processes and open licensing are related to UNIX and POSIX.

2.4 Summary

Systems related to UNIX have historical and technological advantages in support for multiple hardware architectures and in application portability, and in network protocols and services for interoperability. These advantages made these systems popular enough that this system originated by two guys in an attic now runs on every scale of hardware made, is sold by almost every computer vendor in some variant, and is fought over by at least three worldwide consortia of all those vendors. This popularity, together with concerns about licensing and centralized control of the technology, caused development of open processes for standardization of interfaces such as POSIX. These interface standards are used to build open systems, which are used to build distributed computing.

References

Accetta et al. 1986.   Accetta, Mike, Baron, Robert, Bolosky, William, Golub, David, Rashid, Richard, Tevanian, Avadis, & Young, Michael, "Mach: A New Kernel Foundation for UNIX Development," *Proceedings of the 1986 Summer USENIX Conference* (Atlanta, 9–13 June 1986), pp. 93–112, USENIX Association (1986).

Bach 1987.   Bach, M. J., *The Design of the UNIX Operating System,* Prentice-Hall, Englewood Cliffs, NJ (1987).

ISO 1992.   ISO, "ISO Open Systems Interconnection — Basic Reference Model, Second Edition," *ISO/TC 97/SC 16*(ISO CD 7498-1) (1992).

Leffler et al. 1989.   Leffler, Samuel J., McKusick, Marshall Kirk, Karels, Michael J., & Quarterman, John S., *The Design and Implementation of the 4.3BSD UNIX Operating System,* Addison-Wesley, Reading, MA (1989).

Organick 1975.   Organick, Elliot I., *The Multics System: An Examination of Its Structure,* MIT Press, Cambridge, MA (1975).

POSIX.0 1991.   POSIX.0, *Draft Guide to the POSIX Open Systems Environment,* IEEE, New York (September 1991). IEEE P1003.0/D13.

Rozier et al. 1988.   Rozier, M., Abrossimov, V., Armand, F., Boule, I., Gien, M., Guillemont, M., Herrmann, F., Kaiser, C., Langlois, S., Léonard, P., & Neuhauser, W., "Chorus Distributed Operating Systems," *Computing Systems* **1**(4), pp. 305–372, USENIX Association (Fall 1988).

Young et al. 1987.   Young, M., Tevanian, A., Rashid, R., Golub, D., Eppinger, J., Chew, J., Bolosky, W., Black, D., & Baron, R., "The Duality of Memory and Communication in the Implementation of a Multiprocessor Operating System," *Proceedings of the Eleventh Symposium on Operating System Principles* (Austin, Texas, November 1987), pp. 63–76, ACM (1987).

CHAPTER 3

POSIX and Open Standards

In the previous chapters, we traced the path of motivation from the need for distributed computing to the need for open systems to the need for standards. In this chapter, we discuss the standards themselves, starting with their goals and history. Then we define basic technical terms of standardization, from base standards and specifications through extensions, profiles, and implementations, back to open systems and distributed computing. Because these terms are interrelated, we give brief definitions of them at the beginning of the chapter, and more detailed and formal definitions later. Finally, we give some practical reasons why standards are important.

A *standard* is a specification that is produced by a formal process by a formal (accredited) standards body. In this book, we use the term *specification* only for specifications that are not standards, and we use the term *standard* only for formal standards. A specification in this sense may be produced by a vendor or a consortium. IEEE Std 1003.1-1990, the System Interface Standard, is a formal standard, as are X.25 and TP4. NFS is a vendor specification, and DCE is a specification produced by a vendor consortium. A formal standard may be called a *de jure standard* to distinguish it from specifications.

A *de facto standard* is a specification that is widely implemented and used. This has nothing to do with how such a document is produced, and either a standard or a specification may be a de facto standard. A formal standard may be a de facto standard, and such a widely implemented and used formal standard would be the ideal.

A specification produced by an open process is an *open specification*. An *open process* is one that controls the future content of the specification, and that permits input by any interested or affected party. Formal standardization processes are designed to be open processes, and mostly succeed to a large extent in being such. Other open specifications are produced by vendor consortia, such as X/Open, OSF, or UI. There is some contention over whether some such consortium processes are truly open, since consortia may permit direct input only from

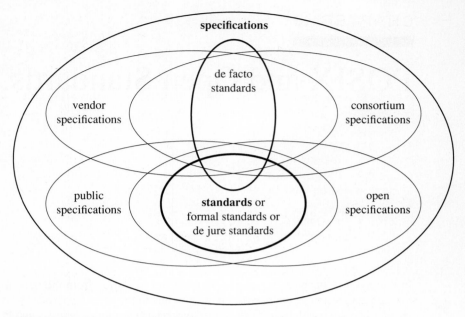

Figure 3.1 Standards and specifications.

member organizations that have paid high membership fees. But a consortium process may be as open as a formal standardization process. The TCP/IP protocols are specified by a group that is neither a vendor consortium nor a formal standards body, yet one can argue that an open process is used, so those protocols would be open specifications. Standards are specifications, of course, as shown in Fig. 3.1, but in this book we try to keep the terms separate to avoid confusion.

The term *public specification* has been invented to cover specifications that are publicly available but were not originally produced by open processes. A standards body or other producer of open specifications will usually require control over future versions of a public specification, or at least a frozen form of a specific version, before using it in producing an open specification or standard. An open specification or a public specification may also be a de facto standard.

A *profile* is a set of standards and specifications, together with certain parameter settings and options, to define an interface or environment to support a set of applications. A profile does not have to be a standard. It may be a specification, produced by a vendor, a consortium, or some other organization, like any other specification. But it may be a standard, and is then called a *standardized profile*. A profile may also be called a *functional standard,* whether it is a formal standard or not. In the international formal standards community, the term *ISP (International Standardized Profile)* is often used interchangeably with functional standard. Properly, an ISP is a standardized profile that is an international standard.

There are still more specialized terms for profiles, according to whether they are standardized, and by whom. Let's leave the specifics to Chapter 12, *Frameworks*. Here, it is enough to discuss profiles in general. Profiles vary in size from particular interfaces for specific applications through those for classes of applications to those for general open system environments.

An *implementation* conforms to a standard or a specification. Most of the standards and specifications relevant to open systems specify interfaces. Implementations that conform to them may vary in their internal details as long as they supply the appropriate interfaces. This provides dependability for the application developer and flexibility for the interface implementer. An implementation may be an open system, if its interfaces conform to standards or specifications that were produced by open processes. Some profiles specify environments for open systems.

We will give more formal definitions for all these terms later in this chapter, and in the glossary; first, let's look at some goals and history of standards.

3.1   Standards for Open Systems

We have shown in the previous chapters how portability and interoperability are critical for open systems. Control of specifications by a single vendor does not provide for the portability and interoperability required by open systems. We will discuss why in the detailed definitions of public specifications and open specifications. Vendor consortia can supply guides or specifications, but not standards. Open interface specifications are needed. Formal standards are needed.

Goals

Some specific goals of standardization are given in this section. Most of these goals are shared by both formal standards and industry specifications. We've mentioned many of them before, as goals of distributed computing or of open systems:

1. Application portability is the most basic open system goal.

2. Interoperability is portability of data and information, and is the most basic OSI goal.

3. User portability is desirable, because retraining users can cost more than purchasing software or hardware.

Here we examine each of them in detail as goals of open system standards, and we add some more goals.

Application Portability

An important goal of standardization is *application portability.* If an application is written with only standard interfaces, it should be portable to other platforms that support those standard interfaces. An application that is engineered for portability is cost-effective, because it won't have to be rewritten for another implementation of the standard interface. If the interface standard is for source code portability, the source code for the application can be moved to a different system, compiled (or translated), and run without being rewritten.

There are several degrees of application portability, as indicated in Table 3.1. The two most common kinds are source code portability and binary portability, but there are degrees within each category, and both categories are points on a spectrum of degrees of portability, which includes other points such as ANDF (see below) and *pseudocode (pcode),* as in UCSD Pascal. Source code portability permits transportation of programs across a wider range of platforms than binary portability. But binary portability requires less effort on the part of the user, since there is no compilation necessary.

Within source code portability, degrees can be distinguished according to the kind of changes that are needed to port a program. The least useful degree involves arbitrary manual changes to the source code. A medium degree involves conditional compilation of parts of a program. This is usually done using compiler facilities like the #ifdef preprocessor facilities in C, that permit the programmer to define a symbol that the preprocessor then uses to decide what to compile. The most useful degree is unconditional compilation, that is, compilation without any changes at all.

Table 3.1 Kinds of application portability.

Category and Degree	Diversity of Systems	Trade Secret Protection	Ease of User Installation	Ease of Migration to New Systems
Source Code Portability				
Unconditional compilation	highest	low	high	highest
Conditional compilation	high	low	high	high
With manual changes	fair	low	poor	fair
Pseudocode Portability				
UCSD Pascal	good	good	good	fair
Binary Code Portability				
ANDF	fair	high	high	fair
Dynamic options	fair	high	high	fair
ABI	low	high	high	low

Unconditional compilation is the ultimate form of source code portability. It is more desirable than the other kinds, because it requires the least effort of the user, but it is also the hardest to achieve.

Binary portability ranges from the loose compatibility of an *ANDF (Architecture Neutral Distribution Format)* through dynamic parameter setting on the same architecture (*sysconf* and *pathconf*), to a true *ABI (Application Binary Interface)* such as MS-DOS. The concept of an ABI was introduced to the UNIX system in 1987 by AT&T. Several vendor consortia pursue it today, including 88Open and SPARC International. ANDF has been popularized by OSF.

An ABI is desirable because there is no need for adaptation of the program to the target platform: the program just runs, because there is only one target. This is rather like unconditional compilation, except there is no source code to compile. But an ABI can put severe restraints on implementations by including very specific hardware characteristics such as byte order or word size. An ABI is clearly not as flexible as source code portability.

The POSIX System Interface Standard provides the functions *sysconf* and *pathconf*. These allow a running program to discover actual settings for parameters required by the standard. For example, *sysconf* can determine how many processes any user may have running, and *pathconf* can tell how long filenames can be on a specific filesystem. In general, *sysconf* is for systemwide parameters. These may change when a new system is configured. Some parameters may change while a system is running, perhaps by mounting a new filesystem with different parameters, and *pathconf* can return some of those that are associated with filesystems, such as the length of a filename. These functions allow unconditional compilation of many applications, which can instead dynamically allocate table space and set other parameters based on limits they discover when they are running. The binary object of such a program can then be moved across machines of similar architectures.

Applications can avoid having to know about some interface details if they are compiled into an ANDF. Such a format hides details of a specific computer architecture, such as byte order and instruction set. An ANDF can provide almost as much flexibility as conditional compilation of source code, but without the source code.

Related topics include internationalization and localization, which will be discussed in Chapter 11.

No matter how carefully interfaces are standardized, and no matter how carefully implementation techniques such as ANDF facilitate portability among *new* implementations, old systems that do not conform to the new interfaces and techniques will still play a role for some time to come. Such an old system is politely called a *legacy system* because it was probably inherited from a previous computing model. Applications must take legacy systems into account, and new specifications, standards, and techniques should attempt to provide upgrade paths [SOS 1991]. Legacy systems were brought to the attention of the standards world especially by SOS and UAOS.

Interoperability

Communication between computers requires standard protocols, and standard interfaces to those protocols promote portability of network and communication applications. This is *information portability,* when it permits information to move among computers without manual intervention, perhaps across a network. Systems that support information portability have *interoperability.* Interoperability is not just interconnectability. A dialup connection from a PC to a timesharing system using Kermit for uploading and downloading software and files does not provide interoperability. Considerable manual effort is needed for this kind of information transfer. The terms *uploading* and *downloading* are evidence that the PC is a lower-class system when used in this manner. True interoperability has to do with systems that use peer-to-peer protocols. A PC connected with TCP/IP over SLIP over a dialup connection can provide interoperability, for instance.

Areas related to interoperability include

• Data interchange format

• Networking protocols

• Distributed file systems

• Access to data on legacy systems

We will discuss interfaces to networking protocols and distributed services in Chapter 8. There is some information about data interchange formats in Chapter 7.

User Portability

A standard user interface enables user portability. Once users have learned the standard interface, they can easily use other hardware supporting the same interface. User training may cost more than software or hardware. Programmers are a kind of user, and programmer portability across systems with standard program interfaces is also desirable. Some user interface standards are described in Chapter 7.

System Engineering

A standard for a system interface affects system engineering. An implementer can no longer make unilateral changes to standardized functions, even to provide useful new facilities. But the implementer may change the supporting implementation in any manner that seems desirable, as long as the interface conforms to the standard. It is easier to implement something that is well defined. As we discussed in the previous chapter, numerous system variants were a big problem in the history of UNIX. If the interface must comply with a standard, the tendency toward "creeping featureism" is avoided. A standard for a basic system interface related to UNIX is described in Chapter 7.

Testing and Verification

A system interface standard makes conformance testing and verification easier, by clarifying exactly what is to be tested. This helps vendors show that a product lives up to its claims, and helps buyers in selecting products. We discuss this in much more detail in Chapter 10.

Marketing and Acquisitions

No matter how good a system is, customers won't buy it if they don't know what it is. Standards are thus also useful for marketing, sales, acquisitions, and procurement, since they provide vendor-independent descriptions of what is being sold or what is wanted to be bought. Vendors need to describe their systems so customers will know how to use them and what will run on them. Customers need to specify system interfaces and applications that will work for them. Vendors use standards and profiles to describe the menu, and buyers use them to select the meal. By permitting variation of implementations of standard interfaces, standards also provide for a diverse market. All this applies to application vendors and value added resellers as well as to platform vendors and end users. We discuss profiles in more detail later in this chapter, and in Chapter 12.

Standards History

From the *usr/group 1984 Standard* (really a specification) to the recently approved International Standard 9945-1 (POSIX 1003.1 Operating System Interface), standards related to UNIX went from idea to reality in four or six years. Whether those were few years or many depends on your point of view. Fig. 3.2 is a standards family tree that indicates how a few standards and specifications have grown from others. Many more standards and groups would have been appropriate for the figure. Only a selection is shown; more are shown in Chapter 7.

The standards shown in Fig. 3.2 are the *1984 /usr/group Standard* and its direct descendents, plus three POSIX standards, plus the three major consortium specifications. All of P1003 (for POSIX), X3J11 (for the C Standard), and AT&T (for the SVID) used the *1984 /usr/group Standard* as a base document. For example, the X3.159 library functions were based on that standard. Standard I/O functions such as *fopen* went to X3J11, and underlying system I/O functions such as *open* went to P1003. All of these documents and X/Open's XPG influenced each other. OSF's AES came too recently to affect the other documents directly, but OSF members had participants in all the relevant standards committees. All of the TCOS POSIX standards shown have related WG15 documents.

3.2   Standard

Most of the standards described in this book were originally produced as voluntary consensus standards. One reference describes voluntary standardization as "the deliberate acceptance by a group of people having common interests or

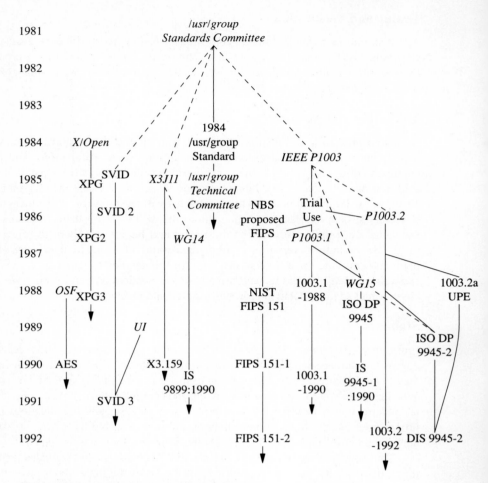

Figure 3.2 A partial standards family tree.

background of a quantifiable metric that influences their behavior and activities by permitting a common interchange" [Cargill 1989, 13]. Some of them may later be required by law for certain purposes, and then would become mandatory or regulatory standards. However, it is important to realize that the organizations that produce standards almost never require anyone to use them.

The range of application of standards may be only internal within a company or agency. One department may even use different standards than another department. Or the range of a standard may be national, regional, or worldwide. Despite all this possible variation, there are certain common categories of standards and related interfaces and implementations.

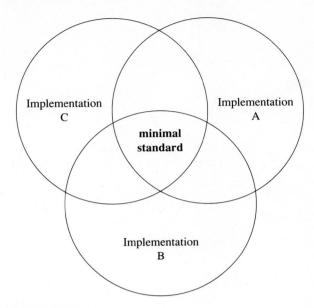

Figure 3.3 Minimal standard.

Formal and de Jure

A *standard* is a document that specifies a technological area within a well-defined scope. It is produced by a formal standardization process by a formal standards body, such as ISO, IEC, ANSI, or IEEE. The term *formal standard* is sometimes used to distinguish a standard from some other kind of specification. A standard is sometimes called a *de jure standard* for the same purpose, and with the same meaning.

Minimal and Compromise

A *minimal standard* is one that was reduced to a small or minimally defined set of features to avoid controversy, as shown in Fig. 3.3. POSIX.1 is a minimal standard, in the sense that many areas were removed from it and were put into projects for extensions, or even into whole other base standards, such as POSIX.2, in the interests of finishing the first POSIX standard.

A *compromise standard* includes features for reasons other than technical merit or how widespread their use may be; this is sketched in Fig. 3.4. For example, IEEE 1003.1 includes both the tar and cpio data interchange formats, even though either one would probably have been sufficient. Sometimes, a standards committee can't even decide to include both variants of a facility, or the variants are in conflict, and the committee decides to put in an option, so that the implementer can select either variant.

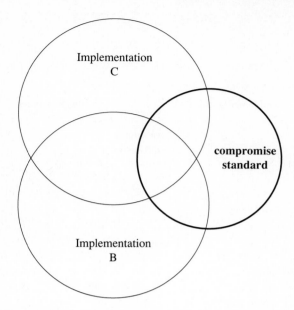

Figure 3.4 Compromise standard.

Much wording in standards gets chosen very carefully to avoid putting in options while permitting multiple variants of a feature. This is known in POSIX standards jargon as *weasel wording,* and is one reason standards can be so hard to read. Compromise is essential to consensus, but it can have obscuring and obscure effects.

It is possible for a standard to be both minimal and compromise, and the POSIX System Interface Standard is both. But minimal and compromise are almost orthogonal concepts, and it is also possible for a standard to be one but not the other.

Base Standard and Extension

The terms *base standard* and *extension* are used for documents that are or modify a single base standard. Examples are given in Table 3.2.

A *base standard* may be modified by an extension or referenced by a profile, but is not itself an extension or profile. The term has to be defined very carefully for use with profiles. One traditional formal definition of a base standard is used by ISO/IETC JTC 1: "an International Standard, Technical Report, or CCITT recommendation used in the definition of a profile" [SGFS 1990a].

A broader and more recent definition is included in the *POSIX Guide*: "A standard or specification that is recognized as appropriate for normative reference in a profile by the body adopting that profile" [POSIX.0 1991]. We'll discuss the implications of this latter definition in detail in Chapter 12, *Frameworks*; essentially, it means that a body like TCOS that does not produce international

Table 3.2 Standards.

Type	Example	Title
base standard	IEEE 1003.1	System Interface
extension	IEEE 1003.4	Realtime and Other Extensions

standards can standardize a profile that uses a base standard that is a national standard, but not an International Standard, TR, or CCITT recommendation. This permits the profile and the base standards it references to progress upwards to international standardization together.

An *extension* adds to a base standard (or to another extension). It may modify facilities or add new ones. It may be called an *amendment* or a *supplement*. It is common for the technical matter of an extension to originate in drafts of a base standard, but to be moved into a separate project to make the base standard more minimal and thus more likely to be approved in a timely manner. Even though an extension may be a separate document, it and the base standard it modifies taken together are still a base standard in the usage of that term for profiling.

3.3   Specification

Standards are specifications in an informal sense, but in this book we use the word *specification* for a document that is not a standard. Such a document specifies a certain technological area, often within a well-defined scope. But it is either not produced by an accredited standards body, or not by a formal standardization process. Specifications are usually produced by vendors, consortia, or users, and may be of several types, as we know from Fig. 3.1. Examples for some of these types are given in Table 3.3. The examples of open specifications and vendor consortium specifications given in the table are merely illustrative, not definitive; no classification of examples in those categories will satisfy all interested parties.

Specifications are sometimes preferable to formal standards. Formal standards have many advantages. They are produced by open processes that take great care to get input from interested parties. They have high standing with standards bodies and procurement agencies. In some cases, they are even required by law. But they also take a long time to produce, and tend to be minimal standards that cover relatively narrow technological areas. They are often also compromise standards that aren't as specific as some implementors or users would like. For these reasons, vendor consortia and even single vendors may succeed in getting nonstandard specifications written more quickly than formal standards can be produced. Some of these specifications may even become de facto standards, which is to say they might as well be formal standards, for many purposes.

Table 3.3 Specifications.

Type	Example	Explanation
de facto standard	UNIX System V	from USL
	4.3BSD	from UCB
open specification	XPG	X/Open Portability Guide
vendor consortium	SVID	UI/USL System V Interface Definition
	AES	OSF Application Environment Specification
vendor specific	Ultrix	manuals from Digital Equipment Corporation
	SunOS	manuals from Sun Microsystems, Inc.
	HP-UX	manuals from Hewlett-Packard
	AIX	manuals from International Business Machines

de facto Standard

A *de facto standard* is a specification that is widely used. A formal standard may also be a de facto standard. The POSIX System Interface Standard, for example, is the de facto standard for the interface functions it specifies. Many de facto standards are not formal standards. Such a de facto standard may be even more widely accepted than formal standards in its area, if any exist. Examples include IBM's *SNA (System Network Architecture)* and Microsoft's MS-DOS operating system.

A de facto standard originating from one vendor may force vendor dependence, since other vendors may have difficulty producing compatible interfaces, or in keeping up with changes. One can even argue that a de facto standard is a specific product implementation. But this book is about specifications, so we choose to consider a de facto standard to be a specification.

Open Specification

An *open specification* is a specification that does not contradict international standards, that is maintained by a public open consensus process, and that is updated to accomodate new technologies and to conform to new standards.

An open specification is often also a de facto standard. It may be used in building open systems. A well known example is the X Window System. Unfortunately, there is no public specification for X, so vendors have diverged from the MIT X Window System interfaces in their implementations. If an open de facto standard exists, there may be no point in creating a formal standard, or at least any formal standard should probably just standardize the de facto standard.

A formal standard should normally be both an open specification and a public specification.

Public Specification

A *public specification* is similar to an open specification, but is not required to have been produced by an open process. It is merely required to have a publicly available and stable specification. Public specifications are useful for reference in other specifications or standards that want to build on them. A standards body that wants to do this will normally require control over future versions of the public specification, at least to the extent of ensuring that there are no legal impediments to the use of its current version [POSIX.0 1991]. Producers of open specifications have the same concern of change control over public specifications. Due to increased pressure to produce standards quickly (partly due to networks; see Chapter 8), some standards bodies and other groups seem to be shifting their emphasis from open specifications to public specifications, as far as what they are willing to reference in their own standards or open specifications. The reason for interest in a public specification may be that it is already a de facto standard, and the referencing body wants to try to use it to make the resulting standard or open specification a de facto standard, too.

3.4   Interface

Most open system standards and specifications are for interfaces. There are three major kinds of interfaces: for writing application programs, for communicating with external environments, and for internal interfaces [POSIX.0 1991]. These are listed in Table 3.4 and depicted in Fig. 3.5.

An *API (Application Program Interface)* is for writing programs to access basic operating system services such as processes or filesystems, or to access facilities of other application programs. An API should not require the application writer to know much, if anything, about the internal details of the operating system or other facility behind the interface. An example is the POSIX System Interface Standard (IEEE 1003.1-1990 or IS 9945-1:1990) for basic operating system functions. Another is the POSIX Shell and Utilities Standard, IEEE 1003.2.

An *EEI (External Environment Interface)* is for communicating with an external environment, such as a network, a monitor screen, or an archive. Three basic kinds are sometimes distinguished, as shown in Fig. 3.5.

• Human to computer EEI examples include IEEE 1003.2a UPE, User Portability Extensions, and IEEE 1201, Interfaces for User Portability.

• Information EEI examples include IS 9945-1 Chapter 10, Data Interchange Format, and the IS 9660 CD/ROM format standard. Communications EEI examples include the IEEE 802 standards, such as 802.3 for *CSMA/CD (Carrier Sense Multiple Access/ Collision Detection)* (based on Ethernet), data bus interfaces such as SCSI, network or data link protocol interfaces such as *FDDI (Fiber Distributed Data Interface),* and even the RS-232-C serial line protocol.

Table 3.4 Interfaces.

Type	Example	Title or Explanation
API		
	IEEE 1003.1	System Interface
	IEEE 1003.2	Shell and Utilities
	GKS	
	SQL	Standard Query Language
EEI		
human	IEEE 1003.2a	User Portability Extensions
information	IS 9945-1 Chapter 10	Archive and Interchange Format
communications	IEEE 802.3	CSMA/CD (based on Ethernet)
	SCSI	Data Bus Interface
SII		
standardized		
non-standardized		

An *SII (System Internal Interface)* is within a platform that supports applications. In Fig. 3.5, the operating system is such a platform, and two SII are shown, between the filesystem and the distributed filesystem, and between there and the protocol module. Such interfaces may or may not be standardized. Most of them aren't, and are thus not of direct interest to this book.

3.5   Implementation

An *implementation* is a software package that conforms to a standard or specification. This term taken alone usually applies to an implementation of an interface to support application programs. That is, an implementation is usually an application platform. An application may also conform to a standard or specification, and is then an implementation of that standard or specification. But an application that conforms to an API standard or specification is called a *conforming application,* not an implementation, to avoid confusion with a platform that implements the interface. We will discuss conformance in detail in Chapter 10, *Conformance Testing.* We are concerned here with interface implementations, that is, application platforms. There are several kinds, as shown in Table 3.5.

A *historical implementation* is an implementation that was used in deriving a standard or specification. 4.3BSD and UNIX System V are specifically cited in the nonnormative parts of the POSIX System Interface Standard as two historical systems whose specifications and documentation were used as base documents for

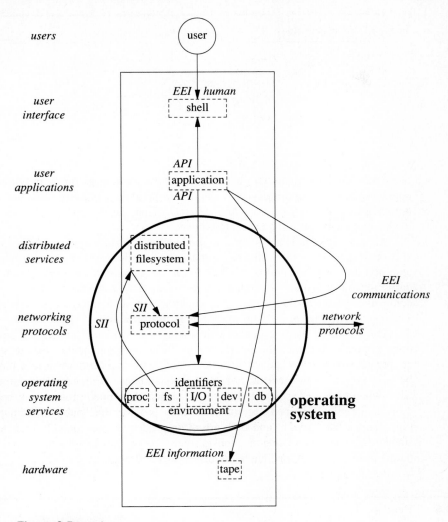

Figure 3.5 Interface types.

that standard. The interface specified by the standard is slightly different from all known historical systems that preceded it, since the historical systems often had incompatible (or flawed) features, and there was no way to reach consensus without some slight compromises and inventions.

A *legacy system* has been inherited from previous computing models of former times, but must be taken into account in developing new computing environments. Open system standards often specify interfaces according to an entirely different computing model than was used for some legacy systems, such as batch or even timesharing mainframe computers. Networked or distributed computing is often quite foreign to such systems. Yet open system standards and models

Table 3.5 Implementations.

Type	Example
historical	UNIX System V
	4.3BSD
open system	GNU?

must take legacy systems into account somehow, at least as far as providing for upgrade paths, and preferably providing interoperability, because most users will not want to switch over entirely immediately. There is too much money invested in legacy systems (thus the name) to do that.

An *open system* is a system that implements interface specifications (preferably open specifications or standards) that promote application portability, interoperability, and user portability [POSIX.0 1991]. This is what open system standards are for. It is also what open system specifications are for. A legacy system could also be an open system, if it implemented such interface specifications. There are some current industry initiatives in this direction.

The end user wants a system that works, and that incorporates the goals of open systems. Whether the interface specifications implemented by the system are formal standards or specifications may not be of direct importance, or may not be as important as whether they are de facto standards. It may become important later, when upgrades are needed; then the utility of an open process will become more apparent. But open specifications may provide this, public specifications may come close enough, and both are often produced more quickly than formal standards. There is an ongoing tension between the advantages of formal standardization and the immediate needs of vendors and users.

3.6   Profile

A *profile* is a suite of standards with specified parameters and options, intended to support an application or a class of applications. A profile is also called a *functional standard* because it helps to support a certain function that the user wants, unlike many base standards, which specify technical areas that were convenient to standardize. Profiles are useful in selecting product specifications. A potential user can build a profile of standards that, taken together, define the necessary interfaces. If vendors say what interfaces their products implement, the user can apply the profile to each product and find ones that fit. Implementations of the same profile should be relatively uniform across vendors' products, giving buyers choices. This uniformity also aids in writing conformance tests [SGFS 1990b].

Most users want systems that will support several classes of applications. Thus, profiles should be *harmonized* so that they do not conflict. This is accomplished by first defining an *OSE (Open System Environment),* which is a very general description of elements that can go into an open system. An actual open system needs to be built out of a subset of these elements. A *profile* is a particular subset of an OSE that can be used to build an open system, together with the option and parameter specifications that make the profiles, standards, and specifications chosen work together. The OSE is a box of pieces from many puzzles, and a profile is a simple puzzle; just enough pieces to make a picture if they're all put in right-side up, in the right place, and turned the right way. The OSE is a set of lenses, and a profile is a subset that will work in a telescope, if held in a certain order and certain distances apart, with a tube (the implementation) to keep them that way.

The OSE is a menu, and a profile is a meal. There may be sandwiches, full course dinners, and coffee all on the same menu. There may be many profiles that can be made from a single OSE, each to support a different application or class of applications. A typical profile of this type is called an *AEP (Application Environment Profile)* because it defines an environment for an application or class of applications.

A *platform profile* specifies an environment for a large environment. The IEEE 1003.18 *POSIX Environment Profile (PEP),* specifies an environment that is much like a traditional interactive multiuser timesharing UNIX system. If the OSE is a menu, a platform profile is a set dinner, and an AEP might be appetizers, bread, or dessert.

A *guide* is a type of document produced by a standards body that is not precisely a standard. In IEEE terminology, at least, there are standards, recommended practices, and guides, in that order of formality. A guide provides contextual material about standardization work not yet finished, partly in order to guide those doing the work. It is an aid to harmonization, in that it describes the context standards should fit in. A guide is also an aid to the vendor or the end user in implementing, selling, and buying applications and systems to build distributed computing.

The guide of most interest to open systems related to the historical UNIX operating system is the IEEE 1003.0 *POSIX Guide*. That particular guide specifies sets of profiles, standards, and specifications to describe an OSE, the POSIX OSE. That guide also provides an overview of related standards work in progress and of nonstandard specifications. The two basic differences between a profile and this guide are the generality of the environment described, and the amount of contextual material. A profile generally describes an application environment, or perhaps a more general environment, such as for an interactive timesharing system. This guide describes an entire OSE. The *XPG (X/Open Portability Guide)* is in some ways similar to the POSIX OSE, on describing a general environment. The *National Institute of Standards and Technology Application Portability Platform (NIST APP)* also performs a similar function.

A *reference model* is a fairly formal statement of elements and their relationships. It classifies standards into general categories, such as external interfaces, program interface, and system interface, and provides requirements for each category. The OSI Reference Model is IS 7498 [ISO 1992]. The POSIX OSE Reference Model is part of IEEE 1003.0, the POSIX Guide [POSIX.0 1991]. Why one is a full International Standard and the other is only intended to be a guide is not clear.

A *framework* is a loosely structured description covering many environments. It is similar to a model, but more general. A model is usually specific to a certain OSE, while a framework can be used to build different models and OSEs to fit them. A model can be viewed as a structured subset of a framework. Some even say a *framework* is just a weasel word to avoid the term *model*. A framework provides context for requirements, standards, and profiles [POSIX.0 1991, Section 3].

A *taxonomy* is a categorization of profiles and standards according to their functions. It may be used in building a framework.

Taxonomies, frameworks, and models can be used to find gaps in existing standards and profiles. This is one of the main reasons for constructing them. These and other profiling issues are discussed in Chapter 12.

Fig. 3.6 shows two models inside a framework. One of the models has two AEPs, which select from several standards. There is apparently no general consensus on this or on any other set of relations among frameworks, models, and profiles. But this way of looking at them is practically useful as a first approximation of how some of them are actually used.

Figure 3.6 Profiles, models, and frameworks.

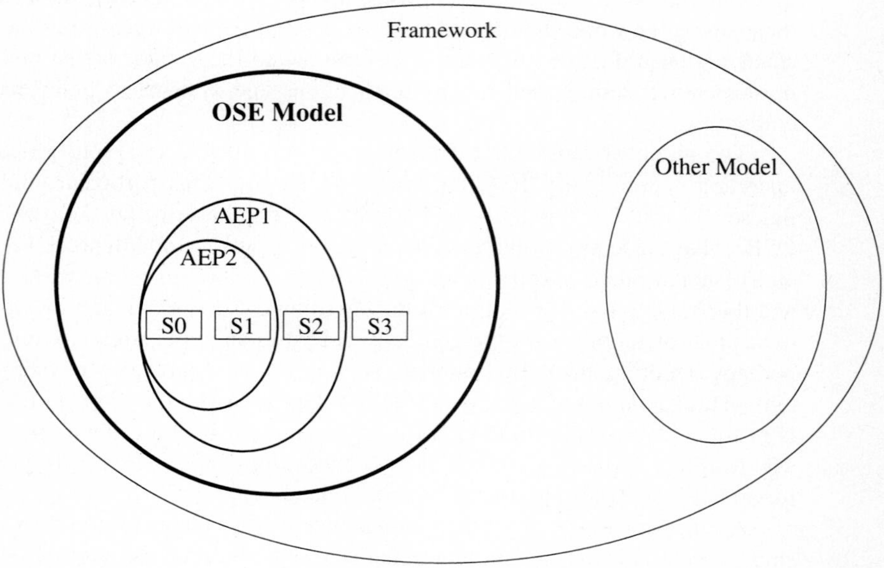

Table 3.6 OSI and open systems profiles.

OSI	Open Systems
framework	framework
protocol model	reference model
protocol suite	OSE
protocol stack	AEP
protocol	standard

There are many analogies between profiles and open systems terminology, as indicated in Table 3.6. People who are familiar with OSI work may find these analogies useful. The idea of a profile or functional standard is in fact derived from OSI work. The basic idea is to use small standards to build hierarchical profiles that specify increasingly comprehensive environments. These are all organized according to reference models that attempt to maintain coherence among the smaller pieces. The framework developed for OSI may be usable for open systems without much change. The OSI framework is actually more general than shown here. Protocols are only one of the kinds of standards included in its taxonomy, for example. And OSI includes several models in addition to the seven layer Basic Reference Model [ISO 1992], including ones for document architecture and distributed processing.

The end user can use profiles and guides in choosing software, and vendors can use them in building applications and open systems. Standardization participants use guides, frameworks, and taxonomies in identifying gaps in existing standards and profiles, and in writing new ones that fit together. We'll discuss specific profiles, environments, guides, frameworks, and taxonomies in Chapter 12.

3.7   Why Standards are Important

Nobody wants a proprietary electrical outlet, but nobody wants their old expensive appliances to stop working in their new house. The proponents of AC and DC power fought economic battles around the turn of this century, before AC became the de facto standard. Today, there are still differences in voltage and alternating frequency in different parts of the world (and sometimes within the same country). These make areas with the same standard open markets for simple utilities. Vendors who want to sell products that work worldwide, or users who want to travel, need utilities that can adapt to multiple standards. This costs more than if there were a single global standard for electrical power delivery. The situation is analogous in computer software.

Many large (and small) companies are interested in "leveraging our investment in people, data, and applications," and they may want to use "vendor neutral standards and enabling technologies" to do so [SOS 1991]. These companies believe that standards can save everyone time and money, in training, hardware, and software. Many governments have similar interests. Because of this economic and sometimes even legal pressure, most vendors will make systems that conform to standards. Whether these standards work correctly or not, and whether you like them or not, they will affect you, whether you are implementing, selling, buying, or using systems [UAOS 1991].

Standards Save Money

Once upon a time, hardware vendors supplied all hardware and all software, and service, supplies, and documentation, too. This was good for the buyers because they had one-stop shopping, and they believed that they had vendor support to fix all their problems. It was good for the vendors because they had loyal customers. But it was mostly simply the way it had always been done.

Then hardware became more powerful and inexpensive. This and networks permitted workstations, fileservers, and other specialized machines. UNIX and networks facilitated application portability and portability of the operating system itself. Personal computers produced expectations of dedicated hardware resources, and a commodity market for software. All these things permitted more capable and more complex applications, often supplied by someone other than the vendor of any given hardware platform.

Nowadays, no single vendor can supply all useful hardware platforms and application packages. And no one vendor can provide all solutions to all problems in all areas, such as networking, security, databases, and languages. So users want to be able to move application packages among a variety of machines, and vendors of applications and of hardware platforms want to be able to meet this need. Standard device interfaces permitted writing device drivers that would work for several hardware devices. Standard application programming interfaces permit writing application programs that will work across several systems that are implementations of the interfaces. Application portability is good for everyone. Vendors save money because they (and their customers) don't have to write new applications for every hardware platform. Users save money by vendor independence: they can buy the most cost-effective hardware for their applications. The bottom line of application portability is better functionality and reduced costs.

New operating systems are too expensive to reinvent for every new hardware platform. Major applications are too expensive to reinvent. Resource sharing and collaboration over networks reduce costs. Training users can cost more than purchasing hardware or software. Standards are independent third party specifications that help ameliorate all these problems. When standardization works as it is supposed to, standards save big money, create markets, and make new hardware and software possible.

This leaves open the question of whether standards really produce such effects. Do they save money, or do they stifle innovation? Probably, to some extent, they do both. Conceivably, to some extent, they cost more money and make some innovations possible. Without ASCII, we probably wouldn't have

UNIX. Yet dependence on ASCII became one of the barriers to the spread of UNIX outside of the United States, and to the transfer of messages other than those in English text over networks. Is ASCII good or evil? That depends on what you want to use it for, and when, and in what context. More complex standards like POSIX are just as hard to characterize. Will they aid or hinder the success of the vendors, the users, or the developers and researchers? Only time, and historians, will know for sure. Meanwhile, they are a practical reality.

The basic intent of standards is to provide a foundation for doing business. The indecision over AC versus DC power made selling electrical utilities difficult. The battle over VHS versus Betamax VCRs left a lot of users with equipment that had a diminishing supply of current software. Similar problems occured with 78, 45, and $33^1/_3$ vinyl records. And all of those are now the data of legacy systems of the sound market. Perhaps software standards can promote better upgrade paths, portability, and interoperability.

Standards Will Affect You

Almost every vendor of a system related to UNIX already claims conformance to POSIX, or is working on conformance to POSIX, and will produce products affected by standards. Those will be what you can buy.

Many users think standards are solely marketing tools of no interest to researchers and academics. But vendors will make systems that conform to standards, and those will be the systems researchers and academics can buy. For example, many users think standards won't affect them because they use a research system such as 4.3BSD, whose authors, CSRG, brag about having no marketing division [Leffler *et al.* 1989, 15]. But even that group is strongly involved in standardization.

One of the biggest problems with many standards committees is that most participants are sent by vendors. These people have to represent their own and their companies' interests. That is a full time job, so they have no extra time to represent users or buyers. If you want to be able to buy what you want to use, you may want to provide input to standards processes. It's not as hard as you might think to influence the contents of a standard. In most cases, you don't even have to attend a single meeting. However, even attending standards committee meetings regularly might be preferable to trying to make systems written to a bad standard work in your environment. Also, changing a standard before it is finalized is often much easier than revising it later. We provide details on how to participate in or influence standardization in Chapter 6, and how to access information for a wide selection of committees and related organizations in Appendix A. Standards will affect you. You can wait and take what you get (and maybe have to fix it afterwards), or you can save yourself and the vendors time and money by getting involved in standardization.

On the other hand, standards will not solve all your problems, and you do not want to dedicate all your resources to them. There are even strong arguments that standards slow innovation both by draining resources from engineering and by getting ahead of themselves and designing untested systems by committee. These things can and do happen, and standards can be very bad. But ignoring them will not make them go away. Your participation in their production could make them more responsive to your needs and interests. Understanding them can certainly make them more useful to you.

References

Cargill 1989.   Cargill, Carl F., *Information Technology Standardization: Theory, Process, and Organizations,* Digital Press, Bedford, MA (1989).

ISO 1992.   ISO, "ISO Open Systems Interconnection — Basic Reference Model, Second Edition," *ISO/TC 97/SC 16*(ISO CD 7498-1) (1992).

Leffler et al. 1989.   Leffler, Samuel J., McKusick, Marshall Kirk, Karels, Michael J., & Quarterman, John S., *The Design and Implementation of the 4.3BSD UNIX Operating System,* Addison-Wesley, Reading, MA (1989).

POSIX.0 1991.   POSIX.0, *Draft Guide to the POSIX Open Systems Environment,* IEEE, New York (September 1991). IEEE P1003.0/D13.

SGFS 1990a.   SGFS, *Information technology — Framework and taxonomy of International Standardized Profiles — Part 1: Framework,* ISO/IEC JTC 1 SGFS, Geneva (15 May 1990).

SGFS 1990b.   SGFS, *Information technology — Framework and taxonomy of International Standardized Profiles,* ISO/IEC JTC 1 SGFS, Geneva (15 May 1990).

SOS 1991.   SOS, "User Requirements Letter," Senior Executives for Open Systems, also known as the Group of Ten: American Airlines, Du Pont, General Motors, Kodak, McDonnell Douglas, Merck, Motorola, 3M, Northrop, and Unilever, Washington, DC (27 June 1991).

UAOS 1991.   UAOS, "Overcoming Barriers to Open Systems Information Technology First Official Report," User Alliance for Open Systems, c/o COS, McLean, VA (27 January 1991).

PART 2

Cutters

This part is about the organizations that cut and shape the puzzle pieces, standards, and specifications, and how they do it. We discuss standards bodies, as well as the many consortia, associations, and user groups that participate in the creation of standards. We have already mentioned the history or models of some of these organizations in Part 1. We will discuss their specific standards and profiles in later parts of the book. This part is about the organizations themselves.

There are different kinds of organizations involved with standards and specifications. For ease of discussion, we have divided these organizations into three categories: formal standard bodies, industry organizations, and user groups. Each kind of organization participates in the standards process in a different way, and each organization may have its own variations in processes.

Only formal standards bodies can create standards. They also maintain liaisons with other formal standards bodies. Industry organizations and user groups participate in the formal standards process, develop specifications, and educate people. We have limited the discussion of standards bodies and organizations to those that participate in the development of the standards required for open systems.

Formal Standards Bodies

The first chapter in this part covers formal standards bodies. A formal standards body is one that produces formal standards, rather than specifications or de facto standards. A formal standards body uses a formal, open process to develop standards. Formal standards bodies are divided into three categories: international, national, and regional.

Some formal standards bodies are recognized by governments, vendors, and users. Such accreditation can come from the government in some cases. For example, in the United States, the *American National Standards Institute (ANSI)* accredits organizations to develop American National Standards. In France, the government has put the *French Association for Normalization (AFNOR)* in charge of standards for France [Cargill 1989, 192]. Technical recognition is also necessary for a standard to be accepted. The committee creating the standard needs to have technical skill and openness that allows affected parties to participate, as well as to exhibit "due process." For example, an appropriate organization to develop electronic standards would be the *IEEE (Institute of Electrical and Electronics Engineers)*.

Industry Organizations and User Groups

The second chapter in this part, Chapter 5, *Industry Organizations and User Groups*, talks about the organizations that are concerned about standards but are not standards bodies themselves. These bodies participate in the standards process, develop specifications, and educate users. When there is market pressure for consensus or when it seems to be in the interest of a group of organizations, vendors or users can get together to define specifications. Some significant industry consortia are the *OSF (Open Software Foundation)*, the *POSC (Petrotechnical Open Software Corporation)*, *UI (UNIX International)*, and X/Open. Each consortium has had a unique influence on the content of standards related to the UNIX system.

User group participation in the standards process is a good way to solicit the input of those people who will eventually have to use a standard. The standards process is unbalanced without user input. Four traditional user groups have participated in one degree or another in the POSIX process. They are *EurOpen (European Forum for Open Systems)*, *jus (Japan UNIX Society)*, *UniForum (The International Association of Open Systems Professionals)*, and *USENIX (The Professional and Technical UNIX Association)*. More recent players include the *UAOS (User Alliance for Open Systems)* and the *POSC (Petrotechnical Open Software Corporation)*.

Organization Description

For each organization, we present a brief description, some key historical events, examples of standards or specifications they have created, and relations to other standards bodies and organizations. Access information for participation and sources for additional information can be found in Appendix A, *Resources*.

Relationship Between Standards Bodies

Standards bodies do not operate in a vacuum. Each body is influenced by other bodies. The relationship between some bodies is hierarchical, but that between others is lateral. An example of lateral coordination is the communication or liaison between working groups. Some liaisons are formal and others informal. There was a liaison between the X3J11 committee that developed the C language standard and the IEEE 1003.1 POSIX committee that developed the System Interface Standard. An example of a hierarchical relationship is that between the POSIX working groups and ISO/IEC JTC 1 SC22 WG15 through ANSI. The following three chapters describe the relationships among these groups.

But here let's sketch how a single standard, IEEE 1003.1, progressed from a user group project to an American National Standard to an International Standard. This descent of the POSIX System Interface Standard is sketched in Fig. P2.1.

In 1981, members of UniForum (then /usr/group) started meeting to discuss an operating system interface standard. This group was called the /usr/group Standards Committee, but it was not a formal standards body by our definition. Its goal was to produce a specification that would enable application portability. The group produced the 1984 /usr/group Standard, which really was a specification. In 1983, the IEEE approved a new project for a similar topic. The driving individual for this project ceased to participate, so work was delayed. Early in 1985, the IEEE POSIX work was revived. The POSIX working group and the /usr/group standard committee merged to continue the work. The 1984 /usr/group Standard

---

Figure P2.1 The descent of the POSIX System Interface Standard.

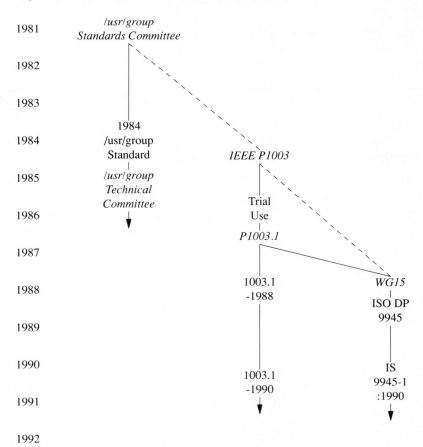

was used as a base document for the new IEEE P1003 standards committee. It was also used as a base document for the library sections of the C Language Standard [POSIX.0 1991]. A Trial Use Standard for IEEE 1003 was approved in 1986, under the name POSIX. The first POSIX System Interface Standard was approved in 1988, as IEEE Std 1003.1-1988.

In 1987, a request was approved to start the process to make POSIX an international standard as well. In 1990, the first international POSIX standard was approved, as ISO/IEC 9945-1:1990. Work on this international standard had been carefully coordinated with the IEEE P1003 work, which meanwhile produced IEEE Std 1003.1-1990. These two 1990 standards differ only in their covers, even though one is an American National Standard and the other is an International Standard.

Processes

The final chapter in this part presents the processes used by the IEEE Computer Society *TCOS (Technical Committee on Operating Systems and Application Environments)* working groups, X3, and ISO/IEC JTC 1. Two standards that these groups are responsible for creating are POSIX and the C language standards. These and other standards bodies use processes similar in concept, but different in detail. Chapter 6, *Processes*, discusses some benefits and drawbacks of several processes.

References

Cargill 1989.   Cargill, Carl F., *Information Technology Standardization: Theory, Process, and Organizations,* Digital Press, Bedford, MA (1989).

POSIX.0 1991.   POSIX.0, *Draft Guide to the POSIX Open Systems Environment,* IEEE, New York (September 1991). IEEE P1003.0/D13.

CHAPTER 4

Formal Standards Bodies

This chapter describes formal standards bodies. We divide them into three groups: international, national, and regional, as shown in Table 4.1. Formal standards accreditation authority derives from either the international or the national level. There are also many direct links in accreditation from international standards bodies to national ones, so national bodies are discussed immediately after international ones. The European regional standards bodies are linked with the European national bodies, but they often have no direct link to international bodies, so they are presented last.

4.1 International Standards Bodies

Information Technology (IT) is an area where the boundaries of international standards organizations become less distinct. This overlap requires coordination. Some of this overlap and coordination is shown in Fig. 4.1, with the merger of the ISO and IEC technical committees. Fig. 4.1 shows the three international organizations discussed: ISO, IEC, and ITU.

Each organization is structured hierarchically. There are many committees and administrative offices that oversee and support the working group that does the research, drafts the standard, and approves drafts for balloting. Depending on the organization, these overseeing bodies are complex or simple. More details about the operation of these groups can be found in [Cargill 1989; Digital 1991], and [IOS 1990].

Each of the voluntary standards organizations takes great care in reaching a consensus. There are many checks and balances in place, as described in Chapter 6, *Processes*, to make sure that all interests have been recognized in the standards creation process. It is a waste of valuable resources to create a standard that will not be used.

Table 4.1 Standards bodies.

Acronym	Expansion
International Standard Bodies	
ISO	International Organization for Standardization
IEC	International Electrotechnical Commission
ITU	International Telecommunications Union
CCITT	International Consultative Committee for Telephony and Telegraphy
National Standards Bodies	
AFNOR	French Association for Normalization
ANSI	American National Standards Institute
IEEE	Institute of Electrical and Electronics Engineers
ASC X3	Accredited Standards Committee for Information Processing Systems
NIST	National Institute for Standards and Technology (U.S.)
BSI	British Standards Institute
CCTA	Government Centre for Information Systems (U.K.)
CSA	Canadian Standards Association
DIN	German Standards Institute
DS	Danish Standards Association
JISC	Japanese Industrial Standards Commission
MPT	Ministry of Posts and Telecommunications (Japan)
Regional Standards Bodies	
CEN	European Committee for Standardization
CENELEC	European Committee for Electrotechnical Standardization
ETSI	European Telecommunications Standards Institute

ISO: International Organization for Standardization

The *International Organization for Standardization (ISO)* is responsible for making standards for industry in a variety of areas. These areas range from Technical Committee 191 for Humane Animal Traps to TC 34 for Food Technology. Other ISO areas are related to open systems.

There are two disciplines at the international level for which ISO is not responsible. The first is electrical and electrotechnical, which is covered by the *International Electrotechnical Commission (IEC)*. The second is telecommunications, which is covered by the *International Telecommunications Union (ITU)*. ISO facilitates international commerce and international academic, research, engineering, and economic areas [Cargill 1989, 126].

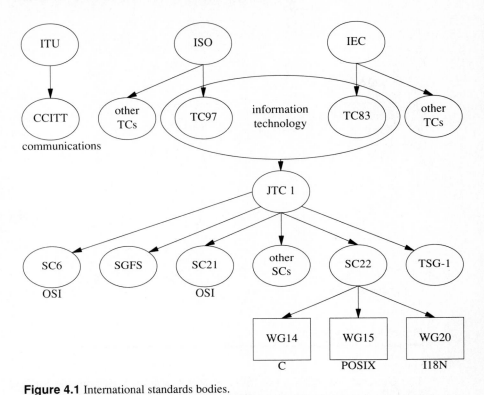

Figure 4.1 International standards bodies.

As you can tell from the diversity, ISO is a very large organization. Since its creation in 1946, it has published more than 7,000 standards. This work is the product of 2,400 technical committees, subcommittees, working groups, and study groups. This requires the participation of over 20,000 experts from around the world. One source estimates at least nine ISO technical meetings occur on any working day [Cargill 1989, 127]. If you translate this into staff, meetings, and travel costs, the investment in international standards is significant.

The ISO Hierarchy

The hierarchical structure of ISO is presented in Fig. 4.2. This structure ensures that the work of ISO runs smoothly and fullfills the purposes set by the General Assembly. The actual creation of the standards happens through the technical committees, their subcommittees and working groups. Membership in the General Assembly is by nation. Within each nation, there is a select group responsible for ISO membership. In the United States, this body is *ANSI (American National Standards Institute);* in Germany, *DIN (German Standards Institute);* in Japan, *JIS (Japanese Institute for Standards);* and, in the United Kingdom, *BSI (British Standards Institute).*

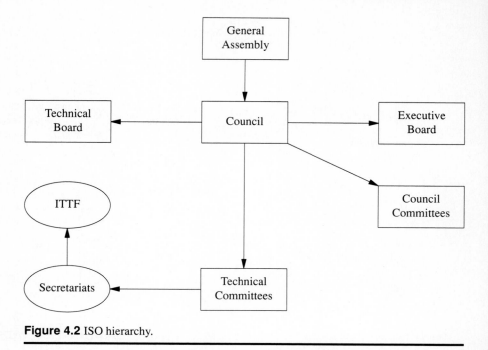

Figure 4.2 ISO hierarchy.

The General Assembly. The ISO *General Assembly* is responsible for ISO policy. It meets infrequently, every three years; the Council carries out the policies of the General Assembly.

Council and Boards. The *Council* carries out the policy made by the General Assembly with the help of two boards, the *Technical Board* and the *Executive Board*. The council meets annually, so the boards take care of running things smoothly throughout the year.

ITTF: Information Technology Task Force. The *Information Technology Task Force (ITTF)* was formed from the ISO *Central Secretariat* and the IEC Central Office "to provide the joint support from the staffs of the two organizations for the activities of JTC 1" [JTC 1 1990, 15]. The ITTF handles the publication and administrative details of creating standards.

Technical Committees, Subcommittees, and Working Groups. A *Technical Committee (TC)* is formed when a topic does not fit within any of the current committees. Beneath a technical committee, a *Subcommittee (SC)* may be more specific. Beneath a subcommittee, there can be *Working Groups (WG)*. Members of the TC, SC, and WGs are national bodies with interest in the topic under consideration. A national body may choose to participate or observe. Observers observe the process and then vote; participating members must attend meetings. Each country chooses how to constitute its national body delegation.

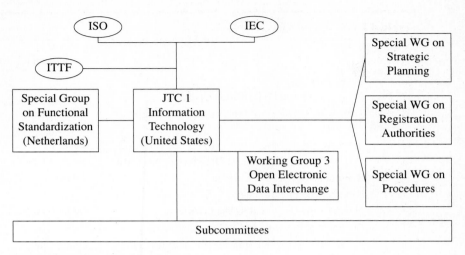

Figure 4.3 JTC 1 organization chart.

JTC 1: Joint Technical Committee One

This book is concerned with a small part of the work of *Joint Technical Committee One (JTC 1)*. JTC 1 is responsible for "Standardization in the field of information technology." This is a joint committee between ISO and the IEC formed in January of 1987 from the former *ISO TC97 (ISO Technical Committee 97)* for information processing systems; *IEC TC47 (IEC Technical Committee 47)* for semiconductor devices; and *IEC TC83 (IEC Technical Committee 83)* for information technology equipment. JTC 1 and related groups are shown in Fig. 4.3.

The United States, through ANSI, holds the JTC 1 secretariat. The secretariat is responsible for administrative support to JTC 1. The secretariat conducts ballots, handles mailings, coordinates meetings, and so on.

Work is carried out within JTC 1 by special working groups that report directly to JTC 1, as well as by the 18 subcommittees. The subcommittees and special groups are listed in Table 4.2, along with the country that supplies the secretariat. The *Special Group on Functional Standardization (SGFS)* is responsible for international standardization of profiles, which are discussed in Chapter 12, *Frameworks*. Work within subcommittees can also be done by working groups reporting directly to the subcommittee. For example, SC22 was traditionally the programming language subcommittee, but has recently expanded its scope to include application environments. Under SC22, WG15 is responsible for POSIX, WG22 for programming language internationalization issues, and WG14 for C.

Some JTC 1 standards for open systems include ISO 9945-1:1990, which is *Portable Operating System Interface (POSIX), Part 1: System Application Program Interface (API) [C Language]*, ISO 7498, *Open Systems Interconnection Reference Model*, ISO 7498-4, *OSI Reference Model Part 4, Management Framework*, and ISO 9899:1990, *Information processing systems—Programming languages—C*.

Table 4.2 JTC 1 subcommittees.

SC	Title	Country
SC 1	Vocabulary	France
SC 2	Character Sets and Information Coding	France
SC 6	Telecommunications and Information Exchange Between Systems	United States
SC 7	Software Engineering	Canada
SC 11	Flexible Magnetic Media for Digital Data Interchange	United States
SC 14	Representation of Data Elements	Sweden
SC 15	Labeling and File Structure	Japan
SC 17	Identification Cards and Related Devices	United Kingdom
SC 18	Document Processing and Related Communication	United States
SC 21	Information Retrieval, Transfer, and Management for OSI	United States
SC 22	Languages	Canada
SC 23	Optical Digital Data Disks	Japan
SC 24	Computer Graphics	Germany
SC 25	Interconnection of IT Equipment	Germany
SC 26	Microprocessor Systems	Japan
SC 27	IT Security Techniques	Germany
SC 28	Office Equipment	Switzerland
SC 29	Coded Representation of Picture, Audio, and Multi-media/Hyper-media Information	Japan

Two JTC 1 subcommittees are particularly active in OSI work. These are SC6, which handles the infrastructure layers, 1 (physical) through 4 (transport), and SC21, which handles higher layers. Their working groups are listed in Table 4.3. For example, SC21 WG1 is working on ISO 9646, which will be a multipart standard for conformance testing of OSI implementations. There is related CCITT work in X.290 [Digital 1991, Chapter 10].

IEC: International Electrotechnical Commission

The *International Electrotechnical Commission (IEC)* is limited to electrical and electrotechnical issues. The commission was formed to prevent problems such as those introduced by the differences between European and North American electric power distribution. The IEC is mentioned here because of the technical committee shared with ISO, JTC 1, which is discussed with ISO.

The IEC is similar in structure to ISO. It has a General Assembly, Council, Central Office, technical committees, subcommittees, and working groups.

Table 4.3 ISO/IEC JTC 1 OSI Working Groups.

Group	Title
SC6	*Telecommunications and Information Exchange Between Systems*
WG1	Data Link Layer
WG2	Network Layer
WG3	Physical Layer
WG4	Transport Layer
SC21	*Information Retrieval, Transfer, and Management for Open System Interconnection*
WG1	OSI Architecture
WG3	Database
WG4	OSI Systems Management
WG5	Specific Application Services
WG6	OSI Session, Presentation, and Common Application Services
WG7	Open Distributed Processing

ITU: International Telecommunications Union

The *International Telecommunications Union (ITU)* is a *United Nations (UN)* treaty agency whose mission is "to promote international cooperation among all members so that all nations, both rich and poor, have access to telecommunication services" [Digital 1991, B-4]. It also sets telephone country codes. Membership is open to all members of the UN. The ITU is the parent organization of the *International Consultative Committee on Telegraphy and Telephony (CCITT)* (discussed next), which is one of its four permanent committees. The CCITT handles matters related to networks for telecommunications. Two of the other committees are the *International Frequency Registration Board (IFRB)* and the *International Radio Consultative Committee (CCIR)*.

CCITT: International Consultative Committee on Telegraphy and Telephony

The *International Consultative Committee on Telegraphy and Telephony (CCITT)* develops recommendations for telecommunications interconnection and interoperability. CCITT specifications for network services begin with the prefix X. (X dot), followed by the recommendation number [Rose 1989, 9]. For example, X.25 is recommendation 25 for a network protocol, X.400 is for message handling systems, and X.121 is for network addresses. These are *recommendations*, not standards, that nonetheless have the force of law in many countries. Many CCITT recommendations become ISO standards, and many CCITT and JTC 1 committees meet jointly to coordinate efforts.

CCITT members are national telecommunications administrations. The U.S. member is the Department of State.

Unlike other processes discussed in Chapter 6, the CCITT publishes recommendations at the ends of four-year study periods. The recommendations from the most recent study period supersede all other study periods. The recommendations from each study period are grouped together in books and named with a color. The recommendations from 1988 are blue. New recommendations will be published in 1992.

4.2   National Standards Bodies

Most industrialized countries have national standards bodies that provide representation to ISO, IEC, or ITU. Examples include *BSI (British Standards Institute)* for the United Kingdom, *DIN (German Standards Institute)* for Germany, and *JISC (Japanese Industrial Standards Commission)* for Japan. We do not attempt to describe every national standards body here. Instead, we pick a few that have been active in the POSIX work, and mention some work they have done, or some influence they have had.

AFNOR: French Association for Normalization

The *French Association for Normalization (AFNOR)* is the national public body that develops French national standards and represents France within ISO. It is also responsible for keeping track of needs for new standards, preparing French standards, training, and managing the national mark of conformity to national standards.

AFNOR was created in 1926. It was a private organization until 1984, when it was decided that creating standards is a public service. At this point, the French

Figure 4.4 AFNOR: French Association for Normalization.

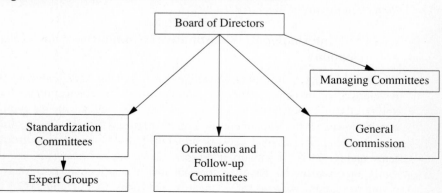

government decided that AFNOR was the appropriate body to carry out the functions of preparing French standards, training, and managing the *NF (French Standard)* certification mark.

The organization of AFNOR is sketched in Fig. 4.4. A board of directors governs AFNOR. The board is responsible for the management of AFNOR and for approving standards. To carry out this responsibility, the board has formed committees. These committees currently handle finances, consumer issues, international affairs, and certification.

AFNOR has two types of working groups. The first is Orientation and Follow-up Committees. These committees handle the administration and overseeing of the standards process. The Orientation and Follow-up Committees determine which areas need work, and assigns them to an appropriate technical committee. The second type of working group does technical development and creates standards.

AFNOR provides an online database, Noriane, that contains references to standards, technical rules, and international projects. This information is helpful to companies that wish to export products.

ANSI: American National Standards Institute

Many standards bodies in the United States, such as those sketched in Fig. 4.5, are related to the *American National Standards Institute (ANSI)*. ANSI was formed in 1918 to handle the problem of manufacturing interchangeable parts. The problem was not the lack of standards but that standards were adopted by a few firms here

Figure 4.5 Standards bodies in the United States.

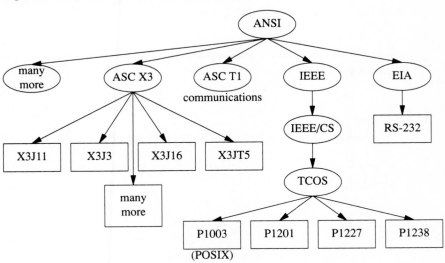

and different standards adopted by a few firms there. Each small group of firms had its own standards. For parts to be interchangeable, standards had to be accepted nationwide. Five of the U.S. engineering societies formed the *American Engineering Standards Committee (AESC)*. The name of this group changed in 1920 and 1960; in 1980, it changed again to be ANSI. Standardization in the United States is different from in other nations, because it is not part of the government. The government uses standards developed by ANSI but is independent from it. ANSI is supported by its membership, which consists of U.S. organizations.

Today, ANSI does not develop standards itself. Instead ANSI coordinates and accredits standards development in the United States. ANSI accredits other groups to develop American National standards. To receive ANSI approval, the standards process used by the group must give anyone and everyone affected or involved in the area addressed by a standard the opportunity to be heard, which is called *due process.* Due process is intended to provide opportunities for any interested or affected party to provide input, either during the creation of a standard, or later, in appeals or challenges [Cargill 1989, 160].

ANSI is the ISO member for the United States. For international representation, ANSI communicates the official U.S. position, which is usually developed by a technical advisory group composed of experts in the area.

ASC X3: Accredited Standards Committee for Information Processing

The *Accredited Standards Committee for Information Processing (ASC X3),* plans, develops, reviews, approves, and maintains American National Standards within the scope of "computers and information processing and peripheral equipment, devices and media related thereto; standardization of the functional characteristics of office machines, plus accessories for such machines, particularly in those areas that influence the operators of such machines" [X3 1990, 4]. X3

Figure 4.6 X3.

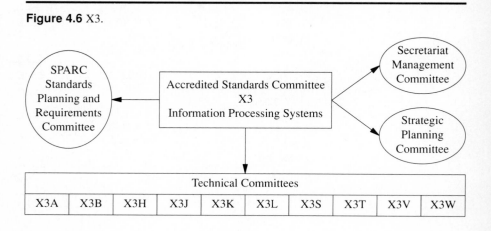

technical committees also act as technical advisory groups to ANSI, the U.S. National Body member of JTC 1. X3 procedures are accredited by ANSI.

X3 was formed in 1961, shortly after ISO formed TC 97 for information processing systems. X3 members are organizations with material interest in the information technology industry. CBEMA (see Chapter 5, *Industry Organizations and User Groups*) holds X3's secretariat. The X3 organization is shown in Fig. 4.6. Three X3 committees take care of planning and management. They are *SPARC (Standards Planning and Requirements Committee), SMC (Secretariat Management Committee),* and *SPC (Strategic Planning Committee).* Standards development takes place within technical committees.

Table 4.4 lists the current ASC X3 technical committees. These committees create approximately 90 percent of the U.S. standards for information technology.

Table 4.4 ASC X3 Technical Committees.

TC	Topic	TC	Topic	TC	Topic
X3A1	Optical Character Recognition	X3J1	Pl/1	X3L2	Codes, Character Sets
		X3J2	Basic	X3L3	Audio/Picture Coding
X3B5	Digital Magnetic Tape	X3J3	Fortran	X3L8	Data Representation
X3B6	Instrumentation Tape	X3J4	COBOL		
X3B7	Magnetic Disks	X3J7	APT	X3S3	Data Communications
X3B8	Flexible Disk Cartridge	X3J9	PASCAL		
X3B9	Paper/Forms Layout	X3J10	APL	X3T2	Data Interchange
X3B10	Credit/Identification Cards	X3J11	C	X3T3	Open Distributed Processing
X3B11	Optical Digital Data Disks	X3J12	DIBOL		
		X3J13	LISP	X3T4	Security Techniques
X3H2	Database	X3J14	FORTH	X3T5	Open Systems Interconnection
X3H3	Computer Graphics	X3J15	DATABUS		
X3H4	Information Resource Dictionary System	X3J16	C++	X3T9	I/O Interface
		X3J17	Prolog		
X3H5	Parallel Processing Constructs for High Level Programming Languages	X3J18	REXX	X3V1	Text: Office
				X3W1	Office Machines
X3H6	Case Tool Integration Models			SC21 TAG	Information Retrieval, Transfer, and Management (ISO)
X3H7	Object Information Management				
				SC22 TAG	Languages
X3K5	Vocabulary				

X3 does not do application-specific standards. They standardize interfaces and the functions required to support applications, like programming languages. Mechanisms specific to an application are standardized elsewhere. For example, X9 develops standards for banking and X12 for electronic business data interchange.

There are more than 200 X3 standards existing or in progress. For example, X3J11 produced ANSI X3.159, X3H3.6 is for windowing, and X3J16 is for C++.

IEEE: Institute of Electrical and Electronics Engineers

The *Institute of Electrical and Electronics Engineers (IEEE)* is an international professional organization. Currently, 25 percent of its membership is from outside the United States. Unlike X3, which produces only *American National Standards (ANS)*, the IEEE creates its own standards and often submits them to ANSI for approval as an ANS. These standards are usable by anyone, and other nations like Canada and Australia have adoped IEEE standards as their national standards [IEEE 1991]. The IEEE is an ANSI *Accredited Standards Developing Organization (ASDO)*.

The actual work of drafting the standard is done in working groups. Membership in the IEEE is not required for participation in the working groups. It is, however, required for voting on a draft standard.

The IEEE produces both formal standards and specifications. Specifications take can take two forms, called *recommended practice* and *guide*. A *recommended practice* is a specification of procedures and positions preferred by IEEE. A *guide* is a specification of good practices, perhaps in several alternatives, without specific IEEE recommendations.

Some examples of IEEE standards include: IEEE 1003.1, *Information Technology—Portable Operating System Interface (POSIX)—Part 1: System Application Program Interface (API) [C Language]*; IEEE 802.3, *Information Processing Systems—Local Area Networks—Part 3: Carrier Sense Multiple Access with Collision Detection (CSMA/CD) Access Method and Physical Layer Specifications*; IEEE 1074, *Standard for Developing Software Life Cycle Processes*; and IEEE 741, *Standard Criteria for the Protection of Class 1E Power Systems and Equipment in Nuclear Power Generating Stations*.

TCOS: IEEE Computer Society Technical Committee on Operating Systems and Application Environments

The IEEE Computer Society has technical committees; *TCOS (Technical Committee on Operating Systems and Application Environments)* is one. Within TCOS, there is a *Standards Subcommittee (TCOS-SS)*, which is responsible for *POSIX (Portable Operating System Interface)*. POSIX is a set of standards that will define a portable interface to the operating system. The term POSIX is a pun on UNIX and on Portable Operating System Interface. All of the POSIX and TCOS standards and standards projects are described in Chapter 7, *IEEE/CS TCOS Standards* and Chapter 13, *TCOS Profiles*.

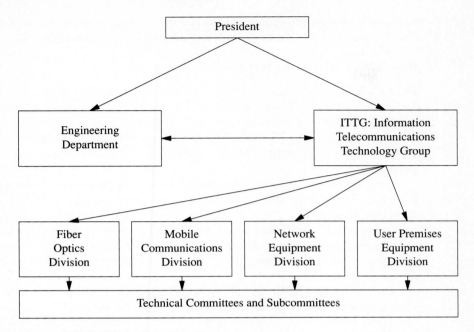

Figure 4.7 EIA Standards Organization.

EIA: Electronic Industries Association

The *Electronic Industries Association (EIA),* sketched in Fig. 4.7, is a U.S. trade organization of electronics manufacturers formed in 1924 as the Radio Manufacturers Association. The EIA is a standards developing organization accredited by ANSI. The EIA produces standards for connectors, wiring schema, and *EDIF (Electronic Design Interchange Format).* EDIF is a standard for the ASCII file format to be shared between a CAE application and a printed circuit board layout application. Most people are familiar with the RS-232-C standard created by the EIA.

Since 1924, EIA has grown to more than 200 standards committees in four divisions. Standards are created by technical committees or subcommittees. These committees fall under the *Information Telecommunications Technology Group (ITTG).* The Engineering Department of the EIA acts like the IEEE Standards Board in overseeing the consensus process and in monitoring progress.

NIST: National Institute of Standards and Technology

The *National Institute of Standards and Technology (NIST)* produces government standards for procurement called *FIPS (Federal Information Processing Standard)* when international or national standards are nonexistent or inadequate. FIPS are used in *Request for Proposals (RFP)* from government agencies for software or hardware. NIST produced *FIPS 151-2 (NIST FIPS 151-2),* the NIST

Applications Portability Profile (APP), and the POSIX Conformance Test Suite (PCTS). NIST was the *National Bureau of Standards (NBS)* until 1990.

BSI: British Standards Institute

The *British Standards Institute (BSI)* is responsible for the coordination of standardization within the United Kingdom. This includes development of national standards and participation in international standards activity. It also includes certification of products to BSI standards. BSI adopts international standards where applicable, and will submit national standards for international standardization when applicable.

For certification, BSI owns and operates the Hemel Hempstead Division testing house. This testing house is able to give a complying product the BSI standards compliance mark.

Organization is by technical committees. Membership in the BSI is open to interested parties, including nationalized industries, professionals, and consulting engineers. Funds are provided by the government, by membership dues, and by the sale of publications.

BSI Information Technology Services (BITS) provides a BITS newsletter that informs readers of current developments. It also provides BITS publications. These publications include copies of draft ISO standards and publications from CEN/CENELEC, as well as BSI standards.

CCTA: Government Centre for Information Systems

The British government invests more than two thousand million pounds Sterling in information systems each year. As part of one government department, HM Treasury, the *Government Centre for Information Systems (CCTA)* is responsible for promoting business effectiveness and efficiency in government through the use of information systems. It gives guidance to other government agencies about how to go about procuring and making best use of information technology. CCTA catalogs standards, develops OSI profiles, and assists other agencies with using standards and creating profiles that suit their needs. "In addition, CCTA represents government departments as users of IS on a range of European committees influencing the formulation of EC policy and legislation and ensuring that IS standards meet stated requirements" [CCTA 1991]. CCTA is also an active participant in IEEE P1003.0. We discuss their M.U.S.I.C. framework in Chapter 12, *Frameworks*.

CSA: Canadian Standards Association

The *Canadian Standards Association (CSA),* along with the government, is responsible for regulatory standards. These standards and conformance testing are used to ensure the safety and quality of goods available to the Canadian consumer.

The organization of CSA is sketched in Fig. 4.8. CSA is governed by a board of directors elected from the membership. The board then appoints a president, who is responsible for carrying out the day-to-day operations of the CSA.

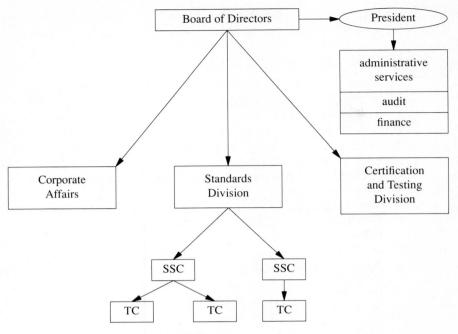

Figure 4.8 CSA: Canadian Standards Association.

Supporting the board are three divisions: the Standards Division, the Certification and Testing Division, and the Corporate Affairs Division.

The Standards Division is managed by the Standards Policy Board. The board forms Standards Steering Committees, which in turn have technical committees that write the actual standards. The Standards Policy Board sets the policy of how standards are developed, and monitors the activities of each of the steering committees.

The Certification and Testing Division is responsible for exactly what its name implies. It certifies that a product or service complies with the appropriate Canadian standard. Certification includes not only the initial certification, but also follow-up audits to be sure that a product and service continues to meet the requirements. These services are provided for a fee.

The Corporate Affairs Division is in charge of membership activities, and provides an interface between the CSA and the government, and between the CSA and the public. Membership is open to any Canadian citizen, business, or organization.

The technical committees do the actual work of writing a standard. Membership in a technical committee is based on technical expertise. The simplified process used by the committees is to write a draft, to develop consensus within the committee, and to rewrite the draft in light of the committee's input. This draft is called a committee draft. The committee is made available for public comment by publication in the CSA Information Update. Any public comments received are incorporated, and the standard is published.

DIN: German Standards Institute

The *German Standards Institute (DIN)* is the national standards body for Germany. DIN is recognized by the German federal government to produce national standards, to represent German interests to ISO, IEC, CEN, and CENELEC, and to test and certify conformance to DIN standards. DIN is very influential both within and beyond Europe, and is perceived as a leader in electrical and ergonomic standards. If a standard is accepted by ISO or CEN/CENELEC, then DIN usually adopts it as a DIN national standard. DIN standards must be written in the German language.

DIN membership is open to any German institution. DIN has a large number of members from the academic community. The internal organization of DIN is sketched in Fig. 4.9.

The DIN testing and inspection mark is a critical component of any product. No insurance company will cover a product without this mark. The inspection mark is mainly used for hardware at this time.

DIN has a large task on its hands with the unification of East and West Germany. The East and West standards do not match, so there is much work to be done before a single set of German standards emerges.

Figure 4.9 DIN: German Standards Institute.

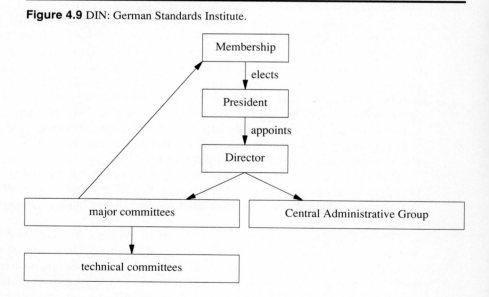

DS: Danish Standards Association

The *Danish Standards Association (DS)* is the Danish national member body of JTC 1. Their main activity is to prepare standards for the manufacture of products. "These standards are used to ensure measures may be coordinated, and that we understand technical words and symbols in the same way" [IOS 1990, 291]. For testing and certification, DS works with the *ECITC (European Committee for IT Testing and Certification)*. The DS is interested in the topic of internationalization; see Chapter 11.

JISC: Japanese Industrial Standards Commission

The main formal standards body for Japan is the *Japanese Industrial Standards Commission (JISC)*, shown in Fig. 4.10. The JISC Secretariat is the *Agency of Industrial Science and Technology (AIST)*, a division of the *Ministry of International Trade and Industry (MITI)*. These bodies ensure that Japan remains an

Figure 4.10 Japanese standardization.

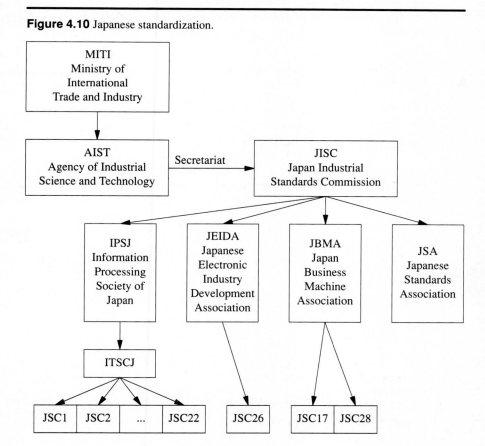

international competitor for information technology and telecommunications [Cargill 1989, 195].

Japan is unique in having centralized planning for standards. Delegates to international standards meetings return to Japan and report to their JISC committee. This contrasts with other nations, where representatives have potentially divided loyalties between company and nation.

Actual standards development in some fields has been delegated to several bodies. They include the *Information Processing Society of Japan (IPSJ)* and its subsidiary, the *Information Technology Standards Commission of Japan (ITSCJ)*, as well as the *Japanese Electronic Industry Development Association (JEIDA)*, the *Japan Business Manufacturer Association (JBMA)*, and the *Japan Standards Association (JSA)*. ITSCJ, JEIDA, and JBMA have Japanese Standards Committees, which are the counterparts of the ISO/IEC JTC 1 subcommittees. JSA does not have counterparts to JTC 1 [Nakahara 1992].

MPT: Ministry of Posts and Telecommunications

The *Ministry of Posts and Telecommunications (MPT)* oversees telecommunications policy in Japan. It is not usually delegated formal responsibility for Japanese standards, but is influential [Quarterman 1990, 181].

4.3   Regional Standards Bodies

In Europe, cooperation among countries is necessary for trade. To facilitate this cooperation and coordination, there are three European standards bodies. Each of them is described in this section, and shown in Fig. 4.11.

Figure 4.11 European standardization.

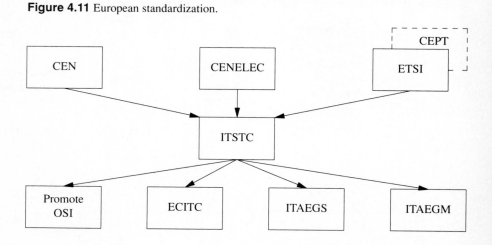

CEN/CENELEC: Joint European Standards Institution

The *Joint European Standards Institution (CEN/CENELEC)* attempts to harmonize European national standards. Members agree to use CEN/CENELEC standards over national standards where possible. CEN/CENELEC is also involved in certification and testing. It is formed from the *European Committee for Normalisation (CEN)* and the *European Committee for Electrotechnical Standardization (CENELEC)*, which are similar to ISO and IEC, respectively, but for Europe. CEN was formed in 1971, but the idea was conceived in 1957. CENELEC was formed in 1973. "CENELEC aims to remove technical barriers to trade which result from conflicting requirements in the technical content of national electrotechnical standards of 18 countries in Europe" [IOS 1990, 282].

Information about CEN and CENELEC can be found in [IOS 1990; Cargill 1989], and [Digital 1991]. CEN members participate in ISO. CEN or CENELEC are not members of ISO, so that dual representation is avoided. If CEN or CENELEC were members of ISO, the 18 CEN/CENELEC members would not be able to participate in ISO. The 18 members of CEN/CENELEC are the national standards organizations of Europe. They are listed in Table 4.5.

The consensus process is used to develop standards, but adoption is by vote of a weighted majority. CEN standards must become national standards regardless of the way in which a member nation voted.

CEN/CENELEC produces *HD (Harmonization Documents)* and *ENV (European Prestandards)* as well as standards. The HD and ENV are more flexible than a standard. An ENV can be developed quickly when an urgent need is seen to exist. Once approved, the ENV then goes through a trial period.

ETSI: European Telecommunications Standards Institute

The *European Telecommunications Standards Institute (ETSI)* was established in 1988 and is responsible for the establishment of technical standards for telecommunications. It produces *European Telecoms Standards (ETS)* for its membership, which consists of network operators, PTTS, manufacturers, users, and research institutes. Some of these functions used to be performed by *European Conference of Post and Telecommunications Administrations (CEPT)* [IOS 1990, 284]. ETSI is roughly analogous to CCITT.

Table 4.5 CEN members.

Austria	Belguim	Denmark	Finland
France	Germany	Greece	Iceland
Ireland	Italy	Luxembourg	The Netherlands
Norway	Portugal	Spain	Sweden
Switzerland	United Kingdom		

ITSTC: Information Technology Steering Committee

The *Information Technology Steering Committee (ITSTC)* was formed by three European bodies: CEN, CENELEC, and ETSI. Information about ITSTC can be found in [IOS 1990].

ITSTC is made up of five members each from CEN, CENELEC, and ETSI. There are observers from each of the CEC and EFTA countries, the secretaries general of CEN, CENELEC, and the Director or EWOS. The convenors of each of the Ad Hoc Expert Groups are invited participants.

Currently, there are two Ad Hoc Expert Groups: *ITAEGS (IT Ad Hoc Expert Group on Standardization)* and *ITAEGM (IT Ad Hoc Expert Group on Advanced Manufacturing)*. ITAEGS is responsible for the process used to create functional standards. ITAEGM is responsible for the areas of *Computer Integrated Manufacturing (CIM)* and *Advanced Manufacturing Technologies (AMT)* as they relate to standardization and certification.

References

Cargill 1989.   Cargill, Carl F., *Information Technology Standardization: Theory, Process, and Organizations,* Digital Press, Bedford, MA (1989).

CCTA 1991.   CCTA, "This is CCTA," CCTA: The Government Centre for Information Systems, London (1991).

Digital 1991.   Digital, *Open Systems Handbook: A Guide to Building Open Systems,* Digital Equipment Corporation, Bedford, MA (1991).

IEEE 1991.   IEEE, "TransCom — Leading the Way to Transnational Standard Development and Adoption," *The IEEE Standards Bearer* 5(2), p. 5, IEEE (October 1991).

IOS 1990.   IOS, *Information Technology Atlas — Europe,* IOS Press and C.G. Wedgwood & Company, Ltd., Amsterdam (1990).

JTC 1 1990.   JTC 1, "ISO/IEC Directives: Procedures for the technical work of ISO/IEC JTC 1 on Information Technology," International Organization for Standardization/International Electrotechnical Commission, Switzerland (1990).

Nakahara 1992.   Nakahara, Yasushi, Personal communication (July 1992).

Quarterman 1990.   Quarterman, John S., *The Matrix: Computer Networks and Conferencing Systems Worldwide,* Digital Press, Bedford, MA (1990).

Rose 1989.   Rose, Marshall, *The Open Book: A Practical Perspective on Open Systems Interconnection,* Prentice-Hall, Englewood Cliffs, NJ (1989).

X3 1990.   X3, "Accredited Standards Committee X3 — Information Processing Systems Master Plan (Overview)," X3, Washington, DC (1990).

CHAPTER 5

Industry Organizations and User Groups

The formal standards process is influenced directly by the participants and by existing practice. This chapter discusses various organizations that have had an effect on the standards process. For each one, we discuss its relations to other groups, its internal organization, and its processes. We pay particular attention to how input is integrated into documents produced by each organization.

The order of presentation follows that in Table 5.1. Organizations are presented in alphabetical order within each category.

Some of these organizations, such as EWOS, have been directly involved in recent restructuring of the high-level processes and frameworks used by formal standard bodies; these effects are discussed in more detail in Chapter 12. Several other groups, particularly X/Open, OSF, and UI, produce specifications that are described in detail in Chapter 14. A few of these groups also deal with distributed management, and their specifications on that subject are discussed in Chapter 14.

Most user groups do not produce standards. However, user groups influence standards by providing a forum for early discussion of potential standards, institutional representation to formal standards bodies, and education of the user population. In this chapter, we describe traditional user groups, and industry user groups. Some industry user groups produce profiles to guide procurement. These profiles are described in Chapter 15. Here, we describe the groups themselves.

5.1 POSIX Process Participants

The open systems market related to the historical UNIX operating system has been divided into two camps for a long time. As discussed in Chapter 2, the nature of the two camps has shifted over time. Through most of the mid-1980s, it was 4.2BSD or 4.3BSD against System V. From about 1988 until the present, it has been mostly OSF versus UI (and USL), plus the neutral third party, X/Open.

Table 5.1 Industry organizations and user groups.

Acronym	Expansion
POSIX Process Participants	
CSRG	Computer Systems Research Group
OSF	Open Software Foundation
UI	UNIX International
X/Open	The X/Open Group, Ltd.
Manufacturers Associations	
CBEMA	Computer and Business Equipment Manufacturers Association
ECMA	European Computer Manufacturers Association
Open System Industry Groups	
MIA	Multivendor Integration Architecture Consortium
POSC	Petrotechnical Open Software Corporation
SOS	Senior Executives for Open Systems
UAOS	User Alliance for Open Systems
Military User Groups	
DISA	Defense Information Systems Agency
PSSG	Protocol Standards Steering Group
NGCR	Next Generation Computer Resources Program
OSSWG	Operating Systems Standards Working Group
Traditional User Groups	
EurOpen	The European Forum for Open Systems
jus	The Japan UNIX Society
UniForum	The International Association of Open Systems Professionals
USENIX	The Professional and Technical UNIX Association
OSI Industry Promotion Groups	
COS	Corporation for Open Systems
POSI	Promoting Conference for OSI
SPAG	Standards Promotion and Application Group
OSI Workshops	
AOW	Asia-Oceania Workshop
EWOS	European Workshop on Open Systems
OIW	OSI Implementors' Workshop
TCP/IP Standardization Bodies	
ISOC	Internet Society
IAB	Internet Activities Board
IETF	Internet Engineering Task Force
IRTF	Internet Research Task Force

CSRG: Computer Systems Research Group

The *Computer Systems Research Group (CSRG)* at the University of California, Berkeley produces *BSD (Berkeley Software Distribution)*. This implementation is discussed in Chapter 2 in the discussion of the evolution of the UNIX system. Its manuals were considered a base document for the development of the POSIX System Interface Standard. Suggestions and contributions are received from many sources to be included in BSD [Leffler *et al.* 1989], for final decisions by CSRG. CSRG dissolved at the end of 1992.

OSF: Open Software Foundation

The *Open Software Foundation (OSF)* is a corporation that produces both specifications and software products. It is a descendent of the *Hamilton Group* that was formed in reaction to a technical and marketing agreement between Sun and AT&T in 1988. The name came from Hamilton Street in Palo Alto, California, which was the location of Digital's Western Research Laboratory, which was where those involved in the original group met.

The original eight OSF sponsors were: *Apollo (Apollo Computer, Inc.)* (now owned by HP), *Digital (Digital Equipment Corporation), Bull (Groupe Bull), HP (Hewlett-Packard), IBM (International Business Machines, Inc.), Nixdorf (Nixdorf Computer AG)* (now merged with Siemens), *Philips,* and *Siemens (Siemens AG).* A somewhat later addition was *Hitachi (Hitachi Ltd.).* There are now about 300 members organizations of OSF [OSF 1991a]. Although all the original OSF members were large vendors, OSF has a strong user orientation, taking into account its own members and input from external sources such as the *Open Systems Directive* from X/Open [X/Open 1991].

OSF is not a standards body, and does not reconcile competing specifications or implementations. Instead, it chooses from "mature, proven technologies...." OSF makes a point of identifying and reviewing all "relevant and promising technology from the worldwide computer industry, educational institutions, government agencies, and end users" [OSF 1991a]. Unlike formal standards bodies such as TCOS-SS with its POSIX standards, OSF does not then produce a consensus interface based on the technologies identified. OSF instead selects a specific technology, including the actual implementation, as well as the interface specifications. OSF has called this choosing a "best of breed" [OSF 1991b]. "The entire process is open to scrutiny, by members, by press, and by the world at large" [OSF].

OSF from time to time issues a *Request for Technology (RFT)* for software and documentation in a particular area. A balanced group of people interested in a specific area generates an RFT. The RFT is distributed to the industry. The industry responds with proposals. Proposals that are accepted are included in the OSF environment. A balanced group would include members from the OSF, users, standards groups, and technical experts in the specific area [OSF 1990]. It is important that the group be balanced, so that technology will meet all of the needs requested. It is important to have user as well as vendor input into the process.

Exactly how an actual decision is finally made is not clear. Apparently, it is by OSF employees after receiving input from the OSF membership. Such an approach can have the advantage of speed, but is not a consensus process. Presumably, OSF is responsible to its membership for such decisions.

The RFT for user interface technology in 1988 led to the OSF adoption of Motif in 1989. This was the first OSF RFT completed. It was followed by the adoption of OSF/1, based on Mach, and OSF DCE [OSF 1991a]; these are described in Chapter 14, *Industry Profiles*. More recently, OSF has been working on a *Distributed Management Environment (DME),* also described in Chapter 14.

OSF has been active in POSIX standardization for a long time, and has an Institutional Representative to TCOS-SS.

OSF also supports the OSF Research Institute, which provides liaison to the academic and research communities.

UI: UNIX International

UNIX International (UI) provides guidance to *UNIX System Laboratories (USL)* on the development of *UNIX System V.* [UI 1992]. UI was formed in December 1988, and currently has more than 245 member companies. These include "a significant base of vendors and end users" [UI 1991]. There are no restrictions on membership. UI has a graduated fee structure, with the companies paying the higher fees getting the most services.

UI itself does not produce software. It provides a framework for a system software environment in its UI-ATLAS. It also provides a *1992 Roadmap for System V and Related Technologies* as a plan to ensure the availability of reference technologies for UI-ATLAS. UI works in conjunction with USL, which produces the *SVID (System V Interface Definition),* a specification, and System V release 4, an implementation. We describe UI-ATLAS and other UI specifications in more detail in Chapter 14, *Industry Profiles*.

The UI-ATLAS framework is intended to assist end users in taking advantage of competition among vendors for components of open systems. The Roadmap helps target not only traditional UNIX markets, but also markets that have traditionally been serviced by proprietary software. UI wants to address all information processing needs of a modern enterprise, including interoperability with legacy mainframes and personal computers, specialized application support such as transaction processing, and high level applications such as spreadsheets and publishing tools. The Roadmap also includes some interesting market projections [UI 1992].

UI technical decisions are overseen by the *UNIX International Steering Committee (UISC).* The UISC *Roadmap Subcommittee (RMSC)* is responsible for examining industry requirements and determining market needs. For detailed market studies, the RMSC charters investigative teams from UI members companies, and evaluates their reports for use in producing feature lists for the Roadmap. These feature lists are reviewed and prioritized by the UISC.

Feature requirements for UI-ATLAS products are created by UI member companies, through UI work groups, which are authorized by the UISC. USL produces more detailed feature specifications in response to feature requirements from UI, and sends them to UI for review. Reference products are developed or selected by USL according to these requirements and specifications, and often include components from other companies. These other companies are selected from responses to a request for technology partners [UI 1991]. UI publishes drafts of feature specifications, usually before USL licenses the corresponding software, so that application and platform developers can write software to those specifications.

Final feature specifications are produced by USL and are published in the SVID and in the USL *ABI (Application Binary Interface)*. USL also makes prerelease versions of software available to UI members (but not to the general public); UI calls this early access. The UI and USL specification and implementation product cycle culminates in licensing of reference software by USL. The Roadmap includes a timeline for deliverables, as well as detailed schedules for feature requirements, feature specifications, early access, licensing, and software delivery.

UI has an Institutional Representative to TCOS-SS.

X/Open Company, Ltd

The purpose of the *X/Open Company, Ltd (X/Open)* is "to facilitate, guide and manage the process that will allow commercial and government users, software vendors, standards organizations and systems makers to solve the information technology dilemmas caused by incompatibilities in their systems and software components" [Gray 1991, 121].

Membership requires a serious committment to producing products that adhere to X/Open guidelines. If all products comply with the guidelines, they are more likely to provide interoperability and portability.

X/Open is organized hierarchically. The board of directors develops the overall strategy, the technical managers develop a work plan to implement the strategy, and the work group does the work. The board of directors comprises one director per X/Open member. For a feature or facility to be incorporated into the XPG, the working group writes a detailed definition, the technical managers agree to the definition, and the board of directors gives final approval.

X/Open was founded by major European manufacturers in 1984. The group was called BISON by the trade press during its formative period because the original founders were Bull, ICL, Siemens, Olivetti, and Nixdorf.

In 1985, Issue 1 of the X/Open Portability Guide was published. Issue 2 followed in January 1987, and Issue 3 was published in late 1988. Issue 4 is expected soon.

In 1988, users and software vendors were given the opportunity for input into the X/Open process with the formation of advisory councils. X/Open now has three associate member councils: the User Council, the *ISV (Independent Software Vendor)* Council, and the System Vendor Council. (The latter are smaller vendors who are not large enough to be able to afford full shareholder membership.)

In 1988, the Software Partners Program was developed. In 1989, the X/Open Requirements Conference (XTRA) was held for the first time. It was held again in 1990 and 1991. The 1991 conference provided input to the "Open Systems Directive" published in 1992 [X/Open 1991].

Today, X/Open includes international computer manufacturers. It used to include both OSF and UI, but OSF is no longer an X/Open member.

The X/Open process relies on the technical expertise of member companies and subcontractors. X/Open's board of directors (one director per member) develops overall strategy. Specifications are also approved by the board; approval requires a 75 percent majority.

The Technical Managers (one per company) meet at least five times per year, in meetings that rotate around the globe. They define a technical work program, which is carried out by technical working groups. Most of the actual work is done at member companies.

There are X/Open technical working groups in the following areas:

• Kernel

• Commands

• Distributed Processing

• Security

• User Interface

• Systems Management

• Internationalization

• Data Management

• Transaction Processing

• PC Interworking

• Object-Oriented Technology

To get a new area of specification incorporated into the XPG, the working group provides a detailed definition. Agreement is sought by the technical managers; the board of directors may settle disagreements. The X/Open staff combines the contributions into a unified whole, and the board of directors approves the new version of the XPG.

X/Open has an Institutional Representative to TCOS-SS, and was the third organization to have one (after UniForum and USENIX). It has long been very active in POSIX standardization, producing many useful ballots. Recently, it has been quite active in the Distributed Services working groups, as well. X/Open also collaborates with other consortia such as OMG, NMF, and the X.400 API Association.

5.2   Manufacturers Organizations

These are trade associations for computer hardware vendors. They are older than the OSI promotion groups, their scope is more general, and their emphasis is more on hardware.

ECMA

ECMA (European Computer Manufacturers Association) is a nonprofit vendor organization that promulgates standards and is also a liaison member of both ISO and IEC [Quarterman 1990, 179]. As a liaison member, ECMA may submit proposals for new work to JTC 1. They may also participate when their proposals are being discussed.

In 1960, IBM and Bull sent an invitation to a meeting to all the known computer manufacturers in Europe. The purpose of this meeting was to address the problem that individual national bodies and single vendors were developing standards without any coordination or cooperation. The result of this meeting and later meetings was the formation of ECMA, with the attending corporations becoming ordinary members.

The purpose of ECMA is "to study and develop, in co-operation with the appropriate national and international organizations, as a scientific endeavour and in the general interest, methods and procedures in order to facilitate and standardize the use of data processing systems. To promulgate various standards applicable to the functional design and use of data processing equipment" [ECMA 1992, 6].

ECMA has technical committees in the areas listed in Table 5.2. These Technical Committees develop ECMA standards. Some Technical Committees also have Task Groups that handle specific areas addressed by the Technical Committee. ECMA produces standards in areas usually not actively addressed by ANSI [Digital 1991, B-14]. For *PCTE (Portable Common Tools Environment),* ECMA coordinates with NIST.

The organization of ECMA consists of a General Assembly, Management, and a Co-ordinating Committee. The Co-ordinating Committee makes recommendations to the General Assembly for coordinating the standards development effort of the Technical Committees. The General Assembly makes the decisions. The Management carries out these decisions.

Membership is of two types: ordinary and associate. Ordinary members may vote in the General Assembly and participate in Technical Committees of interest to them. Ordinary members are companies that make or sell data processing machines in Europe. An associate member is a company with "interest and experience in Europe in matters related to one or more of the TC's" [ECMA 1992, 68]. Associate members have no vote in the General Assembly, but may participate in discussions related to the Technical Committees they are part of.

Table 5.2 Active ECMA Technical Committees.

TC	Subject
TC 1	Codes
TC 12	Product Safety
TC 15	Volume and File Structure
TC 17	Magnetic Tapes and Tape Cartridges
TC 19	Flexible Disk Cartridges
TC 20	Acoustics
TC 29	Document Architecture and Interchange
TC 31	Optical Disk Cartridges
TC 32	Communication, Network and Systems Interconnection
TC 33	Portable Common Tool Environment
TC 34	Office Devices
TC 35	User System Interface
TC 36	Security Evaluation Criteria

CBEMA

CBEMA (Computer Business Equipment Manufacturers Association) is a consortium of mostly American hardware manufacturers. CBEMA "acts as a trade association for the business equipment industry" [Cargill 1989,170], which provides a vehicle for members to discuss common issues. It was formed in 1916 as the National Association of Office Appliance Manufacturers.

Any organization involved with the engineering, manufacture, finance, sale and support of office equipment, computer systems, peripheral devices, telecommunications services, or business equipment may become a member.

CBEMA supports standards work by providing the X3 and ISO/IEC JTC 1 TAG (Technical Advisory Group) secretariats. CBEMA also provides sponsorship for X3, the ASC for computers, information processing systems, and office systems.

5.3   Industry User Groups

Consortia of corporations that are users, not vendors, of computer software and hardware are a relatively new phenomenon. Such consortia have become influential. We have mentioned some of them before. Here we describe MIA, POSC, SOS, and UAOS.

MIA: Multivendor Integration Architecture Consortium

The *Multivendor Integration Architecture Consortium (MIA)* was established in Tokyo in 1988. Its goal is to produce an architecture that can be used to build distributed information processing systems with products from multiple vendors [Digital 1991, B42]. This architecture is called MIA, just like the organization. The importance of this architecture is that, starting in 1993, it will be required for NTT procurements.

The following organizations are members in MIA: *NTT (Nippon Telephone and Telegraph); NTT DATA (NTT Communications Systems Corporation);* Digital; IBM; Fujitsu; Hitachi; and NEC. Each member may vote, and decisions are made by consensus; that is, all members must agree.

MIA produces profiles, which are discussed in Chapter 12. Within these profiles, international standards are used first; when no standard is available, industry specifications are used; if there are no standards or specifications, MIA develops its own.

POSC: Petrotechnical Open Software Corporation

The *Petrotechnical Open Software Corporation (POSC)* POSC was formed in 1990 to develop "a software integration platform for upstream exploration and production (E&P) of petroleum" Its goal is to make this platform an industry standard, open systems platform [Digital 1991, B50].

Membership is open to corporation, business entities, government agencies, nonprofit organization, and academic institutions. POSC had ten members and five sponsors in 1991, and is expanding rapidy. Sponsorship is a three year commitment that provides a seat on the Board of Directors. Membership is a one year commitment that provides the ability to nominate one at-large director.

POSC developed a set of requirements and, in November 1991, issued a request for comment from the industry. The next step POSC plans is to issue an RFT (see OSF) to complete the specifications.

SOS: Senior Executives for Open Systems

The *SOS (Senior Executives for Open Systems)* are also known as the *Group of Ten*. This group is sometimes called *Senior Executives for Standards*. It consists of high level executives from large corporations that use computers extensively. These corporations are American Airlines, Du Pont, General Motors, Kodak, McDonnell Douglas, Merck, Motorola, 3M, Northrop, and Unilever. In June 1992, each member corporation sent a letter, the SOS "User Requirements Letter," to each of its computer vendors, spelling out their perception of a need for user-oriented standards for open systems, and for open system solutions to accomodate legacy systems [SOS 1991]. We have quoted from this letter in the Preface and in Chapter 3, *POSIX and Open Standards*. SOS was influential in the decision of OIW to expand its scope to include OSE, in addition to OSI.

Many of the companies represented in SOS are also represented in UAOS, which is discussed next. The precise relations between SOS and UAOS are unclear, as are any future activities of SOS.

UAOS: User Alliance for Open Systems

The *User Alliance for Open Systems (UAOS)* is a group of major North American users that formed to communicate to vendors their requirements for open systems. This group is creating a process to influence the rapid development of open systems by vendors.

The key goal of UAOS is to overcome barriers to open systems. To do this, it first identifies the barriers, develops strategies to overcome them, and develops a process for specifying the requirements of open systems so that vendors building open systems can meet the needs. The group will produce a set of requirements and specifications that it expects vendors to implement.

This group of end users met for the first time in Atlanta, during February 1990; this first meeting had 17 attendees. The group was thus called the Atlanta 17 at that time. The next meeting was held in Houston, during May 1990, with 30 attendees. After that meeting, the group was called the Houston 30. Then, the UAOS joined with COS (Corporation for Open Systems). COS membership allows participation in UAOS, but UAOS membership does not imply COS membership. Membership in UAOS is open to North American users of information systems. Any COS or UAOS member may vote in UAOS. Members pay dues that vary by organization. The membership is primarily users. Vendor participation is allowed for feedback, but is not permitted to dominate.

Members are from many industries, such as aerospace, finance, banking, chemical, petroleum, pharmaceutical, automotive, and governmental agencies and departments (NIST).

5.4   Military User Groups

The United States *DoD (Department of Defense)* takes a direct role in standards through DISA and PSSG, among other military groups. In addition, the U.S. Navy has its own standardization efforts through its NGCR program and OSSWG within that.

DISA: Defense Information Systems Agency

The *Defense Information Systems Agency (DISA)* was formerly known as the *Defense Communications Agency (DCA)*.

DISA continues standards work through its Center for Standards, which has the mission of providing joint coordination and management of information technology standards across the *DoD (Department of Defense)*.

DISA holds the secretariat for *PSSG (Protocol Standards Steering Group)*. The PSSG is one of several groups through which DISA effects this coordination.

Another group, for example, deals with telecommunications matters [Pasquariello 1992]. PSSG once produced a set of documents called *military standard (MIL-STD)* for some of the major TCP/IP protocols, through PSSG.

PSSG: Protocol Standards Steering Group

The *Protocol Standards Steering Group (PSSG)* is a joint group chaired by *DISA (Defense Information Systems Agency)*. Its members are representatives from U.S. military departments and agencies. PSSG's role is to provide DoD-wide coordination on data protocol matters such as requirements and standards coordination.

In the early 1980s, the PSSG was the approval mechanism for the *MIL-STDs (Military Standards)* that specified some of the major protocols in the TCP/IP protocol suite. These specifications made it easier for the U.S. government to procure TCP/IP software. Some say that such military procurements, in the early years of the Internet (approximately 1983 to 1986) facilitated the growth of the TCP/IP industry, which has now grown beyond the military. The TCP/IP MIL-STDs are listed in Chapter 15.

PSSG decided several years ago to stop publishing these MIL-STDS. Instead, the government now uses the TCP/IP specifications in RFCs produced by the *IAB (Internet Activities Board)* and *IETF (Internet Engineering Task Force)*, which are not military bodies. PSSG and other military groups attempt to ensure that DoD requirements are reflected in those Internet Standards. The PSSG continues to be the principal DoD linkage to the IAB for TCP/IP standards.

PSSG has also been the DoD focal point for GOSIP matters, and for development of the DoD strategy for transition from TCP/IP to GOSIP. PSSG is also the coordination mechanism for establishing the U.S. position on NATO data protocols and profiles [Pasquariello 1992].

This DoD PSSG should not be confused with the *PSSG (POSIX Standards Style Guide)*, which is an internal TCOS-SS document about stylistic issues in writing POSIX standards. The TCOS-SS PSSG is produced by two people, not by a formal organization.

NGCR: Next Generation Computer Resources Program

The U.S. Navy needs standards for procurement of computer software. The Navy may produce standards for this purpose, or may work with outside standards groups. The Navy *Next Generation Computer Resources (NGCR)* program has a charter

> to provide the Navy Mission-Critical Computing Resource (MCCR) applications with a coordinated set of interface standards for both physical and logical computer resources. These standardized interfaces will improve industry's ability to provide computing resources that meet Navy needs. The interface standards are to be widely accepted, non-proprietary, and, if possible, widely used within industry [Small *et al.* 1991].

These goals for standards are quite similar to those of industry users, although the Navy may place somewhat more emphasis on realtime and security issues than do most users.

NGCR's approach to standardization extends to profiling. "NGCR policy is to adopt existing commercial standards whenever possible" [Small *et al.* 1991]. This includes trying to determine which standards need to be adopted together, and where there are gaps that must be filled. In the area of *DBMSIF (Database Management System Interface)* standards, NGCR may even establish a reference model, since none appears to exist.

The NGCR Program works in several areas, one of which is operating system interfaces, which is the purview of the *Operating Systems Standards Working Group (OSSWG),* described next.

OSSWG: Operating Systems Standards Working Group

The U.S. Navy *Next Generation Computer Resources (NGCR)* Program seeks "to establish standard interfaces of several types in order to provide an open system architecture for constructing Navy application systems from compatible components" [Bergman & OSSWG 1991]. One of those types is operating system interface standards, which are handled by the *Operating Systems Standards Working Group (OSSWG).* OSSWG works with standards groups such as TCOS-SS, providing input to the POSIX and other standards. OSSWG was formed in 1989 and produced a formal report in October 1990 [Bergman & OSSWG 1991].

OSSWG has produced a functional specification for an operating system interface standard [OSSWG 1990]. It also has written a "DELTA Document" that describes how existing TCOS-SS standards and drafts, including POSIX, differ from what OSSWG needs [OSSWG 1991]. We have found this latter document particularly useful in writing this book.

5.5   Traditional User Groups

A *user group* is a nonprofit organization related to the UNIX operating system. Each has individual members, and has education as one of its goals. Some are described in the following sections. Examples include jus (Japan), CUUG (China), KUUG (Korea), COSA (Taiwan), AUUG (Australia), NZSUUGI (New Zealand), Sinix (Singapore), MALNIX (Malaysia), USENIX (North America), UniForum (North America), EurOpen (Europe), AFUU (France), UKUUG (United Kingdom), NLUUG (Netherlands), and DUUG (Germany).

EurOpen: The European Forum for Open Systems

EurOpen (European Forum for Open Systems) is an umbrella over the national European user groups, such as UKUUG and AFU. It was formerly known as *EUUG (European UNIX system Users Group).* EurOpen is a joint sponsor with USENIX of the ISO/IEC JTC 1 SC22 WG15 monitor project. Reports from this project are posted to the news group comp.std.unix, as well as published in the EurOpen Newsletter. EurOpen has an Institutional Representative to TCOS.

EurOpen provides a method of coordinating national working groups and developing European working groups. The objectives of all of the EurOpen working groups are [Burbaud *et al.* 1991]:

- To bring people together around specific topics

- To share working outputs among national groups

- To establish EurOpen as a consistent federation

- To help find funds from external organization, and

- To position EurOpen as a major Open Systems actor

The working groups are supported by the EurOpen Secretariat. Information about what the working groups are doing can be read in the EurOpen Newsletter. Some of the current working groups are those for portability, benchmarks, security, and open systems promotion.

jus: The Japan UNIX Society

The *Japan UNIX Society (jus)* was formed in 1983 as "a nonprofit organization whose objectives are: firstly, to promote the sound development of technology, culture and industry in computer-related fields, and especially fields involving the UNIX system; and secondly, to contribute to social development in general" [Imaizumi 1992]. Membership is about 2,000. jus provides a way for those interested in the UNIX operating system to share information. jus cooperates with other UNIX user groups in Asia, Europe, and America.

The network JUNET has long been associated with jus. The mail and news software used on JUNET was converted to handle Japanese Kanji characters by 1988 [Quarterman 1990]. jus is working on public domain implementations of internationalization standards.

UniForum: The International Association of Open Systems Professionals

UniForum (The International Association of Open Systems Professionals) UniForum is the user group with the most involvement in standards. UniForum was formed in 1980 as */usr/group,* in response to the need to "exchange information about UNIX-based products and services, as well as their standardization concerns" [/usr/group 1989]. UniForum is more oriented towards vendor needs than some user groups. It is a user organization as far as standards committees are concerned, since it produces neither hardware nor software. Members are from the United States and Canada, and also from many other countries.

UniForum provided the forum for early discussions of the POSIX work in its Technical Committees. Back when UniForum was called /usr/group, a group of concerned people got together and developed the 1984 /usr/group standard. This standard was based on UNIX System III. This standard was the base for the POSIX and C standard work.

UniForum continues to be active in providing a forum for the discussion of technical areas that are not quite ready for standardization. When ready, this work is moved to a formal standards body. Usually, the UniForum technical committee becomes the standards working group. A list of the UniForum technical committees can be found in Appendix A.

UniForum sends an *IR (Institutional Representative)* to the TCOS meetings. It also participates in the U.S. TAG to WG15. The current UniForum IR is also the U.S. TAG rapporteur for internationalization.

UniForum sponsors informational papers describing the POSIX work. It has written an introductory paper that describes POSIX, and informational papers describing the Operating System Interface, Shell and Utilities, and Internationalization. These papers are written in plain language and explain the standards in these areas, as well as standards jargon.

UniForum provides updates on standards issues monthly in the UniForum monthly magazine, *UniForum Monthly*.

USENIX: The Professional and Technical UNIX Association

USENIX (The Professional and Technical UNIX Association) is the oldest UNIX system user group. Members are from the United States and Canada, and also from many other countries.

USENIX sends an *Institutional Representative (IR)* to the TCOS meetings, as well as to the U.S. TAG to WG15.

USENIX standards activities are planned by the standards committee. The main goal of these activities is to keep standards from preventing innovation.

USENIX sponsors the "Snitch Reports," which are quarterly reports on the progress of standards committees of interest to the membership. Reports are generated for several of the TCOS committees, the ANSI X3B11 (optical disk drives), and the C++ language.

To keep the membership abreast of activities at the international level, USENIX jointly sponsors, with EurOpen, the ISO/IEC JTC 1 SC22 WG15 monitor project. The monitor writes a report about each WG15 meeting, which appears in the USENIX newsletter *;login:* twice a year following the meeting.

5.6   OSI Industry Promotion Groups

Industry organizations can work not only on OSI profiles that might later be adapted by workshops or even formal standards bodies; they can also directly promote the implementation and use of OSI protocols and protocol stacks related to those profiles. These organizations, like the OSI workshops, group themselves by continent. SPAG is European, COS is North American, and POSI is Japanese. They are closely related to the OSI workshops, but maintain separate identities.

SPAG: Standards Promotion and Application Group

The *Standards Promotion and Application Group (SPAG)* is a European group that is perhaps the oldest of the OSI promotion groups, having been formed in 1983 [Quarterman 1990, 199].

COS: Corporation for Open Systems

The *Corporation for Open Systems (COS)* is a user and vendor consortium whose purpose is to help speed the availability of OSI products by defining vendor agreements as to the use of OSI. The *UAOS (User Alliance for Open Systems)* and North American MAP/TOP User Group are both part of COS. COS membership implies membership in UAOS and MAP/TOP, but the inverse is not true.

POSI: Promoting Conference for OSI

The *Promoting Conference for OSI (POSI)* is a Japanese OSI promotion group, analagous to COS or SPAG.

5.7   OSI Workshops

Because *OSI (Open Systems Interconnection)* standards are numerous and have many options, there have long been workshops involved in defining implementation agreements for use developing profiles for OSI standards for various purposes. Two of these workshops, EWOS in Europe and OIW in North America, have recently expanded their scopes to include *OSE (Open System Environment)* work. Some of the effects of this work are described in Chapter 12.

EWOS: European Workshop on Open System

The *European Workshop on Open Systems (EWOS)* has traditionally produced OSI profiles for submission to CEN/CENELEC for European standards or ISO/IEC JTC 1 SGFS for *International Standardized Profiles (ISP)*. Like AOW, EWOS coordinates with other OSI workshops.

EWOS was the first of these three workshops to expand its scope to include OSE, which it did in September 1991. EWOS has been following related OIW activity. EWOS has proposed the concept of public specification (described under OIW) as a way of filling gaps left by missing base standards or profiles [OIW 1991a, App. C].

There was some interesting history behind this expansion of EWOS' scope. The European Commission proposed an EWOS Project Team to study a Framework for Open Systems in October 1989, and the EWOS Technical Assembly approved the project team in that same month. Work with funding began in May 1990. The original team's Final Report was submitted to EWOS in January 1991 [OIW 1991a, App. C]. As mentioned in Chapter 12, X/Open's XPG3 was proposed to CEN as a European *CAE (Common Application Environment)* standard somewhat earlier, in 1988. Even though it was found unsuitable as a formal standard for this purpose, the attempt was the direct impetus for the formation of the *EWOS/EG-CAE (EWOS Expert Group on the Common Application Environment)* whose work has been very influential on TSG-1 and SGFS, as explained in Chapter 12.

EWOS has also been involved in producing an *Open Systems Services Standards Handbook* on behalf of the *Commission of the European Communities (CEC)* [CEC 1991].

OIW: OSE Implementation Workshop

The *OSE Implementation Workshop (OIW)* is cosponsored by NIST and IEEE/CS. It appears that NIST takes the more active role of the two. OIW does not produce standards; its purpose is to produce an *Implementation Agreement* in each area desired by its participants. An implementation agreement is simply an agreement to implement a specific standard or suite of standards in a certain manner and with specified options.

OIW is similar to AOW and EWOS, and coordinates with them. There is evidently a *Regional Workshop Coordinating Committee (RWCC)* for this purpose. These workshops may produce *Memoranda of Understanding* among themselves to coordinate their activities. OIW, for one, is open to "all contributory participants and individuals or organizational expert groups from anywhere" [OIW 1991a].

The most general body of OIW is called the Plenary. Technical areas may be addressed in a *SIG (Special Interest Group)* formed for the purpose, much like a standards working group. Decisions are by majority vote, not consensus. The SIGs are coordinated by a *Technical Liaison Committee (TLC)*. Decisions of the TLC are by majority vote of SIG representatives.

OIW was previously known as the *OSI Implementor's Workshop (OIW)*. Partly due to outside requests [SOS 1991], this OSI workshop expanded its scope in December 1991 to explicitly incorporate open systems [OIW 1991b]. OIW explicitly cited the following as valid business needs underlying user demands:

• Protecting investment in application programmer and user skills across multiple vendor platforms

• Protecting investment in applications by making them portable across present and future vendor platforms

• Providing a neutral architecture for procurement requirements for more equitable procurement, and for procurement of components in parallel

The language used makes it clear that the users providing input are business executives and managers, on behalf of their companies, rather than final end users. The OIW expansion retains the original OIW emphasis on interoperability, while adding development of common application development environments [OIW 1991a]. This is in keeping with the recent trend of redefining open systems to

include interoperability in addition to portability as a goal, and as the now pre-
eminent goal, at that. OIW provides another perspective on this change, remarking that it changes OIW's emphasis from open interconnection of all systems,
whether open or vendor specific, to interconnection of open systems [OIW 1991a,
App. A]. This could be interpreted as an actual narrowing of the final purpose of
OSI. However, it is clearly a widening of the scope technical work that OIW is to
address, since API must now be taken into account.

The specific recommendation was to expand the charter of the OIW to incorporate technical areas consistent with

- The definitions in the TSG-1 final report on interfaces for application portability
  [TSG-1 1991]

- The recent proposed expansion of the SGFS taxonomy in TR1000-2 [SGFS
  1991]

- The ISO *Open Distributed Processing (ODP)* work in SC21 WG7 [OIW 1991b;
  OIW 1991a]

The new name keeps the acronym unchanged. There is also no change in OIW's
sponsorship status with NIST and IEEE/CS, although NIST may eventually have
to contribute more logistical support. Direct funding will continue to be through
attendee registration fees [OIW 1991a, 5].

The new scope of OIW is to be used to establish an *Open System Environment technical committee (OTC)* that will work on scope and framework of an
OSE in response to user requirements. This OTC is expected to respond favorably
to a request from the EWOS/EG-CAE to establish formal liaison.

OIW procedures are also to be revised to permit the use of public domain
specifications, in addition to formal standards. The emphasis of all this is on inte-
grating user requirements submitted by "external mechanisms," in pursuit of an
"internationally harmonized user requirements process" [OIW 1991b]. These
external mechanisms would appear to be those of the COS *Requirements Interest
Groups (RIGs),* the *User Alliance for Open Systems (UAOS),* and the X/Open
Xtra process. The OIW appears to be designed to be the premier coordination
group, at least in North America, for input from these various pre-existing user
requirements processes. The OIW TLC is tasked with handling user requirements
input from them.

The term *public domain specification* as used by OIW appears to be closely
related to the terms *open specification* and *public specification* formerly and currently used by IEEE P1003.0. Unlike an open specification, a public domain specification does not have to have been produced by an open process, although it
apparently does have to have "broad consensus." The point of using public
domain specifications is that, unlike open specifications or formal standards, they
can be produced and deployed faster, mostly because they do not have to go
through an open process. There is insistence on not normally using a public
domain specification where a formal standard exists.

OIW brings in the term *de facto standard* to describe something that could be used even when it overlaps a formal standard [OIW 1991b, App. B]. Presumably this means that a public domain specification does not have to be a de facto standard, that is, apparently a public domain specification's "broad consensus" does not have to, in general, extend as far as that of a de facto standard. In cases of multiple public domain specifications being considered, a decision among them would be made by the OIW Plenary.

There are some interesting provisions for the use of public domain specifications, such as the example that "a public domain specification describing a new networking service and a supporting protocol should be described with a service and protocol specification using the conventions established for OSI standards" [OIW 1991b, App. B]. This would appear to preclude any TCP/IP protocol specifications being used in their native form, as produced by the process described in Chapter 8. The OIW is explicitly interested in minimizing "any risk in jeopardizing the current OSI successes of the OIW," and this was one reason for retaining the former OIW workshop procedures [OIW 1991a, 7], presumably including decisions by majority vote, rather than by consensus.

Otherwise, the OIW's criteria for consideration of specifications are actually quite similar to those of the IAB. The OIW requires

- Specification in conventions, including conformance statements, appropriate for existing related formal standards

- No changes by the OIW except to fix technical and editorial errors, and to make the specification suitable for the formal standardization process

- Sufficient completeness for "useful and predictable implementation of the complete functionality from scratch"; an interface specification to an otherwise proprietary implementation is explicitly disallowed

- At least one actual implementation that has been shown to meet the user requirement

- Availability on terms consistent with ANSI, ISO, and CCITT copyright and patent guidelines

In the insistence on consistency of specification with that expected for formal standardization, OIW is like formal standards bodies, and it intends to forward much work to such bodies. In its insistence on meeting user requirements, it is in line with the recent TSG-1 and SGFS work that it cites. But in its insistence on actual implementation, OIW is much closer to the IAB process than to any formal standardization process. However, OIW and IAB differ markedly on their attitudes towards conformance testing: IAB has no use for it, considering interoperability of implementations to be sufficient and more important, whereas OIW requires it. This may be partly because OIW, after its recent expansion of scope, is concerned with API, as well as with protocols and services. It may also be because of the historical OSI emphasis on conformance testing. In addition to historical differences in orientation, OIW now differs from IAB in having taken the step of incorporating API into its scope.

AOW: Asia-Oceania Workshop

The *Asia-Oceania Workshop (AOW)* is an open public forum for developing International Standard Profiles for OSI. AOW coordinates with EWOS and OIW, both described in this chapter. Information about AOW can be found in [Digital 1991].

Membership in AOW is open to computer or research experts with an interest in creating OSI Functional Standards, which are otherwise known as *International Standardized Profiles (ISP)*. Members must be from Asia-Oceania countries. Some current members are *CSBTS (China State Bureau of Technical Supervision), SA (Standards Australia), ETRI (Electronics and Telecommunications Research Institute)* of Korea, and *INTAP (Interoperability Technology Association for Information Processing)* of Japan.

Unlike EWOS and OIW, AOW has not explicitly expanded its charter to include OSE work in its scope. There is speculation by participants that it will do so, however [OIW 1991a, App. C].

5.8   TCP/IP Protocol Standardization Bodies

The TCP/IP protocols and their uses are described in several books [Comer 1988; Comer & Stevens 1991; Carl-Mitchell & Quarterman 1993; Stallings *et al.* 1988]. But the organizations and processes that produce the protocols have only been sketched in a few books [Rose 1990; Comer 1988; Quarterman 1990], are not widely known, and have changed quite a bit in the last few years. In this section, we describe the bodies that produce the protocol specifications, especially the *IAB (Internet Activities Board)* and the *IETF (Internet Engineering Task Force)*. These organizations are very actively involved in producing protocol specifications, some of which become what they call *Internet Standards*. The processes they use are described in Chapter 8, *Protocols and Standards*.

None of the IETF, IAB, or related bodies are formal accredited standards bodies. The IAB is the top level body, and would thus have to be accredited first. It could delegate authority to some of the other bodies, if it wished. But see the next section, about ISOC.

ISOC: Internet Society

The *Internet Society (ISOC)* is an international nonprofit membership organization, formed in January 1992 to promote the use of the Internet for research and scholarly communication and collaboration [CNRI 1991]. This includes educational activities about the use of the Internet, and exploration of new applications. Individual members can vote. There are several classes of institutional members, but none of them can vote. ISOC holds an annual meeting, and publishes a newsletter, *Internet Society News*.

The initial ISOC organizers were the *Corporation for the National Research Initiative (CNRI)*, EDUCOM, and the IAB. They adopted a charter for ISOC in January 1992 [CNRI 1992], including naming an initial Board of Trustees of three members, who then adopted the Charter. That board appointed more members, and the resulting board adopted bylaws. The board will eventually have about 20 members, and will be elected for three year terms. Terms will be staggered, with a third of the board coming up for election each year. An election for the first third was expected by the end of 1992 [Cerf 1992].

IAB and ISOC decided for the IAB to come under the responsibility of ISOC, at *INET92 (International Networking Conference 1992)* in Kobe, Japan, in June 1992. INET92 was the second in a series of annual international networking meetings. These series of INET meetings will be incorporated into the ISOC annual meeting. This IAB and ISOC decision gives final authority for IAB standardization to the Board of Trustees of ISOC, much as authority for the TCOS-SS Working Groups leads to the IEEE Board of Directors. Whether such association will lead to accreditation or affiliation with an accredited body is unclear. There is no current affiliation of IAB or ISOC with any accredited standards body, such as ANSI or ISO. ISOC and IAB do not attempt to follow ANSI or ISO guidelines.

IAB: Internet Architecture Board

The *Internet Architecture Board (IAB)* is the group responsible for design, engineering, and management of the TCP/IP protocols [Cerf 1990]. The IAB does not attempt to manage the Internet built out of those protocols. The IAB limits itself to two basic functions [Cerf 1992]:

1. Providing a forum for communication and collaboration among network operators; the participants may include anyone who has run networks; typically, this means regional networks

2. Specifying and recommending technology

The IAB does not require anybody to do anything, and is not involved in daily operation of any networks. It does issue standards, but they are voluntary standards. Any of the participant network organizations could presumably issue its own mandatory operational standards, but it is not clear that any of them have.

Unlike the U.S. NSF, the IAB membership is not limited to the United States. In fact, the IAB is not limited in membership to any single country.

The IAB has two Task Forces, for Engineering, and for Research: the IETF and the IRTF. There is no fixed size to the IAB. It currently consists of a Chairman, an Executive Director, the Chairs of the IRTF and IETF, an RFC Editor, and six other Members. The IETF and IRTF each have Steering Groups, the IESG and the IRSG. The IESG consists of the IETF Chair and Area Directors. There may be more than one Director per Area. The IRSG consists of the IRTF Chair and Research Group Chairs. The IRSG has a couple of Members-at-Large with no specific areas. The Chairs of the IESG and IRSG are the Chairs of the IETF and

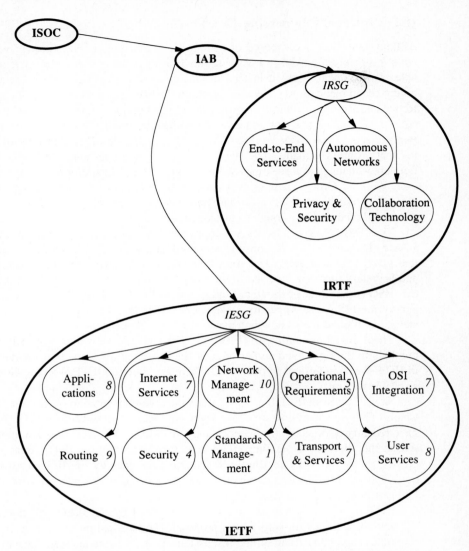

Figure 5.1 Internet working bodies, with working groups per IETF Area, 28 August 1992.

IRTF, respectively. These relations are shown in Fig. 5.1, and we explore them in more detail later. For IAB members, see Appendix A, *Resources*.

The IAB itself is self-perpetuating. The IAB Chair is elected for a term of two years by the IAB members, and IAB members are appointed by the IAB Chair with the advice and consent of the other members. The current IAB Chair is Lyman Chapin of BBN. The IAB was known as the *IAB (Internet Activities Board)* until June 1992, when it was renamed when it came under ISOC.

IETF: Internet Engineering Task Force

Although the IAB is composed of technically competent people, many of whom were intimately involved in inventing the TCP/IP protocols, the IAB itself originates no technical work; it instead originates mostly architectural and technical policy recommendations. Detailed work on TCP/IP protocols and specifications for standardization is done by a group called the *Internet Engineering Task Force (IETF)*. The IETF has working groups that handle specific design and specification projects. Each IETF Working Group has a chair, who is responsible for seeing that progress is made. The IETF met four times a year until 1992, when the frequency changed to three times a year (skipping fall). In addition to meetings of each Working Group, there is a plenary of all attendees. Working Groups may also meet outside of IETF meetings, and they regularly discuss drafts of documents and other issues through electronic mailing lists.

The IETF Working Groups are organized in technical Areas. Each Area has an Area Director who is responsible for coordinating the IETF Working Groups in that given technical area. The Area Directors plus a Chair, Executive Director, and Secretary form the *Internet Engineering Steering Group (IESG)*. The Chair of the IESG is the Chair of the IETF, and is a member of the IAB. For current members of the IESG, see Appendix A, *Resources*. The IESG recommends actions on standardization to the IAB, which makes most actual decisions.

These relations among IETF, IESG, and IAB are shown in Fig. 5.1. The numbers in the right hand corner of each IETF Area ellipse represent the number of IETF Working Groups in that Area. There are about 60 IETF Working Groups, as of this writing.

Areas date from the fall of 1989, when they were invented to offload the IETF Chair. They are administrative oversight entities, not constraints. IETF Areas have recently been added for Security and Operations. The IAB does not approve Areas: the appropriate steering group does that. The original IETF Areas were created by the IETF Chair (Phill Gross), and later ones by the IESG. An Area may also have a directorate, which is an advisory council that assists the Area Director in managing the Area.

IETF Working Groups are sometimes proposed by the IESG, but normally someone else comes forward with a proposal. The instigation may come from a researcher, a vendor, or an online discussion. Usually someone wants a standard way of doing something, and is willing to pursue it into the IETF. The criteria for creation of a Working Group are:

• A goal

• An expectation of success

• A community base (people who want the result)

• A provider base (people willing to work in the Working Group to produce that result)

Every IETF Working Group has a charter with projected milestones. Copies (and related documents) are kept in an anonymous FTP repository at nri.reston.va.us [Chapin 1992].

Participation in the IETF is by individuals, not by representatives of organizations. Membership in the IETF and its working groups is completely open, with no membership registration. Simply attending IETF meetings or contributing to online working group discussions is enough to constitute IETF membership. According to one participant, "IETF membership is thus a state of mind" [Crocker 1992a].

The IAB, IESG, and IETF working groups use different decision processes. The IAB votes, with the usual choices being "ok" or "needs discussion." The latter choice remands a specification to the IETF. Decisions to advance a protocol along the IAB Standards Track must be unanimous; that is, there can be no "needs discussion" votes, although there apparently can be abstentions. Working groups depend on consensus, not voting. Straw polls are sometimes taken, but they are not binding [Crocker 1992b].

Although the IAB makes the final formal standardization decisions, many others get made. The IAB can make a decision, perhaps for policy reasons related to outside organizations, counter to an IETF consensus. However, this is not easy to do, whatever the formalities might be, and IAB attempts to avoid this kind of situation. Ultimate authority is not considered a useful concept in resolving such contention, and usually both sides will see the need for reconciliation. Finally, an online mailing list related to a working group can overrule a decision made in a physical face-to-face meeting [Crocker 1992a].

Many of the usual specific mechanisms used by formal standards bodies are absent. There is no specific percentage of positive votes required for approval, and there is not even any specific membership of either the working group or a balloting group. There is a process for resolution of comments, but it involves none of formal technical reviewers, required balloting forms (such as the yes, yes with comments, or no with objections formats required by TCOS-SS), nor required responses. There is no formal requirement for public notice of meetings. In fact, although IETF meetings are always publicized well in advance, IETF decisions may be made through a working group mailing list at any time with none of the participants located in the same geographical place. There are processes for interpretations and appeals, and they are in outline similar to those used by formal standards bodies, but are perhaps even more vague in specific mechanisms than those used by formal standards bodies. We will discuss all these points in detail in Chapter 8, *Protocols and Standards*.

IRTF: Internet Research Task Force

Another IAB subgroup, the *Internet Research Task Force (IRTF)* is responsible for topics that are more research than operational engineering. Research for this purpose is defined to involve long term or high risk engineering, or real research where the outcome is uncertain, that is, failure is allowed [Cerf 1992]. The IRTF is structured into Areas like the IETF, but there are some members of the IRSG who are neither Area Directors nor officers. For current IRSG members, see Appendix A, *Resources.*

Many IRTF members are also IETF members. The distinction between research and operations is deliberately not strict; often it is a matter of timing.

References

Bergman & OSSWG 1991.   Bergman, R., & OSSWG, "First Annual Report — October 1990," Operating Systems Standards Working Group (OSSWG) Next Generation Computer Resources (NGCR) Program, Naval Ocean Systems Center, San Diego, CA (April 1991).

Burbaud et al. 1991.   Burbaud, P., Cornu, JM, Scheuer, P., & Beaver, S., "EurOpen Working Groups Memento," EurOpen (May 1991).

Cargill 1989.   Cargill, Carl F., *Information Technology Standardization: Theory, Process, and Organizations,* Digital Press, Bedford, MA (1989).

Carl-Mitchell & Quarterman 1993.   Carl-Mitchell, Smoot, & Quarterman, John S., *Practical Internetworking with TCP/IP and UNIX,* Addison-Wesley, Reading, MA (1993).

CEC 1991.   CEC, "Open Systems Services Standards Handbook V5.00," Commission of the European Communities, DG XIII/E.4, Rue de la Loi, 200, B-1049 Brussels, Belgium (December 1991).

Cerf 1990.   Cerf, Vinton, "The Internet Activities Board; RFC1160," *Network Working Group Requests for Comments* (RFC1160), Network Information Systems Center, SRI International (May 1990).

Cerf 1992.   Cerf, Vinton G., Personal communication (March 1992).

Chapin 1992.   Chapin, Lyman, Personal communication (14 April 1992).

CNRI 1991.   CNRI, "Announcing the Internet Society," Corporation for the National Research Initiatives, Reston, VA (July 1991).

CNRI 1992.   CNRI, "Charter of Internet Society," Corporation for the National Research Initiatives, Reston, VA (January 1992).

Comer 1988.   Comer, Douglas, *Internetworking with TCP/IP Principles, Protocols, and Architecture,* Prentice-Hall, Englewood Cliffs, NJ (1988).

Comer & Stevens 1991.   Comer, Douglas, & Stevens, David L., *Internetworking with TCP/IP, Volume II: Design, Implementation, and Internals,* Prentice-Hall, Englewood Cliffs, NJ (1991).

Crocker 1992a.   Crocker, Dave, Personal communication (3 February 1992 and 4 March 1992).

Crocker 1992b.   Crocker, Steve, Personal communication (April 1992).

Digital 1991.   Digital, *Open Systems Handbook: A Guide to Building Open Systems,* Digital Equipment Corporation, Bedford, MA (1991).

ECMA 1992.   ECMA, "European Computer Manufacturers Association Memento 1992," ECMA, Geneva, Switzerland (1992).

Gray 1991.   Gray, Pamela, *Open Systems: A Business Strategy for the 1990s,* McGraw-Hill, London (1991).

Imaizumi 1992.   Imaizumi, Aya, Personal communication (21 February 1992).

Leffler et al. 1989.   Leffler, Samuel J., McKusick, Marshall Kirk, Karels, Michael J., & Quarterman, John S., *The Design and Implementation of the 4.3BSD UNIX Operating System,* Addison-Wesley, Reading, MA (1989).

OIW 1991a.   OIW, "Open System Environment Expansion Final Report," OSI Implementors Workshop Technical Liaison Committee ad hoc Task Group on Open Systems Environment Expansion, Washington, DC (30 October 1991).

OIW 1991b.   OIW, "Open Systems Environment Expansion," OSI Implementors Workshop Technical Liaison Committee ad hoc Task Group on Open Systems Environment Expansion, Washington, DC (13 December 1991).

OSF.   OSF, "The Value of the Open Software Foundation for Users: A White Paper," Open Software Foundation, Cambridge, MA.

OSF 1990.   OSF, "Distributed Computing Environment: Rationale," Open Software Foundation, Cambridge, MA (14 May 1990).

OSF 1991a.   OSF, "Corporate Background," Open Software Foundation, Cambridge, MA (October 1991).

OSF 1991b.   OSF, "Interoperability: A Key Criterion for Open Systems: A White Paper," Open Software Foundation, Cambridge, MA (October 1991).

OSSWG 1990.   OSSWG, "Operational Concept Document Next Generation Computer Resources (NGCR) Operating System Interface Standard Version 1.0," Operating Systems Standards Working Group (OSSWG) Next Generation Computer Resources (NGCR) Program, Naval Underwater Systems Center, Newport, RI (26 November 1990).

OSSWG 1991.   OSSWG, "Delta Document for the Next Generation Computer Resources (NGCR) Operating Systems Interface Standard Baseline," Operating Systems Standards Working Group (OSSWG) Next Generation Computer Resources (NGCR) Program, Naval Ocean Systems Center, San Diego, CA (31 December 1991).

Pasquariello 1992.   Pasquariello, Camillo J., Personal communication (27 May 1992).

Quarterman 1990.   Quarterman, John S., *The Matrix: Computer Networks and Conferencing Systems Worldwide,* Digital Press, Bedford, MA (1990).

Rose 1990.   Rose, Marshall, *The Simple Book: An Introduction to Management of TCP/IP-based internets,* Prentice-Hall, Englewood Cliffs, NJ (1990).

SGFS 1991.   SGFS, *Information technology — Framework and taxonomy of International Standardized Profiles — Part 2: Taxonomy,* 28 June 1991.

Small et al. 1991.   Small, D. L., Butterbrodt, M. C., & Bergman, R. M., "White Paper on the Database Management System Interface Standard for Navy Next Generation Computer Resources (NGCR)," Next Generation Computer Resources (NGCR) Program, Naval Ocean Systems Center, San Diego, CA (July 1991).

SOS 1991.   SOS, "User Requirements Letter," Senior Executives for Open Systems, also known as the Group of Ten: American Airlines, Du Pont, General

Motors, Kodak, McDonnell Douglas, Merck, Motorola, 3M, Northrop, and Unilever, Washington, DC (27 June 1991).

Stallings et al. 1988.   Stallings, William, Mockapetris, Paul, McLeod, Sue, & Michel, Tony, *Department of Defense (DOD) Protocol Standards,* vol. 3 of *Handbook of Computer Communications Standards,* Macmillan, New York (1988).

TSG-1 1991.   TSG-1, "Standards Necessary for Interfaces for Application Portability," ISO/IEC JTC 1 TSG-1, Tokyo (1991).

UI 1991.   UI, "UI-ATLAS Questions and Answers," UNIX International, Parsippany, NJ (September 1991).

UI 1992.   UI, "1992 UNIX System V Roadmap," UNIX International, Parsippany, NJ (January 1992).

/usr/group 1989.   /usr/group, "profile," /usr/group, Santa Clara, CA (1989).

X/Open 1991.   X/Open, "Open Systems Directive," The X/Open Group, Ltd. (1991).

CHAPTER 6

Processes

This chapter describes standardization processes. It defines the terms used to describe various standards bodies, such as *working group, committee,* and *TAG (Technical Advisory Group).* It discusses possible types of participation.

Most standards groups follow similar processes, and the chapter begins with a generalized model of the standardization process. Details follow on the processes of ANSI, IEEE, X3, and ISO/IEC JTC 1. Ways in which the reader can participate are described next, followed by comparisons of some of the processes, including highlights of their advantages and problems. Computer networks have affected the computing and other industries, and we sketch some of those effects. Finally, we mention some drawbacks of standardization, for balance.

Other organizations have other processes, and some of these were described in Chapter 5, *Industry Organizations and User Groups.* Processes specific to network protocol specification and standardization, such as the processes used by the IAB to produce the TCP/IP protocols, are described in Chapter 8, *Protocols and Standards.*

6.1 The Standards Process Model

Standardization based on existing practice and available vendor implementations is supposed to work as follows. The standards body

1. Starts with existing practice

2. Cleans up the rough edges

3. Specifies it clearly

4. Does not change it much

Some people would argue that this is the one and only true way to create a standard. They typically cite the OSI standards as an example of what happens when a second type of standard, called an *anticipatory standard,* is created. OSI has been around for some time, but lack of implementations and costs of implementations have precluded widespread deployment. The OSI standards are called *anticipatory* because the standards are not based on any existing implementation. This anticipatory process is as follows:

1. Users and vendors see a need for a common facility or requirement.

2. They reach consensus on the solution.

3. A standard is written to the consensus.

4. Vendors implement the standard.

In the development of either an anticipatory standard or a standard based on existing practice, the process involves these steps: propose, study, draft, approve, interpret, appeal, and review. These are shown in Fig. 6.1.

Two elements, *due process* and *consensus,* are the keys used in each phase of creating a standard. Due process is

> a concept that provides anyone with a directly or materially affected interest in the proposed standard an opportunity to participate in its development, from its initiation through its completion. Consensus describes that point at which the developers and commentators of a standard merge in agreement; it should not be mistaken for majority or unanimity — consensus can be reached even when objections exist, as long as the developers believe that the objections are not significant enough to prevent the standard from being effective [Cargill 1989, 168].

Figure 6.1 General standardization process model.

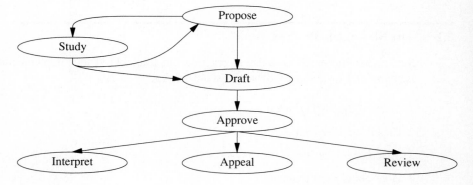

It is these two keys that differentiate a consensus standard from a specification.

The first phase is *Propose*. In the Propose phase, interested parties meet to discuss the need for a standard. This can happen in different ways: one way is at a professional conference, another is within the context of formal standards meetings. The interested parties could be members of a working group, a strategic planning committee, an industry consortium, or a user group. The key is that the parties are interested in deciding whether a standard should be created. If they decide that a standard is required, proposals are drafted and submitted to an appropriate sponsoring body. Sponsoring bodies can provide administrative, financial, publication, and legal support for standards development. Sometimes, a sponsor is called a *Secretariat*. Sometimes, it is decided that further study is required. In this case, proposals to a sponsoring body to form a study group can be developed, or the interested parties may continue to study the area without any formalization.

The second phase is *Study*. In the Study phase, the area is studied to determine what the needs are. An example of a study group is *TSG-1 (Technical Study Group 1)*, which JTC 1 formed to study application portability. Study groups can generate reports and recommendations. They also produce proposals to create new standards.

The transition from the Propose or Study to the *Draft* phase requires approval from the sponsoring body of the proposal to develop a standard. The Draft phase can be either the second or third phase. In the Draft phase, drafts of the standard are written.

When a draft has reached a reasonable degree of stability, it is ready to move to the *Approve* phase. In the Approve phase, the draft is available to a group of people called a *balloting group* to vote and comment on. Depending on the developing organization, the balloting group can be members of the drafting group, the general public, or a professional society. In response to the votes and comments, the draft is modified and is voted on again. This process is repeated until the approval criteria are satisfied. Most standards bodies have requirements on the number of ballots cast and the number of affirmative votes for approval, as well as how negative votes are resolved. After approval by the balloting group, the draft usually must be approved by the sponsoring body. For example, an IEEE standard must be approved by the Standards Board once it has been approved by the balloting group.

After approval, three actions can be taken regarding a standard: *Interpretations, Appeals,* and *Review.* Sometimes, a standard is difficult to understand. Most standards bodies have a formal method of inquiring about the specific meaning of a standard. The IEEE calls these clarifications *interpretations,* and we also call them interpretations. Sometimes, someone believes that their interests were not considered by a standard; an Appeals process is designed to handle these cases. Standards, like most technology, are outdated quickly; the Review process is necessary to make sure a standard remains current and useful.

Most standards bodies go through the phases listed above. ANSI coordinates standards development within the U.S. The ANSI process used was developed to ensure due process for all affected parties, and to ensure consensus. ANSI accredits other bodies to develop U.S. national standards using their own procedures, which are consistent with ANSI rules. First, we discuss two of ANSI's accredited standards developers: the IEEE and X3. Then, we talk about the international process used by JTC 1.

6.2   The ANSI Process

If a standard is to become an American National Standard, it must be developed by an ANSI accredited body. ANSI itself does not develop standards; rather, it accredits other organizations to develop standards. Organizations accredited by ANSI are discussed in Chapter 4, *Formal Standards Bodies*.

There are three methods for developing an ANSI standard. The first method is called the *canvass method*. An example of a standard created using this method is the language Ada. The second method is creation by an *Accredited Standards Committee (ASC)*. X3 is an example of an ANSI Accredited Standard Committee and ANSI X3.159-1989, the C standard, is an example of a standard produced by the X3J11 technical committee. The third method is by *Accredited Standards Developing Organizations (ASDO)*. The POSIX work which is done within the framework of the IEEE is an example of an ASDO.

As we mentioned, there are two keys to ANSI accreditation: *consensus* and *due process*. ANSI approval assures the world that the standards were developed under impartial, democratic procedures and those "directly and materially" affected reached consensus — substantial agreement — on the standards' provisions [ANSI 1987]. Another definition of *consensus* is that any objections raised are not significant enough to prevent acceptance of the standard. Due process ensures that anyone affected by the standard has an opportunity to participate or comment. For example, due process should ensure that there is agreement that any remaining objections are not significant. This agreement assures there is market need and acceptance [Cargill 1989, 169].

An ANSI approved process follows the steps described in the previous section. The Propose phase is initiated with a *Project Proposal*. Any individual can submit a Project Proposal to an ASC. Once it is submitted, the ASC reviews it to determine if this ASC should take on the task of developing the standard. Some of the questions that the ASC would consider are whether there are people to do the work and whether there is a need for this standard. If the ASC decides to accept the proposal, it may then assign the proposal to an appropriate subgroup.

The next phase is drafting. During drafting, the committee listens carefully to everyone's opinion and input. The output of this phase is called a *draft proposed American National Standard (dpANS)*. The ASC reviews the dpANS and the voting results, and checks to see whether it agrees with the original proposal.

The Approve phase includes a public review, lasting for four months. ANSI publishes a description in its publication *Standards Action* and announces the review period [Cargill 1989, 169]. During this phase, the dpANS is changed to reflect the review comments. This phase can take quite a bit of effort, with multiple iterations of the dpANS being commented on. Once consensus is reached, the standard is voted on by the ASC, then is forwarded to the ANSI *Board of Standard Review (BSR)*. The BSR reviews the process that the ASC used to make sure it followed the rules, that everyone had a voice, and that consensus was reached. The dpANS becomes an *American National Standard (ANS)*.

ANSI requires that a standard be reviewed five years after it was approved. Such a review has three possible results: *reaffirmation, withdrawal,* or *revision.* Reaffirmation confirms that the standard is still useful and current. If there is no longer a reason for a standard, it is withdrawn. If a standard is still useful but needs to be updated, the revision process begins with a project proposal and goes through the steps again.

6.3   The IEEE Process as Implemented by TCOS

The following paragraphs describe in detail the process of creating a standard where the work area falls under the IEEE Computer Society *Technical Committee on Operating Systems and Application Environments (TCOS)*. From Fig. 6.2, you can see that TCOS falls under the Computer Society, which falls under the IEEE. Therefore, any procedure followed by a TCOS standards committee must adhere to the rules of the IEEE Standards Board and the Computer Society Standards Activities Board. Because the IEEE is an ASDO of ANSI, ANSI procedures must also be followed. The process used by the *TCOS-SS (TCOS Standards Subcommittee)* is described in the following paragraphs.

Propose

For the TCOS work, the UniForum Technical Committees have provided a forum for early discussion and base documents for POSIX. However, there doesn't have to be a group of interested people to start the Propose phase. A single individual can submit the proposal. To complete the standardization process they will require the support of a working group, but starting the process requires only one person.

A proposal is called a *PAR (Project Authorization Request)*. A PAR is submitted to the *PMC (Project Management Committee)* a subcommittee of the TCOS *SEC (Sponsor Executive Committee); see* Fig. 6.2. The PAR is an IEEE requirement, but the PMC and SEC committees are unique to TCOS. The PAR includes a description of what the new group plans to do. It designates a base document from which to work. The PAR identifies any other groups doing work in the area, and specifies how the new work will be coordinated with it. Two methods of coordination are liaisons between groups, and circulation of documents between groups.

The PMC reviews the PAR, asks any questions, and gets further clarification until it feels satisfied. The PMC makes a recommendation to the SEC for whether to approve the PAR. Once the SEC approves the PAR, it forwards it to the *New*

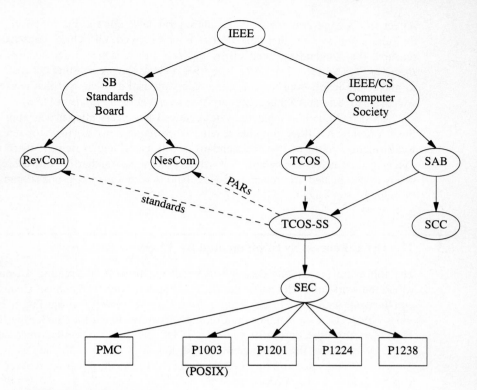

Figure 6.2 TCOS and relatives.

Standards Committee (NesCom) of the IEEE Standards Board, as well as to the Computer Society SAB.

The SEC coordinates and monitors the work. It decides which work is done under its sponsorship, and which is not. For administrative and financial support, the SEC receives assistance from its parents, the IEEE Computer Society and the IEEE. The IEEE standards department coordinates balloting and publication.

Draft

The Draft phase is shown in simplified form in Fig. 6.3, which shows that the process is not necessarily a straight line. There can be loops, with multiple drafts and multiple ballots.

Participation in the working group is open to any interested individual. There are fees for meeting attendance and paper mailings. Proposals are submitted for working group consideration. Participation can be in person at the meetings or by correspondence. A person may participate by receiving the working group mailings and sending in comments by letter.

There is one exception to individual participation within TCOS: the *IR (Institutional Representative)*. An IR represents an organization with an interest in

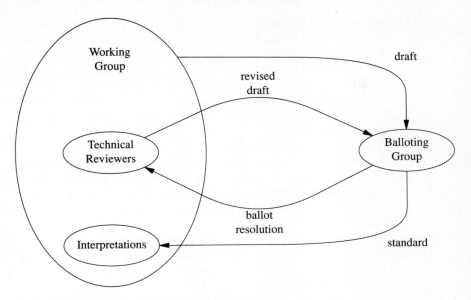

Figure 6.3 TCOS simplified development process.

standardization. IRs speak for their institutions. Some examples of TCOS IRs are those for UniForum, USENIX, the Open Software Foundation, and UNIX International.

Once the working group decides that a draft is almost ready to ballot, it may choose to have a mock ballot first. The mock ballot is unofficial and is a last attempt to identify and clear up any problem areas before actual ballot. Unlike for a real ballot, the participants do not have to join a formal balloting group. Usually, the working group that creates the standard participates in the mock ballot, as do other known interested individuals. Criteria for balanced representation are not considered here. Sometimes a committee will hold an internal mock ballot, with only the working group attendees, before going to an outside mock ballot or to a formal ballot.

Approve

The Approve phase is divided into two parts. First, the balloting group must approve (with sufficient affirmative votes) the draft. Then, the draft must be submitted to the IEEE Standards Board's review committee (RevCom) for its approval.

Ballot groups form when the working group believes that the standard will go to ballot within the next six months. Invitations are sent to members of the TCOS balloting pool. You must request to be placed in the balloting pool. To be eligible for the POSIX balloting pool you must be an IEEE or an IEEE/CS affiliate member, or an *IR (Institutional Representative)*. The IEEE Standards Department sends notices to all members of the balloting pool, asking whether they wish to join an upcoming balloting group. Those who respond to this notice are the people who actually do the balloting. Once the balloting group has closed, additional members are usually not allowed.

Members of the balloting group are placed in three categories: user; producer; and general interest. A balloting group must be less than half providers and less than half users, with the remaining members being classified as general interest. If a balloting group is not balanced, it is thrown out, and a new balloting group is formed.

In addition to individual members in IEEE balloting groups, there are institutional representatives. These representatives vote for a group of people. In the interest of international acceptance of an IEEE standard, members of the appropriate international committees (e.g., JTC 1 SC22 WG15 members) are invited to join the TCOS balloting groups so that international comments can be incorporated early in the process.

The balloting group and the working group chair now have control over the contents of the document. Within TCOS, the working group chair has the support of a group of technical reviewers to respond to the ballots.

There are four types of votes on a POSIX document:

• Yes

• Yes with comments

• No with objections (and possibly comments)

• Abstain

If you ballot no, you must provide specific objections, with sufficient detail that the technical reviewers can tell what, if changed in the document being balloted, would satisfy your objection.

The ballots go out, and the ballots return. For a ballot to be closed, 75 percent of the ballots must be returned. Of the returned ballots, 75 percent of those not abstaining must be affirmative for a standard to be approved.

Technical reviewers look at the ballots to resolve any objections. Even if a draft meets the approval criteria, every objection must be addressed. Each objector must be contacted. If an objection cannot be resolved, it must be documented, along with the reason it cannot be resolved. Unresolved objections with rationale are also circulated to the balloting group, giving its members the opportunity to change their ballot.

The technical reviewers make changes to the document if required, and either send it out to ballot again (recirculation) or forward it to the IEEE Standards Board review committee, RevCom.

The draft standard, along with documentation about the balloting process, is forwarded to RevCom. The documentation is reviewed by RevCom for procedure. If the proper procedures have been followed, the draft standard is placed on the agenda for the next IEEE Standards Board meeting. Once accepted by the Standards Board, the draft becomes an IEEE standard and is published as such.

Appeals, Interpretations, and Review

An appeal can be submitted to the IEEE Standard Board by anyone interested in the standard who objects to the standard content or to the procedure followed to create the standard. This appeal must be filed within a short amount of time following the standard's approval. An interpretations committee is formed from members of the working group to address requests for interpretations. Review occurs every five years per ANSI requirements.

American National Standard

Following IEEE approval, the standard may be forwarded to ANSI for approval as an American National Standard. ANSI reviews the documentation to make sure consensus was reached, that due process was followed, and that there was public review.

6.4   The ASC X3 Process

The following paragraphs describe in detail the process of creating a standard within *X3 (Accredited Standards Committee X3 for Information Technology)*. X3 follows the basic steps outlined in the beginning of this chapter. Details of each milestone in the standard process can be found in [X3 1990].

Membership in X3 is open to anybody affected by the standards that it produces. Usually, X3 members are organizations or corporations. Membership represents producer, user, and general interest groups. As with most organizations, there are membership fees, as well as fees for participation in each technical committee.

Propose

A Project Proposal (SD3) may be formed and submitted by any interested individual to *SPARC (Standards Planning and Requirements Committee)*; see Chapter 4, *Formal Standards Bodies*. SPARC reviews the proposal to determine whether X3 is the right body for the work, and whether the resources are available to do the work. SPARC then makes a recommendation to X3.

At this point, X3 may refer the project to a *Technical Committee (TC)*, establish a study group, or establish a new TC. If the project is approved, the X3 Secretariat issues a press release asking for technical contributions and participants.

Draft

The TC develops a schedule and work plan. Meetings are held and the draft standard is created. Once the TC decides the draft is ready, it forwards the document to SPARC.

Approve

SPARC reviews the document for compliance with the original proposal and makes a recommendation to X3. X3 then votes on readiness for public review. If it is approved, the draft becomes a *dpANS (draft proposed American National Standard),* and is submitted to the ANSI *Board of Standard Review (BSR)* for public review. Comments from public review are addressed by the technical committee, and responses are sent to the submitter. If comments require one or more substantive changes to the dpANS, another public review is required. After public review, the dpANS is forwarded to the BSR for approval and publication.

Appeals, Interpretations, and Review

X3 review occurs 4 years from the approval date of a standard. On approval of a standard, anyone whose objections have not been resolved is notified that they can submit an appeal within the 15 day limit, should they choose to do so. Defect reports are submitted to the X3 Secretariat and are forwarded to the appropriate TC for resolution. The resolution can take the form of an erratum, interpretation, or amendment. Amendment requires another public review.

6.5   The ISO/IEC JTC 1 Process

The following paragraphs describe the process of creating an international standard within *JTC 1 (Joint Technical Committee One)* of both *ISO (International Organization for Standardization)* and *IEC (International Electrotechnical Commission).* The biggest difference between JTC 1 and the two national processes described earlier in this chapter is membership. Participation in JTC 1 membership is by national body. For example, ANSI is responsible for representing the United States. See [JTC 1 1990] for exact details.

Propose

A *New Proposal (NP)* is formed and submitted to JTC 1. New proposals may be submitted by any JTC 1 member. This submission can be made by a working group, through a subcommittee to JTC 1, or by a national body directly to JTC 1 when a new area is being considered. Certain liaison members of JTC 1 also have the power to submit new proposals. JTC 1 reviews the proposal, votes on appropriateness, and assigns to an appropriate subcommittee. Sometimes, study groups are formed directly by JTC 1, such as SGFS, the special group on functional standardization.

Draft

Once the proposal is approved, a subcommittee or working group develops a schedule and work plan. A standard can be written in two ways. In the first and most common method, a JTC 1 working group drafts the standard. The second, called *national body development,* is uncommon. In national body development (discussed later), one of the national bodies actually does the drafting. For POSIX, the TCOS committees draft the standards. With either method, a draft before registration with the ITTF is called a *Working Draft (WD)*. When a WD is ready, and all the main elements are present, JTC 1 or a JTC 1 *subcommittee (SC)* forwards the WD to the ITTF for registration as a *CD (Committee Draft)*. The committee draft used to be called a *DP (Draft Proposal)*. If the work is being done by a *Working Group (WG)* or an SC, the SC requests registration. If the work is being done by a JTC 1 working group, JTC 1 requests registration.

Approve

Now JTC 1 or the SC ballots on the CD. If the ballot is successful, the ITTF is requested to register the CD as a *DIS (Draft International Standard)*. All dissenting votes must be considered, and a disposition of comments developed. If more than two negative votes cannot be resolved, the Secretaries-General will make special enquiry [JTC 1 1990, 29]. Next, JTC 1 (only JTC 1 and not the SC if one exists) ballots on the DIS. If it is approved, the DIS becomes an *IS (International Standard)*.

National Body Development

The ISO POSIX work is being done by national body development. This means that the standard is drafted in a TCOS committee. Once this document is ready, it is forwarded to WG15 for review and comment. Both the U.S. TAG and the TCOS-SEC have to agree that a document is ready to forward to ISO. These comments are fed back into the TCOS committee. Once the document is in TCOS ballot, there are rules for synchronization with ISO ballot, so that both the TCOS and ISO ballot comments and objections are handled at the same time. There is a detailed synchronization plan that describes this. National body development is only recognized by JTC 1 and SC22.

6.6   Participation and Membership

Not only are the processes different in different standards bodies, but who can participate and how they can participate differ as well. Membership is usually required to vote, but to submit proposals and comments does not always require membership. Who may vote is shown in Table 6.1. Usually, individuals are delegated to participate, but who they represent varies widely, from themselves, to their companies, to whole countries.

Voting membership in JTC 1 is by national body. Each national body has one vote and may send a delegation to meetings. Different countries handle their representation with different methods. In the United States, representation is by *TAG (Technical Advisory Group)*. Membership in the U.S. TAG is by U.S. Organization. Any affected or interested U.S. organization may join a TAG. On the other

Table 6.1 Who may vote.

Body	Type of Membership
JTC 1	National bodies
U.S. TAG	U.S. organizations
X3	Affected "persons"
IEEE	Individuals
TCOS	Individuals
IETF	No actual balloting

hand, there are other categories of membership that allow organizations to submit proposals, to observe meetings, and to participate in meetings when their proposals are being discussed. These types of memberships are called liaisons. To participate in JTC 1 activities, contact your national body. For details, see Appendix A. JTC 1 national body members are discussed in Chapter 4, *Formal Standards Bodies*.

X3 membership is by organization. X3 members participate in the work of X3. Committee chairs for X3 do not have to be from member organizations. Each X3 member organization has one vote.

TCOS working group participation is by individual. The individuals do not have to be IEEE, Computer Society, or TCOS members. Working group participation is open to all. During working group meetings, individuals are supposed to represent themselves and not their corporations. The same is true for balloting. Membership in the IEEE or IEEE Computer Society is required for balloting. Each member of the balloting pool has one vote. This could translate into many votes per organization. Membership and participation in X3 and TCOS is open to all organizations or individuals, regardless of nationality.

Participation does not have to mean attending meetings. Written comments can be submitted to working groups. For TCOS, mailings from the working groups are available for a fee.

Collaboration can make participation possible. For example, Institutional Representatives from user groups provide a voice for users and much needed information on the state of a standard. User groups provide updates about different standards groups in their publications. See Chapter 5, *Industry Organizations and User Groups*, for details.

6.7   Differences in Processes

The processes of the various standards bodies can differ in even the most fundamental features, such as how many votes it takes to approve a standard. The following paragraphs look at each phase of the process and highlight the differences among the three processes just presented.

Table 6.2 Terminology differences in standards processes.

Stage	JTC 1	ASC X3	TCOS
Project Proposal	NP	SD3	PAR
new projects	JTC 1	SPARC	PMC
			NesCom
drafts	CD	draft	draft
draft standards	DIS	dpANS	
standards	IS	ANS	IEEE-std

As shown in Table 6.2, the name for a project proposal for JTC 1 is *New Proposal (NP)*. For X3, it is SD3 (named for the X3 standing document number that describes the format of a project proposal). For TCOS, the name is *Project Authorization Request (PAR)*. For work being done in international working groups or subcommittees falling under JTC 1, NPs have to be submitted to JTC 1. SD3s are submitted to SPARC before approval by X3. For TCOS, a PAR is submitted to the PMC, which makes a recommendation to the SEC, which forwards the PAR to NesCom for approval.

During the draft phase, many methods are employed for creating a draft. A proposal is submitted by an interested party for inclusion or revision of the draft. The method used to decide what is included or excluded varies even among working groups within the same body. Some working groups make decisions based on majority, with the safety net that strong objectors still have balloting in which to object. For other committees, all must agree for inclusion or exclusion in a draft.

The criteria used for standards approval are presented in Table 6.3. These numbers are the minimums required for approval. In addition, all comments and objections must be addressed. The objector must be given the reason that their objection was not included. For the IEEE and TCOS members, the rationale is recirculated to the entire balloting group, enabling them to change their votes if

Table 6.3 Standard approval criteria.

Group	Approval*
JTC 1	2/3 of members voting
U.S. TAG	Majority
IEEE	75% of nonabstaining
X3	2/3 of membership

* In all cases, comments must be resolved.

they desire. Within JTC 1 and X3, the communication is directly with the objector. Once it is approved, a standard is usually published. The IEEE publishes IEEE standards; JTC 1 publishes JTC 1 standards. ANSI publishes X3 standards.

Another difference is the type of standardization. As discussed in Section 6.1, some standards, such as the OSI standards, are created by working groups, and are called anticipatory standards. Others, such as ANSI C and POSIX, are really an effort to standardize existing practice. This difference in process may reflect a difference in the level of interest in standards by the industry in general. In contrast, the C standard began with a language that was readily available. This standardization effort smoothed the rough corners and blended conflicting areas of the language to give the community one way to do something. The ANSI C effort took a long time because of the number of people interested and affected by the work. However, it is widely accepted in the industry. The current standardization effort for ANSI C++ is using yet another approach. The originators of the C++ language recognized the need to initiate the effort, rather than to allow C++ standardization to take as long as C standardization did. Their aim is to nip problems in the bud.

6.8   Networks and Standards

Networks are having increasing effects on the information technology industry, and indirectly on requirements for standardization. Probably no computer vendor can compete anymore without an enterprise network connecting its various departments, branches, and levels of management. These networks are used both for resource sharing (file transfer, remote login, supercomputer access, etc.) and for computer mediated communications (mail, news, interactive conferencing, etc.) [Quarterman *et al.* 1991]. Such use of high speed networks reduces costs and increases productivity. It increases product consistency by coordination of offices, and reduces product development times. External access is also important. Even though only about 20 percent of a given company's employees may use external network links, these links are increasingly becoming the arteries of the lifeblood of communications in this industry, for one-to-one mail, for group discussions, and even for publication. They also permit use of supercomputers and other resources that are not available locally [GAO 1991]. Distribution of experimental or free software, or even proprietary operating system releases, is commonly done over USENET and the Internet. A popular definition of portability is "if I can copy it off the Internet and just type 'make'." Currently, this usually implies that the program must be public domain as well as portable, but that is changing as markets come to the Internet (see Chapter 8, *Protocols and Standards*).

Development Intervals

Because networking and other developments have reduced product development and viability times greatly, if standards are to be useful, they need to be completed quickly. A common interval from feasibility to product release is eighteen months, and every lost month costs large sales opportunities [Rutkowski 1991]. Most standards organizations don't move that fast, but they may need to. How can this speed be achieved without losing the benefits of consensus processes?

The networks that are partly driving the need for speed can be part of the solution. It is interesting to compare the degree of practical success of the OSI committees, which do not use actual networks very much, with that of the committees that produce the TCP/IP specifications, which have always used networks built from them.

Online Publication

Online publication of standards is a major issue. Many standards committees, such as ISO and IEEE, copyright their standards, and permit distribution only on paper. Two reasons are usually given for this decision:

1. It maintains the integrity of the documents.

2. It allows revenue to be derived from sales.

These are real concerns. But the purpose of standards is to be implemented, and the success of a standards organization is measured by how much its standards are used, which is related to how easy they are to get. Tradeoffs may need to be made.

Document Integrity. There is concern about the possibility of a vendor modifying an electronic copy of a standard and claiming conformance to it as if it were the real one. Yet the TCP/IP specifications have always been available for free, without copyright, online, and over the worldwide Internet. Document modification problems are countered partly by making the real documents so readily available that it is easy to get them directly from the authorized source. This solution does not always work completely, and there have been problems with vendors having different pinouts when they thought they were implementing the same specifications, because each made incompatible extensions to the base standard (for Multibus). The average Internet or TCP/IP protocol user probably does not know where to get an RFC from the official sources, for that matter. It may be enough for those directly involved in network or system managment, or protocol or system development, to know how to get official specifications.

There is a problem of sales people not understanding that an RFC is not necessarily an Internet Standard, and claiming conformance to something that is actually a draft. This problem is also common with POSIX drafts and standards.

Publication Revenue. ITU once derived 8 million Swiss francs (about 8 million U.S. dollars) from annual document sales [Malamud 1991]. But it is not known what proportion of ITU's annual revenues that figure represents. It is not clear that standards organizations generally derive most of their income from the sale of documents, but it is also not clear that revenue from such sales is not important to standards development. High costs of documents impede their use and thereby impede the practical acceptance of the standards they specify. But a standard that is never developed will not be accepted, either. Difficulty of access is more of an impediment than high cost.

The TCOS-SS working groups are self-supporting on the basis of fees charged to participants for meeting attendance and mailings of working documents. IEEE and ISO derive some income from the sale of POSIX standards, but it does not go back into the actual development effort. However, IEEE document sales do help fund balloting. IEEE could probably still sell paper copies even if networked distribution were possible, since those tend to be separate markets (a programmer will generally want a shelf copy as well as a greppable electronic copy). For example, SRI sells a CD/ROM with all the RFCs (and related documents and source code) on it, even though they are available for free online. And IEEE now makes some of its standards available on CD/ROMs, although for some reason in facsimile format. POSIX and other TCOS drafts are now often available by anonymous FTP. See Appendix A for access details for all these things.

6.9   Drawbacks

Formal standards also have their drawbacks. Writing them can take a long time. Consensus and due process are inherently complex, with many checks and balances to assure that all interests are considered. If there are many people interested in a standard, resolution of public comment or ballot comments can be a very time consuming task. For example, the C language standard had many people interested in it and took a long time to be approved. However, it is a widely accepted standard.

Each standard document tends to cover a limited area. The POSIX System Interface Standard is only a small part of a usable system. If a standard is to be developed in a timely manner, the scope needs to be limited. An example of what can happen when the size of the standard grows is the POSIX Shell and Utilities work. This document is approximately 900 pages. The time to work out the original details and review the document increases as the page count increases.

Writing a standard can be very expensive. When you consider the administrative overhead, the travel and hourly cost of an individual, the amount of money spent on standardization is large. When POSIX began, there was a roomful of people meeting. Now POSIX meetings require all the meeting space in a hotel.

Lack of a standard can injure open systems. In this case, applications are written that do not have standard interfaces. This lack makes the application less portable, and makes it available to end users only on specific platforms. On the one hand, standards make some changes to existing interfaces harder, and thus may impede innovation. On the other hand, standards help to create a solid consensus base from which to build new facilities.

Industry consortia may be very effective here. Since most people need complete systems, and most standards are for narrow parts of a system, specifications developed by a consortium representative of a large portion of the industry can fill the gap. If enough vendors agree to adhere to the specifications, then applications can be made available to a user on a number of platforms. The X/Open Portability Guide is one such specification. The X Window System produced by the X Consortium is another.

Each step in producing a standard can go wrong.

1. Sometimes, a standards body is formed without a clear need for a facility.

2. Sometimes, vendors can't decide what to implement, or can solve only parts of a problem, but market pressures force standardization anyway.

3. Sometimes, market pressures force standardization before consensus is reached.

4. Sometimes, legal issues prevent standardization, even when the consensus is clear. And sometimes standardization shows the consensus is not real.

Failures of the first three kinds are often due to standards politics. The high level process description sounds reasonable, but often there is much bickering, subjectivity, and political maneuvering involved in standards and open systems. Sometimes, a company, or, more commonly, a consortium, decides standardization of its interface is a good way to gain market share and to do away with the competition. This is usually the source of the first kind of failure. The second kind of failure may result from a single vendor stonewalling on changes everyone else can agree to. The third kind of failure, like the first kind, may be due to pressure from a consortium. Perhaps more commonly, the third kind of failure is due to general industry pressure to produce something quickly.

Sometimes vendors wait for a standard before trying their own solutions, to avoid investment in something that will have to change. Sometimes, vendors and users tire of waiting, and put increasing pressure on standards bodies to finish. Ironically, a standard that is completed too quickly may be ignored by many vendors or given minimal support. Other vendors are still hedging their bets with proprietary systems and strategic alliances, despite the existence of standards efforts. This can be extremely confusing to the community at large.

References

ANSI 1987.   ANSI, *American National Standards and ISO International Standards for Information Technology,* American National Standards Institute, New York (1987).

Cargill 1989.   Cargill, Carl F., *Information Technology Standardization: Theory, Process, and Organizations,* Digital Press, Bedford, MA (1989).

GAO 1991.   GAO, "High-Performance Computing Industry Uses of Supercomputers and High-Speed Networks; Report to Congressional Requesters," U.S. General Accounting Office (July 1991).

JTC 1 1990.   JTC 1, "ISO/IEC Directives: Procedures for the technical work of ISO/IEC JTC 1 on Information Technology," International Organization for

Standardization/International Electrotechnical Commission, Switzerland (1990).

Malamud 1991.   Malamud, Carl, "The ITU Adopts a New Meta-Standard: Open Access," *ConneXions — The Interoperability Report* **5**(12), pp. 19–21, Interop, Inc. (December 1991).

Quarterman et al. 1991.   Quarterman, John S., Carl-Mitchell, Smoot, Wilhelm, Susanne, Boede, Jon, & Sheffield, Barbara, "High Speed Networks in Domestic Industry," Texas Internet Consulting, Austin (28 May 1991).

Rutkowski 1991.   Rutkowski, A.M., "Networking the Telecom Standards Bodies," *ConneXions — The Interoperability Report* **5**(9), pp. 26–35, Interop, Inc. (September 1991).

X3 1990.   X3, "Accredited Standards Committee X3 — Information Processing Organization, Rules and Procedures of X3," X3, Washington, DC (1990).

PART 3

Pieces and Patterns

This part is about specific standards and standards projects, particularly those of IEEE/CS TCOS-SS, including POSIX. It is also about issues that affect many different standards; these are patterns that can be found in puzzles. The issues we discuss in this part are network protocol standards processes, programming language issues, conformance testing, and internationalization.

IEEE/CS TCOS Standards

Many open systems standards related to the historical UNIX operating system come from the IEEE/CS TCOS-SS committees. We examine these standards and projects, including POSIX, in Chapter 7. We describe their steering committees and functional groupings. Of the specific standards, we describe the 1003.1 System Interface Standard in most detail. We also describe 1003.2 for Shell and Tools, the P1201 GUI projects, the Distributed Services network interface projects, P1003.4 for Realtime, and P1003.6 for Security.

Network Protocol Standardization Processes

These days many systems are connected to other systems. Networking implementations and standards have made this possible. In Chapter 8, we discuss the processes that produced the OSI and TCP/IP protocol suites. We also discuss the effects that actual networks have had on standardization.

Programming Language Issues

Different communities use different programming languages, such as C, Ada, and Fortran. Users want programs written in each of these languages. Standards now may be written in a language independent form to be used with a language binding. This and other programming language issues are discussed in Chapter 9.

Conformance Testing

Once a standard has been created, how can you determine if the products you buy conform to it? Chapter 10 talks about conformance, IEEE Std 1003.3:1991, the Test Methods Standard, test suites, testing laboratories, and accreditation bodies. It discusses such issues as the difference and relations between a Conforming Implementation and a Conforming Application, as well as between conformance and vendor warrantees.

Internationalization

Internationalization is the process of making a standard or interface independent of human languages, character sets, or cultural conventions. Chapter 11 discusses the work that is being done by POSIX, ISO POSIX, UniForum, and others.

CHAPTER 7

▄▄▄▄▄▄▄

IEEE/CS TCOS Standards

Much open systems standards work originates with the *TCOS-SS (IEEE/CS TCOS Standards Subcommittee)*. TCOS-SS standards include the POSIX family of standards, produced by the IEEE P1003 subcommittees, such as the IEEE Std 1003.1-1990 *System Application Program Interface Standard* produced by the IEEE P1003.1 committee. *POSIX* is a pun on the long name of *IEEE P1003, Portable Operating System Interface,* and on *UNIX*. The POSIX standards specify interfaces for a portable operating system, and the other TCOS standards specify related interfaces for areas such as distributed services and user interfaces. They are important in building open systems.

This chapter gives an overview of all the TCOS standards, with their official titles and numbers. A quick sketch of their history is included, as is a discussion of TCOS-SS steering committees, and of what areas are not covered directly by TCOS-SS standards. Selected TCOS standards, such as the 1003.1 POSIX System Interface Standard, are discussed in more detail. Information that is more time-sensitive, such as expected publication dates, may be found in Appendix A, *Resources*, which also explains how to get standards, drafts, and other documents.

7.1   Overview

TCOS Standards History

Some of the TCOS committees and projects are shown in Fig. 7.1, with some of their interrelations. All of them have related WG15 documents, except for IEEE 1003.3, the Test Methods Standard, which will not be standardized by WG15. Some interesting features of standards history are hard to show in the figure. For example, the original IEEE 1003 PAR existed for two years (since 1983) before work was done using it (the first meeting was late in 1984).

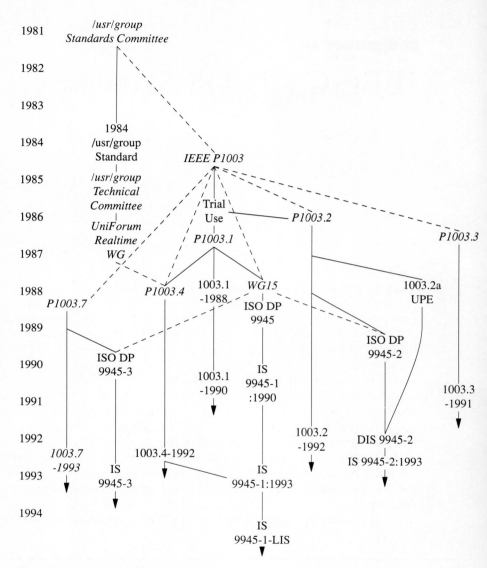

Figure 7.1 TCOS standards family tree.

The standards family tree in Fig. 7.1 is much like Fig. 3.2 in Chapter 3, *POSIX and Open Standards*, but industry specifications are omitted, more TCOS branches are shown, and the timeline is taken several years further to show some projected dates. For example, the Language Independent Standard (discussed in Chapter 9) is not scheduled to become an ISO standard until 1995.

Costs

TCOS standards involve major industry investment. As of the end of 1991, there were 20 working groups and 30 projects. The annual TCOS budget for 1991 was $471,600. More than half of this amount goes into running the meetings, and most of the rest goes into mailings. The funding is just money collected from meeting registration fees, mailing subscriptions, and related minor sources [Hann 1991].

The amount spent by participants is much larger. Given about 400 attendees per meeting, even if you assume that each one is only working about quarter time on standardization, you still get, with about $100,000 for each person's loaded salary (with benefits and taxes), $10 million just in salaries. Travel expenses add about another $3 million, for about $13 million annually. This estimate is very conservative, since some meetings have had 450 attendees, many participants cost their companies more than $100,000, and many of them work more than quarter time on standards work and travel to more than the four TCOS meetings per year on related business. A more likely number would be about $30 million. Dividing by 30 projects, that's about $1 million per project per year. An average project takes two to four years, or $2 to $4 million.

Investment of this kind of money means at least two things. First, the industry takes these standards very seriously. Second, the TCOS-SS process is under a lot of pressure to produce usable standards quickly.

7.2   Functional Groups

The subcommittee numbers of TCOS working groups and projects are assigned in historical order, rather than according to content. Numbers for projects often match those of the committees that are responsible for them, but not always, only by historical accident, and less so as more are approved. A different method of classification than numbers is needed to understand which committees and projects are related. In this section, we list all the TCOS committees, grouped according to the functions that they specify.

Some special marks are used in the tables in this chapter:

*	marks a project that was in balloting (1003.2, 1003.4), or expected to ballot by the end of 1992
IEEE P1003.n	refers to a committee, working group, project, or draft standard
IEEE 1003.n	refers to a standard
POSIX.n	is sometimes used to refer to a working group or to a project

Just because a document has a number doesn't mean that it is a standard. All IEEE standardization projects have numbers. The presence or absence of a "P" before the number isn't a reliable indicator, either, since there is confusion, even

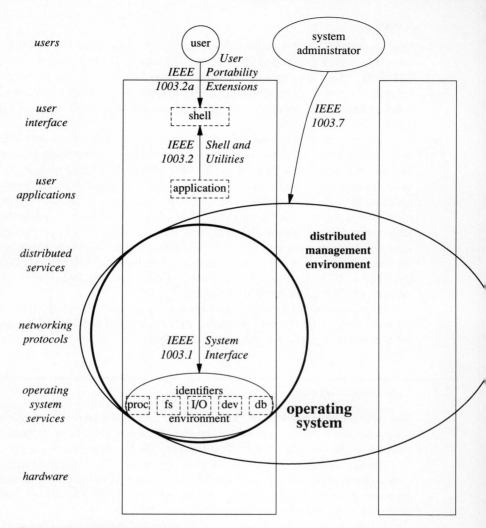

Figure 7.2 POSIX base standards.

among standard producers, about when the "P" is appropriate. Here we follow the official IEEE convention that "IEEE P1003.x" refers to a draft (or project or working group) and "IEEE 1003.x" refers to a standard.

Base Standards

The committees shown in Fig. 7.2 are producing base standards, which the other TCOS standards are grouped around. These standards apply to several basic interfaces. They are listed in Table 7.1.

Table 7.1 TCOS base standards.

Project	Title	Committee	Chapter
1003.1	System API	P1003.1	7
1003.2*	Shell and Utilities	P1003.2	7
1003.7	System Administration	P1003.7	14

1003.1 specifies interfaces to basic system services such as processes, the file system, I/O, devices, and related identifiers and environment variables. The System Interface Standard was the first approved TCOS standard, as IEEE Std 1003.1-1988, followed by IEEE Std 1003.1-1990. It is discussed in this chapter. The Shell and Utilities Standard and its associated User Portability Extensions are also discussed in this chapter. 1003.2 specifies programming interfaces to the shell and related utilities. 1003.2a provides related interfaces for use directly by users. Together, these standards cover traditional interfaces to systems like the historical UNIX timesharing system.

System Administration is discussed in Chapter 14, *Industry Profiles*. It is much more oriented towards networking and distributed computing than are the other two TCOS base standards. 1003.7 applies to the general distributed computing environment, providing a distributed management environment.

Extensions

The projects shown in Table 7.2 are for extensions to TCOS base standards. As each of them is standardized, it should be treated as part of the base standard that it extends.

Table 7.2 TCOS extensions.

Project	Title	Committee	Chapter
1003.1a*	Extensions to 1003.1	P1003.1	7
1003.2a*	User Portability Extensions (UPE) to 1003.2	P1003.2	7
1003.4*	Realtime and Related System API	P1003.4	7
1003.4a*	Threads extensions to 1003.4	P1003.4	7
1003.4b*	Extensions to 1003.4	P1003.4	7
1003.6*	Security extensions to 1003.1 and 1003.2	P1003.6	7
1003.8	(see Distributed Services)		7

Table 7.3 TCOS graphical user interfaces.

Project	Title	Committee	Chapter
1201.1	Interfaces for User Portability	P1201	7
1201.2	Recommended Practice on Driveability	P1201	7
(1201.4	Xlib	P1201)	7
1295.1	Modular Toolkit Environment	P1295	7
1295.2	Open Toolkit Environment	P1295	7

Some of these extension projects, such as 1003.1a, are just later additions or corrections to already-published documents. Others, such as 1003.2a or 1003.4a, cover major technological areas in their own right. Often this happens because the extension was taken out of a larger document because it was delaying the publication of the larger document due to controversy, or simply was taking too much time to specify adequately. This happened with P1003.2a, the User Portability Extensions (UPE) to 1003.2, the Shell and Tools Standard. It also happened with P1003.4a, POSIX Threads, which was extracted from P1003.4, the main Realtime and Related System API extension document. In the case of 1003.6, the Security Extensions to 1003.1 and 1003.2, the idea was introduced late enough in the standardization of the earlier documents that it was clear that there would not be time to address it properly, and security was never taken up as a major topic by the original committees.

User Interfaces

Projects for graphical user interfaces are shown in Table 7.3. They are discussed in this chapter.

Distributed Services

Network interfaces needed a whole group of committees and projects, including 1003.8, which is described in this chapter. The projects in Table 7.4 are for distributed services (sometimes more accurately called distribution services); that is, for interfaces to network protocols and to services that are to be used over networks. They are discussed in this chapter. More general networking and protocol issues are left to Chapter 8, *Protocols and Standards*.

Language Bindings

The committees shown in Table 7.5 are specifying how to do POSIX with particular programming languages. They are all discussed in Chapter 9, *Programming Language Issues*, along with more general programming language issues.

Table 7.4 TCOS distributed services.

Project	Title	Committee	Chapter
1003.8*	Transparent File Access (TFA)	P1003.8	7
1003.12	Protocol-Independent Interface (PII)	P1003.12	7
1003.17*	Directory Services API	P1003.17	7
1238*	Common OSI API	P1238	7
1238.1*	FTAM API part	P1238	7
1224*	Message Handling Services (MHS)	P1224	7
1224.1	Message Handling Services (MHS)	P1224	7
(1237	Remote Procedure Call (RPC) API	into X3T5.5)	7

Testing

The projects shown in Table 7.6 are all performed by IEEE P1003.3. Each other committee should be doing its own test methods. The Test Methods Standard, IEEE Std 1003.3 1991, was the second TCOS standard. It is discussed in Chapter 10, *Conformance Testing*, along with conformance specification and the application of such test methods to conformance testing.

Internationalization

Internationalization is an area that is not directly covered by any single TCOS standard. But it affects all of them, and is covered by a WG15 Rapporteur group, by P1003.0, by a UniForum Technical Committee subcommittee, and by various industry and user groups. These and other groups and issues of internationalization and localization of programs with respect to codesets, human languages, and cultural conventions are discussed in Chapter 11, *Internationalization*.

Table 7.5 TCOS language bindings.

Project	Title	Committee	Chapter
1003.16*	C Binding to 1003.1LIS	P1003.1	9
1003.5*	Ada Binding to 1003.1-1990	P1003.5	9
1003.20	Ada thin LI Binding to 1003.1LIS	P1003.5	9
1003.9*	Fortran 77 Binding to 1003.1-1990	P1003.9	9
1003.19	Fortran 1990 LI Binding to 1003.1LIS	P1003.9	9

Table 7.6 TCOS test methods.

Project	Title	Committee	Chapter
1003.3*	Test Methods	P1003.3	10
1003.3.1*	Test Methods for 1003.1	P1003.3	10
1003.3.2*	Test Methods for 1003.2	P1003.3	10

Profiles and Guides

The projects shown in Table 7.7 are for profiles and guides. These are documents that specify relations, options, and parameters for other standards and profiles. TCOS has quite a few of these. Some cover quite specific areas. Examples include 1003.11 on Transaction Processing and 1003.15 on Superpercomputing Batch Element. Others are more general. 1003.14 is for a multiprocessing system. 1003.18 describes a timesharing system very similar to a traditional UNIX system. 1003.0, the POSIX Guide, describes the elements of a general open system and how they should fit together. 1003.10, on Supercomputing, and the 1003.13 realtime profiles, are for environments of intermediate generality. All these POSIX profiles are discussed in Chapter 13, *TCOS Profiles*.

What TCOS Does Not Do

Because TCOS standardizes interface standards for computer software related to a traditional timesharing operating system, there are many things it does not do. It may define interfaces related to many of them, however.

Table 7.7 TCOS profiles and guides.

Project	Title	Committee	Chapter
1003.0*	POSIX Guide	P1003.0	13
1003.18	POSIX Platform Environment Profile (PEP) AEP	P1003.1	13
1003.14*	Multiprocessing AEP	P1003.14	13
1003.13	Realtime Full Function AEP	P1003.4	13
1003.13	Realtime Embedded Control System AEP	P1003.4	13
1003.13	Realtime Intermediate AEP	P1003.4	13
1003.10	Supercomputing AEP	P1003.10	13
1003.15	Supercomputing Batch Element AEP	P1003.10	13
1003.11	Transaction Processing AEP	P1003.11	13

Here is a list of some things TCOS does not do, and related TCOS interfaces.

implementations   TCOS produces interface standards, and vendors implement them. Some TCOS standards put very detailed constraints on implementations, however. See 1003.4, Realtime and other Extensions (in this chapter), and IEEE 1003.13, Realtime Application Environment Profiles (in Chapter 13).

training   TCOS does not do user training, but it does do user interfaces and related standards that are partly intended to reduce the amount of training users need.

languages   Actual programming language standards are outside the purview of TCOS, and TCOS has avoided modifying or extending language standards. But there are three TCOS language bindings, 1003.5 for Ada, 1003.9 for Fortran, and 1003.16 for C. The System Interface Standard itself is being rewritten to be a Language Independent Standard (LIS). Language issues are discussed in Chapter 9.

test suites   TCOS does not develop test suites, but the Test Methods Standard, 1003.3, helps to structure testing, and two documents, 1003.3.1 and 1003.3.2, provide assertions to test for POSIX.1 and POSIX.2. For actual testing see Chapter 10.

networking   Although TCOS does interface standards, actual network protocols are outside its scope. But interfaces to network protocols and services are within its scope. These are called Distributed Services, and are discussed in Chapter 8.

human languages   TCOS is not a national academy, and does not promulgate vocabulary or grammar. But it is interested in internationalization of software to account for cultural issues, including human languages. This is discussed in Chapter 11.

file servers   At the moment, there are no profiles for networked file servers. Whether this is actually a forbidden area for TCOS is not clear. See Chapter 13 for more discussion. Even the TCP/IP standards have a host requirements document, but no file server requirements document; see Chapter 8.

marketing   TCOS does not market software, but making buying and selling easier is one of the goals of profiles and guides, as discussed in Chapter 12, and especially of IEEE 1003.0, the POSIX Guide, which is described in Chapter 13.

TCOS provides the central standards for open systems. Many of these are related to a historical timesharing system. But they also include interfaces to many other areas.

7.3   SEC Subcommittees

Higher level bodies and processes related to the TCOS committees have already been discussed in Chapter 6. The SEC has established several steering commmittees to manage various areas of TCOS work. We will discuss each of them, but first let's examine the SEC itself.

The *IEEE/CS TCOS-SS Sponsor Executive Committee (SEC)* is the part of TCOS that decides which committees and projects TCOS will sponsor. It is composed of committee chairs, officers, and Institutional Representatives from related organizations. The officer positions are currently Chair, Treasurer, Secretary, Vice Chair Logistics, Vice Chair Technical Editing, Vice Chair Technical Balloting, Vice Chair Technical Interpretations, and Vice Chair Technical Coordination.

The SEC is the executive body for the formal sponsor of the TCOS standards, which is the *Standards Subcommittee (TCOS-SS)* of the IEEE/CS *Technical Committee on Operating Systems and Application Environments (TCOS)*. TCOS is part of the *IEEE Computer Society (IEEE/CS)*, which is in turn affiliated with the *Institute of Electrical and Electronics Engineers (IEEE)*.

The formal U.S. national standardization body, *ANSI (American National Standards Institute)*, accredited IEEE as a standards body. IEEE agreed to do operating system standards (the choice of subject matter does not require top-down assignment by ANSI). IEEE delegated those operating system standards to IEEE/CS, which appointed TCOS-SS to write them. The SEC is the body in charge of making sure that standards are produced.

The SEC may receive recommendations from above, down the hierarchy. These can take the form of requirements, but seldom do. However, the appeals process proceeds back up the same tree that accreditation authority comes down. The first ballot for 1003.1 was appealed as far up as the IEEE/CS Standards Activities Board, for example.

Input may also come from the international level. This is certainly possible, since WG15 is composed of national delegations, and TCOS is perceived as being a U.S. national body (even though there are no barriers to participation from other countries, and there have always been such participants). If WG15 refuses to accept work from TCOS without changes, TCOS has little choice but to make the changes. The language independence work discussed in Chapter 9 was imposed on TCOS in this way by WG15.

Each level of the accreditation hierarchy has its own rules for standardization. The steering committees discussed in this section and shown in Fig. 7.3 are creatures of the SEC, that is, of TCOS-SS. Similar committees will not necessarily be found among other IEEE/CS, IEEE, ANSI, or ISO committees or sponsoring organizations. Some of the rules that these SEC subcommittees are applying are also rules produced by the SEC. The SEC has not, in general, delegated authority to these subcommittees to make new rules on their own, but they can all recommend rules and actions to the SEC, which is likely to accept recommendations.

Given all this structure both above and below the SEC, there is the danger of work being done for the sake of the structure, rather than for the sake of technical

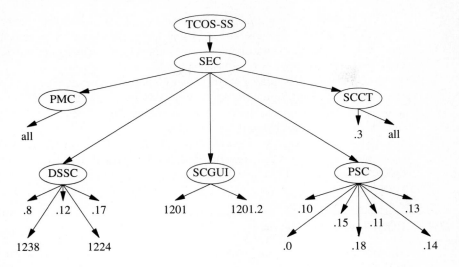

Figure 7.3 SEC subcommittees.

content. Some say language independence is such a case. If so, it is one in which TCOS had little choice. WG15 also imposes a document format, different from the one previously imposed by IEEE, which is different from the one originally preferred by IEEE P1003.1. There have been other, more amusing cases, such as project requests being refused by IEEE NesCom because they were not printed on an actual paper form from IEEE. The SEC is aware of the structure versus content problem, and that is one reason it created the PMC.

PMC: Project Management Committee

The *Project Management Committee (PMC)* is an oversight body for projects and committees. It is responsible for reviewing any new *Project Authorization Request (PAR)* to see whether the PAR meets the New PAR Criteria. The PMC also reviews existing projects or committees from time to time to see whether they are making progress. The PMC can neither prevent a PAR from reaching the SEC, nor otherwise change the status of a project or committee. However, it can recommend actions to the SEC.

Steering Committees

The *Steering Committee on Conformance and Testing (SCCT)* affects almost every working group and project. It coordinates work on assertions and test methods. In that past, this has largely meant trying to persuade committees to include those things in their drafts. The IEEE 1003 projects dedicated solely to these topics have been listed under Testing. Conformance testing is discussed in detail in Chapter 10.

The *Distributed Services Steering Committee (DSSC)* is responsible for coordinating the projects we have already listed under Distributed Services. That is, the DSSC coordinates work on interfaces to network services and protocols. Network interfaces are discussed in this chapter.

The *Steering Committee for Graphical User Interfaces (SCGUI)* has perhaps spent more time on formulating appropriate PARs for new committees than have most steering committees. Its existing committees have been listed under User Interfaces; they are discussed in this chapter.

The *Profile Steering Committee (PSC)* is the newest steering committee. It coordinates committees that are writing profile documents. These have been listed under Profiles; they are discussed in Chapter 13.

7.4   POSIX System Interface

The POSIX System Interface Standard is the central open system standard related to the historical UNIX timesharing system. All POSIX standards and many other standards are related to it. All vendors of systems derived from the UNIX system agree on it, as do many vendors of other operating systems. Most vendor and consortium specifications refer to it. There are viable open systems that do not include POSIX or UNIX, e.g., COBOL + SQL + FIMS, but this book is about standards and open systems related to POSIX and UNIX.

This standard is published under two names. *IEEE 1003.1 (IEEE Std 1003.1-1990),* was produced by IEEE/CS TCOS-SS P1003.1 on behalf of ANSI as an American National Standard. The same document is also an International Standard, *IS 9945-1 (IS 9945-1:1990),* produced by ISO/IEC JTC 1 SC22 WG15. The national and international 1990 publications of this standard differ only in their covers [IEEE 1990]. This will not continue to be the case, because IS 9945-1, as Part 1 of the larger POSIX International Standard, IS 9945, is intended to eventually incorporate other standards originally produced by TCOS-SS, such as IEEE P1003.2 when it becomes a standard. To avoid confusion related to this planned divergence, this chapter often refers to IEEE Std 1003.1-1990 alone, often as IEEE 1003.1 or just 1003.1.

The POSIX System Interface Standard is an *API (Application Program Interface)* standard for basic operating system functions. Two books describe the use of this standard in writing portable application programs [Zlotnick 1991; Lewine 1991]. A shorter guide has been available longer [Jespersen 1989]. We leave details of practical application portability to these other references. This section describes the standard itself, and its effects on other standards. Language independence and language bindings are left to Chapter 9, *Programming Language Issues.* The conformance language in 1003.1 itself is discussed in detail Chapter 10, *Conformance Testing.*

1003.1 is also a minimal and compromise standard. Appropriate combinations of other standards (and perhaps also specifications) are needed for a viable system, and these combinations are often specified in profiles. But all POSIX

Standardized Profiles must be harmonized with this standard, and many other profiles also reference it. We discuss such profiles in Part 4, **Puzzles**.

Goals

No one had tried to formally standardize an operating system interface before IEEE 1003.1. The actual document was very large for a standard. The working group had to take into account several major existing versions of the operating system, while not unduly interfering with numerous other versions. The IEEE P1003.1 Working Group thus had a number of technical, logistical, and political problems to face. One way it addressed them was by spelling out a number of specific goals that appeared to have consensus. Here are some of the main goals:

• Promote application source code portability

• Specify an interface, rather than an implementation

• Consider all major historical implementations

• Keep the interface minimal, with a minimal specification both as part of historical philosophy, and to speed completion, approval, and acceptance.

In other words, IEEE 1003.1 was to be a standard for a minimally specified minimal API based on the major historical systems. Nonnormative text in the standard document names six sets of base documents that were the main sources of the standard: the *1984 /usr/group Standard* [/usr/group 1984] and documentation for UNIX Seventh Edition, UNIX System III, UNIX System V, 4.2BSD, and 4.3BSD.

Consensus among all participants was not always possible. Working group members familiar with UNIX System V or 4.3BSD often did not agree on what should go in the standard. In many areas, the two systems were actually very similar, and the working simply used wording that was inclusive enough that either system fit. Sometimes, this wordsmithing reached the level of *weasel wording*, which is a term working group members used to describe particularly contorted verbiage that had no purpose other than to avoid a breach of consensus among participants.

All of the major options in 1003.1 were put in to permit a choice between UNIX System V behavior and 4.3BSD behavior. Many smaller choices between the behavior of those two historical systems were left to the implementation, either as *implementation-defined* behavior (requiring the vendor to document it), or as *unspecified*. Many working group members, perhaps all of them, intended use of the word *unspecified* in the standard to ensure that the implementation's behavior would *not* be specified, so that an application would have to accept any behavior. Similarly, they often used the word *may* to permit the implementor a choice of implementation behavior that the application must accept. The IEEE P1003.1 Test Methods working group and others concerned with test assertions, test methods, test suites, or actual conformance testing have often seen these choices differently, and have attempted to require implementors to specify choices of behavior specified in the standard with use of the words *may* or *unspecified*. We discuss such issues in Chapter 10, *Conformance Testing*.

One result of the IEEE 1003.1 standard is that many of the vendors who formerly disagreed in the working group now implement systems that conform to the standard, and are very similar to each other in the areas the standard covers. This covergence cannot be attributed solely to the standard, but the standard certainly was a factor.

The working group had a number of subsidiary goals, which were pursued as long as they did not interfere with more primary goals:

• Permit networked, distributed, or secure systems

• Allow limited binary runtime adaptation on similar systems (e.g., *pathconf*, *sysconf*, *setlocale*)

• Minimize changes to historical implementations (use prior art when possible)

• Minimize changes to existing applications

Some of these concerns later produced one or more separate working groups or projects. The actual 1003.1 standard has some careful wording to permit secure implementations, but does not specify what a secure interface might be. For example, 1003.l uses the term *appropriate privileges* wherever someone familiar with UNIX manuals might expect *superuser* or *root access*. The latter two terms appear nowhere in the normative text of the standard. This terminology shift leaves open the possibility of a range of levels of security in implementations, but gives no guidance or direction on what those levels might be. Such direction is provided by the IEEE P1003.6 draft security standard, which we discuss in this chapter.

In the early days of the P1003.1 working group, there were several emulations of UNIX on top of other operating systems, such as VMS. These were called *hosted* systems. This term was always somewhat vague, meaning mostly that the interface was not licensed by AT&T. It has lost almost all meaning it may once have had. Is OSF/1 hosted on top of Mach, or System V on top of OSF/1? The user doesn't care, and it doesn't matter for standards conformance. The interface might be provided by system calls, library routines, or other mechanisms. The specific choices don't matter: if it works correctly, runs fast, and fits into a larger environment, the user is likely to be happy. The IEEE 1003.1 standard is intended to permit just such flexibility.

When the IEEE P1003 Working Group began work, use of UNIX on LANs was just starting to spread. Network or distributed file systems for UNIX were developed by several companies while P1003.1 was in progress. These developments presented the problem of completing standardization of a traditional single system interface while not prohibiting networked or distributed implementations. The normative text of the 1003.1 standard does not use the terms *networked* or *distributed,* yet there are places where it is very carefully worded to avoid prohibiting behavior used by certain distributed services. For example, pathnames beginning with // or /../ are permitted to have special meanings, to accomodate two different historical transparent file access mechanisms. The Distribution Services working groups now deal with such issues. We discuss them in this chapter.

Nongoals

Many other goals were proposed by members of the P1003.1 working group, or by others, but were rejected. In addition, the working group knew from the outset that it did not want to attempt some things. Here are some things the working group specifically did not do:

• Did not try to promote portability of object code

• Did not create barriers to portability of object code

• Did not specify an implementation of the standard interface

• Did not define new interfaces except when necessary (e.g., revised job control)

Each of these points had effects on the text of the standard. In avoiding specification of an implementation, the working group eliminated the distinction between library routines and system calls, including in many cases eliminating references to a potential signal that would only have been produced by a system call. It used symbolic names for constants instead of specifying numbers. It avoided specifying internal behavior wherever possible, even when difficult, e.g., for pipes.

In addition to the more general issues that the working group avoided, it also refused to address or permit several specific issues:

• Excluded system administration functions (because they vary so widely among historical implementations)

• Did not try to solve more than a minimal set of problems (in hopes of getting an acceptable standard finished)

• Did not adhere strictly to any historical implementation (every known pre-existing implementation had to change to conform)

• Did not make concessions for MS-DOS implementations (MS-DOS lacks basic primitives such as fork and links, and does not support long filenames or case-sensitive filenames)

Each of these points spawned or affected later work. IEEE P1003.7 is about system administration, as discussed in Chapter 14, *Industry Profiles*. Most of the other POSIX committees are working in areas that were deliberately left out of the scope of the minimal 1003.1 standard. NIST published its FIPS 151-1 that specified values for all of the major and many of the minor options 1003.1 had left unspecified; this made that FIPS closer to 4.3BSD than to UNIX System V, as discussed in Chapter 15, *Procurement Profiles*. Unlike 1003.1, drafts of IEEE

P1003.2 are implementable on MS-DOS, and conformance to the IEEE 1003.2 standard will not require conformance to IEEE 1003.1, partly for this reason.

History

We sketched the history of the POSIX System Interface Standard very briefly in Part 2, **Cutters**. Here is a somewhat more extensive list of major events related to that standard:

1981:	/usr/group (now UniForum) Standards Committee formed
1984:	/usr/group Standard adopted and published
1984:	IEEE P1003 working group formed
1986:	IEEE 1003.1 Trial Use Standard approved
1987:	ISO/IEC JTC 1 SC22 WG15 formed
1988:	ISO DP 9945 approved
1988:	NIST FIPS 151 and PCTS
1988:	IEEE Std 1003.1-1988 approved First POSIX American National Standard
1989:	ISO DIS 9945-1 approved
1990:	IEEE Std 1003.1-1990 approved
1990:	ISO IS 9945-1 approved First POSIX International Standard
9 May 1990:	FIPS 151-1 signed, based on P1003.1 Draft 13, previous to IEEE Std 1003.1-1988
1991:	IEEE 1003.1 interpretations and extensions continue
1992:	FIPS 151-2 in progress

We will discuss NIST FIPS 151 in Chapter 15, *Procurement Profiles*.

7.5   Contents of the System Interface Standard

The contents of the POSIX System Interface Standard illustrate the structure that is followed by other POSIX documents that are intended to be ISO/IEC standards. The foreword, introduction, and annexes of IEEE Std 1003.1-1990 and IS 9945-1 are informative. That is, they are not part of the actual definition of the standard, and are sometimes called nonnormative for that reason. This informational material is nonetheless very useful for interpreting the standard.

Everything else in the standard is normative. The main body of the standard is organized into sections according to tradtional operating system topics: processes, filesystem, I/O, and hardware devices. There are also sections on programming language services, system databases, and data interchange formats. We include some discussion of the contents of each section and the tradeoffs made. We mention a few examples of facilities derived from 4.3BSD or UNIX System V. This book is not the place to provide an exhaustive list of these; see *POSIX Explored: System Interface* by Hal Jespersen, UniForum, 1989 [Jespersen 1989].

We do not intend here to provide detailed examination of each section of this standard: there is not enough space in this book for that. Instead, we provide some brief comments on the types of information each section of the standard specifies. These comments often refer to basic characteristics of the historical UNIX operating system that are supported by the standard, or to operating system features that might be expected but are not actually found in the standard. These comments do not pretend to be exhaustive.

The foreword and introduction are interesting, but are not particularly informative, in addition to being nonnormative. The introduction does list the goals and nongoals already discussed. It also includes the footnote that claims to give the correct pronunciation of the word *POSIX*. Amusingly enough, the two books previously cited each give a different pronunciation.

General

Section 1 of 1003.1 sets forth the scope of the standard, with emphasis on source code portability of applications. It spells out conformance requirements, which we discuss in detail in Chapter 10, *Conformance Testing*.

Terminology and General Requirements

Section 2 of 1003.1 specifies the conformance terminology used throughout the standard: that is, it defines the words *shall*, *should*, *may*, *implementation defined*, *unspecified*, and *undefined*, as discussed in Chapter 10.

There are subsections on Definitions and General Concepts. The former defines basic terms such as *pathname*. Files are defined to include device special files that provide access to hardware devices, which is a historical characteristic of UNIX. The *portable filename character set* spells out the upper and lower case Latin alphabet, digits, period, underscore, and hyphen. This was the result of protracted discussions in the working group and during ballots. Simply ensuring that upper and lower case are distinct and not folded was a sizeable controversy. The latter subsection, on General Concepts, tends to contain more discursive material, such as explaining how pathname resolution works in a hierarchical filesystem of files and directories.

The subsection on Error Numbers deals with system error reporting, involving **errno**, which we discuss later in this chapter.

This section also specifies names and meanings of configuration parameters. It makes heavy use of the concept of a minimum maximum. For example, the standard specifies the name CHILD_MAX for the maximum number of simultaneous processes a single user may have. If this number is fixed for an implementation, the implementation is required to provide the value of CHILD_MAX to applications in the header **<limits.h>**. The standard does not say what that value must be. An application that wants to take advantage of the actual maximum permitted by an implementation can use the value provided by the implementation.

The standard does specify a minimum maximum, **_POSIX_CHILD_MAX_**, which must be defined in **<limits.h>**. The standard does specify a value for this minimum maximum: 6. Thus, an implementation must set CHILD_MAX to 6 or greater. An application that needs to determine its algorithm according to the number of child processes that will be available can thus know that at least six will always be available on any implementation that conforms to the standard.

The minimum maxima must always be available in **<limits.h>**. The actual maxima may or may not be in that header. Some maxima, such as number of child processes, might vary with system configuration, such as amount of memory. If the implementation permits such a maximum to vary, it must not define it in **<limits.h>**, but will supply it at runtime through *sysconf*. Other maxima, such as the length of a pathname, might differ among different kinds of mounted filesystems. The implementation does not define such maxima in **<limits.h>**, but makes them available through *pathconf*. Regardless of whether the actual maxima are defined in **<limits.h>**, the minimum maxima are always the same, and do not vary among implementations.

This section of the standard also requires the implementation to define values for the major options, in **<unistd.h>** (or, for NGROUPS_MAX, in **<limits.h>**). We discuss these options in Chapter 10, *Conformance Testing*.

Process Primitives

Section 3 of 1003.1 specifies interfaces for some of the most characteristic facilities of the historical UNIX operating system, such as *fork*, which produces a new process with the same memory image as the old one, and six forms of *exec*, which overlay a new program's memory image over the current process. The specification of these *exec* functions includes an interface specification of the *setuid* function of UNIX.

Process termination is supported by specifications of *_exit*, which permits a process to die gracefully; *wait*, which allows a parent process to retrieve status from a deceased child; and *kill* and *sigaction*, which provide asynchronous signalling of exceptional events. A rudimentary timing function is provided by *alarm*; more sophisticated timing and event mechanisms are found in P1003.4.

All these primitives, and the others specified in this section, take into account the idea of a saved user ID, which is derived from UNIX System V. A process may set its effective user ID back to its saved user ID.

Process Environment

Facilities for determining assorted process or system parameters, such as process and group IDs, time of day, or the name of the system, are specified in Section 4 of 1003.1. The standard avoids requiring values for environment variables, but it does specify (in its Section 2) certain meanings for several if they are defined. These include LOGNAME, HOME, TERM, and TZ. The function for retrieving their values, *getenv*, is specified in Section 4, as is the function *sysconf*.

Files and Directories

Section 5 of 1003.1 defines the primitives, *link* and *unlink* that produce and remove links, which are a basic feature of UNIX, in addition to *open* and *close*, which are like similar functions in many operating systems. This section requires some facilities derived from 4.3BSD. These include *mkdir* and *rmdir* for creating and removing directories, and a set of routines for looking through the filenames in a directory. Others are derived from UNIX System V, such as *mkfifo*, which creates a FIFO special file. The function *pathconf* is specified here.

Input and Output Primitives

Another basic characteristic of UNIX is that it uses the same I/O routines to transfer data to and from both files and devices. These functions, such as *read* and *write*, are specified in Section 6 of 1003.1. The *pipe* facility is distinctive to UNIX. In a clear example of weasel wording, the standard carefully avoids saying whether pipes must be simplex, as in traditional UNIX, or may be duplex, as in 4.3BSD pipes.

In one of the longest-running technical controversies surrounding POSIX, the System Interface Standard provides advisory file record locking through the *fcntl* function, but does not provide mandatory locking, such as was provided by the *lockf* function of the *1984 /usr/group Standard*. Some user communities, such as that represented by OSSWG, still consider this lack a defect in the standard [OSSWG 1991]. The working group listed (in Annex B) reasons for not including such a facility, including that anyone could lock any publicly readable file.

Device- and Class-Specific Functions

Section 7 of 1003.1 is mostly about terminal I/O, since that kind of device is used to control processes, and so could not be omitted from the standard. The facilities and parameters specified are based on UNIX System V, but many of the actual functions specified do not occur in historical implementations.

Language Specific Services for the C Programming Language

Section 8 of 1003.1 deals with relations between the system API and the implementation programming language. The present standard is actually written in terms of a specific programming language: C, the historical implementation language of UNIX. For example, 1003.1 does not specify the standard I/O routines *fopen* or *fclose*, which are found in the C standard. Section 8 of 1003.1 instead specifies the relations between those functions and *open* and *close*, which are specified in Section 5 of 1003.1. Similarly, the C standard defines *exit*, 1003.1 defines *_exit*, and Section 8 of 1003.1 specifies the relations between them. We discuss related issues in Chapter 9, *Programming Language Issues*.

In addition to the issue of making the system interface standard independent of a specific language, there are questions of where the boundary should fall between the system interface and any language. For example, the current standard provides only very rudimentary user process memory management routines, *brk* and *sbrk*, leaving the programming language to provide more sophisticated facilities, such as *malloc* in the C programming language. This approach could be advantageous for a Fortran binding, since Fortran does not provide such a facility to the user anyway. It is probably disadvantageous to an Ada binding.

Section 8 specifies the semantics of the TZ environment variable, for timezones. Historical UNIX systems compiled timezone rules into a table in the C library, which was clearly an inadequate method for binary distributions, and certainly inconvenient for implementing worldwide and changing timezone rules. Unfortunately, the working group chose to standardize a version of the less capable and less widely implemented of two solutions to this problem. The specification does carefully permit the other implementation to conform to the standard, however.

System Databases

Historical implementations use files like **/etc/passwd** to define mappings between user login names and numeric user IDs. Section 9 of 1003.1 avoids requiring files, and instead specifies interface routines, such as *getpwuid*, to databases of such information, which the implementation may or may not keep in files. We discuss some related specifications in Chapter 14, *Industry Profiles*.

Data Interchange Format

Portable applications require a data interchange format that can be used to carry them between systems. Section 10 of 1003.1 defines such formats, in terms that avoid specifying the underlying transport medium, which could be disk, tape, network, or something else. Historically, there are two formats for this purpose, named after the programs that implement them: *tar* and *cpio*. Both originated with AT&T, but tar was favored by supporters of 4.3BSD and cpio was favored by supporters of UNIX System V. In one of their more famous and long-running debates (known to participants as *Tar Wars)*, the IEEE P1003.1 working group could not decide on one or the other, and instead included extended versions of both.

The IEEE P1003.2 working group attempted to avoid this controversy by specifying a utility, *pax* (which happens to be the Latin word for peace), that can read and write either format. A public domain implementation of this utility is available.

Meanwhile, potential users of open systems have developed a need for communication with legacy systems, and might expect to find in this section of the standard specifications for representations of data objects to permit transfer of data between dissimilar systems [OSSWG 1991]. This would be essentially a presentation format, in networking terms. Neither of the formats in this section addresses that need, since both are derived from historical formats that were intended for use only on UNIX systems. The P1003.1 working group is examining the possibility of specifying a single new format in a future revision. Whether the scope of the working group includes making such a format deal with legacy systems is not clear.

Annex A: Bibliography (Nonnormative)

This annex gives bibliographic information for books and other publications about historical implementations, and for related standards.

Annex B: Rationale and Notes (Nonnormative)

This annex provides information on the reasoning behind the working group's decisions, on choices considered and rejected, on related historical implementations, on related standards, and on other relevant topics. Much weasel wording is explained here. This annex often states exactly which historical systems had which behavior that is behind strange wording in the standard. The reasons behind many shifts, such as from *superuser* to *appropriate privileges*, are spelled out. The annex provides an extensive list of goals and nongoals of the working group, and often notes where a decision was made about wording because of one or more of them.

The Rationale and Notes annex explains some concepts or facilities that are defined in pieces in several different sections of the standard. For example, job control affects processes (Section 3) and terminal I/O (Section 7), as well as various terms and definitions (Section 2). Any implementation of job control also has to deal with problems such as initializing a terminal session that cannot be completely specified in the standard itself, due to the prohibition of system administration functions. This annex attempts to explain these aspects of job control.

During the development of the standard, this material helped participants recall the context of discussions, and helped familiarize new members with what had gone before. The normative language of the standard itself must be precise, often at the expense of readability. The annex is nonnormative, is written for clarity, and uses terms and concepts deliberately excluded from the standard itself. The annex helps interface implementers and application programmers to understand the meaning and intent of the standard.

Annex C: Header Contents Samples (Nonnormative)

Historical implementations often have *parameter files* or *header files* that specify numeric values for parameters, declare library functions, or define data types. The standard does not use these terms. It requires what it calls *headers,* which are the same things, except that they are not required to be in files. A compiler could have them built in, for example.

This annex gives examples of headers for many of the parameters required in the standard. The normative sections of the standard ordinarily give names for numeric parameters, but avoid specifying the corresponding numbers, which are left as implementation defined. This annex gives examples of what such numbers might be in an implementation, and what they might look like in headers.

Annex D: Profiles (Nonnormative)

This annex gives some guidance on profiling. See Part 4, **Puzzles**, for later developments in this area.

Annex E: Sample National Profile (Nonnormative)

JTC 1 recognizes the concept of a national profile that specifies options in the standard and relations to other standards. This annex provides an example, for Denmark, including additions for character encoding, character display, and locale definitions. For more on internationalization, see Chapter 11, *Internationalization*.

7.6   System Error Interfaces

A historical anomaly and synchronization problem related to 1003.1 and other standards involves system error reporting. Many programs that need to know what kind of error caused a function to fail include and use this external variable definition:

```
extern int errno;
```

It's been left in the System Interface standard for years, even though everyone recognizes it is ugly, because the IEEE P1003.1 working group is supposed to standardize existing practice. Taking errno out entirely would require large numbers of programs to change to conform, even though interface implementations could still have errno. There has been no compelling reason to do this. For example, the X3J11 C Standard committee has complained about errno, yet defined it in X3.159. To date, the 1003.1 standard has required only the existence of a header for the above declaration: **<errno.h>**.

However, the P1003.4a pthreads draft requires a separate errno per thread. This makes declaring errno as extern a real problem. Since **<errno.h>** is already required, no conforming program needs to declare errno explicitly anyway. The P1003.1 working group considered synchronizing with P1003.4a important enough that they decided, at their April 1991 meeting, to deprecate explicit declaration of errno. Another reason the committee was willing to make a change at this late date was the generally increased sensitivity of the TCOS committees to *namespace pollution* issues.

The committee will find out in balloting whether there are strong objections to this change, or even whether enough balloters want to remove errno altogether. Given deprecation, P1003.1 can choose later (probably at their next revision of the document) to remove errno.

The Fortran bindings avoided the concept of errno completely by imposing an error argument on functions that need to return errors. They did this because errno is very specific to C, and rather ugly.

The error handling mechanisms specified by 1003.1, and also by the other parts of POSIX, are not extensive. In particular, no mechanisms are specified for coordinating and reporting errors from several processes, or several threads within a process. There is nothing like the Berkeley *syslog* mechanism, for example. The POSIX working groups considered such facilities to be outside the scope of their project authorizations, although P1003.7, as the system administration group, may find it within scope.

7.7   P1003.1a and P1003.1b

Many things were left out of 1003.1, often for political reasons. Certain features of 4.3BSD were among them. Several of these are in the P1003.1a draft standard for extensions to 1003.1. These include symbolic links, which require the addition of the functions *symlink*, *lstat*, and *readlink*, as well as clarification of whether various existing standard functions follow symbolic links. Other proposed new interfaces include *fchmod*, *fchown*, and *ftruncate*, which are like the existing standard functions that change the permission modes, the owner, or the size of a file. Some previous compromises produced ambiguities in the standard, particularly in what NGROUPS_MAX means, and how effective and saved user IDs interact. The 1003.1a standard should clear these up. There are also a few clarifications for things that the standard wording simply doesn't specify quite accurately enough, such as the atomicity of read and write operations. The P1003.1b draft is for things that didn't get into P1003.1a in time for various deadlines. There is no point in providing an exhaustive list here of the contents of either of these extensions. These examples should give a flavor for how such extensions are used to correct, clarify, or actually extend a standard.

7.8   POSIX Shell and Utilities

The previous section described POSIX 1003.1, which defines an application programming interface to system functionality. 1003.1 covers a narrowly defined area. For a system to be useable, additional interfaces are required. You would not want to work on a system that only provided a POSIX 1003.1 interface. The POSIX 1003.2 standard for shell and utilities and the user portability extensions (UPE) provide additional interfaces. These interfaces are defined independent of 1003.1 to enable 1003.2 interfaces to be written for a wide variety of systems. In

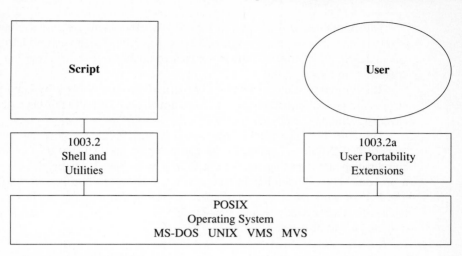

Figure 7.4 POSIX 1003.2.

additional to application portability 1003.2 has as its goal user portability.

POSIX 1003.2 has two parts, as shown in Fig. 7.4. The first and largest part describes the facilities required for the portability of shell scripts. It excludes interactive features. This first part, 1003.2, is sometimes referred to as .2 (dot 2) classic. The second part, 1003.2a, is called the User Portability Extensions (UPE). The UPE includes interactive commands required for user portability, such as vi. P1003.2 and P1003.2a should be published together in 1992; they will form a large document. POSIX 1003.1 was considered a large IEEE standard at 376 pages; 1003.2 is 1300 pages. The combined document of 1003.2 and 1003.2a is in the process of becoming the second part of the international POSIX standard as 9945-2.

History

As occurred with 1003.1, the ideas for 1003.2 began with the UniForum (then /usr/group) Standards Committee in 1981. The 1003.2 TCOS committee was formed in early 1986 to address shell functionality in a formal standard. In late 1987, work on an additional document, 1003.2a, the UPE, began. The UPE addresses the interactive commands that most users expect from a UNIX system but that were excluded from 1003.2.

Balloting on 1003.2 began in late 1988. Balloting on 1003.2a began in mid-1990. Approval for both occurred during 1992. The length of balloting is attributable to two basic factors: the size of the documents, and the addition of internationalization functionality during balloting for international acceptance.

Internationally, 1003.2 was registered as a Committee Draft in 1991. Draft International Standard registration of both documents occurred in 1992. 9945-2 should become an international standard in 1992.

Overview

The scope of 1003.2 is to "define a standard source code level interface to command interpretation, or 'shell' services and common utility programs for application programs" [IEEE 1992, 1]. The UPE extends the scope of 1003.2 to include utilites and features "to provide a common interactive environment for system users and program developers" [IEEE 1991, 1]. Together, these two documents provide an environment the POSIX user environment.

Three base documents were used in the development of the 1003.2 standard: *System V Interface Definition (SVID)*, [AT&T 1986]; the *X/Open Portability Guide (XPG)*, [X/Open 1987; X/Open 1989]; and the *UNIX User's Reference Manual, 4.3 Berkeley Software Distribution (4.3BSD Manual)*. The *KornShell Command and Programming Language* and *The AWK Programming Language* were used as references. These texts described most of existing UNIX practice in this area.

Parts of the environments described in the base documents are not included in this work. Fig. 7.5 shows a Venn diagram of the relation between the standard and the base documents. For example, the commands lp and pr are included for printing; however, the commands lpq, lprm, or lpstat, those which deal with queue and spool management, are not included. These management facilities are the domain of 1003.7 for system administration.

Figure 7.5 IEEE P1003.2 and IEEE P1003.2a.
From Jespersen, POSIX Update: Shell and Utilities, *Santa Clara, CA: UniForum.*
© *1989. Reprinted with permission.*

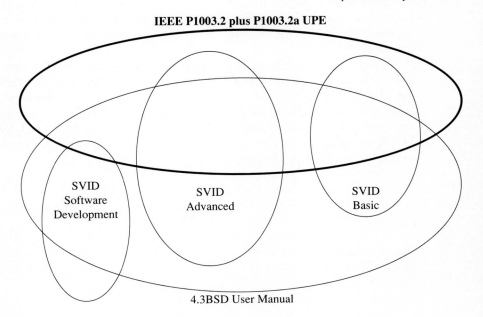

IEEE P1003.2 plus P1003.2a UPE

SVID
Software
Development

SVID
Advanced

SVID
Basic

4.3BSD User Manual

The working group was very careful in defining 1003.2 features so that most do not assume a 1003.1 compliant operating system. This was done to enable a 1003.2 conformant interface to be developed for many different platforms. An example is the MKS Toolkit from Mortice Kern System, which provides a shell interface on DOS platforms. But 1003.2 enumerates specific 1003.1 features when they are required.

Most major vendors will have a shell and command interface that complies with 1003.2 soon after it is published. Many vendors have developed implementations according to the drafts that have been available.

Ongoing Work

The work in this area continues. This work consists of improving the clarity of the original documents, developing test assertions (see Chapter 10), adding new facilities required by other working groups, and developing the file interchange and archiving format. One of the new facilities required by the work of another group is user access to symbolic lines, as is being defined in P1003.1a.

7.9   Graphical User Interface

These days, a user may interact with a computer by using a number of different devices. No longer are keyboards and terminal screens the only accepted means. An action may be initiated through a mouse click, or graphic objects may be manipulated using a special glove. This chapter is devoted to the standards that are being developed to support *Graphical User Interfaces (GUI)*.

There are two parts to this area. The first is windowing systems. The second is graphics: drawing pictures, rather than simply text. With the exception of user interface driveability, the standards discussed are for application programming interfaces.

Windowing system standards are being developed around the X Window System [Scheifler *et al.* 1988]. Where each standard fits in the layer cake between user and machine is shown in Λb. IEEE P1201.1 is working on a look and feel-independent API to the X Window System. The X Window System data stream encoding is being standardized by X3H3.6. Two toolkits, Motif and OPEN-LOOK, are being standardized by P1295. IEEE P1201.2 is working on a recommended practice to assist in user portability.

The X Window System produced by the X Consortium is the de facto standard for building windowing systems. OSF, UI, and X/Open all endorse the X Window System [Dryar *et al.* 1991, 80]. NIST has adopted the data stream encoding and Xlib layers as FIPS 158 [Digital 1991, 7-8].

Standards for graphics libraries and device interfaces have been around longer. We discuss two standards in this area: the *GKS (Graphical Kernel System)* and the *Programmer's Hierarchical Interactive Graphics Standard (PHIGS)*.

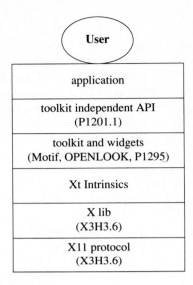

Figure 7.6 GUI layers.

P1201.1 Window Interface for User and Application Portability

This committee was formed in 1989. P1201.1 is developing a *LAPI (Layered Application Programming Interface),* which is a user interface API usable with several different toolkits and interfaces. Some (but not P1201.1) call this a *LAFI API ("look and feel" independent API).* Programs written to this API would be usable with many different toolkits. The scope of the project includes making the standard implementable on Motif, OPENLOOK, Macintosh, MS Windows, and Presentation Manager. The resulting document would specify more than the intersection of those existing interfaces.

The P1201.1 draft standard uses the *XVT Programmer's Reference Guide* as a base document. XVT is a commercial product of XVT Software. Reference documents include Visix Galaxy and Army THINGS, which is a C++ toolkit. Test implementation are being done by both XVT and VISIX. The standard itself will be a language independent specification, and there will eventually be language bindings for C, Ada, Mumps, and C++. The C and C++ bindings will probably be specified first [Walker 1992].

X3H3.6 Window Management

X3H3.6 is working on X3.196, "Computer Graphics — X Window System Data Stream Definition; Part I: Functional Specification, Part II: Data Stream Encoding; Part III: KEYSYM Encoding. This corresponds to the bottom layer shown in Fig. 7.6. It is also preparation for work by ISO JTC 1 SC24, which is about graphics standards, such as GKS.

Motif and OPENLOOK

The standards projects currently in progress under IEEE P1295, and sponsored by TCOS-SS, have a curious history, sometimes known as *GUI Wars*. Each of these two projects was originally developed by a vendor consortium: *Motif* by OSF, and *OPENLOOK* by UI. Each was proposed to P1201.1 as a solution to the need for a GUI API. They were debated in that working group for more than a year, and eventually turned elsewhere. Their proponents took them to the TCOS-SS SEC, which politely deferred acceptance. Their proponents then moved up the standards appeal process, to the *IEEE/CS Standards Activities Board (SAB)*, which asked the SEC for clarification on the previous SEC decision. The SEC clarified that they had declined to accept PARs for either project. The SAB referred the projects to the *IEEE/CS Standards Coordinating Committee (SCC)*. At this point, the SCC could have sponsored the work. However, since the TCOS-SS was already in a position to be able to sponsor the work, they were asked to do so. The SEC then approved a PAR for each of the projects, under a new committee, P1295. P1295.1 is for Motif based *MTE (Modular Toolkit Environment)*, and P1295.2 is the OPENLOOK based *OTE (Open Toolkit Environment)*.

This scenario is similar to the multiple network management projects that the *Internet Activities Board (IAB)* dealt with somewhat earlier, as described in Chapter 8, *Protocols and Standards*. In that case, there were three contending protocols, SGMP, CMIP, and HEMS. One was withdrawn by its authors, and the other two were given their own working groups. Each of the two continuing projects eventually became an Internet Standard: SGMP as SNMP, and CMIP as CMOT. The IAB deliberately left the final choice of protocol to the market. That is essentially what TCOS-SS finally did, as well.

P1201.2 Drivability

P1201.2 is developing a recommended practice for driveability. Driveability enables a user to switch among user interfaces with minimal interference from error-provoking inconsistencies, misleading expectations about the results of user actions, gross inconsistencies in the high-level user model, and incompatible motor control tendencies. In short, if you know what to expect, you can switch among user interfaces and avoid the frustrating period of learning what each button on the mouse will do. The specification is all about user actions; it does not include an API.

To describe user interface behavior, P1201.2 is collecting *Driveability Analysis Data (DAD)*. DAD is divided into seven categories: keyboard, user guidance (help), menus, buttons, mouse or pointing device, tasks or actions, and windows. DAD includes, for each category, a definition, recommendation, and summary of current industry usage.

A DAD example in the menu category, subcategory for behavior, and the item for describing choice feedback, would look like this. Choice Feedback is defined as the indication to the user that a particular menu item has been selected, and that a particular menu item has been activated. For each item, P1201.2 makes a recommendation regarding the behavior expected. Industry practice is described, relevant standards are cited, and human factors research and practice results are also listed for each item.

Graphics

Two graphics standards are *GKS (Graphical Kernel System)* and *PHIGS (Programmer's Hierarchical Interactive Graphics Standard)*. Each provides an interface for application programmers. The X Window System provides very basic graphics support. These two standards provide more complete toolkits than X, for more functionality. Each of these standards provide functionality for managing graphics devices and image storage. Both have as their goal to facilitate portability of graphics applications. See [Digital 1991, Chapter 8] for more information on these two graphics standards.

GKS. ISO 7942-1985 is the international GKS standard. It was approved in 1985. It is also NIST FIPS 120-1. GKS was developed to give the application programmer a toolbox from which to create graphics applications. It provides the application programmer an interface to many different hardware devices, such as color displays, printers, plotters, mice, or digitizers. This standard is for two-dimensional pictures only. In 1988, *GKS-3D (Graphical Kernel System for Three Dimensions)* ISO 8805-1988 was approved.

Because this standard was written in a programming-language-independent manner, it has two parts. Part 1 describes the functional aspects, and Part 2 provides language bindings.

PHIGS. PHIGS is the result of work started by X3H3.1 and continued in ISO/IEC JTC1 SC24 WG2. PHIGS is ISO 9592 and also NIST FIPS 153. PHIGS is a set of standards. "PHIGS provides a set of functions and programming language bindings (or toolbox package) for the definition, display and modification of two-dimensional or three-dimensional graphical data" [Dryar *et al.* 1991, 65]. Since PHIGS is based on the work done by GKS, there is a flatter learning curve for application programmers familiar with GKS.

The PHIGS standard is divided into three parts: 9592.1 is the functional description, 9592.2 is the archive file format, and 9592.3 is clear-text encoding of PHIGS archive files.

PEX (PHIGS Extension to X) is designed to provide PHIGS graphics capabilities to X Window System applications. Because of the popularity of both PHIGS and the X Window System, work is being done is this area.

7.10   Network Interfaces

Interoperability requires interfaces to network protocols and services. Here, we discuss the TCOS standards for Distribution Services.

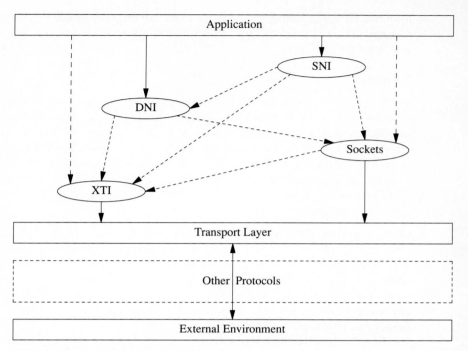

Figure 7.7 SNI, DNI, XTI, and sockets.
Figure adapted from IEEE Draft Standard, P1003.12/D0.2, Information Technology—Portable Operating System Interface (POSIX)—Part xx: Protocol Independent Interfaces (PII), *copyright © 1992 by the Institute of Electrical and Electronic Engineers, Inc. with the permission of the IEEE. This is an unapproved draft, subject to change.*

TCOS Distribution Service Interfaces

TCOS is the Technical Committee on Operating Systems and Application Environments. It doesn't do networking, but it does standardize operating system interfaces (both API and EEI) for what it calls *distribution services.* The TCOS working groups in this area are listed in Table 7.4. Most of them are described in this section, except for P1237. P1237 was about an API for *RPC (Remote Procedure Call),* but that working group was dissolved by the SEC at its own request to avoid duplication of effort with X3 TC5.5. TCOS maintains a liaison to that latter group.

The interfaces produced by these working groups may be API, EEI, or a mixture. *DNI (Detailed Network Interface)* is perhaps the key interface. It is a general interface to the transport layer, and can be used for most kinds of network programming. *SNI (Simple Network Interface)* is a simpler transport interface for applications that don't need the flexibility of DNI. As shown in Fig. 7.7, SNI may be implemented on top of DNI, and either SNI or DNI may be implemented on

Table 7.8 TCOS API and OSI layers.

OSI Layer	TCOS API	Committee
7 Application	ONI	P1238
	TFA	P1003.8
6 Presentation	DRI	
5 Session		
4 Transport	PII: DNI and SNI	P1003.12
3 Network		
2 Data link		
1 Physical		

top of the historical sockets or XTI interfaces. A program may also use either sockets or XLI directly, but such a program would not be as portable as one that used only SNI or DNI.

ONI (OSI Network Interface) is an interface to OSI application services such as MHS (mail) and FTAM (file transfer). SNI can be used above it, but DNI cannot be. SNI can be implemented on top of DNI, ONI, or underlying transport protocols. *DRI (Data Representation Interface)* is a presentation interface that can be used above either SNI or DNI. Where all these interfaces fit in the OSI layers is shown in Table 7.8.

Fig. 7.8 may provide a more useful way of looking at these interfaces. TCOS isn't really interested in anything below the transport layer, since application protocols generally need transport services. Both DNI and SNI provide transport layer access. The figure shows several protocol suites (OSI, TCP/IP, and XNS), but an application using SNI or DNI should not, in general, have to care about which suite is in use.

The application also has other options, such as using the transport layer through historical transport interfaces. There are at least two of these: sockets and TLI or XTI. The existence of multiple historical interfaces is one of the main reasons DNI and SNI were invented. We discuss these interfaces later, under P1003.12.

We don't see *Transparent File Access (TFA)* in Fig. 7.8, because it really is transparent, and is used through the ordinary filesystem interface specified in the System Interface Standard. We discuss some of the work necessary to make it transparent, under P1003.8.

In addition, ONI allows access to all the facilities in the OSI stack, and can also be used through SNI, as we discuss under P1238. Like TFA, Directory Services as defined by P1003.17 will probably be implemented using DNI, but perhaps in combination with ONI. The MHS interface by P1224 and the FTAM interface by P1238.1 would be more likely to be implemented using ONI alone.

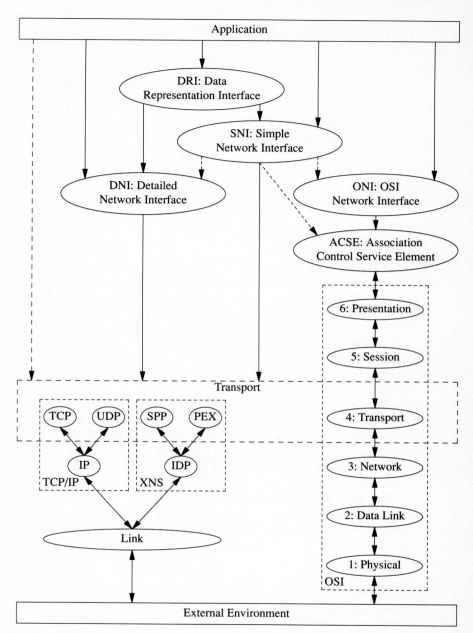

Figure 7.8 Distributed services model.

Figure adapted from IEEE Draft Standard, P1003.12/D0.2, Information Technology—Portable Operating System Interface (POSIX)—Part xx: Protocol Independent Interfaces (PII), *copyright © 1992 by the Institute of Electrical and Electronic Engineers, Inc. with the permission of the IEEE. This is an unapproved draft, subject to change.*

DSSC: Distributed Services Steering Committee

The *Distributed Services Steering Committee (DSSC)* is responsible for coordinating the projects we have already listed under Distributed Services. That is, the DSSC coordinates work on interfaces to network services and protocols. The Distributed Services working groups need to be mutually aware of what they are doing, so that they do not duplicate effort, and so that they can coordinate ballots on one another's draft standards. Many topics are common to these working groups and projects, and they need to coordinate, for example, namespace harmonization.

The Distributed Services working groups also need to be aware of efforts by one of their number to affect projects of other working groups, such as proposals by P1003.8 to make modifications to P1003.2. In addition, a Distributed Services working group may consider splitting into two, so that a new group or project can be formed to pursue another topic. The DSSC provides a forum for these kinds of discussions.

In addition, the DSSC chair sits on the *Project Management Committee (PMC),* and the DSSC thus acts as a channel to the PMC and the SEC. The SEC or PMC may also use the DSSC as a channel in the other direction.

IEEE P1003.12 PII

The *Protocol-Independent Interface (PII)* committee had a hard time choosing between *Berkeley sockets (sockets)* and *XTI (X/Open Transport Interface).* The socket interface for general networking services was first available in 4.2BSD. XTI is the X/Open version of AT&T's *TLI (Transport Layer Interface),* which is an interface for general networking services, derived in part from Berkeley sockets. Instead of picking either sockets or XTI, P1003.12 chose to incorporate both, plus two new interfaces, DNI and SNI, which we have already mentioned.

Some of the implementation possibilities are shown in Fig. 7.7. SNI can be implemented on top of DNI. Either SNI or DNI can be implemented directly on top of either XTI or sockets. Sockets can be implemented on top of XTI. The application can use either SNI or DNI, or it can use either sockets or XTI directly.

But to be portable, an application should use either SNI or DNI, and should not be concerned about what lies underneath. This is analogous to the concept of language-independent specification that we examine in Chapter 9, *Programming Language Issues.* DNI or SNI would be the LIS, which would then be bound in a particular implementation to either sockets or XTI, as the underlying transport interface language.

Neither SNI nor DNI support unreliable virtual circuits, reliable datagram transfer, or unreliable broadcast or multicast [OSSWG 1991]. The P1003.12 working group concentrated on more common application services, such as reliable virtual circuits and unreliable datagram transfer. These services correspond to those provided by the Internet protocols TCP and UDP, respectively, or the OSI protocols TP4 and TP0, respectively.

IEEE 1003.8 TFA

The *Transparent File Access (TFA)* committee had a lot of prior art to choose from, such as:

• *NFS (Network File System)*, a stateless network file system developed by Sun Microsystems, Inc. and now widely distributed by other vendors

• *RFS (Remote File System)*, a stateful distributed UNIX file system developed by AT&T

• *AFS (Andrew File System)*, a stateful distributed file system developed by Carnegie Mellon University and now distributed by Transarc, Inc.

• *FTAM (File Transfer, Access, and Management)*, the ISO-OSI protocol

P1003.8 chose not to standardize directly on any of those historical implementations of TFAs related to the UNIX system. Instead, it specified TFA behavior in more generic terms, in several levels of functionality.

Core TFA The most basic kind of TFA supports basic POSIX functions for file access, such as *execl, open, close, read, write, fseek*; some capabilities of *fcntl*; the directory access routines; *access*; *pathconf*; and getting permissions for reading and writing from *stat*.

Full TFA This more complete kind of TFA supports POSIX functions related to setting user permissions on files, such as *umask, chown, chmod, utime*; the full semantics of *fcntl* and *stat*; and all the functions supported by Core TFA. Full TFA also supports behavioral characteristics such as advisory locking, append mode writes, controlling terminals, errors returned with the call that produced them, consistent reads and writes, and defined behavior on last close of a file.

Subset TFA A given file may be accessable by some set of mechanisms intermediate between those of Core TFA and Full TFA.

The kind of TFA supported by a given file may be determined with *pathconf*. For example, behavior of a file on last close may be determined using *pathconf* _PC_LAST_CLOSE parameter. If last close behavior is in effect on a regular file, and a process has that file open, the file stays usable to that process even if any or all of several unusual conditions occur. The process may change its effective user ID or effective group ID; the process may change its supplementary group IDs; the same or another process may change the file access permissions of the file, or even remove the file. None of these conditions affect usability of the open file in a historical UNIX system, and none of them affect that usability when POSIX last close behavior is in effect.

Some historical TFAs, such as NFS, do not support these semantics in full. Modifications may be needed for conformance.

7.11   Realtime

Some extensions to IEEE 1003.1 are being developed by IEEE P1003.4 for real-time support. P1003.4 contains the main extensions.

P1003.4a is a project for threads extensions, that is for threads of control within the memory space of a traditional UNIX process. This specification of a threads interface is commonly known as *pthreads,* for POSIX threads.

P1003.4b is a project for other extensions, perhaps including a user process memory management mechanism similar to the C language *malloc* facility.

In addition, IEEE P1003.13 is for realtime profiles:

• P1003.13 Realtime Full Function AEP

• P1003.13 Realtime Embedded Control System AEP

• P1003.13 Realtime Intermediate AEP

We will come back to those profiles later, in Chapter 13, *TCOS Profiles.*

IEEE P1003.4 is not just realtime. Here are the major topics in it:

• Asynchronous event notification and response

• Scheduling and priority interrupts

• Preemptive scheduling

• Memory locking

• High-performance file system

• Nanosecond timers

• Shared memory

• Semaphores

• IPC (message passing)

• Synchronized (not synchronous) I/O

The addition of the P1003.4 specifications to 1003.1 produces a capable real-time system interface. Its derivation from a nonrealtime historical system shows, as in the overloading of *kill* to do many things other than kill processes, and the lack of an explicit ability to assign attributes such as priority to a process when it is created. The composite interface also still lacks some features that might be desirable, such as a direct way to trigger an event at a given clock time, rather than after an interval [OSSWG 1991].

Here are some major milestones in the history of P1003.4:

1989   Threads separated into P1003.4a, usually known as pthreads.

1989   1003.4 in balloting.

June 1990   WG15 refused to consider 1003.4 because it was not language independent.

October 1990   Compromises reached between WG15 and TCOS-SS on language independence.

The current plan is for IEEE to publish a single 1003.4 standard, which will by used by WG15 to modify both IS 9945-1 (the equivalent of 1003.1 and related TCOS standards) and IS 9945-2 (the equivalent of 1003.2). The eventual 1003.4a and 1003.4b standards will be treated similarly.

7.12   Security

There are several groups dealing with security related to the POSIX System Interface Standard. Some of these groups are doing extensions and others are producing security specifications or software in related areas. They include

• The IEEE P1003.6 Security working group, which is the group we discuss in the most detail in this section.

• The ISO/IEC JTC 1 SC22 WG15 international security rapporteur group, also discussed in this section.

• The Open Software Foundation, with their DCE and DME, which are discussed in Chapter 14, *Industry Profiles*.

• UNIX International, with their UI-ATLAS framework, which is also discussed in Chapter 14.

Several groups deal with network security, a topic we do not discuss in detail in this book. The Kerberos authentication mechanism has become a de facto standard, and is used by both OSF and UI.

Important documents related to security in POSIX include

• The *Information Technology Security Evaluation Criteria (ITSEC)* harmonizes security criteria from France, Germany, the Netherlands, and the United Kingdom in ten security classes. It was published in May 1990.

• The U.S. DoD *Orange Book* specifies four basic levels of security, and is widely influential. For example, NIST has a specification dealing with *Orange Book* C2 security. We examine this book in more detail in the next section.

Orange Book

The *U.S. National Computer Security Commission (NCSC)*, produced the *Trusted Computer Security Evaluation Criteria (TCSEC)*, commonly known as the *Orange Book. TRUSIX (NCSC specification and evaluation of trusted systems)* is a testing organization for the *Orange Book*. The *Orange Book* specifies four levels of security, from minimal protection at level D to formal proofs at level A.

A   Verified protection and formal proofs

B   Mandatory protection

B3   Access control lists

B2   Trusted facility management, configuration control

B1   Mandatory access control and labeled output

C   Discretionary protection

C2   Controlled access, authentication, auditing

C1   Discretionary access control

D   No protection

The *Orange Book* only deals with single-machine systems. Distributed security such as is needed in distributed computing is beyond its scope. Distributed security is treated by UI, OSF, and X/Open, as described in Chapter 14, *Industry Profiles*.

IEEE P1003.6

The IEEE P1003 Security working group is a descendant of the UniForum Technical Committee Subcommittee on Security. The IEEE group was formed in 1987, and formation of a balloting group for it began in 1991, with the first ballot in that same year. During balloting the group is working on creating a language independent interface and test assertions.

Overview. P1003.6 is specifying programmatic interfaces to services specified by the NCSC in their *Orange Book* (TCSEC). P1003.6 has divided its work into the following four areas:

1. *DAC (Discretionary Access Control):* TCSEC Level C2 security

2. *MAC (Mandatory Access Control):* TCSEC Level B1 security, involving security labels

3. Privileges

4. Audit

DAC: Discretionary Access Control. P1003.6 is defining *ACL (Access Control List)s* to operate with the traditional UNIX user/group/other file permission mechanism. An access list is associated with each file. This is a security mechanism used with discretionary access control. It is called discretionary because access is determined by the user. It corresponds to *Orange Book* level C2 protection. Traditional file permissions are simply an ACL with three entries.

MAC: Mandatory Access Control. Mandatory access control is determined by the security administrator, not the user. All system objects get a security label; all system users have a security classification; and users have no control over the access. Access cannot be granted to a user of a less restrictive class; the traditional System V *chown* function is thus obviously a problem. An option was introduced into 1003.1 as long ago as 1987 to allow an implementation to prohibit users from giving away files with *chown*.

This kind of security corresponds to *Orange Book* level B1 protection. An example is the top secret, classified, and unclassified categories used by the U.S. government. Another example is departmental categories, such as engineering, marketing, and sales, where none may be higher than another, but each may want to keep some information confidential from the others.

Privileges. One of the first changes made to IEEE 1003.1 in the initial stages of the work that led to IEEE P1003.6 was the removal of all occurrences of the term *superuser,* or root access. This traditional form of UNIX security might better be referred to as insecurity, since a process with root access can do almost anything.

Instead, the term *appropriate privilege* was substituted into 1003.1. This new term could be defined to be identical to superuser, so that a user with it could do almost anything, as usual. But it could also be redefined later by IEEE P1003.6 and reimplemented for more detailed security mechanisms.

IEEE P1003.6 allows a list of privileges. It is developing a mechanism to inherit, assign, and enable privileges.

Audit. The audit subgroup of IEEE P1003.6 is creating a standard interface for a logging mechanism, a standard format for logging records, and a list of system calls and commands to log.

Liaison with other groups. IEEE P1003.6 coordinates with TRUSIX. It also coordinates with P1003.7 and P1003.8, since security depends on administration and network access.

ISO/IEC JTC 1 SC22 WG15 Security Rapporteur Group

The *ISO/IEC JTC 1 SC22 WG15 Security Rapporteur Group (SRG)* provides a forum for coordination for security work. At the international level, representation to standards bodies is usually possible only for countries. This forum permits other representation, as well.

References

AT&T 1986.   AT&T, *System V Interface Definition (SVID), Issue 2*, UNIX Press, Morristown, NJ (1986).

Digital 1991.   Digital, *Open Systems Handbook: A Guide to Building Open Systems*, Digital Equipment Corporation, Bedford, MA (1991).

Dryar et al. 1991.   Dryar, Cindy, Glaze, Kymberly, Kosinski, Peter, Silverman, Andy, & Wade, Erni, *The World of Standards: An Open Systems Reference Guide*, 88open Consortium, Ltd., San Jose, CA (1991).

Hann 1991.   Hann, Quin, "Finance Report," *TCOS SEC Standing Documents*(TCOS/SEC/SD-14) (23 August 1991).

IEEE 1990.   IEEE, *Information Technology — Portable Operating System Interface (POSIX) — Part 1: System Application Program Interface (API) [C Language]*, IEEE, Piscataway, NJ (1990). ISO/IEC 9945-1; IEEE Std 1003.1-1990(E); ISBN 1-55937-061-0.

IEEE 1991.   IEEE, *Draft Standard for Information Technology — Portable Operating System Interface (POSIX) — Part 2: Shell and Utilities — Amendment 1: User Portability Extension (UPE)*, IEEE, Piscataway, NJ (1991). ISO/IEC 9945-2; IEEE Std 1003.2-1992(E), Draft 8.

IEEE 1992.   IEEE, *Draft Standard for Information Technology — Portable Operating System Interface (POSIX) — Part 2: Shell and Utilities*, IEEE, Piscataway, NJ (1992). ISO/IEC 9945-2; IEEE Std 1003.2-1992(E), Draft 11.3.

Jespersen 1989.   Jespersen, Hal, "POSIX Explored: System Interface," UniForum, Santa Clara, CA (1989).

Lewine 1991.   Lewine, Donald, *POSIX Programmer's Guide: Writing Portable UNIX Programs*, O'Reilly & Associates, Inc., Sebastopol, CA (1991).

OSSWG 1991.   OSSWG, "Delta Document for the Next Generation Computer Resources (NGCR) Operating Systems Interface Standard Baseline," Operating Systems Standards Working Group (OSSWG) Next Generation Computer Resources (NGCR) Program, Naval Ocean Systems Center, San Diego, CA (31 December 1991).

Scheifler et al. 1988.   Scheifler, Robert, Gettys, James, & Newman, Ron, *X Window System: C Library and Protocol Reference*, Digital Press, Bedford, MA (1988).

/usr/group 1984.   /usr/group, "1984 /usr/group Standard," UniForum, Santa Clara, CA (1984).

Walker 1992.   Walker, Amanda, Personal communication (April 1992).

X/Open 1987.   X/Open, *X/Open Portability Guide, Issue 2*, Elsevier Science Publishers, Amsterdam (1987).

X/Open 1989.   X/Open, *X/Open Portability Guide, Issue 3*, Prentice-Hall, Englewood Cliffs, NJ (1989).

Zlotnick 1991.   Zlotnick, Fred, *The POSIX.1 Standard: A Programmer's Guide*, Benjamin Cummings, Redwood City, CA (1991).

CHAPTER 8

███████████

Protocols and Standards

Large segments of the open systems market can agree on the POSIX standards as one of several common elements for application program interfaces. When it comes to networking, there is no such agreement about what to use. There are two major open protocol suites, OSI and TCP/IP, produced by radically different processes, each with its own proponents. In this chapter, we do not discuss protocols in detail, since they are treated thoroughly in many other texts [Tanenbaum 1988]. We also avoid detailed discussion of actual networks, for the same reason [Quarterman 1990]. What we do discuss is the processes used to create specifications and standards for the OSI and TCP/IP protocol suites.

The chapter begins with an overview of the network protocol models and suites, including their layering models, and of the general processes that produce them. Then, there is a section on OSI standardization, and one on TCP/IP standardization, giving general strong and weak points of each.

Most of the rest of the chapter is about TCP/IP, because the bodies and processes involved are less well known and have changed markedly in the last few years. The bodies directly involved in TCP/IP standardization have already been described in Chapter 5, *Industry Organizations and User Groups*. To understand TCP/IP, it is useful to understand the worldwide Internet built out of those protocols, so that network of networks is discussed first here. The TCP/IP standardization process itself is described in detail. Some comparisons are made between TCOS and TCP/IP standardization processes (some others have already been made in Chapter 6, *Processes*). The major TCP/IP specifications are listed, along with related profiles, in Chapter 15, *Procurement Profiles*.

Since this is a process chapter, we leave network interfaces to Chapter 7, *IEEE/CS TCOS Standards*, and we leave network management to Chapter 14, *Industry Profiles*.

8.1   Layers and Processes

We've already discussed the relations of open systems and open systems interconnection in Part 1. In this chapter, we are concerned with programming interfaces to actual protocols.

The Basic Reference Model for *Open Systems Interconnection (OSI),* or OSI Model, was specified by the *International Organization for Standardization (ISO).* It and the protocol suite that fits it are becoming increasingly important. Several of the OSI protocols were originally specified by *CCITT (International Consultative Committee on Telegraphy and Telephony).* CCITT has also adopted the OSI Model. The CCITT numbers begin with "X." For example, parts of X.25 have the corresponding International Standards IS 8878 and IS 7776. The X.400 series of recommendations are also specified in IS 10021, for *MHS (Message Handling System).* X.500 is Directory Services, and is also known as IS 9594. Some ISO OSI specifications do not have corresponding CCITT specifications; for example, CCITT does not support all the connectionless mode features that ISO does.

OSI standards are written by formal international standards committees [Rose 1989; Stallings 1987] under ISO/IEC JTC 1 SC21 and SC6, which we have listed in Chapter 4, *Formal Standards Bodies.* As we have already seen in Chapter 6, the ISO POSIX work is performed by ISO/IEC JTC 1 SC22 WG15, which is a peer subcommittee to SC21 under JTC 1.

TCP/IP (Transmission Control Protocol/Internet Protocol) is the most widely implemented and used protocol suite worldwide [Comer 1988; Comer & Stevens 1991; Carl-Mitchell & Quarterman 1993; Stallings *et al.* 1988]. It began in government and academia, but has for some years been widely used in industry. By one estimate, the TCP/IP market did about $3 billion to $10 billion in business in 1992 [Lynch 1992]. The specifications for TCP/IP are written by the *IETF (Internet Engineering Task Force),* which is overseen by the *IAB (Internet Activities Board),* which we have described in Chapter 5, *Industry Organizations and User Groups.*

Many UNIX machines are connected to CSMA/CD, token ring, or token bus networks. The IEEE 802 standards govern communication at this level. ISO has the corresponding IS 8802 standards. IETF working groups may produce interface or management specifications for these media level protocols, but they do not normally specify the latter directly. The one exception so far is the *Point-to-Point Protocol (PPP).* In this chapter, we are mainly interested in protocols at the internet layer or higher. These are protocols that can be used across several physical networks.

The OSI and TCP/IP groups fall on either side of the TCOS committees in formality, as shown in Fig. 8.1. OSI working groups are more formal than those of TCOS, since they operate at the international level of formal standardization, and are composed of national delegations, whereas the TCOS working groups are composed of individual technical experts. The IETF working groups are less formal; many of their rules and procedures are only now being written down. There

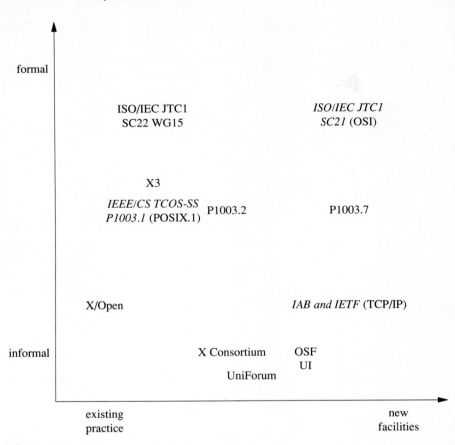

Figure 8.1 Formality and innovation.

has always been international participation in specification and implementation of Internet protocols, but the Internet community has perhaps been less international than the OSI community (although that appears to be changing). Both OSI and IETF working groups tend to originate more new specifications not drawn directly from base documents than do TCOS working groups. Of course, that depends on the TCOS working group, with P1003.1 (System Interface) including the least new facilities, P1003.2 (Shell and Utilities) somewhat more, and P1003.7 (System Administration) many, since it has little prior art to draw from. Also, POSIX work at the international level is governed by the same rules and procedures as the OSI work, since both come under ISO/IEC JTC 1, with POSIX under SC22, and OSI under SC21, as we have discussed in Chapter 4 and Chapter 7. However, SC22 WG15, the ISO POSIX committee, mostly depends on the TCOS commit-tees for draft documents, whereas the SC21 OSI working groups tend to either write their own, or get them from CCITT, which usually writes its own documents directly. So the same rules and procedures (for both TCOS-SS and ISO/IEC

JTC 1) may lead to different degrees of innovation in final specifications, depending on the subject matter and the source of draft documents. The IETF working groups are driven by a need for innovation similar to that of the SC21 OSI working groups. Yet IETF works under much less strict procedures than does SC21, and that is related to the main difference between IAB and SC21, and between IAB and TCOS.

TCOS places a strong emphasis on standardizing existing practice. A POSIX committee usually does not specify a complete new interface, unless there is no prior art, and then there may be a question as to whether the committee should exist. Most of the OSI protocols are specified by ISO or CCITT working groups, rather than being adapted from previous specifications. Most of the specifications produced by IETF working groups are also not drawn from previous specifications.

But the IAB and IETF place a very strong emphasis on implementation before standardization. TCP/IP protocols are often implemented in parallel with the development of their freely available specifications, and interoperable implementations must exist for a protocol soon after it enters the IAB standards track.

OSI protocols are seldom implemented before specification. They may rarely be based on something that already exists, but changes are always made during standardization. OSI standards exist solely on the basis of paper, not of implementations.

Figure 8.2 Protocol models and layers.

ISO-OSI Model		Internet Model	User Model
7 Application		Process	Network
6 Presentation		/	
5 Session		Applications	Applications
4 Transport		Transport	Network
3 Network	internet	Internet	
	convergence	Network	
	subnet		
2 Data Link		Link	Infrastructure
1 Physical		Physical	

User programs and implementations of distributed services are more interested in getting bits, bytes, and data structures from here to there than in learning
what protocol religion the underlying network infrastructure supports. The two
main protocol models disagree on many points, even on their basic layering divisions, as shown in Fig. 8.2. The problem gets even more complicated when specific protocol stacks to support applications are considered [Malamud 1992].
However, there are some important points in common. For example, the transport
layer is essentially the same in both models. The OSI model has a network layer
(now including an internet sublayer) and a data link layer, and the Internet model
has an Internet layer, a network layer, and a link layer. These cover approximately
the same functions together. ISO has recently adopted three formal sublayers to
their Network layer.

internet   This is formally the subnetwork independence sublayer, with an
              subnetwork-independent convergence protocol (SNICP), which is
              often null for the *Connection Oriented Network Service (CONS),*
              i.e., over X.25, but can be the *Connectionless Network Protocol
              (CLNP)* (also known as ISO-IP) for the *Connectionless Network
              Service (CLNS).*

convergence   This is formally the subnetwork dependent sublayer, with the *sub-
              network-dependent convergence protocol (SNDCP).*

subnet   This is formally the subnetwork access sublayer, in which is used
              an *subnetwork access protocol (SNAcP),* containing an encoding
              of the network protocol [Rose 1989], for example, the Ethernet
              type field.

The OSI internet sublayer corresponds to the Internet layer, and OSI CLNP (ISO-
IP) has the same general functions as the Internet Protocol (although they differ in
details such as address format). The existence of this OSI internet sublayer
removes one of the major points of disagreement in the ISO OSI and TCP/IP layering models. Since IP is always encapsulated in a network layer protocol (except
for point-to-point links), the TCP/IP Internet layer may be considered to be a sublayer of the Network layer, like the OSI internet sublayer within the OSI Network
layer. However, if we consider Ethernet, token ring, X.25, BBN 1822 (the old
ARPANET network protocol), ISDN, SMDS, frame relay, and ATM all to be network layer protocols, then IP fills a separate Internet layer above the Network
layer [Cerf & Cain 1983; Cerf & Kahn 1974]. CCITT has not followed ISO in
adopting an internet sublayer, so ISO OSI and TCP/IP are now actually closer
than ISO and CCITT in this respect.

We can simplify the picture by thinking of the protocol layers as being
divided above the transport layer into application protocols above and infrastructure including the transport and lower layers [Quarterman 1991a; Quarterman
1991b]. In addition, although the TCP/IP model has no formal presentation layer,
there are presentation protocols sometimes used with TCP/IP, such as Sun's *XDR*

(External Data Representation). However, the Internet transport layer has some features of the OSI session layer. For example, the Internet *FTP (File Transport Protocol)* uses two data channels, and these are handled as two transport channels. In the OSI model, these would properly be handled by the session layer, but there is no Internet session layer. One could instead argue that the application layer is handling the missing session functions. The point remains that layer boundaries are somewhat arbitrary. The important thing about layering is not the number of layers or exactly where the boundaries are, but that there are layers that permit substitutable protocols and simplify understanding and programming.

The layering points in common would lead the programmer to expect a common programming interface. The network protocol committees do not really address this issue. OSI defines service interfaces requirements, but not specific programming interfaces; theoretically, OSI layers indicate functional requirements, but not necessarily actual protocol implementation interaction points. IETF usually does not do API, and there has been no attempt to create a common API for lower layers (or even the application layer), since operating system designs vary a great deal and no single API would work for all of them [Cerf 1992]. The occasional exceptions, such as for *CAT (common authentication protocols)*, are rare. Nonetheless, there are two UNIX programming interfaces, at least for the transport layer: sockets and TLI or XTI. These need to be reconciled. Standards for a common *PII (Protocol Independent Interface)* and for related API and EEI are being produced by TCOS; we have discussed them in Chapter 7, *IEEE/CS TCOS Standards*. In this chapter, we discuss how the OSI and TCP/IP protocol standards are produced.

8.2   OSI Standardization

The OSI standards are produced by the ISO and CCITT processes that have already been described in Chapter 6, *Processes*. Here, we only mention some interesting features of those processes as applied to the OSI protocol standards, and as compared to the TCOS-SS and IAB (TCP/IP) processes. Many OSI protocol and service specifications actually originate with CCITT. CCITT processes were also discussed in Chapter 6. More detail on ISO and CCITT OSI processes may be found in [Digital 1991, Chapter 10] and [Rose 1989].

Strong Points

OSI has a great deal of support from governments and high-level industry executives [SOS 1991]. It has an international network of workshops (EWOS, OIW, and AOW) and industry consortia (COS, SPAG, POSI, etc.) that permits collaboration among companies involved in OSI work. Those involved in OSI have done a very good job of marketing the need for open systems interconnection, and for open systems.

OSI technical design and specification work is often quite good. In some areas, including multimedia mail, OSI has had ambitious goals in addressing important technical areas and user requirements before any other networking bodies. OSI also does not have the address space limitations of IP.

Practical implementation and deployment have often lagged behind, but some OSI standards, such as the X.500 directory protocol, appear to be spreading widely in actual use, although interconnection of the various deployed implementations may be lagging in that case.

The concept of layering was not invented by OSI. It is a common research heritage used by both OSI and TCP/IP, among others, and much of the early work was done on the ARPANET, the early U.S. research network that preceded the Internet (discussed later), and on other research networks such as CYCLADES, in France. For example, CYCLADES substituted protocols in the same layer, and was the first to use pure datagrams [Pouzin 1982; Quarterman 1990]. However, the careful attention paid by OSI to interfaces, and to the distinction between protocol and service, has had effects on protocols, services, and specifications of most other protocol suites, and on standards in other areas. OSI has been most notable in architecture, vocabulary, and upper layer protocols.

The concept of profiles as it is being adapted by TCOS for the POSIX OSE originated with OSI. The OSI Basic Reference Model was first drafted as early as 1977. The various OSI workshops and industry support groups have been developing OSI profiles for a long time, as have national bodies like NIST, in GOSIP. The IETF and IAB seem to have independently reinvented profiling, but OSI certainly did it first.

Problems

Implementations of many OSI protocols do exist, and some of them are openly licensed, or even available for cost of distribution. But a distinctive feature of OSI standard specification documents for a long time has been that they are expensive, and relatively hard to get [Rutkowski 1991]. They are, for the most part, available only on paper, and the cost per document is very high. This contrasts with the ready availability of TCP/IP specifications has been attributed by some to U.S. government financial support for TCP/IP and not for OSI, but that doesn't account for European Community and national government support for OSI. However this state of affairs originated, what is not clear is how long it can be maintained, given current inexpensive photocopying and even scanning. An experiment in online distribution was attempted for about three months in 1991 [Malamud 1991], using CCITT specifications (which often precede and parallel ISO OSI specifications). This involved scanning copies of the paper documents and converting them into troff (a UNIX text formatter) source, then distributing that source over the Internet. Usage was considerable. However, permission was withdrawn at the end of the year, and the online originals were supposed to be returned to *ITU (International Telecommunications Union),* the parent body of CCITT. This does not account for the copies already distributed, however. How does one return an online original that is already mirrored in dozens of countries?

A particularly unfortunate feature of the OSI process is that many of those involved do not use the protocols. In addition, many of those who write the OSI specifications do not implement them. There are also no really widespread vendor-independent OSI networks. Some networks implement a few application protocols, such as X.400; none support a full set of applications, except for small-scale or experimental networks. The data processing department of ISO uses TCP/IP internally, as does the *COS (Corporation for Open Systems)*. Meanwhile, the Internet built from the TCP/IP protocols grows exponentially, and is already the largest in the world.

Some OSI work has been done using development packages such as the *ISODE (ISO Development Environment)*. The key technology is defined in RFC1006, which specifies a "transport service convergence protocol" resembling TP0, for use on top of TCP, on top of IP [Rose & Cass 1987]. ISODE is an implementation that includes RFC1006 [Rose 1989]. About a dozen other implementations of RFC1006 also exist. Such implementations permit OSI work to be done on the Internet and other IP networks. The ISODE Consortium was formed in 1992 to oversee the evolution and distribution of ISODE software [Chapin 1992a].

Some say there is little direct input from the Internet community into OSI protocol development. For example, few people involved in IETF attend CCITT or *RARE (Réseaux Associés pour la Recherche Européenne)* meetings, although interaction between RARE and IETF is increasing. But the current IAB chair, who is one of the authors of the original OSI Reference Model, has chaired the U.S. (ANSI) committee responsible for Network and Transport layer OSI standards for ten years, and is the ISO editor for the OSI internetwork protocol (CLNP). He asserts that "in general, in the Network and Transport layer work, there is almost one hundred percent cross-participation in OSI and IETF" [Chapin 1992a].

Ironically, many, if not most, people and organizations involved in OSI protocol development now have Internet access and exchange electronic mail over that network. The main exceptions tend to be the standards bodies themselves. It will be interesting to see what effect competition among standards bodies has on this situation. Some of them, such as CCITT and CCIR, have already adopted fast-track approval procedures, so it is clear they are aware of the need for speed [Rutkowski 1991].

OSI standards are generally written in advance of widespread implementation. Sometimes they are even adopted as International Standards before they have been tested. Even when they have been implemented and tested, there are often great variations in options or interpretations among different companies or countries. OSI attempts to include everything that might be useful, as options. Meanwhile, TCP/IP includes only what makes it work. Each approach is both a strength and weakness.

Numerous implementer's workshops and commercial consortia have sprung up to address problems of OSI options, variations, and protocol stacks [Rutkowski 1991]. Examples include the workshops *EWOS (European Workshop on Open Systems)*, the *AOW (Asia-Oceania Workshop)*, and the *OSE Implementation Workshop (OIW)*, in the United States. Industry OSI promotion consortia include COS, already mentioned, SPAG, and POSI (see Chapter 5). Some of these groups, such as EWOS and OIW, have expanded their scope to include *OSE (Open System Environment)* in addition to OSI; see Chapter 5 and Chapter 12 for details.

OSI standards are generally very hard to read, due to a great deal of specialized terminology. This problem has been alleviated somewhat by books published recently that explain these standards in plain English [Rose 1989; Rose 1991].

8.3   TCP/IP Standardization

The TCP/IP protocols are standardized by the IAB and IETF standardization processes. IETF emphazises experience and interest over standardization status, in marked contrast with the OSI approach. Some IETF participants like to say that OSI has standards for the future, while the Internet has standards for today. To which OSI proponents may respond by asking what are we to do now that the future is here. TCP/IP proponents may respond by remarking that we add to existing functionality. The debate continues.

Strong Points

The IAB and IETF standardization process has been successful. The TCP/IP industry, which amounted to a few million dollars in 1986, was projected to gross $3 billion to $10 billion by the end of 1992 [Lynch 1992].

Many vendors of UNIX and related systems supply TCP/IP software with their hardware. TCP is not specific to UNIX, and is available for most operating systems platforms of all kinds. But UNIX is responsible for much of the popularity of TCP/IP, because of the reference implementation in 4.2BSD, and the wide availability of UNIX workstations. Because IP works across diverse lower layer network protocols and hardware, most network hardware (such as modems, routers, and local area network cables and transceivers) will support TCP/IP.

The commercial market for TCP/IP has been very strong in Europe for the last several years, and the Internet in Europe is currently growing twice as fast as the Internet worldwide. OSI did the world a massive favor in terms of education. OSI did a very good job of sales, but didn't have the software to back it up. TCP/IP had the goods, and they sell [Crocker 1992].

A major part of the secret of this success is that the people who write the specifications also implement and use the protocols they specify, and are thus sensitive to the abilities and limitations of the technology. This situation is quite similar to that of UNIX, especially in earlier years.

Another reason for success was informal cooperation by technologically sophisticated researchers, most of whom know each other and attend three annual IETF meetings, as well as meeting at other conferences and functions. A high level of trust was achieved. There are still few formal rules for the creation of new IETF Working Groups or IESG Areas, for example. There was no need to spell out such things in more detail, because the process worked.

Problems

Growth has brought technical problems. The IP address space has only 32 bits, and is partitioned into network and host parts in a rather complicated manner. The number of connected networks in the Internet was about 7500 in January 1992, and had about the same exponential growth rate as for hosts worldwide. Technical work is underway to allocate network addresses more efficiently, but the whole address space is still going to be exhausted in a few years. There are ways to work around this limitation without every implementation of TCP/IP having to change, but it is still a problem. Similarly, more networks mean harder routing, and new routing algorithms are being developed. And network speeds are increasing dramatically. The ARPANET had 56Kbps links; 1.544Mbps is common now, and 45Mbps is also used. Gigabit speeds are expected in a few years. This introduces software efficiency problems, which have mostly already been dealt with for TCP, and packet size and round trip latency problems, which are being studied.

The exponential growth of the Internet caused a sudden jump between 1988 and 1991 in the number of attendees at IETF meetings, from around fifty to about four hundred. And the Internet is no longer used only by researchers, academics, and government employees. Many IETF attendees are no longer well versed in what has gone before, and some of them are more interested in marketing than in technical development.

This is very similar to what happened to TCOS meetings about two years earlier. In both cases, the sponsoring organizations had to start levying meeting attendance fees. Even $100 per attendee per meeting for 400 attendees is $40,000 quarterly, which is enough money to require accountability. IETF hasn't reached TCOS levels of cash flow, but both groups have had to promulgate more formal procedures. Fiscal accountability is still a minor point for the IAB. The primary motivating factor is standards decision making capability. If they make the wrong decision, and it looks unfair, a vendor might sue. The IAB considers process more important than meeting logistics as a motivating factor for procedures. It will be interesting to see whether they can keep these things separate.

The IAB insists on change control over documents used in its Standards Track. It does not insist on actually inventing every protocol that becomes an Internet Standard, but it does insist that such protocols not be proprietary, (i.e., controlled by someone else). This makes it difficult for commercially specified software to become an Internet Standard even if it has already become a de facto standard.

We can see this in the case of the rlogin remote login protocol, which was developed by UCB CSRG and commercialized by various vendors. Almost every UNIX vendor with TCP/IP has it, but it is only now being integrated into the TEL-NET protocol. The usual reason given for this is that rlogin was never documented. Some say it was never documented because it would not be accepted anyway. We can call this ancient history.

A more recent situation involves two candidates for an Internet standard transparent file access protocol: *NFS (Network File System)* from Sun and *AFS*

(Andrew File System) from CMU and Transarc. NFS is documented in an Informational RFC [Sun 1989]. But it is dubious that either NFS or RFS will ever become an Internet Standard. There is an IETF working group on distributed file systems, but it seldom meets.

The Internet community suffers from *NIH (Not Invented Here)* syndrome just as much as does any other community. The TCP/IP protocol suite is quite functional from the transport layer down. The applications it has are rather robust, but haven't changed much in many years. For example, there is no standard way to handle mailing lists, and software to automatically add and remove subscribers at their own request is not widespread. Internet mailing lists often involve redistribution points and nested lists, which cause many maintenance problems [Westine & Postel 1991]. In addition, there are a number of ad hoc ways to retrieve messages from archives of mailing lists, but no standard. Yet BITNET has had a single way of doing both those things for years: LISTSERV. LISTSERV is not only widely available throughout BITNET, but the nodes that run it are also linked together in a LISTSERV service network, so that someone wanting to use a LISTSERV needs only to use the closest one, and redistribution is handled automatically.

The Internet community seems to feel that the existence of several partial UNIX implementations of LISTSERV lookalikes solves the problem for the Internet. Even though the implementations are partial, they are not documented in any RFC, the nodes running them are not linked together in a BITNET LISTSERV-style service network, and there is no standard for what they should do. Reasons given in public forums for why the Internet doesn't need LISTSERV have also included these: we already have mailing lists (despite the problems mentioned); we already have newsgroups (but they don't provide privacy and they can't reach as far); and even we already have FTP (which doesn't have anything like the sophisticated retrieval mechanisms of LISTSERV). Others feel that all that is missing is a specification, and the rest will follow automatically.

None of these problems were tolerated for mail, nameservice, file transfer, or any of the other basic Internet applications. Yet the Internet community, and the IETF in particular, depends heavily on mailing lists, and suffers from the lack of facilities and standards for handling them. One conclusion is that nothing like LISTSERV exists in the Internet because that would require admitting that BITNET had something better first. Another view is that this mailing list situation is a symptom of the more general problem of the lack of application protocols and services in the Internet, or at least the lack of integrated services that are usable and maintainable by nonexperts. This seems to be slowly changing. Perhaps the increasing involvement of industry, in such projects as EINet [MCC 1991], will accelerate the development of more usable applications on the Internet. In a less monolithic approach, many network service providers are trying to reach lower end user communities, including libraries, elementary schools, and ordinary private individuals. Such users are interested in usable applications, not protocols, so new applications may result.

8.4   The Internet

To describe standardization of the TCP/IP protocols, it is important to distinguish them from the worldwide Internet built out of them [Quarterman 1990]. The Internet was expected to have about ten million users by the end of 1992, and is the largest electronic network of any kind in the world, except for the telephone system. If you can FTP to nis.merit.edu, nic.ddn.mil, ftp.psi.com, or ftp.uu.net, you are on the Internet. (If you can FTP to some but not others of those hosts, you are on one of several subsets of the Internet, but that is a long, political, and separate story [Quarterman 1991c].) The *Internet* is an internet, which is a network of networks. All the networks in the Internet use the *Internet Protocol (IP)* and are interconnected for end-to-end interactive information interchange. The Internet now also includes major parts that support CNLP (the OSI connectionless network internet protocol). Nonetheless, direct interactive connectivity is necessary to be part of the Internet.

The Matrix

The Internet is often confused with the worldwide Matrix of all interconnected computer networks that exchange electronic mail or news. The Internet is the largest and fastest-growing network in the Matrix, but it is not the Matrix, which also includes USENET, UUCP, FidoNet, BITNET, thousands of enterprise IP networks within corporations, and numerous other entities [Quarterman 1992].

DNS: The Domain Name System

The Internet is even more often confused with all hosts and networks that use the Internet *DNS (Domain Name Service),* which defines and implements domain names like tic.com, so that mail to addresses like jsq@tic.com works. DNS is primarily intended to map domain names to IP addresses (with DNS A records), for use by machines that are directly connected to the Internet. However, DNS can also support domain names for machines that are not on the Internet. For such a machine, DNS can provide an IP address of a mail forwarder that is on the Internet and that knows how to reach the machine that is not on the Internet. DNS *MX (Mail Exchange)* records are used for this purpose. DNS names are widely used on UUCP, BITNET, FidoNet, and other networks. One name for all such hosts that use DNS names for their hosts and the interchange mail is the DNS Mail System. The DNS Mail System is that is closely related to the Internet, but it is not the Internet. It is larger, and many of the hosts on it cannot provide Internet services such as FTP for file transfer or TELNET for remote login.

The ARPANET

Long before the Internet, there was the ARPANET (1969–1990, R.I.P.). The ARPANET was created by the United States *Defense Advanced Research Projects Agency (DARPA)* (formerly known as ARPA) as an experiment in and platform for research in packet switched networking.

Internet History

The proper name, the *Internet,* was first applied to a research program in 1973, and an implemented system involving four networks was demonstrated as early as 1977, including packet satellite, packet radio, ARPANET, and an Ethernet at XEROX [Cerf 1992]. DARPA created the nonexperimental Internet in January 1983, when it simultaneously mandated the split of the original ARPANET into ARPANET and MILNET, and required the use of TCP/IP instead of earlier protocols throughout what was then called the ARPA Internet. There were originally two transcontinental national backbones in the Internet: ARPANET and MILNET. Other backbones were added by other government agencies such as the *National Aeronautics and Space Administration (NASA).* The name of this composite internet changed with the growing participation of other government agencies, from ARPA Internet (and then DARPA Internet) to Federal Research Internet, to TCP/IP Internet, and to its current name of just the Internet.

The Internet is run by a federation of organizations, each with its own operational arm. Policy for the Internet moved from DARPA to a succession of committees of government agencies. More recently, the *National Science Foundation (NSF)* has taken a leading role in setting policy for the Internet in the United States, partly due to its funding for NSFNET, which is another major transcontinental backbone network in the U.S. Internet. Each of the major federal agency or departmental networks have their own usage and other policies set by their sponsoring organizations. DARPA, *DOE (Department of Energy),* NASA, *NIH (National Institutes of Health),* and NSF participate in the *Federal Networking Council (FNC),* which is the coordinating body for Internet related issues in the Federal government.

NSFNET is the most prominent of the backbones with policies set by the government because about a dozen regional networks connect to it, and thousands of more local networks at companies, universities, and agencies connect to the regionals. There are now several other national backbones, such as PSINet, Alter-Net, and ANSnet, most of which are not run by the government. Other backbones, such as EBONE in Europe or WIDE in Japan, may or may not be related to national or international governments, but are certainly not controlled by the U.S. government. Even NSFNET is a derived service [Cerf 1992] of ANSnet. NSF is just one of several U.S. government agencies currently involved in the Internet.

The Internet itself has grown far beyond the U.S. government, or any government. Most of it consists of thousands of local, metropolitan, state or provincial, regional and national networks owned and operated by a very diverse array of corporations, universities, networking companies, nongovernmental organizations, and governments. In some regions, there are coordinating bodies, such as *RIPE (Reseaux IP Européens)* in Europe; RIPE is now formally a part of *RARE (Réseaux Associés pour la Recerche Européenne),* which is itself affiliated with the *European Commission (EC).* In some countries, there is a national governmental lead organization, such as for CA*net in Canada. But no single organization, or even set of organizations, has overall responsibility for the worldwide Internet.

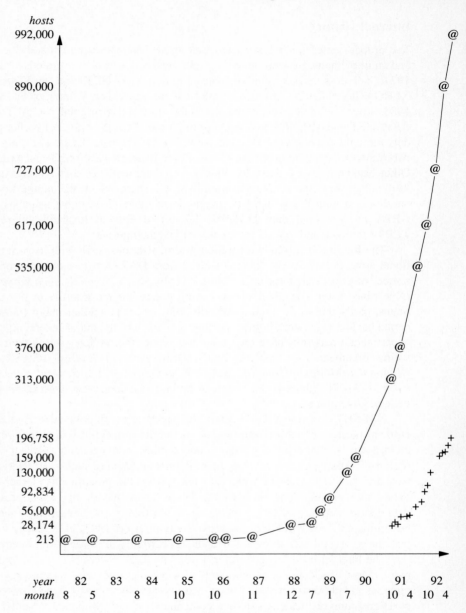

@ Worldwide (see RFC 1296), by Mark Lottor <mkl@nisc.sri.com>.
+ Europe, for RIPE (see RFC 1181), by Marten Terpstra <terpstra@ripe.net>.

Figure 8.3 Internet hosts, worldwide and in Europe.
From Quarterman, "Sizes of Four Networks in the Matrix," Matrix News, *Vol. 2, No. 2, Matrix, Inc., Austin, mids@tic.com, July 1992. Copyright © 1992 MIDS. Reprinted with permission.*

Internet Growth

Starting about 1986, the size of the Internet has been more than doubling every year, and promises to continue doing so for quite a while. The approximate numbers of hosts on the Internet from 1981 to 1991 is shown in Fig. 8.3 [Lottor 1992]. The numbers shown for dates since late 1986 were produced by walking the DNS domain tree over the Internet. They exclude domains with only *MX (Mail Exchange)* records. Domains included have associated IP addresses. Whether they are actually directly connected to the Internet is not known (that would require actually attempting to exchange traffic with each host). But it is reasonable to assume that almost all of them are. There are anomalies such as compuserve.com, which is one domain for CompuServe that serves a few hundred thousand users. And there are enterprise IP networks like the HP Internet that do not use DNS, but are also not directly and interactively connected to the Internet. Neither CompuServe nor the HP Internet are properly part of the Internet [Quarterman 1991c]. So these numbers are probably reasonably accurate for the size of the Internet.

The number estimated for January 1992 was 727,000 hosts. Given a factor of 5 to 10 users per host (plausible in an era of more PCs, workstations, and file-servers than large timesharing machines), that means something like 3.5 to 7 million Internet and DNS users, worldwide, which is consistent with estimates from other sources and methods [Partridge 1991]. Call it 5 million, and doubling each year or less. That means 10 million by January 1993, 160 million by 1997, and 5 billion by 2002. Such growth has to slow down eventually, but there's no sign that it will for several years yet. There are not 5 million computer scientists in the world; the technology has spread to a much wider community.

The TCP/IP protocols and the Internet built from them mostly began in the United States, but have not been limited to one country for a long time. Norway and England were connected from the earliest days of IP development. Much technical input for IP and TCP came from France and the United Kingdom. For example, the original TCP retransmission algorithm was known as the *RSRE (Royal Signals and Radar Establishment)* algorithm for the organization of the people in the United Kingdom who developed it [Partridge 1992].

8.5   The IAB Standards Process

The TCP/IP protocols have historically been specified and implemented without much formality. The IAB and IETF see that informality as a major factor in the success of the protocols. Yet, because there are many more people participating in creating TCP/IP protocols and still more involved in implementing and using those protocols; IAB and IETF see a need for more formal, or at least more codified, processes. They are modifying and codifying the historical process carefully, to avoid killing the spirit of it.

This section describes the current state of the IAB standardization process. There are necessarily divergent opinions, due to the current state of flux. For some technical or political points, several such opinions are described.

So far as we know, this is the first published in-depth examination of the current processes used by these bodies. For that reason, it is worth reemphasizing that this book is not the official source for procedures for any standardization process. In the case of TCP/IP standardization, the IAB document about the Internet Standards Process [Chapin 1992b] is an attempt by the IAB and IESG "to describe the procedures as we now understand them" [Cerf 1992]. "The Internet evolves, and the procedures evolve" [Postel 1992a]. This book describes some aspects of those procedures that are not documented in any RFCs. Current practice by the IAB, IESG, and IETF may differ from the book.

Costs

The minimum cost of producing a standard through the IAB process is at least $100,000 for relatively trivial standards, is more usually about $250,000 to $500,000, and often is $1 million or more. The values in Table 8.1 are for time spent in various phases of IETF work, including time spent at meetings and time spent elsewhere [Crocker 1992]. The IESG and IAB have to approve each specification for each of the three standardization steps of Proposed Standard, Draft Standard, and Internet Standard, so the totals include a factor of 3 over the IESG and IAB numbers. Let's say 1 year for completion and $220,000 for the average working group, and approximately 60 working groups. That's $13.2 million

Table 8.1 IAB standardization costs.

	Staff * Time (in staff months)		
Phase	**Simple**	**Usual**	**Complex**
Development	1	2 * 6	5 * 12
Review	10 * 1	10 * 1	20 * 1
Proposed			
IESG	0.5	1	1
IAB	0.25	0.5	1
Draft			
IESG	0.5	1	1
IAB	0.25	0.5	1
Standard			
IESG	0.5	1	1
IAB	0.25	0.5	1
Totals	13.25	26.5	86
Cost	$110,416	$220,833	$716,666

dollars per year in time alone. Table 8.1 shows only time, not meeting logistical expenses or travel costs. Three IETF meetings per year and about 400 attendees at each would account for about $2.25 million in travel expenses. We don't know how much CNRI handles in meeting money, but let's guess $150 for each of 400 attendees three times per year, or $156,000. The total then would be about $15 million per year.

These costs are supported by the volunteers who do the work, or the organizations they work for. Several U.S. government departments or agencies subsidize the operation by CNRI of an IETF secretariat, and the cost of some IAB functions. These departments and agencies are *DOE (Department of Energy), DARPA (Defense Advanced Research Projects Agency),* which is part of the *DoD (Department of Defense), NASA (National Aeronautics and Space Administration),* and *NSF (National Science Foundation).* But the standardization activities of IAB and IETF, like TCOS, are primarily funded by participants [Cerf 1992].

These figures are very loosely derived, but they are clearly in the same general cost range as for TCOS standards, as explained in Chapter 7. An Internet Standard probably costs less to make than an average TCOS standard. There are twice as many IETF projects as TCOS projects, so if the total annual figures are approximately equal, the average IETF project would cost half as much as the average TCOS project, per year. Reasons for this difference might include greater IETF use of electronic media, smaller tasks, or simpler procedures; we don't know for sure. Some say that all the real IETF work is done by electronic mail, so the IAB process may be more expensive than is indicated here.

Since the IAB limits the IAB standardization process to two years, and TCOS standards often take four years or even more, a TCOS standard could cost quite a bit more than an IAB standard. However, the two year IAB limit is slightly misleading, since a project may be set back to the beginning, or may split into several, just like a TCOS project that fails a ballot or is split into several projects. Generally, it seems clear that the IAB and TCOS processes have costs on the same order of magnitude, but the IAB process is less expensive per project, and perhaps less expensive overall.

RFC: Request for Comments

Any IETF document is normally published online as an *RFC (Request for Comments).* That acronym originated in the early days of the ARPANET when members of the group designing and implementing the ARPANET protocols (the ARPANET Network Working Group) published RFCs to ask for input from one another and from others. The RFC series of documents contains a wide variety of material, from network demographic surveys to poetry. Many important protocols related to distributed computing are codified in RFCs. For example, the *Simple Network Management Protocol (SNMP)* is RFC 1157.

Not all RFCs are standards. But all Internet standards are RFCs. Each *Internet Standard* is named in an RFC, "IAB Offical Protocol Standards" [Postel 1992b], also known as STD 1. SNMP is an Internet Standard, for example. Internet Standards usually originate with the IETF. Work produced by the IRTF that should become an Internet Standard is first funneled through the IESG, and then into an IETF Working Group (usually formed for the purpose) once the work is ready for the IAB Standards Track [Cerf 1992]. The recent *PEM (Privacy Enhanced Mail)* work originated in the IRTF Privacy and Security Research Group, for example. Protocols from outside sources can become Internet Standards, but they have to be sponsored by an IESG Area Director or the IESG Chair, or submitted to a working group.

Essentially, anyone can submit a document for standardization. The constituency of the submittor may affect how the document is dealt with. For example, the IAB consists of technically and politically knowledgeable people, so a document originating with the IAB would probably have an easier time getting through the process. This has been called "rule by credibility" [Crocker 1992].

There is an RFC Editor, who is a member of the IAB. Informational and Experimental RFCs (see below for definitions of these terms) are published at the discretion of the RFC Editor, except for RFCs originating with the IAB, all of which are always published. RFCs on their way to becoming standards require decisions by the IAB before being published. Otherwise, almost anything that is not libelous or dangerous can be published as an RFC, and the RFC Editor takes a permissive approach to publication.

Attempts are made to coordinate with IETF Working Groups. If a draft RFC intersects with a draft in progress by an IETF Working Group, the RFC Editor will encourage the WG to incorporate the new draft somehow. The author of the new document may insist on separate publication anyway, and in that case will usually get it, but it may not wind up on the Standards Track [Cerf 1992].

Historically, collections of RFCs have been issued in paper volumes by organizations associated with RFC publication, but paper is not the normal means of publication of an RFC. Publishing an RFC means putting it on about half a dozen Internet hosts scattered around the world. These hosts make RFCs available by file transfer using anonymous FTP. Some of them also make RFCs available through electronic mail, in automatic response to an electronic mail request. Others provide access to RFCs through AFS, NFS, or other means. The RFC editor announces availability of a new RFC by electronic mail to an online mailing list of interested parties. Details on how to get an RFC may be found in Appendix A.

There is no consensus within the Internet community as to who is the publisher of RFCs for purposes of bibliographic citation. At least one organization distributes paper copies: *SRI (SRI International)*. SRI publishes a six volume set called the *Internet Technology Handbook*, containing RFCs and related material [Cerf 1991]. SRI also publishes a CD/ROM with all the RFCs and various related documents and software [SRI 1992].

USC-ISI (University of Southern California, Information Sciences Institute) is the location of the master online RFC database and of the RFC Editor, and the RFC Editor is considered the online publisher of record.

Multiplicity and distribution of publication is a feature of this publication series. Since bibliographic formats for books were not evolved to deal with it, we have chosen a single organization to cite: SRI. ISOC apparently plans to become the publisher of record.

Internet Draft

There is another online series of documents, also available from a number of well-known Internet hosts scattered around the world. These are Internet Drafts. A document intended to be an RFC will often first be put online as an Internet Draft. However, the IAB does not consider the Internet Draft series to be "archival" publications [Cerf 1992]. They think of that series instead as volatile storage for access to working documents. When a version of an Internet Draft is published as an RFC, it is removed from being available as an Internet Draft. These documents may be withdrawn for other reasons, such as their authors deciding they have served their purposes. An Internet Draft is always removed after six months.

Internet Drafts are not archived: when they are removed from their normal means of accessibility, they are deliberately thrown away. This is quite different from the usual methods of other standards bodies, which normally number and keep large numbers of working documents at least during the lifespan of the corresponding working group. (Some formal standards bodies, such as X3, mandate the destruction of working notes after a standard is completed, to avoid any possibility of lawsuits against individual members.) There are apparently no plans to make previous Internet Drafts available to historians, or even to later implementers of Internet Standards that succeed them. There is a backup archive at CNRI, but it is not intended for online access.

States and Statuses

Internet Standards follow the IAB Standards Track from Proposed Standard to Draft Standard to Internet Standard [Chapin 1992b; Postel 1992b], although some early specifications were grandfathered to standards status when the current procedures were defined. This is similar to many other standards processes, such as the ISO process, with its states of Committee Draft, Draft International Standard, and International Standard. But this IAB Standards Track also has an applicability status or requirement level, in addition to the standardization state dimension. This leads to a two-dimensional standards track, as shown in Fig. 8.4.

The states on the IAB Standards Track are Proposed Standard, Draft Standard, and Internet Standard. The goal for a protocol on the IAB Standards Track is to become an Internet Standard. A protocol first enters the Standards Track as a Proposed Standard. It normally moves to Draft Standard, and finally to Internet Standard, where it stays indefinitely until it is superseded by a later protocol or is otherwise retired. Protocols on the IAB Standards Track are intended for eventual operational use in the worldwide Internet. For this reason, IAB standardization has a very strong emphasis on implementation and testing by actual interoperation with other implementations, preferably on existing networks, where feasible. A Proposed Standard needs implementation by and interoperability testing between at least two groups before it is likely to be promoted to be a Draft Standard. A Draft Standard needs widespread testing, some operational experience, and widespread comment before it can be promoted to be an Internet Standard. This might seem likely to be a slower path than for anticipatory standards, but in general that does not seem to be the case.

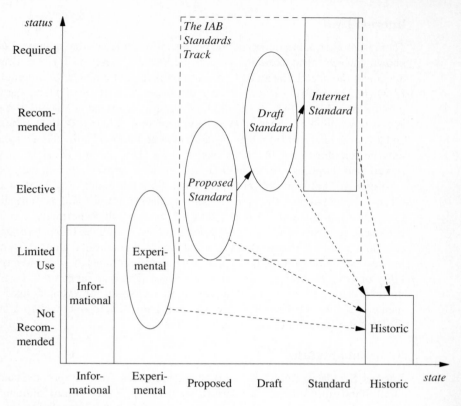

Figure 8.4 IAB Standards Track.

There are other, offtrack, states. A protocol whose time has passed may be reclassified as Historic, whether or not it has ever become a standard. Two states, called Informational and Experimental, are for protocols that are not intended for the Standards Track.

The Informational, Internet Standard, and Historic states (shown as boxes in Fig. 8.4) are permanent; the others (shown as ellipses) are temporary. Classification of a protocol as a Proposed, Draft, or Internet Standard requires a recommendation from the IESG and approval by the IAB. As already mentioned, the RFC Editor may at discretion publish Informational or Experimental RFCs. A protocol may enter the final Historic state from any of the other states. This is normally done with IESG recommendation and IAB approval, and usually applies only to those protocols that were widely used or were Internet Standards.

The requirement levels are, from highest to lowest, Required, Recommended, Elective, Limited Use, and Not Recommended. A protocol is more likely to be higher on this status scale the further along it is in standardization state. There are very few Required protocols, and not many Recommended ones. Most are Elective.

At one time, the status of a protocol was kept in the protocol specification document. Currently, status information is kept in a related RFC called "IAB Official Protocol Standards." That document is reissued frequently as a new RFC, with a new number, so depending on knowing the current RFC number for it is usually a mistake [Postel 1992b]. There is a new series of Internet Standard numbers, partly to simplify this problem; STD 1 is always the official protocol document, regardless of its current RFC number [Cerf 1992]. Assigning statuses in a separate status document avoids the need to reissue a protocol specification or other document as a new RFC just to change its status.

The requirement level of a protocol is increasingly context dependent. An RFC may also be assigned a status, or a set of statuses for various uses, by another document called an *AS (Applicability Statement)*. The most general ASes are the Requirements Documents, of which there are currently two: for hosts, and for routers. An AS is basically a profile, and we will describe such AS RFCs later, when we discuss profiles.

Offtrack States

The three states off the Standards Track are nonetheless important. Let's describe them first, so that it will be clear what they are for and why they are not on the Standards Track. According to one interpretation of the most current IAB standardization procedures, neither Informational nor Experimental RFCs have statuses [Chapin 1992a].

• Informational protocols are usually taken from some other source, such as OSI or a vendor's proprietary protocol suite. This state, unlike the others, is also used for documents that do not describe protocols. Informational RFCs can describe procedures, practices, or perspectives. It is possible for an Informational RFC to become Experimental, but that is not the usual case. The only statuses permitted to Informational RFCs are Limited Use and Not Recommended. But an AS may reference an Informational RFC and make the Informational RFC mandatory. This is how the IAB adopts specifications from outside sources without requiring that the original sponsoring body assign change control to the IAB: the IAB instead controls an Informational RFC that specifies a snapshot of the outside specification [Cerf 1992].

• An Experimental protocol is usually just that: a protocol for which its author, the RFC Editor, or the IAB thinks experimentation is appropriate. An Experimental protocol may not be intended ever to see operational use. An Experimental protocol is intended to be of interest to, and to be used by, the participants in the experiment [Chapin 1992a]. The Experimental state is not normally on a path to the Proposed Standard state. However, a specification that might otherwise be a candidate for Proposed might instead go to Experimental if there is a view that the technology is not well understood or the user constituency is not well established. Yet Experimental is not a consolation prize. If it's a good idea and the IESG or IAB doesn't understand it well enough, they believe that the appropriate action is to find a way to understand it better. If the protocol is really experimental, it should go to the Experimental state, for experiments. In addition to experimenting with the technology itself, that can include getting people to use it to see whether they want it. In other words, the IETF does not only development but also popularization. An Experimental protocol can have Elective, Limited Use, or Not Recommended status.

• The idea of a Prototype state has recently been introduced for a protocol slightly different from an Experimental one. A Prototype is intended for eventual production use, and is not a research experiment, whereas an Experimental protocol is not intended (or at least not ready) for moving into any production track [Cerf 1992].

• The Historic state is one of the few IAB concessions to history. It is for protocols that are no longer (or never were) recommended for operational use. A protocol may move into the Historic state from any other state. The IAB is aware that the name of this state, grammatically, should be Historical, but they have chosen to retain the spelling Historic for historical reasons: that's what it has always been called. Historic protocols may have only a status of Not Recommended.

A good example of a specification made into an Informational RFC so that it could be referenced by other RFCs is MD4, currently documented in RFC 1320 [Rivest 1992]. MD4 is message digest algorithm that uses encryption to produce a 128 bit "fingerprint" of an arbitrary length message. It was wanted for use in security protocols. This algorithm had apparently been published previously only as an internal memo, and the RFC cites no previous references. Many in the Internet community prefer documents that are easy to obtain, and there are few things more easy to obtain than an RFC. IEEE standards are apparently considered easy enough to get that it's not necessary to make them into RFCs before referencing.

The document that specifies the IAB standards process [Chapin 1992b] is not a standard, and gives its own status as an "informational memo." But Informational RFCs can have at most Limited Use requirement status. There appears to be a bootstrapping problem. Of course, none of the RFCs have legal standing, and any IAB policy suggestions have been nonstandards track documents. Perhaps this particular document will become associated with an agreement between ISOC and IAB about standards processes [Cerf 1992]. Such an outcome is considered very likely by some [Chapin 1992a].

The IAB Standards Track

To enter the Standards Track as a Proposed Standard, a protocol must have a good specification. To become a Draft Standard, the protocol specification must be implemented and tested by more than one organization. To become an Internet Standard, the protocol specified must be stable and must see actual use. Let's examine these three states of the Standards Track in detail, together with some interesting features of how a specification progresses through them. Although we have indicated status ranges for each of these states, only an Internet Standard normally has a fixed status. The status of a specification is given in the separate "IAB Official Protocol Standards" document [Postel 1992b], or in an *Applicability Statement (AS)*. A protocol specification is called a *Technical Specification (TS)*. Either a TS or an AS may be any of Proposed Standard, Draft Standard, or Internet Standard. We will discuss the difference between a TS and an AS further under Profiles.

- To become a Proposed Standard, a specification should be stable technically and should have no known bugs or holes. For example, a basic algorithm cannot be left for later selection. There should be sufficient community interest to predict or suggest community usage. If the nature of the specification is sufficiently complicated to be hard to understand, or if the specification has an important effect on technical infrastructure, the IESG (or IAB) can require that the specification first be implemented and tested. An example of a specification with effects on technical infrastructure would be a modification to IP. Exactly how many implementations might be required is an open question. Functionality may not be added once a specification becomes a Proposed Standard. A hole (a missing ancillary function) may be split into a separate specification; this is what TCOS would call an extension. Otherwise, a standard that has reached Proposed state should only be debugged in that state: anything else requires reentering the Standards Track with a new specification. A protocol must stay in Proposed state for a minimum of six months. A Proposed Standard will not normally have Required status, and usually does not have a status lower than Limited Use.

- To become a Draft Standard, a protocol must have at least two independent and interoperable implementations that test all specified functions. There is no conformance certification. A protocol must stay in this state for a minimum of four months before being promoted to become an Internet Standard. A Draft Standard can be Required, and usually has no status lower than Elective.

- Full standards in the IAB Standards Track are called Internet Standards. To reach this state, a protocol must have had significant field use and there must be clear community interest in production use. There is no limit on the time a protocol may remain in this state. There is no mandatory review after a preset period; in fact, there is no mandatory review at all. An Internet Standard can have any status from Elective to Required, and does not normally have any lower status.

The minimim time for a specification to reach Internet Standard status is ten months. A protocol specification may take a maximum of 24 months from entering the Standards Track as a Proposed Standard to becoming an Internet Standard. After this time, it will be "reviewed for viability."

A protocol may fail to progress in the standards track. It does not then become Experimental, since that state is for experiments. If a document fails to pass its review after its timeout period has elapsed, it gets decommissioned. This can mean that its working group gets canceled. The IESG or IAB can do this, and sometimes working groups dissolve themselves. The status of the document then changes, possibly to Historic, in the next revision of the Official Protocols RFC.

A protocol specification already on the Standards Track may undergo significant or destabilizing changes, rendering it incompatible with previous versions. In this case, the status of the protocol will probably be moved back to Proposed Standard. The original RFC specification document will be decommissioned. This does not normally mean that it will be reclassified as Historic, as mentioned earlier, since that state is usually reserved for protocols that actually became Internet Standards and were later retired. An Internet Standard that saw widespread use may be reclassified as Historic according to the judgment of either the IAB or the RFC Editor [Chapin 1992a].

When an RFC is decommissioned with the intent of its protocol being put back into the Standards Track, a new RFC will be issued and assigned a status of Proposed Standard. Even though the new RFC may have the identical text of the RFC that has been retired from the Standards Track, the new RFC is treated as a new specification entering the Standards Track. All the timeouts start over for this new specification. A recent example is *PPP (Point-to-Point Protocol)*. The original PPP specification did not become Historic. It is simply marked in the RFC index as "superseded" by the new RFC.

Looking at it as a protocol, it moves backwards. Looking at it as a specification document, the old one retires and a new one enters the process. This distinction is probably not of interest to the end user, but is important for those involved in the standardization process. For example, consider an FTP revision that supports the same user functionality as an old FTP version, yet uses a different protocol over the network. Most people would consider this to be the same protocol, but it has two different specifications. The new version must start as a Proposed Standard if it is ready for the Standards Track, or it may be given a status of Experimental.

The specification for an old version of a protocol may remain an Internet Standard while a new version moves through the Standards Track. When the new version becomes an Internet Standard, what happens to the old version depends on the nature of the new protocol revision. There may be a switchover, or a transition in which both protocols are used for a period of time. This is an operational decision, but the standards process can help support either mode. For example, if the new protocol specification is a strict superset of the old, the old specification may be reclassifed as Historic on the same day that the new protocol becomes an Internet Standard.

Sometimes precision is avoided in Internet Standards to encourage human input. The Internet process has succeeded because of individual effort, and the roles and skills and integrity of the people involved in the effort are essential. Above all, interoperating protocols and systems are more important than formalities. A common phrase (attributed to David Clark) used to sum up the intent of the IETF and IAB is "rough consensus and working code."

Table 8.2 Applicability Statements and profiles.

IAB	TCOS
Technical Specification (TS)	Base Standard
Applicability Statement (AS)	Profile
AS for restricted domain of applicability	Application Environment Profile
Requirements Document (comprehensive conformance specification)	Platform Profile
Official Protocol Standards	Model

Profiles

The word *profile* is never used in any IAB standardization documents. This is apparently because the IAB and IETF invented the concept independently of ISO, TCOS, or other bodies, and invented new terminology with it. There are IAB standardization terms that are strikingly similar in their meanings to profiling terms defined by SGFS [SGFS 1990], EWOS [EWOS 1991], and TCOS [POSIX.0 1991]. The basic terms are listed in Table 8.2 [Chapin 1992b]. The term *Technical Specification (TS)* is very similar to a base standard. An *Applicability Statement (AS)*, is much like a profile or functional specification. There is an AS for a restricted domain of applicability, which is very like an *AEP (Application Environment Profile)*. A Requirements Document is essentially a platform profile. The IAB does not consider these subtypes of ASes to be anything more than clarification of what an AS is. But the way the IAB terms parallel the TCOS terms is quite striking.

There are also differences in emphases. An AEP usually coordinates APIs for application portability, whereas an AS coordinates protocols. But the protocols required by an AS may be used in building an application environment. Also, many (if not most) TCOS AEPs include requirements for network protocols. Similarly, a TCOS platform profile may be more general than a Requirements Document, because the platform profile includes many APIs. But a host that uses TCP/IP needs the protocols specified in the "Host Requirements" documents for interoperability, and to serve as a platform for use of other protocols, and for portable applications, particularly distributed applications.

Profiling is actually not new in Internet protocols. As a trivial example, *RFC 1036,* which specifies the format for USENET articles, draws on *RFC 822,* which specifies the format for Internet mail messages. RFC 822 permits several variant syntaxes for the format of the From: header. RFC 1036 permits only one of them. However, the term AS and its applications are new in Internet Standards.

A *Requirements Specification* is a platform profile. It can incorporate by reference, amend, correct, or supplement the primary protocol standards documents. For each protocol, this kind of AS provides an explicit set of requirements, recommendations, and options. Two Requirements Specifications are currently kept up to date: "Host Requirements" (actually a pair of RFCs) [Braden 1989a; Braden 1989b]. and "Requirements for IP Routers" (a single document) [Braden & Postel 1987].

The closest thing to IEEE 1003.0, the POSIX Guide, with its reference model, may be the "IAB Official Protocol Standards" RFC [Postel 1992b], which is periodically updated with a new RFC number, but the current RFC is always also known as STD 1. It categorizes all the published Internet protocol specifications, with indications of their standardization state and applicability status. It also includes some contextual information about the Standards Track, and some access information.

Any AS (platform profile) may assign a requirement level status to a TS (base standard). This "IAB Official Protocol Standards" Requirements Specification gives statuses for every RFC on the Standards Track (and most others). It makes *IP (Internet Protocol)* and *ICMP (Internet Control Message Protocol)* Required, for example. That is, any implementation of the Internet protocols must include both IP and ICMP. Even though the protocol suite is usually called TCP/IP, *TCP (Transmission Control Protocol)* is not Required, presumably because many useful applications use the other transport protocol, *UDP (User Datagram Protocol)*, instead. TCP and UDP are Recommended, like most of the standard application procotols, such as TELNET, FTP, and SMTP. Any real login host or server implementation of TCP/IP will include all of these. Any real router implementation will also include several Recommended routing and management protocols.

There is also an RFC called "Assigned Numbers" that lists all assigned protocol numbers, port service numbers, and other parameters needed for actual operation of Internet protocols [Reynolds & Postel 1990]. This RFC is constantly updated and reissued: do not depend on knowing the correct RFC number. The numbers in this RFC are assigned by an *IANA (Internet Assigned Numbers Authority)*, commonly known as the *Number Czar.* This document corresponds more to implementations than to interfaces. However, the minimum requirement to get a transport protocol port number from IANA for an application protocol is a specification describing the protocol that will use it. This specification no longer has to be an RFC, and can require nondisclosure agreements. But the need for a specification often leads protocol implementers into the IAB standards process.

The "Assigned Numbers" RFC may have no equivalent in other standards processes. It could be compared to object registration. It could be considered to be similar to ISO 3166, which records a character name and a three digit number for each country or nationality in the world. Option declaration, as recommended by ISO/IEC JTC 1 TSG-1, is somewhat similar (TSG-1 doesn't require option registration).

There is no requirement that a TS and an AS must be in separate documents. In addition to option and parameter value selection, these documents can subset or extend their base standards. Subsetting and extension of base standards by profiles have been major issues in TCOS and other standards bodies, as discussed in Chapter 12. TCOS and SGFS do not permit a profile to do either of these things.

For a new subset to be introduced into a base standard, the original working group for that base standard must specify an option that the profile can choose. An extension must be specified in a separate document from a profile. There is no discussion of these issues in the documents that spell out the IAB standards process. These subsetting and extension capabilities of ASes appear to be assumed for historical reasons. The router and host Requirement Documents do both subsetting and extensions, for example. One point of view is that one of these requirements documents does these things, it is acting as a TS, and elsewhere it is acting as an AS. Or, to look at it from the other direction, a Requirements Document should be only a set of domain and restrictions statements, and anything else in it is actually a TS. At least one reader thinks this mixing of AS and TS in the same document is needlessly confusing. The important question is how to get two or more systems to actually implement an interoperable set of protocols.

An AS can clarify or revise, since the host and router requirements documents do that. That is, they interpret and extend the original specifications for even such basic standards as IP. The current "Host Requirements" AS interprets and extends many protocols, because the alternative was to modify all the TSes referenced in its predecessor AS documents. The new AS had already taken two years to produce, and this would have delayed it even more [Cerf 1992].

An AS may not have a higher standardization status than any TS to which it applies. That is, an AS with a status of Internet Standard is not permitted to cite an unfinished document, but it can do so when it is a Draft Standard or a Proposed Standard. This draws an interesting analogy with the problems of an ANSI standard (such as a TCOS POSIX document) simultaneously being standardized at the international level. The old definition of a base standard would not permit a document in the international standardization process to reference a national standard, much less a draft national standard. This and related problems led to a new definition of base standard, as discussed in Chapter 12.

There is no explicit discussion of this problem in the IAB standardization documents. Yet an Internet Standard AS cannot reference an unfinished draft IEEE or ISO standard, even though reference to a stable published vendor specification is explicitly permitted. What is wanted is a "fully stable specification." If the specification is on a standards track, it must be a full standard to be considered fully stable. A standards track for this purpose must have public participation, public decision making, and public availability. In practice, this means any of the formal standardization processes used by accredited standards bodies such as ISO or ANSI, or the IAB standards process [Crocker 1992]. These rules are very similar to those recently adopted by the *OSE Implementation Workshop (OIW),* and described in Chapter 5. This leads to the question of whether the OIW process would be considered to be a standards track.

Making an external document into an RFC on the IAB Standards Track is relatively easy. This can be advantageous, because an RFC is considered stable. For example, NFS is specified in an RFC. This wasn't necessary for references by Internet Standards, since there were already appropriate stable and available proprietary specifications for NFS. But Internet Standards old or new (such as secure

NFS) can continue to refer to the NFS RFC even if the proprietary specifications for NFS change [Crocker 1992]. There has been online discussion more recently about incorporating external specifications.

There is no IAB equivalent to the TCOS-SS SEC *PSC (Profile Steering Committee),* which helps the SEC establish guidelines for profiling.

The IETF Development Process

As we have already noted in discussing Fig. 8.1, IETF uses an informal development process, compared to many other standards organizations. The working group chair has a job to get done, and members of working groups are there to help get it done. This is similar to the way CCITT does it, especially in that the chair is the most responsible person. The IETF working group process has more to do with negotiated consensus, called "general consent." Anyone with an objection must be heard, but it is difficult for a single person to block the process.

This approach is similar to the TCOS emphasis on consensus, although perhaps with a bit more emphasis on progress. An IETF working group chair has the gavel, and can attempt to close discussion and recommend a decision by force of position. Unlike in TCOS, there are no formal rules of process to back up the working group chair, and the members can decide not to decide. In addition, since there are no formal rules of membership, there can be no formal votes (straw polls are sometimes taken, but are not binding). However, a working group chair can generally move the process forward.

The IESG has line management responsibility for management of the IETF. Since managers have to make decisions, this generally means that the Area Directors or the IESG as a whole make decisions on creating new projects and on quality control of existing ones, without waiting for approval by the IAB, although they keep the IAB informed. The IESG is not really a policy making group, but it can set precedents in getting its job done. The IAB is the final arbiter, but many things do not go up to the IAB for approval, and don't need to. Most normal operations of the IETF are managed by the IESG.

A request for creation of a new working group actually goes to both the IESG and the IAB, but the IESG often acts to form it without waiting for an opinion from the IAB. Any IAB member may comment or object at any time, and the IAB can then decide.

But the IAB has sole authority over decisions to advance an RFC into the three states of the Standards Track. The IESG recommends such advances, but the IAB must make the actual decision. So, for operations, the IESG acts more like line management, but for standardization state decisions, it acts more like a subcommittee of the IAB.

The IAB does reserve some other decisions to itself. These include creation of new task forces (such as IETF and IRTF), maintenance of formal liaison with other standards groups, and creation of policies on use of other standards, including formal reception of change responsibility for a protocol from a vendor or other standards body [Cerf 1992].

The IAB Internet Standard Adoption Process

The Internet Standard adoption process is much more formal than the IETF development process. There are the stages, criteria, and timeouts that we enumerated when we discussed the Standards Track. However, the final arbiter is the community, not a manual. IAB adoption of an Internet Standard is more by consensus of community than is TCOS standardization. The IAB makes the final decision, after a recommendation by the IESG. But the IESG sends out a "last call" message by electronic mail over a well-known distribution to which anyone may subscribe. The IESG makes its final recommendation after observing responses.

The state changes upwards along the IAB Standards Track are determined solely by recommendation of the IESG and decision of the IAB. There is no balloting group, and there is no ballot involving other people or organizations. However, protocol specifications in each of these states are available for free, in electronic form, over the worldwide Internet itself. The IESG announces a proposed change of state over an electronic mailing list (ietf@isi.edu) that anyone with electronic mail access on the Internet or in the worldwide Matrix of interconnected computer networks may subscribe to. Discussion may be either in an open IETF meeting or by electronic mail, or both. The interval for review is rather short: two weeks. This reflects a desire by the IESG and IAB (and many other participants in the development of the TCP/IP protocols and the Internet) to keep formalities and bureacracies to a miminum, to use the Internet itself for communication and publication, and to get things done quickly.

The IAB tries for consensus even during adoption. The two week period is the final interval before the IESG makes a recommendation to the IAB on an RFC becoming an Internet Standard. The IAB does not consider this a review period; they consider it "last call" and the message sent out to announce it is so labeled. This final interval is a safety net, a catchall, not normally expected to produce problems. It assumes previous opportunities for collaborative review and change, that is, the whole working group sequence and related online discussion [Chapin 1992b]. It is specifically based on an assumption that those with a major interest in a specification will track details in the working group. In other words, if you care a lot, you should be involved, and this is easy due to the online mailing lists and drafts. (Remember that a decision of a working group meeting can be overridden by its online mailing list.)

This approach is radically at variance with the way TCOS-SS works. The first ballot of IEEE 1003.1 failed, partly because of a short balloting interval. More than one more ballot followed, even with thirty day balloting periods. The final standard had changed quite noticably in ballot. IEEE 1003.2 balloted for years. The balloting group for a TCOS standard is normally much larger than and quite different in composition from the working group.

However, making an Internet Standard takes much less time (minimum ten months, maximum two years) than making an ANSI standard by the TCOS-SS process (usually at least about two years; often as many as four, and products often emerge before final standard status is approved). Thus, a specification for an alternative protocol can be put forward to become a Proposed Standard. However, it has no guarantee that it will become one. Opinions on the relative importance of the three Standards Track states vary among IAB and IESG members, but there seems to be a consensus that they each serve a purpose. Entering the Proposed Standard state is a major public event. The intention is to weed out specifications with bad goals or lack of community interest at the start, not the end. Entering Draft Standard state is also a public event, since Proposed state is too early to determine the viability of a protocol, and some of those should fail. The final acquisition of Internet Standard state is also important, since it indicates acceptance of the protocol for operational use. Which state change is the highest hurdle depends somewhat on the protocol being standardized. The IAB prefers to retain flexibility on this.

Objections to IETF working group results and IAB standardization decisions generally fall into two categories:

1. The specification is technically or philosophically unacceptable to the objector.

2. The objector asserts that the specification can't be implemented or won't work correctly.

In the first case, there is probably something wrong with the goal of the specification. The high threshold for entering the Proposed Standard state, with the requirement for a community of interest, is intended to weed out this kind of problem. This is good, and should be listened to, but in the working group.

The second case is a matter of quality control, which is always listened to. The IETF and IAB consider a sudden delay at the end of the process to be bad, because of a desire to make progress. Thus, they are not very sympathetic to any problems a short final review period might cause.

The working group is for goals; the standards track is for tuning. If the final standard is not good, it will not be used, and something else will start through the process. If something useful but not essential was left out, it can be added later. In any case, the IAB is the arbiter of the Internet architecture, and is comfortable in asserting quality control and architectural integration control.

The IAB Appeals Process

Handling of minority views is an interesting phenomenon in the Internet. Such views tend to reflect either a purist concern for a small point, or a fundamental disagreement in approach. There is an appeals process for recourse. It is informal, personal, and very forceful. The parties concerned can go to these arbiters, in order:

• Working Group Chair (generally too close to the issue)

• Area Director

• Standards Area Director

• Chair of IESG

• Members of the IAB (last resort)

All of these tend to bend over backwards to thoroughly investigate any complaint that comes in, even when the complaint is not fully substantiated. An electronic mail message or a verbal complaint is generally enough. The threshold is low enough that there is no need for massive logistical backing to bring a complaint.

There are many opportunities for noting a problem and bringing it to view. Specifications get quite a bit of public review, both online and generally at a plenary session at an IETF meeting. Each standards status change recommendation is announced to the IETF, often at a plenary. Nonetheless, responsibility for detecting a conflict and getting resolution for it falls on the person who raises it. This is a challenge that some people have a hard time adapting to. It is also one reason the people in the line of recourse are responsive to complaints. There doesn't seem to be any other standardization appeals process quite like this, although it is not extremely different from that of, for example, TCOS-SS or IEEE/CS, except perhaps in degree of responsiveness. It is certainly different from the IEEE 802 majority voting method.

Occasionally, an IETF working group will split into two or more fundamentally different camps on a technical issue. The IETF solution is not to try to spend arbitrary time trying to reconcile the two camps, nor to include both solutions in a single specification. It is instead to split the working group. An example of this is *SNMP (Simple Network Management Protocol)* versus *CMOT (Common Management Information Services and Protocol over TCP/IP)* (see Chapter 14.) The two resulting working groups were left to produce their own specifications, with the community to decide among them by using them. To date, SNMP is widely used and CMOT seems to have stalled.

The SNMP versus CMOT debate was actually the case in which IETF learned to split a working group. Until that was done, productive work was stalled for at least a year, perhaps two. There were actually three proposals. The one that later developed into SNMP was called *SGMP (Simple Gateway Management Protocol)*. The proposal that led to CMOT was to use the OSI *CMIP (Common Management Information Protocol)* in the Internet. The third was called *HEMS (High-Level Entity Management System)*. The debate became sufficiently problematical that the IAB convened a special review board to resolve the problem.

HEMS was technically interesting [Partridge 1988; Partridge & Trewitt 1987], and many of its ideas appeared in other protocols, including CMIP. HEMS had actually been commissioned by the IAB, and was judged by the review board to be the best of the three proposals, technically, according to some accounts. But SGMP was simple, was proposed by a group of engineers responsible for line management of some networks in the Internet, and was already relatively widely deployed. And CMIP was OSI, which at the time had the air of inevitability. HEMS had neither the Internet management community support, nor the OSI advantage [Rose 1989, 593–594]. The authors of HEMS withdrew it from consideration for the standard Internet management protocol. They did this to break the lengthy debates [Partridge 1992]. Many consider this to have been an act of statesmanship, and some would even say an extraordinary one. The IAB then decided to have SGMP upgraded slightly to reflect experience gained in network operations, and to have the result become the short term network management solution for the Internet. SNMP was resulting protocol. Meanwhile, the OSI solution was studied and experimented with, in the expectation that it might become the long-term solution [Rose 1989, 593–594].

The IAB made CMOT a standard, in addition to SNMP, in April 1989. This could not have happened under the current IAB standardization rules, because there were no implementations of CMOT. Apparently, all previous Internet standards had had implementation before standardization, even before the recent codification of the standardization rules [Rose 1989, 593–594]. The experience with CNMP and CMOT was one of the most important motivating factors leading the IAB to develop its current standards procedures [Chapin 1992a].

There is sentiment that an impasse like that among the competing network management protocols would be unlikely to happen now, because the IETF learned from that incident [Crocker 1992]. Apparently, there are dissenters from this view, however [Rose 1989, 593–594].

There is a striking similarity to the impasse in IEEE P1201.1 in 1990 and 1991 over choosing between Motif or OpenLook (two *LAFI (Look and Feel Interface) GUI (Graphical User Interface)* specifications). Progress was held up for quite a while, until the working group rejected both. That did not stop the problem, however, since the proponents of the two packages proposed them again at increasingly higher levels of the standardization process until TCOS-SS was apparently finally forced to do something with them anyway. See Chapter 7 for more about these *GUI Wars.*

In a more recent example, Internet mail is seven bit, which is bad for multiple human languages. There are two possible approaches to fixing this:

1. Make the application transport protocol, *SMTP (Simple Mail Transport Protocol),* handle eight bit characters.

2. Extend the mail format, RFC822, to handle eight bits.

Both sides had strong arguments, so two working groups were formed. There is an RFC822 Extensions Working Group, and an SMTP Extensions Working Group.

The basic idea is to not insist on resolving fundamental differences. Try to do so, but if that fails, make two working groups, proceed, and see who the community prefers (both, one, or neither). "The IAB/IETF process really does believe in the free market system" [Crocker 1992]. Given people and a project, they will probably standardize it, and will certainly pursue it. The IETF had about forty meeting attendees at each meeting in 1987, and about 350 in 1991 (530 in March 1992). They feel quite a bit of learning has been done along the way.

8.6   IAB and IETF and TCOS

In detail, the reactions of TCOS and IETF to various problems, such as greatly increased attendance, have been rather different, although they seem to be converging on similar overall solutions.

Rationale and Notes

The TCOS-SS SEC requires each Working Group to develop a Rationale and Notes appendix with each standard. This appendix contains information about base documents, choices made and not made, and other contextual material that helps the interface implementor or application writer determine what the standard is supposed to mean. The IETF has no such requirement, although some such material sometimes appears in any given protocol specification. An IETF working group charter may contain some information on goals, but this is not usually carried through into the specification document, nor are notes added on the rationale for decisions, nor notes on historical background or expected implications. There seems to be a misconception that a request for rationale is a request for excess verbosity in text of the actual normative specification. What is actually needed is additional *nonnormative* text, whether in an appendix or marked in the main document, that *explains* the normative text.

The IAB even requires the removal of drafts after the corresponding protocol is moved elsewhere in the standardization process [Chapin 1992b]. The IAB view is that Internet Drafts are not part of the formal record. It will be interesting to see how well future implementers will understand some Internet Standards after a few years.

Newcomers and Electronic Media

TCOS recognized that there would be many newcomers who would have to be educated, and set up a system for getting paper mailings to whoever wanted them. IETF stoutly resists paper mailings because they want participants who actually use the networks. TCOS has been making increasing use of electronic mailing lists and electronic mail, and even the IEEE Standards Department is now online. Actual IEEE standards are still not available electronically, however, even though the POSIX standards, for example, are all developed online in troff. But TCOS drafts are available online; see Appendix A.

New Projects

The IETF has Area Directors, and their function is much like the Steering Committees the SEC has developed over the last few years. The IESG performs review and recommendation functions much like the SEC PMC, and the IAB has approval authority for new projects and status of existing ones much like that of the SEC.

There are currently about sixty IETF Working Groups, compared to the approximately twenty TCOS-SS Working Groups and thirty or so projects. The

TCOS-SS SEC adopted their PAR Approval Criteria in reaction to the approval of 11 new projects at one SEC meeting. There is no exact IETF equivalent, although there are specific criteria that a Proposed Standard has to meet, with review by the IESG for approval by the IAB. One criterion, operational impact, is evidently more important than the others, since it is also cited as necessary to consider before revising an Internet Standard. But the TCOS Criteria include many practical points, such as a plan of work and a set of objectives, that are not spelled out by the IAB. The IESG apparently recognizes that an arbitrary number of IETF working groups can be a problem, in meeting logistics, tracking progress, costs, and the like. But they consider that, as long as there are adequate constituencies for the output and input of a working group, there will be a reasonable self-selection process.

External Relations

TCOS has an elaborate set of liaisons and interrelations with other bodies. The IAB and IETF have no formal mechanisms for external relations, except for incorporation of standards or vendor specifications produced by other bodies. There is no representative of the IETF on the TCOS *DSSC (Distributed Services Steering Committee)* or the P1003.12 *Protocol Independent Interface (PII)* committee, for example. One reason given for this is that IETF does not generally do API, so PII is irrelevant. Nonetheless, many people writing applications to use TCP/IP protocols will be using PII. The usual purpose of a liaison is to keep an eye on a standards body that is working in an area outside of ones own scope, but that is nonetheless related. There seems to be some concern with the IETF about funding liaisons, but IETF doesn't fund working group chairs, either. There are also no representatives from TCOS to IETF, even though several people attend meetings of both.

The current view of the IETF on using outside specifications is that modifications will be avoided. If modifications are essential, an appropriate IETF working group will do so, but there is an obligation to pursue the change back to the originator. The IAB or IETF may try to set up joint working groups where appropriate, for example, with IEEE or ANSI [Cerf 1992]. "In any area where IETF WGs overlap with other standards bodies, we will attempt as much coordination and integration as possible" [Crocker 1992].

There is a long chain of bodies above the SEC, but there was traditionally no authority higher than the IAB, although the IAB recognized the concept of Internet sponsors, which are mostly governmental agencies funding parts of the network. The IAB is interested in more formal status; see the section on ISOC.

Base Documents and Historical Implementations

Weeding out bad goals at the beginning of projects would not work in general for TCOS-SS (although such weeding has been tried for some working groups that later formed and some that were actually prevented or at least delayed). An IETF working group normally writes its specification from scratch, or starts from a single or set of coordinated sources. A TCOS working group usually starts from multiple base documents representing multiple divergent historical implementations that must be resolved. It is very difficult to predict what the working group will produce, and massive review by a balloting group is appropriate. TCOS-style balloting group issues related to historical implementations usually don't come up in IAB process. Situations like the protracted discussions over job control and process groups during the IEEE 1003.1 ballots, that still ended with an option, not a single decision, do not normally occur during the IETF process. Granted, comparing an interface standard group with a protocol standard group is not entirely fair, but the comparison is still interesting.

However, protection of installed bases produces similar issues, and changes are made in ways as compatible as possible with that. For example, the extensions being made to the RFC 822 mail format will work with an old mail *UA (User Agent)*. The old UA will not be able to display the new enclosures so they will look like they would with a new UA that implements the extensions, but the new enclosures will not break an old UA. Also, the RFC 822 extensions say how to structure the message body using a format that is compatible with the old one. An IETF working group has access to all the specifications for the previous formats (they're in RFCs online), so it can handle backwards compatibility relatively easily. A TCOS working group generally has to seek out such specifications. Also, because IETF deals with networking, implementations must interoperate, and historical implementations of protocols do not tend to diverge as much as do operating system interfaces.

It can happen, even in IETF, although that is quite unusual. For example, the RFC for NETBIOS started with the IBM NETBIOS programmers' manual. Different companies had different implementations. The IETF working group tracked down some of the people who did the implementation (when they worked at Sytek), and got them to comment on why they did things. This would be an argument for keeping notes on the rationale for decisions along with the affected specifications, as TCOS requires.

Internationalization

There is an IETF working group on extensions to the Internet mail format specification, RFC 822 [Crocker 1982]. The original format is very widely used, both throughout the Internet and also on other networks, such as UUCP. One reason it is so widespread is that it is very simple. An RFC 822 mail message is all in plain text in seven bit ASCII. This is fine for American English, but not very useful for other languages, graphics, or binary files. The 822ext Working Group is adding capabilities for such different formats by permitting encapsulation. A header in a message specifies an escape sequence that will be used in the body of the message to surround data in a certain format.

One kind of data that is needed is codesets for other languages. Several are in use in Europe for European languages. Several others have been used with RFC 822 for years in Japan. Each such codeset could be handled as a different type of encapsulation. But considering how many possible character sets there are, it would be useful if the original seven bit ASCII codeset could be augmented with a single character set that would handle a wide variety of human languages. Such a codeset has been proposed: DIS 10646. However, that codeset is not used very much in real applications yet. It is also currently only a Draft International Standard, not a full International Standard. And other codesets have their own groups of proponents and established users, for example, IS 8859-[1-9].

This is an interesting example of something IETF usually does not have to deal with: existing historical documents in an area of standardization, many with historical implementations, all of which have to be taken into account. IETF is quite willing to copy or reference existing technology where possible. IP was originally invented to take advantage of existing lower level networking software, for example. A solution that is an International Standard is of more interest to IETF than others, because that indicates consensus. However, IETF is more interested in experience with implementations in the field, and in community interest. The problems of this situation are quite similar to those normally faced by TCOS and other standards organizations. And IETF seems to forget that many of their standards depend heavily on a standard they did not produce: ASCII.

Voluntary Standards and Accreditation

The Internet standards process has been viewed by its participants sometimes as producing recommendations and sometimes as producing standards. The IAB apparently sees a recommendation as a description of how anyone using the technology should use it, if they choose to use it. The IAB apparently sees a standard as an indication that the technology is appropriate for use within the connected IP Internet, including specifications for how to use it there. This would appear to make Internet Standards voluntary standards in the same sense as formal standards, except that the IAB is not an accredited standards body. There may be a minority view within the IAB that the word *standard* has a connotation of being mandatory. But the IAB has no jurisdictional authority for policy in operational networks, and does not seek any. Its real expectations of its standards are that they be precise and stable. The IAB can and does declare that certain technical requirements are necessary to achieve an interoperable architecture. If this is a mandate, the IAB considers it driven by technical need, not by policy [Cerf 1992].

CCITT produces similar specifications, and chooses to call them recommendations. The IAB thought standard was a good word and chose to call their own recommended specifications Internet Standards. What the IAB produces are essentially voluntary standards, much like what TCOS, or even ISO, produces.

It appears that the only mandatory standards are actually made mandatory by governments. The mandating body seldom, if ever, actually produces the standard it is requiring. For example, NIST FIPS pick and choose from other bodies, but are not new specifications, as we will discuss further in Chapter 10. Thus it is reasonable to view all standards specifying organizations as producing voluntary standards. An exception might be IEEE standards for national electrical codes, and parallels in other countries. These may not be ANSI standards, and neither ANSI nor IEEE are governmental bodies, anyway, but such codes often have the force of law.

Lack of accreditation of the IAB and IETF is a problem for international bodies such as SC22 WG15, which have difficulties specifying conformance to documents that are not formal standards, as we discuss in Chapter 12. In fact, this seems to be the main meaning of *accreditation* of a standards body: accreditation makes it easier for other accredited standards bodies to specify conformance.

A few Internet protocols have also been published as military standards (MIL-STD) by the U.S. government, but most have not. The existence of these MIL-STD versions makes reference by formal standards groups somewhat easier, but not much, since MIL-STDs are only national government standards, not national or international formal standards that have been through a full consensus process of the types required by TCOS, X3, or ISO. Yet some accredited standards bodies do not work by consensus, whereas IETF and IAB do.

Even though they are not formal standards because they are not produced by accredited standards bodies, the Internet protocols and standards are nonetheless very widely used. This is partly because they work, and are widely implemented. That is partly because their specifications are easy to get.

Alliances

Open systems standards such as POSIX are being produced by bodies such as TCOS-SS that are increasingly allied with groups such as EWOS and SGFS that were organized to deal with questions of OSI standardization. Yet all these bodies are becoming increasingly dependent on TCP/IP networking. Government agencies such as NIST require OSI procurement, while using the TCP/IP Internet. Industry user groups such as SOS and the User Alliance for Open Systems demand OSI [SOS 1991], but their companies depend on TCP/IP [Quarterman *et al.* 1991]. Meanwhile, the bodies that produce the TCP/IP specifications do not seem to be interacting much with traditional standards bodies. Is this a three way conflict? Will it be resolved? Is the competition between OSI and TCP/IP unfortunate, or just an example of market forces at work? Time will tell.

References

Braden 1989a.   Braden, Robert, "Requirements for Internet Hosts — Communication Layers; RFC1122," *Network Working Group Requests for Comments* (RFC1122), Network Information Systems Center, SRI International (October 1989).

Braden 1989b.   Braden, Robert, "Requirements for Internet Hosts — Application and Support; RFC1123," *Network Working Group Requests for Comments* (RFC1123), Network Information Systems Center, SRI International (October 1989).

Braden & Postel 1987.   Braden, Robert T., & Postel, Jon B., "Requirements for Internet gateways; RFC1009," *Network Working Group Requests for Comments* (RFC1009), Network Information Systems Center, SRI International (June 1987).

Carl-Mitchell & Quarterman 1993.   Carl-Mitchell, Smoot, & Quarterman, John
S., *Practical Internetworking with TCP/IP and UNIX,* Addison-Wesley,
Reading, MA (1993).

Cerf 1991.   Cerf, Vint, *Internet Technology Handbook,* SRI International, Network Information Systems Center, Menlo Park, CA (November 1991).

Cerf 1992.   Cerf, Vinton G., Personal communication (March 1992).

Cerf & Cain 1983.   Cerf, Vinton G., & Cain, Edward, "The DoD Internet Architecture Model," *Computer Networks* **7**(5), pp. 307–318 (October 1983).

Cerf & Kahn 1974.   Cerf, Vinton G., & Kahn, Robert, "A Protocol for Packet
Network Interconnection," *IEEE Transactions on Communications*
COM-22(5), pp. 637–648 (May 1974). Also in Partridge, *Innovations in
Internetworking*, 1988.

Chapin 1992a.   Chapin, Lyman, Personal communication (14 April 1992).

Chapin 1992b.   Chapin, Lyman, "The Internet Standards Process; RFC1310,"
Network Working Group Requests for Comments (RFC1310), Network
Information Systems Center, SRI International (March 1992).

Comer 1988.   Comer, Douglas, *Internetworking with TCP/IP Principles, Protocols, and Architecture,* Prentice-Hall, Englewood Cliffs, NJ (1988).

Comer & Stevens 1991.   Comer, Douglas, & Stevens, David L., *Internetworking
with TCP/IP, Volume II: Design, Implementation, and Internals,* Prentice-
Hall, Englewood Cliffs, NJ (1991).

Crocker 1992.   Crocker, Dave, Personal communication (3 February 1992 and 4
March 1992).

Crocker 1982.   Crocker, David H., "Standard for the Format of ARPA Internet
Text Messages; RFC822," *Network Working Group Requests for Comments*
(RFC822), Network Information Systems Center, SRI International (13
August 1982).

Digital 1991.   Digital, *Open Systems Handbook: A Guide to Building Open Systems,* Digital Equipment Corporation, Bedford, MA (1991).

EWOS 1991.   EWOS, *EWOS/TA/91/08, EWOS/EG-CAE/91/31,* EWOS, Brussels (1991).

Lottor 1992.   Lottor, Mark, "Internet Growth (1981-1991); RFC1296," *Network
Working Group Request for Comments* (RFC1296), Network Information
Systems Center, SRI International (January 1992).

Lynch 1992.   Lynch, Dan, Personal communication (16 May 1992).

Malamud 1991.   Malamud, Carl, "The ITU Adopts a New Meta-Standard: Open
Access," *ConneXions — The Interoperability Report* **5**(12), pp. 19–21,
Interop, Inc. (December 1991).

Malamud 1992.   Malamud, Carl, *Stacks,* Prentice-Hall, Englewood Cliffs, NJ
(1992).

MCC 1991.   MCC, "EINet Services," Microelectronics and Computer Consortium, Austin (November 1991).

Partridge 1988.   Partridge, Craig, "A UNIX Implementation of HEMS," *Proceedings of the Winter 1988 USENIX Conference* (Dallas, Texas, 9–12
February 1988), pp. 89–96, USENIX Association (1988).

Partridge 1991.   Partridge, Craig, "How Many Users are on the Internet," *Matrix News* **1**(3), p. 1, Matrix Information and Directory Services, Inc. (MIDS) (June 1991).

Partridge 1992.   Partridge, Craig, Personal communication (August–November 1988 and February 1992).

Partridge & Trewitt 1987.   Partridge, Craig, & Trewitt, Glenn, "HEMS Variable Definitions; RFC1024," *Network Working Group Request for Comments* (RFC1024), Network Information Systems Center, SRI International (October 1987).

POSIX.0 1991.   POSIX.0, *Draft Guide to the POSIX Open Systems Environment,* IEEE, New York (September 1991). IEEE P1003.0/D13.

Postel 1992a.   Postel, Jon, Personal communication (April 1992).

Postel 1992b.   Postel, Jon ed., "IAB Official Protocol Standards; STD-1/RFC-1360," *Network Working Group Requests for Comments* (STD-1/RFC-1360), Network Information Systems Center, SRI International (September 1992).

Pouzin 1982.   Pouzin, Louis, *The CYCLADES Computer Network—Towards Layered Network Architectures,* Elsevier, New York (1982).

Quarterman 1990.   Quarterman, John S., *The Matrix: Computer Networks and Conferencing Systems Worldwide,* Digital Press, Bedford, MA (1990).

Quarterman 1991a.   Quarterman, John S., "Network Applications," UniForum, Santa Clara, CA (January 1991).

Quarterman 1991b.   Quarterman, John S., "Network Substrata," UniForum, Santa Clara, CA (January 1991).

Quarterman 1991c.   Quarterman, John S., "Which Network, and Why It Matters," *Matrix News* **1**(5), pp. 6-13, Matrix Information and Directory Services, Inc. (MIDS) (August 1991).

Quarterman 1992.   Quarterman, John S., "How Big is the Matrix?," *Matrix News* **2**(2), pp. 1,5-11, Matrix Information and Directory Services, Inc. (MIDS) (February 1992).

Quarterman et al. 1991.   Quarterman, John S., Carl-Mitchell, Smoot, Wilhelm, Susanne, Boede, Jon, & Sheffield, Barbara, "High Speed Networks in Domestic Industry," Texas Internet Consulting, Austin (28 May 1991).

Reynolds & Postel 1990.   Reynolds, Joyce, & Postel, Jon, "Assigned Numbers; RFC1060," *Network Working Group Requests for Comments* (RFC1060), Network Information Systems Center, SRI International (March 1990).

Rivest 1992.   Rivest, Robert, "The MD4 Message-Digest Algorithm; RFC1320," *Network Working Group Request for Comments* (RFC1320), Network Information Systems Center, SRI International (April 1992).

Rose 1989.   Rose, Marshall, *The Open Book: A Practical Perspective on Open Systems Interconnection,* Prentice-Hall, Englewood Cliffs, NJ (1989).

Rose 1991.   Rose, Marshall, *The Little Black Book: Mail-bonding with OSI Directory Services,* Prentice-Hall, Englewood Cliffs, NJ (1991).

Rose & Cass 1987.   Rose, Marshall T., & Cass, Dwight E., "ISO Transport Service on top of the TCP: Version: 3; RFC1006," *Network Working Group*

Requests for Comments (RFC1006), Network Information Systems Center, SRI International (May 1987).

Rutkowski 1991. Rutkowski, A.M., "Networking the Telecom Standards Bodies," *ConneXions — The Interoperability Report* **5**(9), pp. 26–35, Interop, Inc. (September 1991).

SGFS 1990. SGFS, *Information technology — Framework and taxonomy of International Standardized Profiles,* ISO/IEC JTC 1 SGFS, Geneva (15 May 1990).

SOS 1991. SOS, "User Requirements Letter," Senior Executives for Open Systems, also known as the Group of Ten: American Airlines, Du Pont, General Motors, Kodak, McDonnell Douglas, Merck, Motorola, 3M, Northrop, and Unilever, Washington, DC (27 June 1991).

SRI 1992. SRI, *TCP/IP CD,* SRI International, Network Information Systems Center, Menlo Park, CA (February 1992).

Stallings 1987. Stallings, William, *The Open System Interconnection (OSI) Model and OSI-Related Standards,* vol. 1 of *Handbook of Computer Communications Standards,* Howard W. Sams, Indianapolis (1987).

Stallings et al. 1988. Stallings, William, Mockapetris, Paul, McLeod, Sue, & Michel, Tony, *Department of Defense (DOD) Protocol Standards,* vol. 3 of *Handbook of Computer Communications Standards,* Macmillan, New York (1988).

Sun 1989. Sun, "NFS: Network File System Protocol Specification; RFC1094," *Network Working Group Request for Comments* (RFC1094), Network Information Systems Center, SRI International (March 1989).

Tanenbaum 1988. Tanenbaum, Andrew S., *Computer Networks,* 2d ed., Prentice-Hall, Englewood Cliffs, NJ (1988).

Westine & Postel 1991. Westine, Ann, & Postel, Jon, "Problems with the Maintenance of Large Mailing Lists; RFC1211," *Network Working Group Requests for Comments* (RFC1211), Network Information Systems Center, SRI International (March 1991).

CHAPTER 9

Programming Language Issues

Different communities want to write programs in different languages. Physicists and mathematicians want may Fortran, many commercial and academic organizations want C, and U.S. Department of Defense contracts require Ada. Yet they all want their programs to interface with the same basic operating system services. For this reason, a base standard written in terms of a single programming language is not adequate. Such a base standard would force other languages to make interlanguage calls to that one language. Current programming languages differ sufficiently to make that very difficult.

The database interface standard SQL is written to accomodate different programming languages. SQL is an abstract base standard, which avoids specifics of programming languages. The SQL base standard is used with a language binding that describes the interface more precisely in terms of a given programming language. This approach is also being used with POSIX and other TCOS standards, largely due to insistence from the international level through WG15.

Necessary pieces for a whole standard are sketched in Fig. 9.1. The specification of a base standard that does not depend on a specific programming language is called a *language-independent standard (LIS)*. An LIS has *language independence (LI)*. For it to be useful in writing an application or an implementation, it must be used with a *language binding*. The standard for the language used in the binding must also be taken into account. That is, where the language standard defines a facility, the language binding should refer to that definition, rather than repeating it. The binding should also take care not to contradict facilities of either the language standard or the language independent service specification. When all three are taken together, the result is a base standard with language support. An implementation that conforms to all three provides access to system services by conforming means.

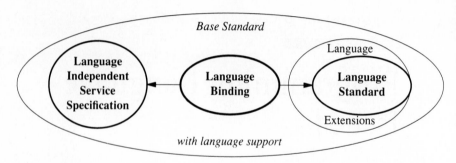

Figure 9.1 Language binding.

It is worth remembering that the ISO POSIX committee, WG15, is under SC22, which is the ISO/IEC JTC 1 subcommittee for programming languages. This could be convenient for any necessary language extensions, although so far no such extensions have proved necessary.

As an example, the American National Standards Institute (ANSI) C standard X3.159 drafted by the X3J11 committee (or IS 9989) may be used in conjunction with the language independent version of IEEE P1003.1, and with the C binding, IEEE P1003.16, to produce a complete system interface base standard with language support.

An LIS and a binding are not the same thing as a base standard and an extension. Many existing base standards and extensions are language specific. But an LIS, language binding, and language standard together can *form* a base standard, or an extension.

An LIS is similar to an internationalized version of a facility, and a binding is like a localization of that facility. That is, programming language independence and internationalization (I18N), including human language independence, are somewhat alike in general features. There is an abstract standard, the language independent standard, or the internationalized standard, that must then be made more specific by use with a language binding, or by localization. The analogy can't be carried too far. For example, the language binding is chosen at compile time, whereas localization is done at runtime, but there are similarities. Language independence and internationalization cut across many standards, in much the same way as does testing and verification.

Although some of the specific issues of language independence discussed in this chapter may be of only momentary interest, the general issue will affect more people as more standards are rewritten to be language independent.

9.1   Interfaces

LI and bindings are just another special case of the general issue of interfaces. Other interfaces of relevance to open systems are for data representation, network protocols, and user interfaces. It is possible to specify a data representation independently of a specific representation. This is the function of the OSI presentation layer. It is also an area where POSIX is lacking, since the only data representation format (in 10031.) is not sufficiently independent or general to communicate with legacy systems. Network protocol layering requires specification of interfaces between the layers. These interface specifications must be independent of the specific protocols used within the layers for it to be possible to substitute a protocol within a layer. The LI work is an attempt to apply similar abstract interface specification ideas to APIs.

9.2   History

Here are some milestones in POSIX language independence history:

1984:   The *usr/group 1984 Standard* is published, and is written wholly in traditional C language.

1987:   ISO requires TCOS-SS to supply language independent standards.

1988:   IEEE Std 1003.1-1988 is published; it is still written using C, but has language elements separated out.

1989:   ANSI X3.159 *Standard for Programming Language C* is approved and published by ANSI X3J11.

January 1990:   TCOS SEC requires LI for all but a few standards already in ballot.

June 1990:   WG15 refuses to accept P1003.4 (and others) for international standardization, because it is not language independent. WG15 also refuses the Ada (P1003.5) and Fortran (P1003.9) bindings to 1003.1, because they are not bound to a language independent standard.

December 1990:   IEEE Std 1003.1-1990 published, using Standard C function prototypes, but still written in terms of the C language.

December 1991:   Mock ballot: P1003.1LIS/D2 and P1003.16 C binding.

9.3   How Language Independence Affected POSIX

The language independent standard most often mentioned is P1003.1-LIS, currently in progress, but LIS work affects other TCOS standards, as well. Affected standards or projects include 1003.2 (shell and tools), P1003.4 (realtime), P1003.6 (security), plus most of the Distributed Services projects, including P1003.8, P1003.12, P1003.17, P1224, and P1238.

IEEE P1003.1-LIS

IEEE Std 1003.1-1988 was defined in terms of common reference C as in Kernighan and Ritchie's first edition [Kernighan & Ritchie 1978] because there was no C standard yet. IEEE Std 1003.1-1990 uses Standard C function prototypes and refers to the C standard.

The next revision of P1003.1 will be an LIS, currently in draft form as IEEE P1003.1-LIS. The C binding will be separated into IEEE P1003.16.

Other TCOS LIS Work

It might seem that language bindings wouldn't affect IEEE P1003.2, since it specifies higher-level programming interfaces. However, there are a few C language routines currently in P1003.2. These will move to 1003.1 by way of P1003.1a, presumably before the publication of the actual 1003.2 standard. When TCOS-SS SEC required all TCOS standards to be made language independent, it explicitly excluded P1003.2 because it was then (and is still) in ballot. So the first published IEEE 1003.2 standard will not be language independent. Nonetheless, certain facilities that originated in 1003.2 will be in the language independent version of 1003.1. In addition, P1003.2 specifies the compiler calls *c89* and *fort77* (but none for Ada) as well as language specific development utilities such as **lint**. These are also expected to move to the appropriate language binding to 1003.2.

Since IEEE P1003.4 includes many programming-language level interface functions in its realtime and other system interface extensions, it needs an LIS. This is in progress.

P1003.6, the security document, also contains system interface extensions, and must be made into an LIS to ballot.

The P1003.8 Transparent File Access (TFA) work involves new interfaces, which may be written simultaneously in an LIS and a C binding.

The P1003.12 Protocol Independent Interface (PII) work has to produce an LIS for both sockets and XTI, plus two new interfaces. Merging sockets and XTI into an LIS of one generic interface would be useful, but is quite difficult, since their functions and interface elements do not match.

P1003.17 NS/DS was, in July 1991, near to doing an LIS mock ballot based on XDS.

Other distribution services documents, such as P1224 (MHS) and P1238 (Common OSI API) must also convert to LIS.

9.4   Language Binding

Language bindings have certain required features, and come in two thicknesses. Five are in progress for the System Interface Standard: for C, Ada, and Fortran, as shown in Table 9.1. Of the five TCOS binding projects listed in Table 9.1, P1003.19 and P1003.20, the Fortran 1990 and Ada bindings to P1003.1LIS, were authorized in January 1992, and are not described in detail here. The projects

Table 9.1 TCOS language bindings.

Project	Title	Committee
1003.16	C Binding to 1003.1LIS	P1003.1
1003.5	Ada Binding to 1003.1-1990	P1003.5
1003.20	Ada thin LI Binding to 1003.1LIS	P1003.5
1003.9	Fortran 77 Binding to 1003.1-1990	P1003.9
1003.19	Fortran 1990 LI Binding to 1003.1LIS	P1003.9

described in more detail in this chapter are those that are further along: P1003.16 (C), P1003.5 (Ada), and P1003.9 (Fortran 77).

New Zealand has proposed to WG15 to do a Modula-2 binding; this is an experiment in doing a binding at the international level. The general consensus seems to be that bindings to other TCOS or WG15 standards, such as IEEE P1003.4, should be produced by the committee that writes the LIS. It is probably sufficient for that committee to produce only one binding with the LIS; other bindings can be written from the LIS.

Required Features

Each language binding may have two parts, shown in Fig. 9.2:

• A standardized interface for accessing core system services

• A standardized interface for accessing language specific services, if any exist

Core system services are services to be provided across all language bindings. For the System Interface Standard, the core system services are defined in IS 9945-1, and will be abstracted into an LIS in the next revision of that standard, in draft now as IEEE P1003.1-LIS. The language specific services are taken from the appropriate programming language standard, as needed.

Figure 9.2 Language binding features and conformance.

Both parts of the language binding must be specified in the language binding document. Any application claiming conformance to that binding must conform to both parts of the binding. Such an application must also conform to the core system services specification. In other words, an application that conforms to the C binding of the System Interface Standard will have to conform to both:

• The core system service interface of the language binding (IEEE 1003.16)

• The standard interface for services specific to the C language

Such an application must also conform to the core system service standard itself (IEEE 1003.1-LIS).

Thick Versus Thin

Language bindings may be thick or thin, as sketched in Fig. 9.3. Thick is analogous to call by value, and thin to call by reference. A *thin language binding* does not specify core services beyond the required interface to them. Specification of the core services is left to their LIS.

Figure 9.3 Thick and thin language bindings.

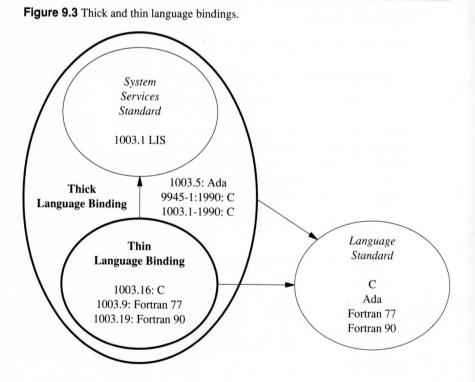

Thin bindings are strongly preferred by WG15. IEEE P1003.16 (C) will be a thin binding, and IEEE P1003.9 (Fortran 77) is a type of thin binding (P1003.9 actually binds to the C version of 1003.1, not to an LIS.) IEEE P1003.19 will be a thin binding for Fortran 90 to IEEE P1003.1LIS.

A *thick language binding* has the required interfaces but also includes a language independent description of the actual system services the binding needs. This was necessary before IS 9945-1 was rewritten to be language independent. IEEE P1003.5 (Ada) is a thick binding. IEEE P1003.20 will be a thin binding for Ada to IEEE P1003.1LIS.

A thick binding may be easier for an application developer to use. In it, system services will be specified in terminology familiar to the application writer, because such terminology will be consistent with that normally used with the programming language. It may also be easier if the LIS is not truly language independent, and the resources need to be restructured to be appropriate for a given language. But there is danger in having two separate specifications of the core system services. This danger is multiplied by each thick binding. It is hard enough to make language bindings refer to the same core services even with thin bindings.

9.5   LIS and Binding Goals

The IEEE P1003.1-LIS work has helped to clarify some goals that are generic to all TCOS LIS work, and probably to all LIS work in general.

General LIS Goals

As sketched in Table 9.2, the eventual language bindings for the languages, plus the language standards themselves, when added to IEEE P1003.1-LIS, should produce a standard identical in functionality to the current IEEE 1003.1-1990, with nothing new and nothing missing. There are many complications to overcome before this goal can be reached.

Table 9.2 TCOS LIS and bindings.

Base	1003.1-1990	1003.1LIS	1003.1-1990	1003.1LIS	1003.1LIS
+ binding	1003.5	1003.20	1003.9	1003.19	1003.16
+ language	Ada	Ada	Fortran 77	Fortran 90	X3.159
+ extensions					
= functionality	1003.5	1003.5	1003.1+1003.9	1003.1+1003.9	1003.1-1990

For example, you may not need to require the whole language standard to have an implementation conform to POSIX. Presumably, the binding specifies what parts of the language standard are wanted.

On the other hand, you do want all of IEEE P1003.1-LIS, except those parts explicitly specified as optional. That is, a language binding is not permitted to subset the base LIS.

The IEEE P1003.1-LIS should be necessary and sufficient not only for a C binding, but also for bindings to various other programming languages. In particular, it had to be necessary and sufficient for Ada and Fortran bindings, since expertise in those languages was available for review. This involved not only the elimination of obvious C programming language features from the LIS, but also the elimination of some basic terminology. For example, Ada has no concept of a "manifest constant," such as a C preprocessor macro definition. So a manifest constant could be assumed to be a C language concept, defined in the C Standard. Or it could be taken to be a system interface concept, and defined in P1003.1-LIS. But it should not be left to the language binding to define. An Ada binding might want to omit the concept of a manifest constant entirely. If the concept is left to the C standard, the Ada binding can ignore it. If the concept is defined as a requirement in the LIS, the Ada binding must take it into account. One or the other must be done, and those writing the Ada binding would of course prefer that manifest constants be left to the C standard.

On the other hand, POSIX is derived from historical systems that were written in the C programming language. Total elimination of all C bias from POSIX is probably not possible, for that reason. It is probably not even desirable, because many of the basic features of the core system services were designed with C in mind, and attempting to recast them to be completely linguistically unbiased might well alter the core services themselves beyond recognition.

The goal is not eliminating C orientation; it is eliminating C exclusivity. It should not be impossible or unnecessarily difficult to implement POSIX in Ada or some other language, but not necessarily as easy as in C. Making everything easy to implement in, for example, Ada, would change the C orientation to an Ada orientation. For example, Ada permits null characters in filenames, and Fortran does not exclude them. The current 1003.1-1990 standard requires null terminators for filenames: this is clearly a C orientation, and a somewhat controversial one. However, permitting nulls in filenames could make a C binding impossible, and would certainly be counter to a great many historical implementations.

LIS and Binding Goals

Here is a list of some desirable goals for LIS and bindings:

• Ensure that there is nothing new, and nothing missing. This includes no subsetting.

• Avoid redundancy. That is, if it is specified completely in the LIS, don't respecify it in the binding. In some cases, such as specifications of return values, the language being bound to may force redundant specification. This is because some POSIX functions return values of different types, depending on essentially arbitrary conditions, and not all languages permit that. The LIS should separate such cases into different specifications that can be combined back together by a given binding if that is desirable in the target language.

- Separate the LIS from the original language, that is, from C in the case of P1003.1-LIS. This applies to the Rationale and to all other related material, as well as to the normative text of the LIS standard.

- Keep a clear relationship between the LIS and the binding for the original language (i.e., P1003.16 for P1003.1-LIS), since that binding will be used as a model for others. This relationship should be reflected in the phrasing of the standard, the notation, the cross references, and other paraphenalia of specification.

- Follow general guidelines (e.g., the TCOS-LIS guidelines), objecting to them where necessary, instead of just ignoring them.

9.6   LIS and Binding Conformance

Ideally, the whole package of LIS, binding, programming language, and programming language extensions should clearly and unambiguously specify interfaces for use by the interface implementer and by the application writer. Each of the four pieces of the package may require (with the word "shall") or recommend (with the word "should") normative features of the implementation or the application.

LIS and Binding Requirements

As shown in Table 9.3, the LIS can directly make requirements on the binding, the implementation, and the application. The binding can directly make requirements on the implementation and the application, but not on the LIS (except by being developed along with it). The language standard (with possible extensions) can

Table 9.3 LIS and binding conformance.

Standard	Binding	Implementation	Application
LIS	X	X	X
Binding		X	X
Language	X	X	X
Extensions	X	X	X

directly make requirements on the implementation and the application, and indirectly on the binding, but not on the LIS (except by helping to define by example what language independence means).

This is a more elaborate interpretation of which document can affect which than is the case for, for example, SQL, where the LIS and binding speak only to the application writer, not to the implementer. But POSIX includes a system interface, so more elaborate mechanisms of specification are necessary.

LIS as OS Definition

These requirements may make more sense if the LIS is thought of as an operating system definition, and the binding as the operating system interface definition. For example, the LIS defines separate *fork* and *exec* operations, but the Ada binding provides a combined interface function. As long as the Ada binding for the combined function provides all the functionality of the LIS *fork* and *exec* functions, there is no problem. Unless it also provides other, similar, functions not found in the LIS or the language specification; then conflicts can arise.

There are also many functions in the existing System Interface Standard C language specification that do two different things, depending on whether a parameter is null. These functions should be broken into their functional parts in P1003.1-LIS, but may remain undivided in P1003.16 to match historical C language interface functions.

The file descriptor (fd) type in the C binding is an integer. Some other language bindings say it is an opaque type. The current LIS does not specify that an fd is an integer. Yet C applications that know it is an integer are portable over all existing C implementations. This example makes it clear that implementation conformance is to the binding, not to the LIS. Conformance to an LIS could not be meaningful, anyway, since an LIS by definition does not make specific programming language requirements. Since testable assertions need to be written in terms of a specific programming language, conformance to an LIS could not readily be tested.

This level of detail probably doesn't matter much to an application, which must be rewritten to move to another language anyway, even on the same machine. An application might be prototyped in one language, because it is easier to write in that language, and later translated into a more efficient language. This will usually involve redesign and reimplementation of data types, functions, and so on, anyway.

But some applications want to interoperate with applications written in other languages. Many of them will do this over networks, using network protocol interfaces designed for the purpose, and that poses no new problems. But some will want to exchange information on the same system, using interprocess communication mechanisms such as files or pipes, or that support interchange of file descriptors. Problems of interoperability can arise even with two programs written in the same language, if different compilers use different size integers for basic types. Thus, there is a need for the LIS and those who specify language bindings to balance flexibility of language bindings against strictness of specification to permit interoperability.

Conformance to a language binding, rather than to an LIS, is important to implementations. The underlying software that supports the implementation of the interface often also supports multiple programming languages, and thus may practically need to support conformance to all the language bindings to the LIS. The number of bindings may grow, and add new requirements that are not in the LIS, such as additional constraints on the fd type. A new binding should stay within the set of requirements defined by previous bindings, where possible, to avoid forcing changes to the underlying interface implementation that might affect other bindings. For example, an Ada binding could say file descriptors are enumerations, that is, like integers but with no defined order. This fits within the LIS definition of file descriptors, and does not add any new constraints.

There is really nothing to stop a new binding from requiring, for example, floating point file descriptors, except that no one would implement it. Such a binding would adversely affect interoperability, because a program that expects integer file descriptors would not know how to deal with floating point file descriptors passed from a program written to use the new binding.

The LIS can try to explicitly state what the binding is not permitted to do. For example, it could say that file descriptors cannot be of a floating point type. But it cannot anticipate everything that might be natural or practical in any new programming language. Where the LIS does make restrictions, a binding must enforce them. If the restriction is not statable in the programming language of the binding, the binding document must state the restriction in English in terms meaningful to that language.

LIS Assertions

In writing assertions for conformance testing, it is very useful if there is a "shall" or "should" for any given facility or feature in only one place, that is, in only one of the LIS, binding, or language standard. In practice, many things will be specified in two places, because if the LIS makes requirements on the binding, the binding must usually make corresponding specifications.

Since a binding can have requirements on the implementation, it should also have test assertions that should be used with those of the LIS in testing an implementation for the language of the binding. It may be possible to have all test assertions specified by the binding. This may be desirable, since test assertions specified by the LIS have to eventually be specified in the target language anyway. As of summer 1991, WG15 had asked the U.S. member body for a plan for writing a plan for how to deal with test assertions and language independence. Some work has already been done in IEEE P1003.5 (the Ada binding).

A given language binding may be intended to be used directly by an application writer, without further explanatory material. The P1003.5 Ada standard is an example. However, there are already two books explaining how to program to the published System Interface Standard, IEEE 1003.1-1990, which is still written in C, before being split into LIS and binding (P1003.16). It seems likely that the average application writer (and possibly interface implementer) will read such a book for the language binding of interest, and refer to the actual LIS and binding only for abstruse details.

9.7   Other LIS Issues

A number of other issues have come up during the TCOS LIS work. Some of them may, in the end, be of interest only to those doing that work. Others may still be of interest to the interface implementer or the application writer. Here is a brief list.

Object Model

In 1003.1-1990, it was often adequate to define basic objects, attributes, and manipulations largely in terms of C functions or data structures. Since P1003.16 must be the actual C interface, P1003.1-LIS must be more of a generic operating system description, and such things must be spelled out more clearly. For example, is st_atime (the access timestamp that can be retrieved with the stat() function) a named attribute of files? That is, is st_atime an operating system attribute, or is it an artifact of the traditional C interface? The same question arises about other file attributes.

At least two problems are known to arise with this need for generic specification:

1. It requires treating English as a formal language, which it clearly is not. However, this problem has had to be addressed with test assertions already.

2. Previous attempts to describe objects, attributes, and manipulations in this manner were discarded as being too tutorial for a standard. But times have changed, and more experience and more understanding of the goal now exist, so another attempt, with more prescribed wording, might succeed. There are also some existing partial examples of the kind of description that is needed, for example, in the specifications of process groups and job control in 1003.1-1990. A concerted effort was made to separate out the concepts of process, process group, and session, and to define them clearly, together with related concepts such as controlling terminal. User-level facilities were then defined in terms of these basic concepts. The success of this attempt at abstraction may be debatable, but it does provide some historical examples of relevant problems.

In making P1003.1-LIS into an operating system model, the more basic goal of keeping the result close to the existing standard has to be preserved. This is not only for the benefit of the final application and interface implementors, but also simply so that it will get through the necessary balloting and review processes.

Event Model

UNIX signals are somewhat different from event models in other operating systems or in languages other than C. What exactly is an interrupt handler in some other language? How can you describe one in the LIS so that it will come out in recognizable form in an eventual language binding? How do you handle subtle effects with multiple processes, when the basic notion of a process may be different?

Use of Datatypes

There is a whole spectrum of integerlike data types: integer, ordinal, enumerated, and opaque. Each may have different sizes. Which is appropriate for, for example, a file descriptor? For st_atime?

What characters are permitted in strings, and how are they delimited? What are record data types? What are unions?

How can these things be specified at a level of abstraction far enough from C that they can be more tightly specified by a language binding, but not so far from C that a language binding may inadvertently specify something other than was intended? How far is far enough, and how far is too far?

1003.1 Section 8

IEEE Std 1003.1-1990 includes a Section 8 that specifies details of some functions required from the C standard, including augmentations to some of them and explanations of how some of them map to similar functions in the rest of 1003.1. Whether a given language binding should have such a section, or whether the whole binding is the equivalent of such a section, is constantly under debate, and probably will be even after all the relevant standards are balloted and published. (Someone has even pointed out that Army regulations have a Section 8 that deals with discharges for the insane. :-)

In most languages other than C, there are few language features that map closely to POSIX features, and thus a Section 8 might not be needed for this. However, new routines may be needed to fill gaps in the capability of a language to access all POSIX functionality. IEEE P1003.9 used Section 8 to define routines which provided pointer and structure functionality, because such features were not defined in Fortran 77. The facilities mentioned in 1003.1-1990 Section 8 must be dealt with by each binding.

Take file descriptors and their associated functions. Must a binding provide a mechanism to map its underlying I/O system to POSIX I/O? Or must file descriptors be basic, for interoperability of applications?

Since the mechanism POSIX defines for interchange of information is POSIX I/O, that is the only way of making two POSIX applications interoperate. Except that an application reading data does not see what the other application used to write it; it sees only the form of the data. But 1003.1-1990 doesn't really say much about the format of the data (other than things like atomicity of pipe writes). It just says it is treated as a stream of bytes, which doesn't even mean it really has to be a stream of bytes in the underlying implementation.

The Ada binding actually has two I/O systems: one native Ada I/O, the other POSIX I/O. Would an Ada I/O binding with no POSIX I/O be a 1003.1 binding? Ada allows an arbitrary number of open files (fortunately, 1003.1 allows that). What if the Ada equivalent of open (in the Ada I/O system) decrements the number of available file descriptors (in the POSIX I/O system)?

What about an Ada implementation that caches file descriptors to allow arbitrarily many open Ada files with only 20 file descriptors, where 20 is the 1003.1

minimum maximum (floor)? The underlying system could be System V, in which there may be only 20 fds, so there would be no extra file descriptors to cache.

What to do with Fortran structured I/O? Can it coexist with byte I/O?

What about discrepancies between 1003.2 (which has text files) and 1003.1 (which does not)? Must a binding to P1003.1-LIS include them? Perhaps they should be moved to P1003.1-LIS to avoid the problem. This is a good example of a distinction between something (text files) that is basically an LIS feature instead of a language (P1003.16 + X3.159) feature.

In some languages, the equivalent of reading or writing would be a type conversion.

What is visible to the user? Does it include time sequences?

TZ

What about TZ? Can something that peculiar and broken be modeled in an LIS?

9.8   C

The POSIX System Interface Standard was originally written in terms of the C programming language, so there was no need for a separate standard for a C binding to it.

IEEE P1003.16

IEEE P1003.16 will be a thin binding to IEEE P1003.1LIS.

The C Language

Language bindings are no good without languages to bind to. The traditional implementation language for the historical systems and for POSIX interfaces so far is the C programming language. Let's discuss it, and then the other languages currently being bound to the POSIX System Interface: Fortran and Ada.

We can distinguish three major historical variants of the C programming language.

K&R C   *K&R C* is also known as *common usage C,* this variety of the language is described in the first edition of a book by Brian Kernighan and Dennis Ritchie [Kernighan & Ritchie 1978].

ANSI C   *ANSI C* was the first standardized form of the language, and is specified in ANSI X3.159, produced by ANSI X3J11. X3J11 started with a popular language and attempted to standardize it without changing it much. This turned out to be more time consuming than expected, because the language is used on widely differing platforms, such as MS-DOS and UNIX, and because many compilers had extended K&R C in incompatible directions.

ISO C   *ISO C* is ISO 9899:1990 was produced by by ISO/IEC JTC 1 SC22
          WG14. It extends ANSI C from a national standard to an internation-
          alized standard. Character sets and symbols used in C conflict with
          national languages, at least in ASCII. ISO 9899 deals with this prob-
          lem.

9.9   Fortran

Fortran is one of the most venerable of programming languages, but also one that
continues to evolve. Two bindings to IEEE 1003.1 are in progress: IEEE P1003.9
to Fortran 77, and IEEE P1003.19 to Fortran 90. We will discuss P1003.9 first
and most, and the other binding and the two language standards briefly.

IEEE P1003.9

IEEE P1003.9 (Fortran 77) is a type of thin binding. P1003.9 actually binds to the
C version of 1003.1, not to an LIS. So it's a standard way of doing C under Fortran. It could be called an "ultra thin" binding [Hannah 1992]. This approach
corresponds to one way in which implementations of C and Fortran have historically been interrelated.

The P1003.9 document has gone through three phases:

1. The original base document came from the /usr/group Technical Committee
   Supercomputing Subcommittee. There were two alternative approaches. The
   one not used was a single function of the form:

        call system(...)

   The one used has separate Fortran functions for most of the C functions and
   structures in IEEE 1003.1-1990.

2. The second form of the document attempted to be more generic, rather than
   having one routine per structure.

3. The third form of the document was caused by the balloting group. A major
   area of contention was I/O. Fortran I/O is radically different from POSIX I/O.
   Should the binding standard put a "sheepskin over the wolf of POSIX," or
   should it simply permit two different I/O systems?

The original P1003.9 document was strongly influenced by a long history of
making Fortran look like C. The LIS issue was first raised in P1003.9 as a specification method, not as a separate document. The intention was to address problems such as unsigned int being too large for Fortran.

It was WG15 that caused a separate Fortran LIS binding document to be proposed. Some consider this to be a good example of POSIX as "bureaucracy in
evolution" as the original technical participants with real world concerns become
overruled by abstractions such as LIS [Hannah 1992].

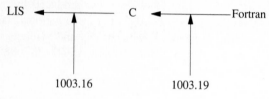

Figure 9.4 Fortran bindings and LIS.

IEEE P1003.19

IEEE P1003.19 will be a thin binding for Fortran 90 to IEEE P1003.1LIS. The essential distinction in approach between P1003.16 (C) and P1003.19 is shown in Fig. 9.4.

The original PAR for P1003.9 covered any and all bindings from any and all Fortran standards to any and all POSIX interfaces. When P1003.9 proposed a new project for a binding to Fortran 90, the PMC required a rewrite of the P1003.9 PAR to restrict its scope, and the new PAR that became P1003.19.

Fortran 77

There is no ISO equivalent of Fortran 77, which is one reason P1003.19 is needed instead of P1003.9.

Fortran 90

Fortran 90 is the most recent standardized version of the FORTRAN language.

9.10   Ada

The Ada binding committee has produced some interesting perspectives on the TCOS process. The UNIX timesharing system was designed to support multiple concurrent users, each of whom might have multiple concurrent processes. Users were expected to be doing much text processing and I/O. I/O calls are normally synchronous and block a whole process. Ada is more oriented toward large scale, long lived, and reliable applications, that is, more towards single-user, realtime, or multiprocessor environments. It has process management, synchronization, and scheduling built into the language, rather than into the operating system. Some Ada compilers are intended to run directly on the hardware and to be the operating system. Others use underlying operating systems to provide system services.

Unlike POSIX processes, Ada tasks share memory, inherit attributes differently, and cannot continue executing after their parents die. The P1003.4a Pthreads draft standard specifies threads of control that are more like Ada tasks. However, Ada puts much more emphasis on monitoring the execution status of a task than is common in UNIX or C environments. Similarly, Ada expects to be able to manage the memory of a user process to an extent that is not directly supported by the System Interface Standard, which leaves such facilities to the language binding. And Ada expects to be able to receive hardware interrupts at the user level, which is a concept alien to UNIX and not supported by POSIX [OSSWG 1991].

IEEE P1003.5

IEEE P1003.5 is a thick binding, partly because of the basic difference between the Ada and POSIX task and process models, and partly because it was begun before much of the Pthreads work.

IEEE P1003.20

Unlike P1003.5, IEEE P1003.20 will be a thin binding for Ada to IEEE 1003.1LIS. This is possible because P1003.20 can build on the P1003.4, P1003.4a, and P1003.4b work, which supplies many of the primitives that were formerly missing from POSIX and were needed to support Ada tasks. The existence of a draft of P1003.1LIS also makes creating a thin binding easier, since the LIS eliminates much of the C orientation of the previous System Interface Standard. However, the P1003.20 working group continues debates already in progress in P1003.5 as to the advisability of providing Ada bindings to POSIX interfaces that duplicate or conflict with Ada facilities [OSSWG 1991].

Ada Standard

The Ada standard is ISO 8652 [ISO 1987].

References

Hannah 1992.   Hannah, Michael J., Personal communication (January 1992).

ISO 1987.   ISO, *Programming languages—Ada*, ISO 8852 1987; ANSI/MIL 1815A-1983; the Ada standard. 1987.

Kernighan & Ritchie 1978.   Kernighan, Brian W., & Ritchie, Dennis M., *The C Programming Language*, Prentice-Hall, Englewood Cliffs, NJ (1978).

OSSWG 1991.   OSSWG, "Delta Document for the Next Generation Computer Resources (NGCR) Operating Systems Interface Standard Baseline," Operating Systems Standards Working Group (OSSWG) Next Generation Computer Resources (NGCR) Program, Naval Ocean Systems Center, San Diego, CA (31 December 1991).

CHAPTER 10

Conformance Testing

Specifying a standard is not enough, and implementing it isn't enough. Application writers and buyers want evidence that the implementation conforms to the standard. Getting that evidence for applications or interface implementations requires testing and verification. In software testing in general, most of the things tested are applications. POSIX system interfaces and application platforms are also tested. Interoperability testing for network protocols is a different topic, often uses different methods, and is examined in Chapter 8, *Protocols and Standards*.

This chapter begins with a brief sketch of some historical motivations for conformance testing. It uses the conformance requirements of the POSIX System Interface Standard as examples of the different levels of conformance that implementations and applications must meet. It uses the IEEE 1003.3 POSIX Test Methods Standard to motivate an overview of assertions and test methods. Practical testing is a major topic. The chapter examines methods of accreditation, validation, and certification that are applied to testing laboratories, test results, and systems under test. Several open issues, including international ones, are examined. Finally, the chapter includes brief sketches of some current test suites.

10.1 Overview

Real systems usually require pieces that have not been standardized. Many of these pieces can eventually be replaced by full standards, but current procurement specifications must refer to some de facto standards, or even vendor-specific specifications or actual products.

In this context, it is necessary to distinguish among terms such as UNIX, SVID, SVVS, and POSIX. UNIX is a licensed product, and the word UNIX is a trademark of *USL (UNIX System Laboratories)*. UNIX could be called a brand name. The *System V Interface Definition (SVID)* is a description of the interfaces of UNIX System V; that is, the SVID is specific to a certain vendor. The *System V*

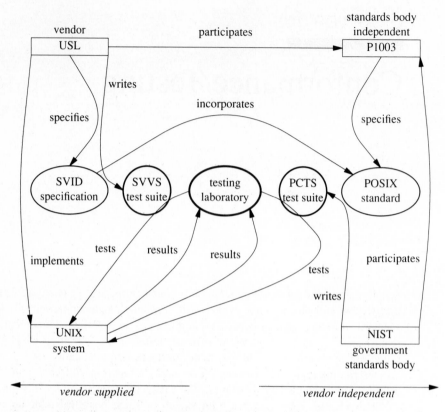

Figure 10.1 Products, standards, and testing.

Verification Suite (SVVS) is a vendor-specific test suite produced by AT&T (the original parent of both USL and UNIX).

POSIX is a set of interface standards, written by the IEEE P1003 standards committees. The POSIX standards are not tied to any specific vendor's products. A government agency (or corporation) wanting to do open procurement rather than sole source procurement would usually prefer to require an implementation conformant to a generic interface standard such as POSIX than to name a particular vendor's system, system interface description, or test suite. It might prefer to use an independent test suite derived from the *NIST POSIX Conformance Test Suite (NIST-PCTS)*, which was written by the *National Institute of Standards and Technology (NIST)*. *POSIX Conformance Test Suite (PCTS)* is actually a generic term, defined in the Test Methods Standard. NIST wrote the first one, but there are other PCTSes from other sources than NIST. A PCTS tests a POSIX system, which may or may not be based on UNIX. The client might employ a testing laboratory to run such a test suite to produce conformance results. These and other names and terms are sketched in Fig. 10.1. Actual conformance testing is even more complicated than is reflected by the figure. This chapter attempts to separate out major topics in standards conformance, and to explain them one by one.

Several other vendors' products, specifications, and even test suites would fit the figure just as well. We are using UNIX, SVID, and SVVS here because that combination is of historical significance, as we will discuss next.

10.2 History

Standardization of software conformance testing is a relatively new area, and the POSIX committees are to some extent pioneering it. However, ANSI testing standards exist for topics such as carpet pile and asbestos, and there is a European Standardization 45000 series on testing. In addition, the U.S. *GSA (General Services Administration)* once did testing for COBOL (NIST now does compiler testing). And several companies on different continents do testing for compatibility to *OSI (Open Systems Interconnection)* networking software standards. In North America, a principle organization for this purpose is the *COS (Corporation for Open Systems)*. (There is no direct relation between COS and TCOS, and the two should not be confused.) The *Federal Aviation Agency (FAA)* has software standards for testing.

Testing is more common for hardware. For example, the United States *Federal Communications Commission (FCC)* sets various physical standards and requires tests for them.

The government agency perhaps most closely involved with POSIX conformance standardization and testing is *NIST (National Institute of Standards and Technology)* (pronounced N I S T). Personnel from the NIST *Computer Systems Laboratory (CSL)* are directly involved in POSIX standardization, and CSL writes POSIX *FIPS (Federal Information Processing Standards)*. NIST also accredits testing laboratories in a wide variety of areas, under the auspices of the *National Voluntary Laboratory Accreditation Program (NVLAP)*, as we will examine later. (NVLAP is pronounced Nav Lap.)

Milestones in POSIX Testing

1986:   IEEE P1003 Trial Use Standard. This was the first POSIX standard, even though it was not a full standard.

1986:   IEEE P1003.3 Test Methods Working Group. This committee was formed by TCOS at the encouragement of NIST and other users [Martin 1992].

1987:   AFCAC 251. This U.S. Air Force procurement specified a particular vendor's make and model of software (UNIX System V Release 3.2), and the same vendor's test suite (SVVS) to determine conformance. This led to protests and a court case.

1988: NIST FIPS 151. NIST produced a procurement specification from a draft of an incomplete (but, in the opinion of NIST, sufficiently mature and stable) POSIX standard. This FIPS was used in some government procurements.

1988: IEEE Std 1003.1-1988. This POSIX System Interface Standard was the first full POSIX standard.

1989: TMAC. *TMAC (Treasury Multiuser Acquisition Contract)* was a major RFP by the United States Department of the Treasury. It was one of the first procurements to deal with specifying POSIX, with POSIX conformance, and with other functionality from UNIX, all independent of any specific vendor. It used FIPS 151 for this purpose. The entire procurement is still not finished.

1990: NIST FIPS 151-1. This FIPS was originally written about the time IEEE Std 1003.1-1988 appeared, but was actually based on Draft 13 of P1003.1, not on the final standard. FIPS 151-1 was not formally approved as a FIPS until 9 May 1990, after IEEE Std 1003.1-1990 had been published. It is essentially an update of the original FIPS 151 intended to match the published POSIX System Interface Standard. However, it was based on a draft of P1003.1 prior to the 1988 standard, and was not published until after the 1990 standard. For details of what is in FIPS 151-1, see Chapter 15.

1990: TCOS testing resolution. Because the number of TCOS committees was becoming too large for IEEE P1003.3 to write test assertions and test plans for all of them, and because the working group producing a standard has the best expertise for writing test assertions about that standard, the TCOS SEC directed all TCOS committees to develop their own test methods, instead of expecting P1003.3 to do it for them. Projects already in ballot at the time, namely P1003.2a, P1003.4, P1003.4a, P1003.5, P1003.6, and P1003.9, were directed to propose plans for developing test methods. New projects submitted for sponsorship by the SEC must include "an evaluation of the requirements for the development of appropriate test methods as part of the standard" [SCCT 1990]. It is not clear how motivated the other TCOS committees are to produce test methods, but many have become motivated after seeing the benefits. The resolution itself is considered by some involved to be a turning point in the history of standards.

1990: IEEE Std 1003.1-1990. The updated revision of the System Interface Standard.

1990: IS 9945-1:1990. The ISO version of the System Interface Standard.

1991: IEEE Std 1003.3-1991. The POSIX Test Methods Standard.

1992:   NIST FIPS 151-2. This is an update of FIPS 151-1 to be consistent with the 1990 version of the System Interface Standard, and to incorporate some other updates. Adoption was expected by June 1992. For details of what is in it, see Chapter 15.

1992:   TCOS testing standards renumbering. Since P1003 is not going to be doing all test methods standards, a new series of numbers has been allocated for such standards.

AFCAC 251

The *AFCAC (U.S. Air Force Computer Acquisition Center)* put out an *RFP (Request for Proposal)* in 1987. This was the first RFP for more than a billion dollars. The U.S. federal government uses standards in this order, when available:

• U.S. government FIPS or *MIL-STD (military standards)*

• International standards

• National Standards

But there were as yet no standards for operating systems or their interfaces: IEEE 1003.1 was not yet standardized, and there was no *FIPS (Federal Information Processing Standard)* from NIST (then known as NBS) to guide procurement by U.S. government agencies. So this RFP, AFCAC 251, required System V Release 3, as specified in the SVID, to be verified by SVVS. That is, it required a specific vendor's make and model of software, to be verified by a test suite from the same vendor. The RFP also required vendors to become compliant with IEEE P1003.1 when the latter became standard.

Several companies, including Digital and Wang, formally protested the RFP to the *GSBCA (General Services Administration Board of Contract Appeals)*. The protesters said, in effect, that the Air Force was specifying not just a particular vendor's proprietary product, but a specific model number. This would be counter to federal government regulations requiring competitive procurement whenever possible.

Relevant regulations include the Brooks Act of 1965, which is a federal law that covers IT procurements [Congress 1965]. The *Office of Management and Budget (OMB)* circular A-130 [OMB] directs government agencies to use off-the-shelf software and compatible systems, and to rely on the private sector as much as possible. There are also *Federal Aquisition Regulations (FARs)* that implement the Brooks Act.

AFCAC 251 was defended by the Air Force, AT&T, and others. The final decision was that the RFP could require the SVID, but not SVVS. Thus, the Air Force won, in some sense, but had to pay court costs. The other side also won, in the sense that USAF couldn't require the use of SVVS. Neither side won all its points.

Effects of AFCAC 251

The AFCAC 251 case was widely perceived by industry and government as a problem. Because of this much greater visibility of needs for testing and conformance testing, AFCAC 251 had important effects on testing and evaluation. NIST had been trying for visibility, but this case was much higher profile. It exposed a whole range of issues, since it required not only implementation specific software, but also verification testing according to a single vendor's specification, much like ordering a brand name from a single source. This is not what the U.S. government is supposed to do in procurements, since the government is not supposed to favor specific companies. In addition, AFCAC 251 required use of a test suite developed and controlled by the same specific vendor.

No proposals submitted in response to the RFP were approved during the legal contention. Many other government agencies delayed issuing RFPs involving UNIX or SVID for fear of similar suits. Billions of dollars of procurements were held up due to the lack of standards.

If NIST had already produced a FIPS, the Air Force probably would have used it. If there had been a nonvendor test suite, they probably would have used it. Given those two changes to the RFP, it probably wouldn't have been contested for the reasons for the actual protest, nor would all the other similar incipient RFPs have been delayed due to the lack of a standard.

AFCAC 251 affected NIST's approach to standards. NIST became more willing to adopt drafts of formal standards as FIPS; they did this for the original FIPS 151, derived from a draft of IEEE 1003.1. This permitted government agencies to specify the FIPS in RFPs even before the IEEE standard was completed. This avoided the specification of the SVID, as AFCAC had done. It is not clear that many agencies actually used FIPS 151 this way, and not many vendors actually implemented FIPS 151, since the vendors knew that FIPS 151 was based on a draft standards that would change. But the possibility spurred the 1003.1 committee to complete its work more quickly and caused the 1003.2 committee to adopt an aggressive schedule in anticipation that NIST would do a FIPS in that area.

NIST pushed harder on development of its *NIST POSIX Conformance Test Suite (NIST-PCTS)*, which tests for conformance of implementations to FIPS 151-1. This prototype test suite in turn influenced development of other test suites. Some of them were based directly on its software, and others had to provide at least comparable functionality.

Finally, AFCAC 251 gave the IEEE P1003.3 committee greater incentive to finish their specifications of POSIX test methods, and the Test Methods Standard eventually became the second POSIX document to be standardized. The P1003.3 committee also had greater incentive to finish test assertions (descriptive testable requirements) for 1003.1.

The precedent of NIST producing FIPS 151 before 1003.1 became a standard was remembered among TCOS-SS participants. A strong argument for the formation of the P1003.7 System Administration committee was that if there were no TCOS-SS standards committee, NIST might do a FIPS anyway.

TMAC

The Department of the Treasury urged NIST to go forward with specifying FIPS 151 even before the System Interface Standard was completed. Their *TMAC (Treasury Multiuser Acquisition Contract)* used the resulting FIPS.

TCOS Renumbering of Test Method Standards

TCOS test methods were originally published as documents under the 1003.3 series, with, for example, P1003.3.1 as test methods for IEEE 1003.1, and P1003.3.2 as test methods for 1003.2. The TCOS SEC testing resolution of 1990 meant that most TCOS standards had to incorporate test methods in the main standard document. In 1992, the SCCT and SEC agreed to publish the test methods for the major base standards, such as 1003.1, 1003.2, and so on, as separately numbered standards. They probably will be in the 2003 series of standards. So P1003.3.1 would become P2003.1 for 1003.1; P1003.2 would become P2003.2 for 1003.2, etc. The dot numbers may continue to correspond, or may diverge. The main point is that most readers of the main standard have no interest in reading the test methods, and, with this approach, they will not have to. Yet a test method standard may, and probably will be, balloted along with its base standard. Profile test methods will probably be an exception, in that they will probably be incorporated into their main document as an annex.

This approach is modeled after the IEEE 802 networking standards, and their corresponding 1802 test method standards. The 802.3 CSMA/CD standard has test methods in 1802.3, for example. At the ISO level, 8802-3 has test methods in 18802-3.

10.3   System Interface Conformance

Let's consider conformance to the POSIX System Interface Standard (IEEE Std 1003.1-1990 or IS 9945-1:1990). This was the first POSIX standard, and most terms and methods that apply to it will apply to related standards. Conformance for implementations of the standard interface and conformance for applications that use it are specified separately, but they are closely interrelated. Let's look at those interrelations first. Like so much else in computing, understanding of standards conformance involves circular definitions of terminology. To discuss the basic conformance specification terms, we need to know that the System Interface Standard distinguishes three levels of application conformance:

1. Strictly Conforming POSIX.1 Application (can use only features from the interface standard or from a related language standard)

2. Conforming POSIX.1 Application (can use other standards)

3. Conforming POSIX.1 Application Using Extensions

We'll discuss these application conformance levels in more detail later. First, we must examine the key terms that are used in the standard to specify conformance requirements. These words are deceptively simple, but they are not, unfortunately, specified very clearly or unambiguously, and they have far-reaching connotations that need to be spelled out.

Shall, Should, and May

Several small words are extremely important in conformance and conformance testing: *may, should,* and *shall.* These words all have precise meanings in their usage in standardization, and these meanings may not be precisely the same as in common English usage. These may be used in a standard to apply to either the implementation or an application, and they mean different things for implementations and for applications, and sometimes for different kinds of applications. For example, the word *should* is a recommendation when referring to a Conforming Implementation, but a requirement when referring to a Strictly Conforming POSIX.1 Application, but not necessarily a requirement for the other kinds of conforming applications. Here are the meanings for these words as used in the POSIX System Interface Standard.

The use of *shall, should,* and *may* to refer directly to applications, as listed in Table 10.1, must be carefully distinguished from the implications for applications when those words are used to apply to the interface, as listed in Table 10.2. Only the first two of these words are applied directly to applications. All three of them have implications for the application when they are applied to the interface.

The word *shall* usually applies to the implementation, and indicates a requirement on the implementation. When it is applied to an application, as in "the application shall," it indicates a requirement for a strictly conforming application, but not for the other kinds of applications. But when the word *shall* is applied to the implementation, it has implications for all three kinds of applications. This is the most specific and clear of the three words *shall, should,* and *may,* and is preferred for that reason. However, some standards still use simple

---

Table 10.1 Shall, should, and may applied to the application.

Application Type	Shall	Should	May
Strictly Conforming POSIX.1 Application	requirement	requirement	—
Conforming POSIX.1 Application	—	recommendation	—
Conforming POSIX.1 Application Using Extensions	—	recommendation	—

Table 10.2 Shall, should, and may applied to the implementation.

	Conformance Type	Shall	Should	May
The Interface	Language Binding	requirement	shall permit	shall permit
	Conforming Implementation	requirement	recommendation	option
The Application	Strictly Conforming POSIX.1 Application	shall accept	shall accept	shall not use
	Conforming POSIX.1 Application	shall accept	shall accept	may accept
	Conforming POSIX.1 Application Using Extensions	shall accept	shall accept	may accept

declarative language (words such as *will* and *is)* to specify requirements. Such language should usually be interpreted as though the word *shall* were used instead.

The word *should* usually applies to the application, and indicates a requirement for strictly conforming applications, but only a recommended programming practice for applications in general. When the word is applied to the implementation, it indicates a recommendation, but not a requirement. Implementation recommendations using the word *should* are not normally tested according to the methodology recommended by the POSIX Test Methods Standard. However, if the word is used in specifying an option, and the option is implemented, the word *should* is interpreted as a requirement on the implementation, and testing should be done.

The word *may* is not applied to applications; only to the implementation. It indicates an optional feature of an implementation. An implementation is not required or recommended to support it, but may do so. If the option is included in an implementation, it must behave as specified. A strictly conforming application shall not use such an option. There is no indication of what applications in general should do about the option. Because *may* is somewhat ambiguous (what does *may not* mean?), it is avoided wherever possible. Where it occurs, it specifies an implicit option, since it normally implies the implementation may do one specific thing or another specific thing, but not a third thing. This kind of option is tested by conformance test suites. The 1003.3 standard uses the phrase *need not* to mean "is not required to," which is one of the possible meanings of *may not,* but with less ambiguous phrasing. The same meaning for *need not* is used throughout POSIX and ISO.

Options are more commonly defined using the word *shall* in feature test macros; these are called explicit options. A *feature test macro* has a name, e.g.,

_POSIX_OPTION, and language of the form "if _POSIX_OPTION is defined, the implementation shall do one specific thing; otherwise, it shall do another specific thing."

From Implementation Defined to Undefined

Other important phrases that specify degrees of conformance: *implementation defined, language binding defined, unspecified,* and *undefined.* These terms are not used to refer directly to applications. They apply only to the interface, and sometimes to the language binding or the implementation of the interface. These four terms have implications for applications, however, according to the level of conformance of the application. Together with *shall, should,* and *may,* these four terms give a range of seven terms for conformance specification. The four terms are shown in Table 10.3, and all seven in Fig. 10.2.

The phrase *implementation defined* does not mean only "defined by the implementation." It also requires the implementation to define and document program and data constructs and behavior.

The specification of an interface may be separated into an abstract specification and a language binding, as we have discussed in Chapter 9. A facility may also be determined by the language binding, not by either the abstract specification or the implementation. The term *language binding defined* is used for this.

Table 10.3 From implementation defined to undefined.

Conformance Type	Language Binding Defined	Implementation Defined	Unspecified	Undefined
The Interface				
Language Binding	shall define and document	shall permit	may specify	may specify
Conforming Implementation	shall accept	shall define and document	may specify	may specify
The Application				
Strictly Conforming POSIX.1 Application	shall accept	shall accept	shall accept	shall not use
Conforming POSIX.1 Application	may accept	may accept	may accept	shall not use
Conforming POSIX.1 Application Using Extensions	may accept	may accept	may require specific behavior	may use specific behavior

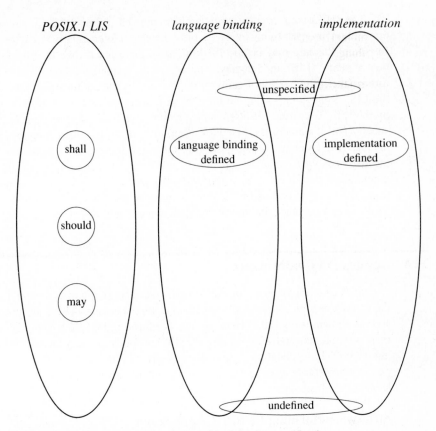

Figure 10.2 Conformance terms and interface behavior specification.

The word *unspecified* indicates that an application should accept any plausible behavior, and an implementation may specify a behavior. The implementation is not required to document the behavior of unspecified features, which is the main difference between those features and those specified in the standard as implementation defined. The term *unspecified* is usually used for behavior that *cannot* be specified, such as which signal arrives first. An application that depends on a specific behavior is using extensions. Wherever the standard does not explicitly define behavior, the word *unspecified* should be inferred, not *undefined* or *prohibited*.

Finally, the word *undefined* says that the standard does not define a behavior, and that an application should not depend on any definable behavior, although an implementation may define it. An application that uses behavior specified by the standard to be undefined is using extensions. Such an application is among the least portable of conforming applications.

The meanings of these four conformance terms for the language binding and the implementation are listed in Table 10.3, together with their implications for applications.

The seven conformance terms are summarized in Fig. 10.2. Behavior of the application programming interface provided by implementations of the System Interface Standard may be specified in one of three places: the language independent standard (LIS), the language binding, or the implementation. Which of these three makes the final specification is determined by the conformance terms used in the LIS. Behavior specified in the LIS with *shall, should,* or *may* is determined by the LIS. But if the LIS uses *implementation defined,* the implementation must specify and document the behavior. Similarly, if the LIS uses *language binding defined,* the language binding must specify and document the behavior. Where the LIS uses *unspecified* or *undefined,* either the language binding or the implementation is permitted to specify the behavior, but is not required to. Implementation features specified using these terms may be used by applications with some levels of conformance, but not with others; we will come back to this point later.

10.4   Application Conformance

A *conforming application* for the System Interface Standard conforms to any of the three levels of conformance specified in that standard. These are proper subsets, as shown in Fig. 10.3, from Strictly Conforming POSIX.1 Application as the most portable, through Conforming POSIX.1 Application, and finally to Conforming POSIX.1 Application Using Extensions as the most inclusive and least portable. *Portable application* is another general term for any of the these three levels of conformance.

Strictly Conforming POSIX.1 Application

A *Strictly Conforming POSIX.1 Application* uses only POSIX System Interface Standard facilities and applicable language standards, such as the C Standard. It also accepts all implementation-defined or unspecified behavior, and all ranges of constants allowed in ISO/IEC 9945-1. It cannot use any undefined behavior, nor any options specified in the standard with the word may. Any behavior specified for an application by the standard with the words *shall* or *should* must be supported by the implementation, and also by any application that uses the behavior.

The wording in the standard says a Strictly Conforming application is one "that requires only the facilities described in this part of ISO/IEC 9945 and the applicable language standards." As of this writing, IS 9945-1 incorporates only IEEE 1003.1-1990, not IEEE 1003.4. However, 1003.4 will be incorporated into IS 9945-1, and then that wording will apply to the latter.

This mismatch between the intuitive and actual meanings of conformance to the System Interface Standard is perhaps an artifact of the dual use of the same text as an ISO/IEC standard and as an IEEE (ANSI) standard. Nonetheless, the words in the standard are as above. This mismatch is also one reason we use the term *POSIX System Interface Standard* instead of *POSIX.1.*

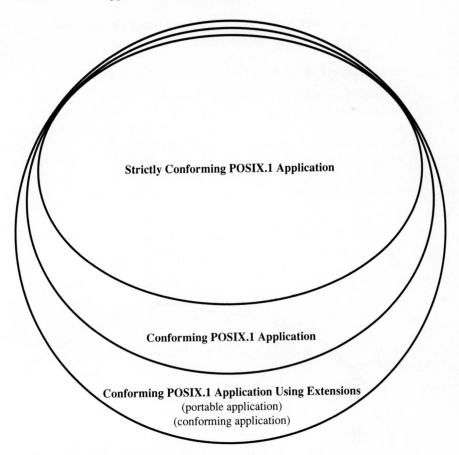

Figure 10.3 Application conformance.

Conforming POSIX.1 Application

A *Conforming POSIX.1 Application* is like a Strictly Conforming POSIX.1 Application, but may also use facilities from standards other than the System Interface Standard. It must document all standards used, together with options and limit dependencies. In addition, it may use options specified with *may*. It is permitted, but not required, to accept implementation defined or unspecified behavior. It shall not require behavior unspecified by the standard but determined by the implementation, and it shall not use undefined behavior.

The word *should* is a recommendation on a Conforming POSIX.1 Application, not a requirement, but the word *shall* is a requirement, just as for a Strictly Conforming application.

There are several subclasses of conforming applications, depending on what kinds of other standards they use. An *ISO/IEC Conforming POSIX.1 Application* uses only ISO/IEC standards, not national standards. Such a *<National Body>*

Conforming POSIX.1 Application also uses standards produced by a national body. The standards used in either case must be documented.

Conforming POSIX.1 Application Using Extensions

A *Conforming POSIX.1 Application Using Extensions* uses not only standards, but also may use nonstandard facilities, as long as they are consistent (in the sense discussed at the beginning of this chapter) with the System Interface Standard, and their use is documented. Like a Conforming POSIX.1 Application, a Conforming POSIX.1 Application Using Extensions may use options specified with *may,* and may accept implementation defined and unspecified behavior. In addition, it may require behavior unspecified by the standard but specified by an implementation.

Figure 10.4 Applications are permitted to accept.

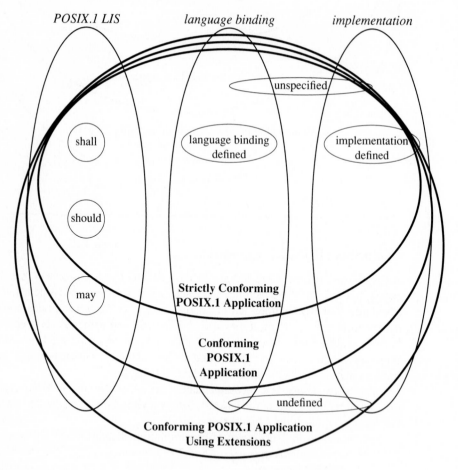

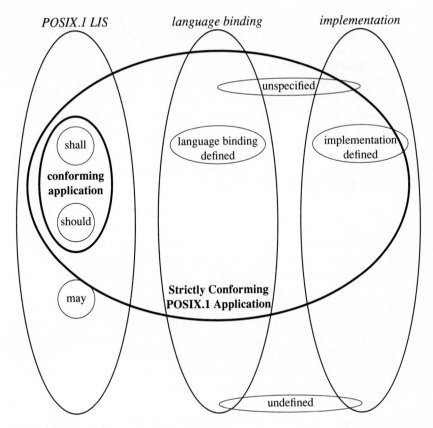

Figure 10.5 Applications are required to accept.

It may also use behavior not specified by the standard but defined by an implementation, that is, vendor-supplied additional features (extensions) beyond the scope of the standard. The word *should* indicates a recommendation, and *shall* indicates a requirement, just as for Conforming POSIX.1 Applications.

We have defined and discussed the seven conformance terms used in the System Interface Standard. We have shown, in Table 10.3, which of the LIS, language binding, or implementation defines application programming interface behavior, according to which of those seven terms is used in the LIS. We have just shown, in Fig. 10.3, the three levels of application conformance defined in the System Interface Standard. Now we show, in Fig. 10.4, which of the seven conformance terms an application conforming to of the three levels is permitted to accept, and, in Fig. 10.5, which it is required to accept.

A Strictly Conforming POSIX.1 Application is permitted to use behavior specified with any of the seven conformance terms except for options specified with may and for undefined behavior. A Conforming POSIX.1 Application is in addition permitted to use options specified with may, but is not permitted to use undefined behavior. A Conforming POSIX.1 Application Using Extensions is permitted to use behavior specified in the LIS with any of the seven conformance terms, even undefined behavior.

It's also interesting to look at what an application is not just permitted but required to accept for each of the three levels of conformance. A Strictly Conforming POSIX.1 Application is required to accept the same behavior that it is permitted to accept. Applications with the other two levels of conformance are only required to accept behavior specified in the LIS with *shall* or *should.*

10.5   Implementation Conformance

There is one basic kind of implementation conformance for the System Interface Standard, but it may be modified by language bindings, options, and parameters.

Implementation conformance as defined in the POSIX System Interface Standard is similar to that defined in the ANSI C standard. A strictly conforming ANSI C program uses only standard facilities. A conforming ANSI C implementation accepts any strictly conforming program, but is not limited to implementing only the standard. "A conforming implementation may have extensions (including additional library functions), provided they do not alter the behavior of any strictly conforming program" [X3J11 1989 §1.7]. Similarly, any real implementation of ISO/IEC 9945-1 needs facilities beyond the standard. For example, most system administrations functions are excluded from IS 9945-1. There is not even any specified way to mount a filesystem. So there is no idea of strict conformance for implementations in the System Interface Standard. This is one reason that a vendor's warranty of what a system does has to guarantee more than implementation conformance, even if that conformance has been tested and certified.

Conforming Implementation

A *Conforming Implementation* supports the execution of all Strictly Conforming POSIX.1 Applications. It has all the interfaces and behavior of IS 9945-1. Any additional functions or facilities must be described in a conformance document, must not change IS 9945-1 behavior, and must not require changes to any Strictly Conforming POSIX.1 Application.

Implementation conformance also involves the idea of language binding. The original IEEE Std 1003.1-1988 was written in terms of what it called Common-Usage C [Kernighan & Ritchie 1978]. IEEE Std 1003.1-1990 and IS 9945-1 use some of the features from Standard C [ISO/IEC 1990], most notably function prototypes, but have not been updated to use the whole language standard. The next revision of the System Interface Standard will be an LIS, specified first as IEEE 1003.1-LIS, or POSIX.1-LIS.

More detail on the C and other language bindings can be found in Chapter 9, *Programming Language Issues.*

Conforming Implementation Options

A conforming implementation may have several options, which we list here:

{NGROUPS_MAX}

Multiple groups per process. Traditionally, a UNIX process had one numerical file access group, which was used along with the numerical user identifier of the process in determining permissions to open, read, or write files. Some historical implementations, starting with 4.2BSD, added multiple groups per process, to facilitate participation in multiple projects. This option provides such multiple file access groups.

{_POSIX_JOB_CONTROL}

Job control. A job is a group of processes being used to accomplish a task. A UNIX pipeline is a typical job. Each process in a job is in the same process group. Job control permits stopping or starting all the processes in a process group by sending a signal. Job control was first introduced in 4.1BSD. This optional facility provides the terminal interrupt characters and signals for process group manipulation.

{_POSIX_CHOWN_RESTRICTED}

Permissions for *chown*. The *chown* function changes the ownership of a file. System V permits any user to use this function. This option limits the use of *chown* to processes with appropriate privilege, for example, what is traditionally implemented as superuser access. This is just one example of many issues related to appropriate privilege. Appropriate privilege is also a serious test suite portability issue.

There are other options, specified with the word *may*. The full list can be found in the IEEE 1003.3.1 standard. There is some debate regarding whether these other options are really options, or, rather, variants. Many of them were put in the System Interface Standard by deliberate decisions not to choose between variants of facilities as found in various historical implementations, usually 4.3BSD and System V.

In addition, the *sysconf* and *pathconf* functions provide runtime values of certain per-process or per-file system parameters. This allows these parameters to vary within limits set by the standard and further specified by the implementation and documented in the conformance document. This makes it easier for a program to be compiled on one system running the implementation and moved to another without recompilation. The *pathconf* function is also useful when a new file system is mounted on the same computer.

Conformance Document

A conforming implementation must have a *conformance document* that specifies limits and options (from **<limits.h>**and **<unistd.h>**), specifies implementation defined behavior, may define otherwise undefined or unspecified behavior, and has any other documentation required in the standard. It is structured like the standard itself.

A conformance document can be very useful in determining what a system actually implements before buying it. The document has to spell out exactly which options are implemented, and what implementation defined behaviors are supported. Because it is structured like the standard, you can just flip to the corresponding section in the conformance document and see immediately what is implemented.

10.6   IEEE 1003.3: Test Methods

There is a TCOS POSIX committee, IEEE P1003.3, on Test Methods for Measuring Conformance to POSIX. It has several subprojects, as shown in Table 10.4. There will be no further P1003.3 subprojects. Other POSIX committees are supposed to be developing their own test methods, without waiting for P1003.3 to do it for them. There is a steering committee, the *Steering Committee on Conformance and Testing (SCCT),* which is responsible for seeing that this is done.

We have already discussed this and other steering committees in Chapter 7, *IEEE/CS TCOS Standards.*

Table 10.4 TCOS test methods.

Project	Title	Committee
1003.3	Test Methods	P1003.3
1003.3.1	Test Methods for 1003.1	P1003.3
1003.3.2	Test Methods for 1003.2	P1003.3

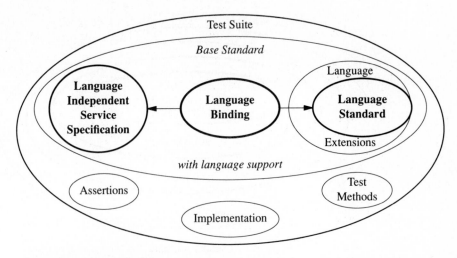

Figure 10.6 Language binding.

Assertions and Test Methods

As we saw in Chapter 9, *Programming Language Issues*, a base standard can be composed of an LIS, a language binding, a language standard, and relevant extensions. All of these things together are not enough alone for testing. Test methods and assertions are also needed for conformance testing.

An *assertion* specifes what to test. Assertions are essentially a codification of the standard document in the form of logical assertions written in stylized forms that are readily implementable in test suites.

A *test method* performs tests. It may be a program that implements assertions. An audit of the conformance document required by the System Interface Standard might be a test method. Other test methods may check for configuration parameters that are beyond the scope of the actual standard or assertions. For example, a test suite may check to see whether the files that exist in the directory **/usr/include** on a certain implementation correspond to the headers required in the standard, even though the standard doesn't say where the headers are or whether they are actually found in files.

Test methods used in test suites must deal with the actual implementation of the standard, by definition. Yet most parts of test suites for POSIX testing are Strictly Conforming POSIX.1 Applications, making them easier to move to a new system so it can be tested.

These relations are sketched in Fig. 10.6. They are somewhat difficult to represent graphically. For example, the language standard is not tested, although the figure might seem to imply that it is. However, the base standard is tested with a specific language binding. This means that conformance of the implementation to the language standard is required, even though that language conformance is not directly tested.

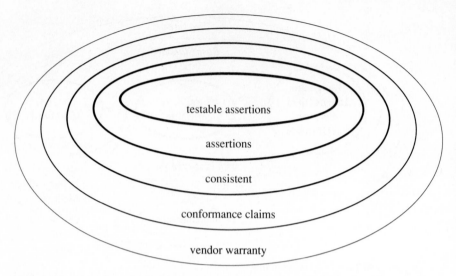

Figure 10.7 Testing and conformance.

Compliance and Conformance

Two words, *compliance* and *conformance,* have a confusing history as related to the POSIX standards. A third word, *consistent,* is sometimes also used.

The term *compliance* is not actually defined in any TCOS or related standard document. It was in drafts of 1003.3. The intent was to distinguish between the theoretical ideal of complete conformance and the practical measurement of that conformance. The latter would indicate compliance. Anyone may claim that any interface implementation or application program conforms to any standard. Such a claim means essentially that the person claiming it says that the software follows the standard, but there is no inherent implication of third party verification or strictness of compliance. The term *compliance* would indicate tested conformance. Unfortunately, the two words are very similar in their ordinary English meanings, and the term *compliance* was dropped in the final standard because it was judged to produce too much confusion.

The standards documents use the term *conformance* in precise degrees, such as the levels of conformance we've discussed for the System Interface Standard. A vendor might claim any degree of conformance, and it would be up to the potential buyer to determine the validity of such a claim. General claims like *POSIX conformant* mean very little.

A vendor may implement a standard, but have no adequate test suite to show that the implementation is conformant. The vendor may nonetheless say the implementation is *consistent* with the standard. It is not clear how valuable a claim of consistency is to the end user, but at least it indicates that the vendor believes the implementation matches the standard.

Some degrees of certainty are shown in Fig. 10.7, from testable assertions (the smallest circle), through assertions, to consistent, to conformance claims (the largest circle). Certification of a vendor product against a test suite, as recommended by NIST, is a good thing, but is not all that is implied in a vendor warranty of what is in the product.

Levels of Testing

The IEEE 1003.3 Test Methods Standard classifies levels of testing along two axes:

1. *Thoroughness:* from identification, through thorough, to exhaustive

2. *Complexity:* from simple, to intermediate, to complex

Likely locations of actual features under test on these two axes are shown by the curved line in Fig. 10.8, with guesses at ranges shown by error bars.

Exhaustive testing attempts to verify everything about the item being tested, from special cases to general cases. Automatic exhaustive testing, with no human intervention, would be desirable, but is almost never attained. Identification testing just verifies that the item exists, and that it does something verifiable. Thorough testing is a reasonable compromise between the two extremes. These are engineering tests, not logical proofs. Thoroughness will vary between test suites, and among tests within a single test suite.

Simple features can be clearly defined and have few variations to test. The more complex a function or other item being tested, the less thorough the possible testing. The *close* function of the System Interface Standard is a simple feature, and it can be tested thoroughly, perhaps even exhaustively. The *open* function, on the other hand, is at least of intermediate complexity, and even thorough testing

Figure 10.8 Testing levels.

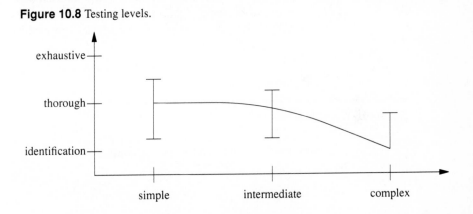

may be difficult. For really complex items, such as the shell or awk languages found in the POSIX Shell and Utilities Standard, identification testing is probably all that is practicable, although there are indications that more than that will be attempted.

Extended and Conditional Assertions

The Test Methods Standard has two ways of classifying specific assertions:

1. *Optionality in the tested standard:* required feature or conditional feature.

2. *Ease of testing:* base assertion or extended asssertion;

The letters A, B, C, and D are used widely by people writing assertions or test suites or doing testing to refer to the four classifications that can be made from these two methods of classification, as shown in Table 10.5. These letters are in fact required by the Test Methods Standard.

A required feature must be present on all conforming implementations. It may be a single facility or behavior, or it may be one of a pair of alternative facilities of behaviors required by a POSIX standard. Required features are usually given base assertions, except for required features that are untestable.

A conditional feature does not have to be present on all conforming implementations. It is usually an option in the standard to which conformance is being tested. It can be conditional because it has a *feature test macro,* or because it is specified using the word *may.* The term *conditional* is deliberately used in the Test Methods Standard, instead of *optional,* so that assertions for a given standard may be written to interpret more things as options than were explicitly designated as such in the standard. In addition, any implementation defined feature is conditional.

The base or extended label applies to an assertion. The Test Methods Standards includes a list of seven reasons for classifying an assertion as extended. But an extended assertion is really just one that is hard to test; it is often a complex item according to the levels discussed in the previous section. A base assertion is really just one that is easy to test; it is a simple or perhaps an intermediate level item.

Table 10.5 Assertion classifications.

Feature	Base Assertion	Extended Assertion
Required Feature	A	B
Conditional Feature	C	D

Table 10.6 Assertion test result codes.

Feature	Base Assertion	Extended Assertion
Required Feature	A	B
	PASS	PASS
	FAIL	FAIL
	UNRESOLVED	UNRESOLVED
		UNTESTED
Conditional Feature	C	D
	PASS	PASS
	FAIL	FAIL
	UNSUPPORTED	UNSUPPORTED
	UNRESOLVED	UNRESOLVED
		UNTESTED

These four A, B, C, D letters are used to classify assertions as they are written, including the test result values that the assertion may return.

A test case does not have to correspond exactly to a single test result. That is, a test case in an actual test suite can test several assertions and return several results. A test may also be accomplished by manual inspection, instead of by software. But neither of these things is important for a basic understanding of the relations between assertion classifications and test results.

The permissable test results are shown in Table 10.6. Any assertion test may return PASS, FAIL, or UNRESOLVED. The most desirable result is PASS, for a *true test* (the word *successful* is avoided because it could mean merely that a bug was found). Conditional assertion tests may return UNSUPPORTED, and extended ones may return UNTESTED: these are acceptable results that still permit the system under test to conform, except that UNSUPPORTED can mean nonconformance to a profile, if the profile requires the unsupported feature. If FAIL or UNRESOLVED occur in actual tests, the system under test does not conform to the relevant standard. UNRESOLVED may later be resolved to PASS, and FAIL may be due to a test suite bug, but these result values indicate the test suite says the system under test is not conformant.

10.7 What Is Tested

An application may be tested for just the runtime actions of its software. But when an implementation is tested for conformance to the POSIX System Interface Standard, a combination of hardware, software, and documentation is tested.

Hardware for this purpose means a specific configuration, including details such as memory size (a different size might uncover a kernel bug). Disk and terminal controllers tend to be more critical.

Software for testing must also be very specific. Precise release and configuration parameters are needed for an implementation of the standard, and for any larger software environment needed to run the implementation.

Documentation must also be precisely specified. The POSIX Conformance Document required in the POSIX standard is the document that is tested. This documentation requirement comes from the standard being tested, not from the Test Methods Standard.

The sum of these parts may be called a *product,* a *system under test,* or a *test item.*

10.8   Accreditation, Validation, and Certification

Actual conformance testing involves organizations, such as vendors, testing laboratories, accreditation agencies, and validation agencies. Three key terms are especially relevant to the relations of these organizations: accreditation, validation, and certification. The interrelations of these terms are sketched in Fig. 10.9. Here is a simplified scenario for how testing can work:

1. An accreditation body accredits testing laboratories.

2. A validation body validates test results produced by an accredited testing laboratory.

3. The accredited testing laboratory certifies the products it tested. (Or, in some countries, the validation body must do that.)

Testing Laboratories

A *testing laboratory* supplies an opinion on the conformance of software to a standard. This is much like an accountant applies an audit, which is an opinion on correctness of accounts. A testing laboratory may function without accreditation. Because *accreditation* is a finding of laboratory competence (for specific test methods in specific fields of testing) [NVLAP 1991, 3], it increases the credibility of the testing laboratory. A vendor may thus be more likely to choose an *accredited testing laboratory* to test its products.

In addition, validation bodies will only work with accredited testing laboratories, so a vendor that wants certification will go to an accredited laboratory.

Incidentally, accreditation and certification of this kind are not related to the ISO 9000 family of quality process management standards, which are for factory operations.

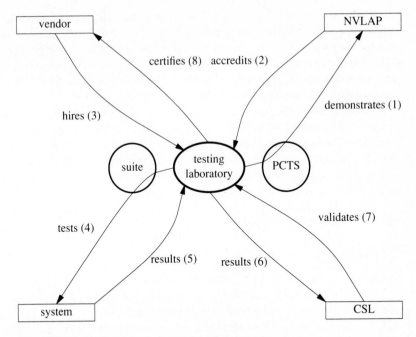

Figure 10.9 Accreditation, validation, and certification.

Accreditation Bodies

This credibility of an accredited testing laboratory accrues largely because the *accreditation body* is an unbiased third party that can provide independent evaluation and recognition of the performance of the testing laboratory, and perhaps assistance in upgrading that performance.

In the United States, the appropriate body to accredit testing laboratories is *NVLAP (National Voluntary Laboratory Accreditation Program),* which is part of NIST. NVLAP offers accreditation for one year, renewable annually, after a laboratory meets a list of criteria. It accredits testing laboratories in a wide variety of areas, ranging from carpet testing and solid-fuel room heaters to electromagnetic compatibility. Under a general category of Computer Applications Testing, they accredit laboratories for testing X.25, HLP, POSIX, and GOSIP. In POSIX conformance and all other areas, NVLAP actually accredits testing of conformance to FIPS, not direct conformance to other standards, such as POSIX.

FIPS 151-1 is a U.S. government procurement standard. It is closely related to the international standard IS 9945-1. Since NIST usually adopts, rather than adapts, the FIPS merely specifies option values, and otherwise requires conformance to the POSIX System Interface Standard. Nonetheless, accreditation is based on the ability to run the FIPS test suite, which tests for the option values specified in the FIPS. An implementation could conform to IS 9945-1 with option values that are not permitted by FIPS 151-1. It could omit job control, for example. A test suite that did not test for detailed behavior of the job control facility could still establish conformance of such an implementation to IS 9945-1. But such a test suite could not establish conformance of another implementation to FIPS 151-1. So that test suite would probably not be acceptable for testing laboratory accreditation by NVLAP for POSIX FIPS conformance. NIST/CSL determines what test suites may be used to test conformance to a FIPS.

NVLAP disclaims responsibility for test results, but their own credibility is involved, because the NVLAP name appears on test reports of accredited laboratories. NVLAP even makes their logo available for use by accredited testing laboratories. NVLAP usually uses outside technical experts, contracted as required, as *assessors* to conduct on-site assessments of laboratories, and as *evaluators* to conduct general reviews of the laboratories.

NAMAS (National Measurement Accreditation Service) is the U.K. national accreditation body for testing laboratories.

Accreditation Criteria

Accreditation for POSIX FIPS testing is a message to the consumer that a testing laboratory is technically qualified to run tests for conformance to FIPS 151-1 for the POSIX System Interface Standard. It is also authorization for the laboratory to sell its services as being so qualified. Accreditation by NIST also involves a requirement for review of test results.

Accreditation criteria evaluated by NVLAP include quality assurance, staff, training, competency, facilities and equipment, test methods and procedures, records, and test reports. In addition to these relatively static characteristics, actual proficiency in test methods is evaluated. For POSIX conformance testing, the testing laboratory should be able to configure a test system that implements the System Interface Standard, run a PCTS for IS 9945-1 on it, evaluate the test results, and fix problems with the tests. They should report known test bugs, and should be willing to retest.

The U.S. Code of Federal Regulations permits internal accredited testing laboratories (previous industries lobbied for it). If the laboratory is not independent, its visibility within the organization is relevant, as are some personnel questions.

- To whom do the testers report (e.g., are they part of the marketing department)?

- How are they funded (do they have their own budget)?

- What is the funding hierarchy (is it buried in overhead?)

- Do they have other duties such as marketing or development that may take up their time or present potential conflicts of interest?

Validation

An accredited testing laboratory produces test results, and a test validation body validates them, providing a certificate of correctness. Such validation is for acceptable test results. Validation is not a certification of the vendor's product.

Since the validation body cannot establish the absence of errors, or even fraud, it validates only the actual test results.

The U.S. national test result validation body for POSIX is *CSL (Computer Systems Laboratory)*, which is also part of NIST. NIST only accepts results for validation from accredited testing laboratories. It requires the laboratory to produce such results with the test suite that was used in accreditation of the laboratory. Specifically, that test suite would be the latest version of NIST PCTS-151.

Certification

An accredited testing laboratory takes validated test results and certifies them to the customer as correct. In some countries, the validation body (perhaps called a certification body) must do this, instead.

Certification is not properly a function of accreditation, or even of validation. A testing laboratory can issue its own certificates, on whatever basis it deems appropriate. However, it cannot issue a FIPS conformance certificate without validatation of its test results by NIST. And NIST will not validate results except from testing laboratories it has accreditted.

10.9   Issues

There are a number of open issues surrounding conformance testing. These include the effects of profiles on testing, specifications that are not standards yet, and international coordination of testing efforts.

Since a profile can specify values for options and parameters of a standard, are test results for conformance to a base standard relevant to conformance to the profile? Probably, as long as the option and parameter values shown by the test suite match those required by the profile. FIPS 151-1 is a kind of simple profile, an option set, so this part of the problem is not new. (See Chapter 12 for definitions of terms related to profiles.) However, unlike FIPS 151-1, most profiles require conformance to more than one base standard. Test results may show conformance to a single base standard with the appropriate values for the profile. But the system under test may not implement some other base standard required by the profile. Or the system under test may act differently when configured for another base standard required by the profile, just as it may act differently with a different hardware configuration. So test results for a single base standard do not necessarily show even partial conformance to a profile. Yet having a test suite for every profile is not practical.

Some profiles may require conformance to specifications that are not yet standards. Testing laboratories want to start implementing drafts of standards before they are finalized. How can such specifications and drafts be obtained, and when is testing appropriate? These issues are being addressed in several forums, including the *OIW (OSE Implementation Workshop)*. OIW recently expanded its charter to include *OSE (Open System Environment)* work as well as *OSI (Open Systems Interconnection)* work. More on OSE can be found in Chapter 12, on OSI in Chapter 8, and on OIW in Chapter 5.

There appears to be general consensus that most testing issues should be resolved at the international level, to avoid duplication of effort and confusion. Several specific goals appear to have consensus. Here they are, in descending order of importance:

1. There should be a single mutually agreed on test suite for each standard. This is preferable to, for example, a test suite per country for each standard. For the System Interface Standard, that test suite might be NIST-PCTS.

2. Otherwise, test suites for the same standard should be equivalent. NIST-PCTS and VSX might be examples. These different test suites may produce different results, however.

3. There should be reciprocity in the use of results. For example, results of VSX should be usable in the U.S. and results of NIST-PCTS should be usable in Europe. Ideally, such results should be equivalent for the two test suites.

Many discussions have been held on these issues among the WG15 *RGCT (Rapporteur Group on Conformance Testing)*, NIST, the *Commission of the European Communities (CEC)*, between bilateral national groups, in OIW, and elsewhere.

RGCT: Rapporteur Group on Conformance Testing

The ISO POSIX Working Group, WG15, has a *Rapporteur Group on Conformance Testing (RGCT)*.

ECITC: European Committee for IT Testing and Certification

The *European Committee for IT Testing and Certification (ECITC)* manages the European System for IT Testing and Certification, which is based on a Memorandum of Understanding signed by the representatives of 16 Western European countries. The signatories were jointly nominated by the CEN, CENELEC and CEPT members of each country. The System is a framework for *recognition arrangements (RA)* in different technical areas. Each RA is a group of testing laboratories or ceritification bodies that have agreed on the mutual recognition of their reports or certificates. The mutual recognition is in turn based on mutual confidence achieved through open technical harmonisation within the RA, thus guanteeing the quality of the RAs. So far, two RAs are accepted, one for testing in the WAN area, the other for MAP/TOP testing [IOS 1990, 283].

10.10 Test Suites and Test Scaffolds

Several national standards bodies are involved in testing. In Chapter 4, *Formal Standards Bodies*, we specifically mentioned BSI (U.K.), CSA (Canada), DIN (Germany), and DS (Denmark), as well as the European body ECITC. In this section, we mention some current and historical test suites that are directly related to POSIX. Most of these test suites are for testing application platform conformance to POSIX standards, rather than for application testing. We list here only a sampling of all the test suites or testing houses associated with POSIX.

A *test suite* tests conformance to a standard or specification. A *test scaffold* is a set of programs, libraries, directory structures, and configuration files that are used to run test suites. A test scaffold may be used to run more than one test suite. NIST-PCTS, SVVS, and VSX are test suites. IBM CTS and TET are scaffolds. A scaffold may be supplied with an API for writing test suites, or with some actual test suites. Much more could be said about the contents and relative merits of various test suites and scaffolds [Quarterman 1991].

NIST-PCTS

NIST-PCTS (NIST POSIX Conformance Test Suite) is a test suite for FIPS 151-1 and IEEE 1003.1-1988, developed by NIST. It is the test suite NIST NVLAP expects testing laboratories to use for accreditation, and that NIST/CSL validates test results of. As of 15 June 1992, NIST NVLAP had accredited eight *Accredited POSIX Testing Laboratories (APTL):* Applications Software Inc., BULL SA/Laboratoire POSIX, DataFocus Inc., Hewlett-Packard Company, Mindcraft, Inc., National Computing Centre Ltd, PERENNIAL, and UniSoft Corporation. These APTL had tested many products for FIPS 151-1 conformance with NIST-PCTS. For 52 of these products, NIST/CSL had issued a Certificate of Validation. Of these 52 products, 30 had been tested by Mindcraft, 13 by DataFocus, 3 (all CDC products) by Applications Software Inc., 3 (all Hewlett-Packard products) by Hewlett-Packard, and 3 by UniSoft. For current information, send an electronic mail message to the NIST POSIX Electronic Mail File Service, like this:

```
To: posix@nist.gov
Subject: posix

send register
```

SVVS

SVVS (System V Verification Suite) is a test suite for System V developed by AT&T; it tests for consistency with the *SVID (System V Interface Definition).* It is not actually a POSIX test suite, but it does include NIST PCTS as an option.

VSX

VSX (Verification Suite for X/Open) is a test suite for the X/Open Portability Guide, developed by X/Open and written by UniSoft. It covers many more technological areas than NIST PCTS, and somewhat more than SVVS. But it cannot be used for NIST POSIX FIPS conformance certification.

IBM CTS

IBM CTS (IBM Conformance Test Suite) is a scaffold that runs test suites to measure conformance of a computer system to software standards. It was developed by IBM and written by Mindcraft. It tests for IEEE 1003.1-1990, and is used by BSI for certification in the United Kingdom. It also tests for conformance to the current draft of IEEE 1003.2, and for XPG3 conformance.

TET

TET (Test Environment Toolkit) is a scaffold for the development and execution of information processing system conformance and system tests. It was produced by Project Phoenix of OSF, UI, and X/Open. It doesn't include any test suites, although participating companies have written some for it. It is not based on POSIX assertions, but can be used (perhaps with enhancement) for POSIX testing.

STE

STE (Standard Test Environment) is an assertion-based test suite from *STI (Software Testing International)*. STI is not precisely a consortium. Rather, it is a mechanism for sharing costs of developing test suites. Participants do not have to pay membership fees; they can simply fund projects they are interested in.

References

Congress 1965.   Congress, "Brooks Act," Congress, Washington, DC (1965).

IOS 1990.   IOS, *Information Technology Atlas — Europe,* IOS Press and C.G. Wedgwood & Company, Ltd., Amsterdam (1990).

ISO/IEC 1990.   ISO/IEC, *Information processing systems—Programming languages—C,* International Organization for Standardization/International Electrotechnical Commission, Switzerland (1990). ISO/IEC 9899: 1990.

Kernighan & Ritchie 1978.   Kernighan, Brian W., & Ritchie, Dennis M., *The C Programming Language,* Prentice-Hall, Englewood Cliffs, NJ (1978).

Martin 1992.   Martin, Roger, Personal communication (15 January 1992).

NVLAP 1991.   NVLAP, *Program Handbook: Computer Applications Testing POSIX Conformance Testing,* NIST, Gaithersburg, MD (March 1991).

OMB.   OMB, "OMB circular A-119," Office of Management and Budget (OMB).

Quarterman 1991.   Quarterman, John S., "Scaffold Comparison: Project Phoenix Test Environment Toolkit (TET) and IBM Conformance Test Suite (IBM CTS)," Mindcraft, Inc., Palo Alto, CA (24 June 1991).

SCCT 1990.   SCCT, "TCOS/SEC Testing Resolution," TCOS SCCT (23 April 1990).

X3J11 1989.   X3J11, *Programming Language C,* ANSI (1989).

CHAPTER 11

Internationalization

Internationalization (I18N) makes a standard or interface independent of

- Coded character sets
- Human languages
- Cultural conventions

An internationalized interface needs *localization (L10N)* for use with local conventions, such as those in Table 11.1. Sometimes *internationalization* is used loosely to denote both pieces.

Table 11.1 Traditional American English locale.

Type	Area	Example
Code Sets	ASCII	American English
		Swahili
		Hawaiian
Languages	character set	Roman
	collation	dictionary
	informational messages	English
Cultural Conventions	numeric formats	1,000.00
	monetary formats	$1,000.00
	date formats	mm/dd/yy

Internationalization lets the user determine, for example, the format for displaying numbers. The actual format of commas for the decimal point and periods to separate thousands is an example of localization. Because conventions can differ within nations, *interculturized* is another word used for this. An application that has been internationalized can be combined with many definitions of local conventions, so that it is useable in each culture. A set of definitions for a culture is called a *locale*.

The abbreviation *I18N* is commonly used for internationalization because there are 18 letters between the *i* and the *n*, and *I18N* is much easier to say or type. Similarly, localization is abbreviated as *L10N*.

Internationalized systems and programs, shipped with data and programs for localization, can yield systems and applications that are usable worldwide. A single binary distribution of a system may be usable in Europe, Japan, and the United States, thus achieving the goal "to take the same program and compile it and have it run anywhere in the world without change and without recompilation for different languages and local cultural conventions" [Radoff 1990, 16]. Several locales, including codesets for languages such as French, Japanese, or English, may be usable simultaneously, in different processes, or even in the same process. Tools based on I18N and L10N standards and specifications can even permit users to develop their own locales at their own sites.

11.1 Traditional Environment

Traditionally, an application was a complete entity, as shown in Fig. 11.1. It interacted with the user directly. It prompted for information, warned when responses were questionable, formatted output, all for a single cultural environment. This single cultural environment is called a *locale*.

The traditional UNIX locale is described in Table 11.1. The coded character set used was ASCII which is also ISO 646. This coded character set supports three languages: English, Swahili, and Hawaiian, although two of them were probably not supported by design. The language used is American English. The cultural conventions used are listed in the table.

Figure 11.1 Traditional application.

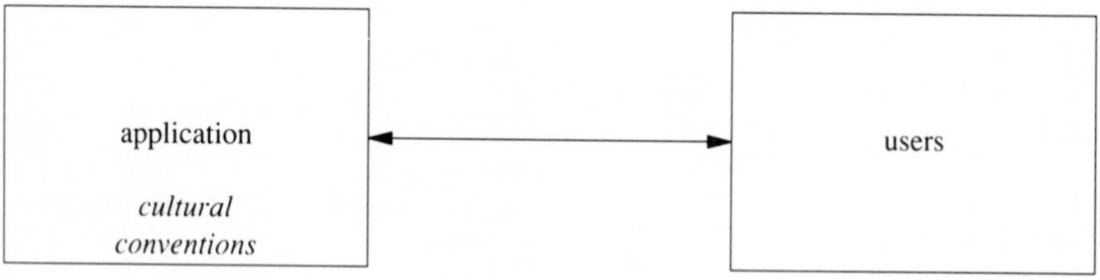

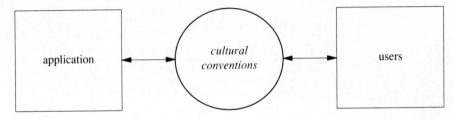

Figure 11.2 Internationalized application.

If an application written for the traditional UNIX environment was to be used in another culture, there were only two choices: modify it or require the users to learn the language and cultural conventions that the application was written for. Modifying these monolithic applications was a difficult task. The modifications were spread throughout the entire application. This made finding all the areas needing modification hard, as well as increasing the probability of new bugs. Operating in a nonnative language can be problematic and error prone.

Sometimes the modifications weren't easy because of the assumptions used for traditional UNIX. For example, the ASCII coded character set uses only seven bits. This limits the number of characters possible to 128. This is hardly sufficient for East Asian languages, where most characters represent words. Such pictographic languages need thousands of characters, not just hundreds. Most European languages can be expressed using eight bits. Since ASCII only used seven bits, several applications would use the eighth bit for their own purposes, making the transition to using eight bit codes difficult as well.

The cost of monocultural applications would vary depending on the size of the market. If there were many users with the same cultural requirements, the cost of the application was less. How could an application developer write an application and not have the rewrite expense for an international marketplace like the one we find today? By internationalization and localization, as sketched in Fig. 11.2 and Fig. 11.3.

Figure 11.3 Localized application.

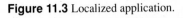

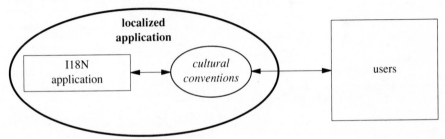

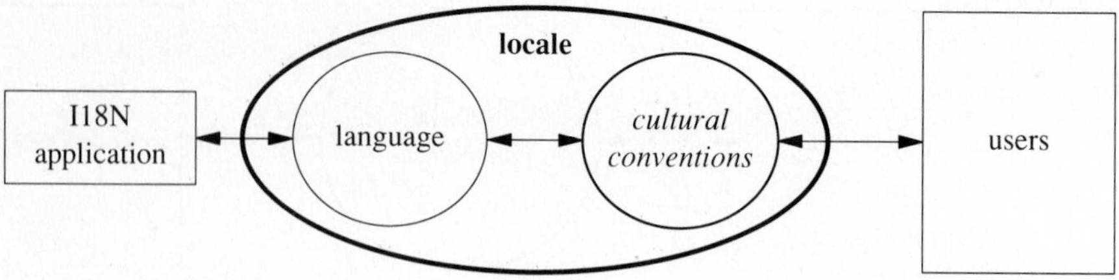

Figure 11.4 Locale.

A common technique used for application portability is to limit the application's interaction in anything machine dependent or culture dependent to well-defined interfaces; for machine independence, this is done with operating system interfaces. Many of the standards described in this book specify such interfaces to computer systems. For cultural independence, limiting an application's interaction can be done by placing the cultural dependencies outside of the application and interfacing with them, as in Fig. 11.2. The cultural dependencies may be implemented in library routines, files, or even other programs. An application that uses interfaces to such external implementations of cultural dependencies is an internationalized or interculturized application.

When an I18N application is used with specific local cultural conventions, the two together are called a *localized application.* Such an application is shown in Fig. 11.3.

From the word *localized*, the term *locale* is derived. A locale is depicted in Fig. 11.4. A locale comprises the attributes of communication with a user, such as language, character set, and cultural conventions. The user views the application through a locale.

Each user of an application can specify their own locale, as shown in Fig. 11.5. Each user may thus get messages from the application in a different language. Some implementations of internationalization even permit users to define their own locales.

Figure 11.5 Locales and users.

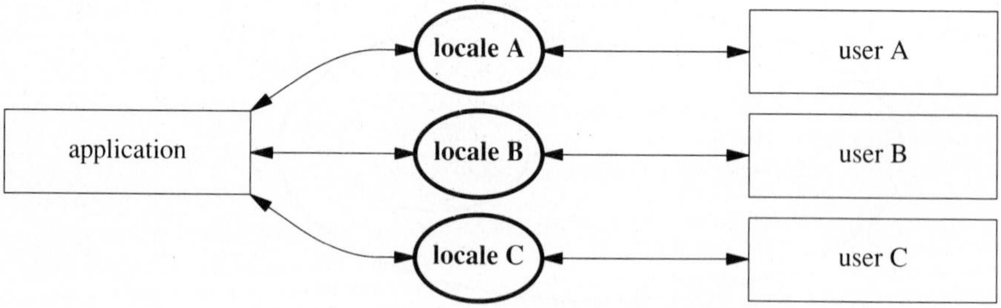

11.2   Languages

For each human language, there are choices in the following categories; examples are shown in Table 11.2.

• Character set

• Collation

• Regular expression

• Informational messages

Character Sets

It may be confusing that a codeset is a basic feature of internationalization, yet a character set is an attribute of a human language, which is another basic characteristic of internationalization. It is useful to distinguish a *character set,* which is a set of graphic characters used in a human language, from a codeset which is a set of numeric encodings of one or more character sets. Characters in a character set are letters, such as you may write with a pen or a computer may display on a screen. Character codes are numbers in codesets that computers use as representations of letters in storing and manipulating text.

Thus, when a human language is chosen in localization, it implies a character set, and a codeset that can implement that character set must be available. English, Hawaiian or Swahili imply ASCII (or EBCDIC). French, German, or Dutch imply ISO 8859-1 or some other eight bit codeset (or one of the extensions to ISO 646). Japanese, Chinese, or Korean imply a sixteen bit codeset, such as ShiftJIS or HCC. Supplying a capable set of codesets is thus an aspect of internationalization, even though the selection of a character set is an aspect of localization. Codesets will be discussed in the next section.

Table 11.2 Languages.

Area	Example
Character Set	coded character sets
Collation	dictionary
	phonebook
	phonetic
Regular Expressions	
Informational Messages	prompts
	error messages

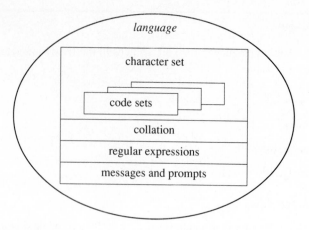

Figure 11.6 Language.

Some of these relations among the pieces needed to support a human language are shown in Fig. 11.6. Let's consider two aspects of human languages that can be localized: messages and collation.

Informational Messages

Several kinds of output messages should be varied by language:

- System error messages
- Program error messages
- Prompts for input
- General text output

In the traditional UNIX environment, which used the ASCII coded character set, collation was built in. The numeric code for each character was in the appropriate order, so a numeric comparision was all that was required. For example, the character A was the decimal value 48, and B was 49. Other coded character sets are not as simple.

Collation

There are at least two kinds of collation sequences for European languages: dictionary order and telephone book order. They are mostly the same, but some non-Latin characters or accents may be sorted differently. Some European languages also have characters that consist of several letters. These include ll and ch of Spanish, and œ of French. There is the question of whether accented characters should be treated as several characters or a single letter, as in Norwegian ø, which is considered by Norwegians to be a basic letter of their alphabet. And there is the question of how to map (or even to detect) upper and lower case. The uppercase version of Spanish ll is Ll, unless the whole word is capitalized, when it is LL. Then, there are letters that may have multiple spellings, such as German ü, which may also be spelled as ue. Letters in languages such as Greek and Arabic may vary according to their position in a word or sentence. Languages such as Arabic and Hebrew are written right to left. A really satisfactory localization facility would account for all these properties of human languages, and for others.

The *strcmp* function is used by the C language to compare strings. It assumes that each character will have a numeric value in the right order. The C standard provides two functions to handle comparison problems when this is not the case, as with the German ü described previously. These functions use the collation rules defined in the locale instead of the characters numeric value. The first function, *strxfrm*, takes the originating string and transforms it into a string which when passed to *strcmp* produces the correct results. The function *strcoll* does the transformation and comparison both. This function is table driven, so it takes longer than *strcmp*.

Asian languages traditionally have three collation sequences:

1. phonetic order: according to pronunciation

2. radical order: according to root components, that is, smaller constituent characters

3. stroke order: according to writing order, that is, the order in which the pen touches the paper

A dictionary will normally have three indexes, one for each of these orders.

In addition, there are numerous homonyms. There are more than a dozen ways of writing the Chinese name pronounced *Lee*; these are normally distinguished in conversation by drawing the appropriate Hanzi character. Some East Asian languages also have multiple writing systems. Japanese is particularly complicated, with two syllabaries and Latin characters in addition to Kanji.

There are also higher level syntactic linguistic cultural conventions. The first or last name written may be the surname, and there is no way to know, unless it is possible to tell by other means that the name is Chinese, Vietnamese, Korean, and written in Asian or European order. This can make bibliographies and indexes including proper names rather difficult.

11.3   Coded Character Sets

A *coded character set,* is a set of numeric encodings of one or more character sets. It is used for representing the characters of a language on the computer's side of the monitor glass, as electronic ones and zeros that can be stored on magnetic media and transferred over a network.

This section talks about the different coded character sets that are available or in development at this time. Some codesets are listed in Table 11.3.

Western Languages

For coded character sets, we've seen how the seven bit *ASCII* has served for years in the United States. But in Europe and Canada, multiple languages, with accents and characters beyond the basic Latin character set of American English, are necessary. Even British English has a different currency symbol, and sometimes uses accents. Such a simple thing as an e with an acute accent as in the word resumé are beyond representation by the ASCII coded character set. Although some of these needs can be met by remapping some of the punctuation characters of ASCII, at least eight bits are really needed.

The ISO 8859 family of standards provide support for most European languages. There are ISO 8859-1 through ISO 8859-9, which have common names of Latin-1 through Latin-9. These coded character sets use seven bits to represent the ASCII characters. For ASCII the eighth bit is zero; otherwise, it is one.

Asian Languages

For languages based on ideographic characters, such as those in China, Japan, and Korea (CJK), at least sixteen bits are needed to handle languages with a total of around 50,000 characters. In addition, there are questions of what to do with filenames and input through scanf, where the character set to use may not be obvious.

Table 11.3 Coded Character Sets.

Codeset	Bits	Comments
BCDIC	6	English
EBCDIC	8	English and most European languages
ASCII	7	English only
ISO 646	7	Same as ASCII
ISO 8859-1	8	Most European languages
ISO 8859-n	8	Other codesets for other languages
ISO 2022	—	Framework for switching four codesets
JIS X02028	16	6353 Japanese characters
Shift JIS	16	MS-DOS, Japanese
EUC	multi	Extended UNIX Codes
UJIS	16	Japanese implementation of EUC
Unicode	16	Multilingual
ISO 10646	32	Groups, planes, rows, and cells

Current popular coded character sets to support these languages are JIS, Shift-JIS (SJIS) and *EUC (Extended UNIX Code)*. UJIS is an implementation of EUC for the Japanese language.

One of the more recent character set is the Han Characters Collection [Wada 1990, 3]. *HCC (Han Characters Collection),* with all known Hanzi (traditional and simplified), Kanji, and Hangul characters. *Kanji* characters are ideograms used in Japanese, which also uses two syllabaries, *Hiragana* and *Katakana,* plus foreign words in Latin characters, known as *romaji*. Other alphabets, such as Greek or Cyrillic, are also sometimes used in Japanese texts [Hadamitzky & Spahn 1981]. *Hanzi* are Chinese characters. Simplified Hanzi are used on the mainland, and traditional Hanzi are used elsewhere. *Hangul* characters are used for a Korean syllabary. The *CJK JRG (China, Japan, Korea Joint Research Group)* was formed to address issues raised by this unification. The results are incorporated in two coded character sets, UniCode and ISO 10646.

Universal Codesets

UniCode defines character codes, in sixteen bits, to support most languages. It attempts to define a single character set that is a superset of all character sets in wide use for commercial purposes. It doesn't cover obsolete character sets, and its coverage of modern sets is controversial in some areas, such as Han unification. This coded character set was developed by a consortium of vendors. Two major participants were Apple and Xerox. This coded character set was seen as important enough to delay the approval of ISO 10646 while work on incorporating Uni-Code as the multilingual plane was completed.

The ISO 10646 structure uses four bytes per character. Each byte is named by group, plane, row, and cell. Plane 32 of Group 32 is the multilingual plane and UniCode was proposed for this plane.

The SC22 WG14 C and WG15 POSIX working groups were dissatisfied with the merger of UniCode, particularly with the second DIS of 10646. The Latin 1 ASCII characters are encoded as two byte characters, each with null first byte. Traditional C programs, including implementations of UNIX and POSIX filesystems, will probably read such a null byte as an end of string marker. Also, slashes can appear in a character, making pathname encoding difficult.

The WG15 U.S. TAG sent a comment through the JTC 1 U.S. TAG about this. SC2 responded that the *UTF2 (Universal Transformation Format 2)* that converts characters into one or more bytes that can pass cleanly through a system. Plan 9 from Bell Labs has implemented a UniCode interface by doing all file I/O in UTF2. This imposes no penalty for ordinary ASCII. Some codesets, such as for Japanese Kanji, can turn into up to five bytes per character [Sigma 1989a; Sigma 1989b]. Since the Plan 9 implementation is an existence proof that ISO 10646 can be implemented in a system related to C and UNIX, the problem is now less controversial [Jespersen 1992].

Table 11.4 Examples of cultural conventions.

Type	Example	Geographic Location
Numeric Formats	10.1	United States
	10,1	Europe
Monetary Formats	$50	United States
	50USD	Europe
Date Formats	July 4 1991	United States
	4 July 1991	Europe
	1991.07.04	ISO
	Showa 15	Japan

11.4   Cultural Conventions

Cultural conventions are extremely varied, but those that can be addressed in standards include

• Numeric formats

• Monetary formats (ISO 3167)

• Date formats

Examples of cultural conventions are shown in Table 11.4.

11.5   Locale

The combination of language, coded character set, and cultural conventions forms a locale. A *locale* is an execution environment selected from the characteristics for localization described previously. A locale may involve the selection of a human language and cultural conventions, as well as other attributes. The entire locale or parts of it are settable by the user at runtime. The American English locale was described in the beginning of this chapter.

A locale is made up of the categories: LC_ALL, LC_COLLATE, LC_TYPE, LC_MESSAGES, LC_MONETARY, LC_NUMERIC, and LC_TIME. The common method of setting and querying a locale from an application program (used by all the standards, profiles, or guides that have such a facility) is the *setlocale* function from the *C Standard*. From the shell, the command "locale" is used to query the locale settings. The categories are environment variables withing the shell and can be set like any other environment variable.

Each of the five variables LC_COLLATE, LC_TYPE, LC_MESSAGES, LC_MONETARY, and LC_NUMERIC specifies behavior for a specific category. The variable LC_ALL affects all of the categories. LC_ALL, if set, will override the setting of any other category. For example if LC_ALL is set to Japanese and LC_MONETARY is set to French, monetary output from an application would be in yen. There is nothing to prevent a user from setting different categories to incompatible types such as Italian and Hebrew, so the user needs to be cautious when mixing types.

An *internationalized* utility supports output and input formatting according to local conventions selected by the user at runtime. By using the locale environment variables, a user can change the behavior even for different applications. For example, the user could run one application in American English, change the LC_NUMERIC variable, and run the next in French. The first application would output 1,000.00; the second, 1.000,00.

Associated with each locale is a name. Two locale names are defined in standards. These are C and POSIX defined in their respective standards. X/Open has suggested a format for locale names, but there are no standards defining how a locale is named. The X/Open format uses a combination of language name, territory name, and coded character set. The language name is taken from ISO 639. The territory name is taken from ISO 3166 [OSF 1990, 13–14]. Some examples are en_US.ASCII for the English language, as used in the United States, with the ASCII coded character set, and fr_CH.88591 for the French language, as used in Switzerland, with the ISO 8859-1 coded character set.

In a distributed environment, the lack of a naming standard for locales becomes problematic. The situation where a server has one name for a locale and a client a different name for the same locale can cause unexpected results.

Work is being done in this area in the internationalization rapporteur group of ISO/IEC JTC 1 SC22 WG15. One idea is to provide registration for locale names.

11.6   Internationalization Organizations

Because the topic of I18N affects many areas of standardization, there are many organizations involved in defining techniques for internationalization. Some of them are shown in Fig. 11.7. Each of these groups was described in detail in Chapter 5, *Industry Organizations and User Groups*.

UniForum and X/Open Working Groups

At the least formal level are the X/Open I18N Working Group and the *UniForum I18N (UniForum Technical Committee Working Group on Internationalization)*. The UniForum Technical Committees started work on internationalization in 1983 when the need for these facilities was recognized. These two groups meet jointly to discusss I18N problems and possible solutions. They have been meeting for quite some time and have been working on this problem longer than the standard committees have been. Since they are not bound by consensus rules, they can

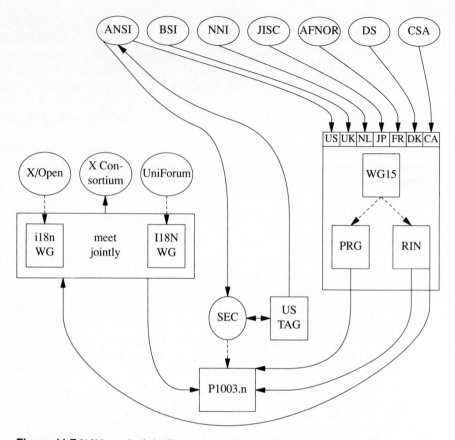

Figure 11.7 I18N standards bodies.

provide vendors and users specifications to use until formal standards are
developed. The vendors and users can try the solutions and determine whether the
latter are suitable.

Several I18N functions have originated with this group, such as the *setlocale*
function, the locale and localedef shell commands, and regular expression pattern
matching. The UniForum group originated the I18N form of regular expressions
and pattern matching, which were first specified in XPG3 and implemented in systems that implement XPG3. The UniForum group also specified a message catalog scheme, which was different from the one XPG3 specified. The P1003.1
working group couldn't decide among those two and another proposal, and
included no message scheme in P1003.1a. UniForum provided something called
colldef, in draft 8 of P1003.2. P1003.2 ended up calling it localedef. Localedef
defines a locale that you can use *setlocale* to invoke [Jespersen 1992].

UniForum and X/Open are discussing how to name locales so that systems
from different vendors behave the same way for the same locale name, and how to
make locales function in a distributed environment.

X Consortium

The X Consortium is responsible for the development of the X Window System, which is the basis for several graphical user interfaces. Most locale functionality was intended for a single program to interface with a single user. With X, one server provides services to many clients. Each client could be operating on a different machine with a different locale. The X/Open and UniForum working groups are proposing a solution for these problems to the X Consortium.

References

Hadamitzky & Spahn 1981.   Hadamitzky, Wolfgang, & Spahn, Mark, *Kanji & Kana: A Handbook and Dictionary of the Japanese Writing System,* Charles E. Tuttle Company, Rutland, Vermont; Tokyo, Japan (1981).

Jespersen 1992.   Jespersen, Hal, Personal communication (June 1992).

OSF 1990.   OSF, "Internationalization Made Easy: A White Paper," Open Software Foundation, Cambridge, MA (September 1990).

Radoff 1990.   Radoff, David, "Toward A Global Operating Environment," *CommUNIXations* **X**(6), pp. 15–19, UniForum (August 1990).

Sigma 1989a.   Sigma, "Multi-byte Character Processing on UNIX, part 1 (Background and Concept)," Sigma, Tokyo (March 1989).

Sigma 1989b.   Sigma, "Multi-byte Character Processing on UNIX, part 2 (Implementation on SigmaOS)," Sigma, Tokyo (March 1989).

Wada 1990.   Wada, Eiiti, "ISO 2nd Draft Proposal 10646 and Unicode," *NEWSSITE*(5), pp. 1–4, Center of the International Coorperation for Computerization (CICC) and Japanese Standards Association (JSA) (Autumn 1990). Japanese National Body for JTC 1/SC2.

PART 4

Puzzles

Users want working systems: viable applications, and interface implementations to support them. Individual standards only define narrow areas. Even when two standards are intended to be used together, neither may say how. Profiles do that, and this part of the book is about profiles.

The first chapter in this part, Chapter 12, gives detailed definitions of terms and examples of frameworks and models. Succeeding chapters describe specific profiles and environments. This book itself is a high level guidebook to specifications, standards, and profiles.

Frameworks

We have already discussed profiling terms, such as base standard, environment, profile, AEP, platform profile, and framework, in general in Chapter 3. We define them in more detail in Chapter 12, with specific examples. We also sketch the organizations, such as SGFS, EWOS-CAE, and TSG-1, responsible for high level profiling documents. The chapter ends with overviews of profile issues and of processes of profiling.

TCOS Profiles

TCOS profiles are described in Chapter 13. Some, such as the IEEE P1003.10 supercomputing profile, are to support specific environments. Others, such as P1003.14 for multiprocessing and P1003.18 for an interactive timesharing system, are for larger platforms. This chapter also describes the P1003.0 POSIX Guide, which is not a profile, rather it is a guide to the POSIX Open System Environment.

Industry Profiles

We describe industry profiles for open systems and distributed computing environments in Chapter 14. The chapter starts with brief descriptions of X/Open's XPG, USL's SVID, and OSF's AES. It continues with details of UI-Atlas and OSF DCE, including UI's OLTP and OSF's ANDF. Also, BSDI, 88open, SPARC International, and ACE are briefly mentioned. The chapter concludes with distributed management standards and profiles.

Procurement Profiles

Chapter 15 is about acquisition and procurement profiles from government agencies, such as NIST, CCTA, and the CEC, and from other organizations, such as POSC, UAOS, and Bellcore. Networking standards and profiles are described, including the NIST GOSIP OSI procurement profile, the obsolete PSSG TCP/IP MIL-STDs and current U.S. DoD work, and the current, nonmilitary, TCP/IP specifications, which are IAB RFCs and Internet Standards.

CHAPTER 12

Frameworks

This chapter defines profiling terms in detail, then describes some specific frameworks, taxonomies, models, guides, and other high-level documents related to profiles.

A standard or specification for how to fit standards together to define an environment is called a *profile*. A profile lists a set of base standards, together with specific option and parameter values.

Unlike *base standards,* profiles are usually more application oriented than component oriented. That is, whereas most base standards describe technical areas that could be separated out for ready standardization, most profiles are designed to support particular classes of applications. Such a profile is often called an *Application Environment Profile (AEP)*. A profile defines a jigsaw puzzle that requires the pieces that are base standards to fit together in certain orientations to show a picture of an environment. An actual environment that looks like the picture is an implementation of the profile.

A profile is selected from a more general *Open System Environment (OSE)*. An OSE is based on a *reference model* that categorizes standards into areas. An OSE fits in a *framework* that indicates how profiles should be constructed out of standards, while still being harmonized with each other and with the OSE. There may be several OSE models for the same framework. There are usually many profiles per OSE. If a model is a menu, a framework is a set of ingredients and sauces, an AEP is a combination dinner that many diners may like, and a profile is a meal à la carte for a particular patron.

A guide is a document that is less formal than a standard or a recommended practice. It may include a reference model, or even a framework. It usually includes other contextual material. The guides of most interest to profiles related to the historical UNIX operating system are the *IEEE P1003.0 POSIX Guide,* which includes a reference model for the POSIX OSE, and the *X/Open Portability Guide (XPG),* which describes a similar large environment.

Profiles provide clear definitions of applications and system interfaces, making implementation and conformance testing easier. They simplify targetting applications for environments [Digital 1991]. And they ease standards development by identifying missing standards and profiles (gaps).

Constructing a profile is called *profiling*. The purpose of profiling is to build environments to support applications within open systems. This allows clear communication about such environments for acquisition and procurement. We discuss profiling issues and guidelines at the end of the chapter.

12.1   Profile Hierarchies

There are many different kinds of profiles, of varying degrees of scope and complexity, to fit various user requirements.

OSI and Open Systems Profile Hierarchies

It may be useful to draw analogies between open system profiling terms and some terms used with the OSI protocol model, as in Table 12.1. OSI profiling is intended to promote interoperability and conformance testing. OSE profiling adds application portability and user portability, but many of the methods and terms are similar, and were to some extent derived from those used for OSI.

If we take a standard to be equivalent to a protocol, then a profile is like a protocol stack, because it groups together smaller elements to support a particular application. IEEE 1003.1, IEEE 1003.2, and IEEE 1003.2a might be used in describing an interactive shell programming environment, just as TP0 might be used with X.25 to support FTAM. An OSE is like a *protocol suite,* which is a set of protocols that can be used together in various protocol stacks to support various applications. A *reference model* is like a *protocol model,* which describes the properties protocols need to satisfy to work together. The standards and profiles of an OSE should fit the corresponding OSE model, just as the protocols in a

Table 12.1 OSI and open systems profile hierarchies.

OSI	Example	Open Systems	Example
Framework	TR10000-1	framework	TR10000-3
Taxonomy	TR10000-2	taxonomy	EWOS taxonomy
Protocol model	IS 7498	reference model	P1003.0 Reference Model
Protocol suite	OSI protocols	OSE	POSIX OSE
Protocol stack	GOSIP	profile	P1003.10
Protocol	X.25	standard	1003.1

protocol suite should fit the protocol model. The analogy is straightforward to this level of complexity, and is shown in Table 12.1.

A *taxonomy* describes partitions of an environment that profiles might want to describe. TR10000-2 is one for OSI [SGFS 1991]. A *framework* describes in general the properties needed by reference models, using a taxonomy to do so. TR10000-1 is the OSI framework [SGFS 1990].

Open System Profile Hierarchy

We can group profiles together with standards in a rough hierarchy of standards, profiles, models, and frameworks. The basic terms are shown in Table 12.2, ranked according to levels of abstraction. Each of these things describe an environment of some sort. The higher levels tend to describe objects from the lower layers. Profiles describe environments or platforms to support application programs or users. These smaller environments should fit into a larger environment, called an *Open System Environment (OSE)*. An OSE should be comprehensive and consistent; its profiles and standards should specify interfaces, services, and formats for interoperability and portability of applications, data, and people. Where there is no standard for a part of an OSE, an open specification may be used instead. A reference model categorizes profiles and standards and explains their relations in an OSE.

The OSI framework, TR10000-1, is almost general enough to include the OSE model as well as the OSI model, and may be extended to do so. There is no formal standardized taxonomy for open systems yet, but the *European Workshop on Open Systems (EWOS)* has constructed a less formal one [EWOS 1991a]. This categorizes parts of a *CAE (Common Application Environment)*.

The term *CAE* is used by X/Open and other industry groups to describe something very like an OSE, except that it is an industry specification, rather than

---

Table 12.2 Open system profile hierarchy.

Specification	Describes	Example	Describes
Framework	models	TR10000	OSI (and OSE?)
Taxonomy	profiles	EWOS taxonomy	OSE profiles
Reference model	OSE	P1003.0 Reference Model	POSIX OSE
Platform profile	platform	P1003.18 PEP	timesharing system
AEP	AE	P1003.10	supercomputing
ASED	ASE	P1003.15	batch processing
Option set	API	NIST FIPS 151-1	system interface
Extension	EEI	P1003.12	network interface
Base standard	API	1003.1	system interface

a formal standard. Some of the specifications included in a CAE may themselves be less formal than would be permitted in an OSE. A CAE may cover a broader technological area than an OSE, and, because standards processes take a long time, vendor consortia may describe an open environment in a CAE before it is standardized as an OSE. Because a CAE may be available sooner and may be broader than an OSE, a CAE may be more useful in some procurements. A CAE is otherwise much like an OSE. The best-known CAE is probably the one described by the *X/Open Portability Guide (XPG)*.

A *guide* specifies an OSE or CAE, usually including a reference model and some contextual information, such as descriptions of standards work in progress that cannot yet be used in constructing the environment. The IEEE P1003.0 POSIX Guide specifies the POSIX OSE. The XPG describes the X/Open CAE. However, the term *CAE* is being replaced with the term *OSE* [EWOS 1991b].

12.2   Profiles

In this section, we describe some kinds of profiles, starting with the simplest, and working up to the most complex. This section is thus a very short taxonomy of profiles. A profile describes an environment. For each kind of profile, we sketch the kind of environment it is intended to describe. Many of the terms, acronyms, and examples defined here have already been listed in Table 12.2.

Here are a few more general terms. ISO documents often use the term *functional standard* for a profile. The process of getting international agreement on functional standards is called *harmonization*. This process is more commonly called *coordination* in TCOS documents. For a profile to be harmonized with the POSIX OSE, it should take into account the IEEE P1003.0 POSIX Guide, the IEEE P1003.18 *PEP (POSIX Environment Profile)*, TR10000, and the TSG-1 Final Report.

Base Standard

We've already discussed base standards and extensions in Chapter 3, together with the types of interfaces they may specify. Table 12.2 shows the example extension as an EEI and the example base standard as an API, but of course either could be an *Application Program Interface (API)*, an *External Environment Interface (EEI)*, or even a *System Internal Interface (SII)*. And an extension taken together with the base standard it modifies forms a combination base standard for the purpose of profiling.

The interesting question is how standard a base standard has to be to be used in a profile. According to the 1990 edition of TR10000, a base standard is "an International Standard, Technical Report, or CCITT recommendation used in the definition of a profile" [SGFS 1990]. This kind of strictness is a problem in for OSEs, where sufficient international base standards do not yet exist, but national or de facto standards often do [EWOS 1991a]. The new definition, found in the POSIX Guide, and apparently adopted by SGFS, is "A standard or specification that is recognized as appropriate for normative reference in a profile by the body adopting that profile" [POSIX.0 1991]. This new definition permits TCOS, for example, to say that any ANSI standard is good enough to be a base standard in a TCOS profile, even though it is not an International Standard. TCOS can even decide to permit industry specifications as base standards. Other bodies can make their own decisions. By choosing appropriate rules for normative references in profiles, a national body such as TCOS (acting for ANSI) can standardize a profile that uses a national standard, or even a draft of one, as a base standard. The profile and the base standards it references can thus progress upwards to international standardization together.

Simple Profile

An *option set* is a set of specifications of parameters and options to apply to a single base standard. Because it modifies only to a single standard, it is a degenerate form of a profile.

A simple *profile* may be an unadorned list of standards. The intended use may be that a *request for proposals (RFP)* should require that a vendor or vendors supply products that fit all the listed standards. This kind of profile tends to be very short, and to specify only very basic standards. The earliest form of the NIST *Application Portability Profile (APP),* was such a simple profile.

Anyone, from a single user to a department to a company to a vendor or user consortium, may write a profile. There is really no secret to profiling, and we will discuss how it is done in the final section of this chapter. The term *Component Profile* is sometimes used for a relatively simple profile that may be used in building other profiles [EWOS 1991a].

Application Environment Profile

An *Application Environment (AE)* supports a class of applications. An *Application Environment Profile (AEP)* describes an environment for a class of applications. An AEP might describe an environment for supercomputing (as in IEEE P1003.10), whereas an ASED might describe a more specific environment for supercomputing batch processing (as in IEEE P1003.15). The definition comes from TSG-1, and is for OSEs [TSG-1 1991].

AEPs are particularly useful in finding gaps in base standards. They are also good for discovering whether the options specified by a base standard are the ones really needed by users. A set of AEPs in the same area, such as all POSIX AEPs within the POSIX OSE Model, should ideally lead to a set of common options and parameters being found for each base standard.

An *Application Specific Environment (ASE)* is an environment for a particular application. It should be a complete and coherent subset of an environment described by an AEP. An *Application Specific Environment Description (ASED)* describes an ASE in detail for successful operation of the application. It includes any additional options, parameters, formats, or resource requirements that are necessary for successful operation of the application in the ASE.

An *OSE profile* is defined by reference to a set of component profiles and platform profiles. The idea is to define a few large profiles for vertical markets, such as CIM, banking, or medical information. Only a few OSE profiles are wanted, because too many would provide too many choices and cause confusion in the market. The OSE profile classes actually listed in one taxonomy include ones for supercomputing, transaction processing, and realtime [EWOS 1991b], corresponding to IEEE P1003.10, IEEE P1003.11, and IEEE P1003.13. This would seem to make an OSE profile the same as an AEP.

Platform Profile

Some profiles are designed not only to describe a specific environment, but also to serve as examples for writing other profiles. Some AEPs even serve as platforms from which other AEPs or ASEDs may be created by addition and greater specification. Such an AEP is called a *platform profile*. A platform profile normally references other AEPs, rather than trying to specify the whole environment directly from base standards.

The simplest example of a platform profile is the NIST *APP (Application Portability Profile)* The IEEE P1003.18 PEP profile is a more general example. It specifies an AEP for a traditional timesharing system, and an early version of it was called *TIMS (Traditional Interactive Multiuser System)*. PEP is meant not only to be an AEP for such a system, but also to serve as a platform from which other, related, profiles may be built.

National Profile

National profiles are basically profiles for localization after internationalization. In addition to base standards, options, and parameters, they include concepts such as locale, character size, and character set. Some of them may be harmonized by language, such as perhaps all national profiles that use French [WG15 1991a]. These profiles may require extensions to TR1000. The WG15 *RIN (Rapporteur Group for Internationalization)* might be an appropriate body to assist in such extensions, and JTC 1 SC22 WG20 may also want to contribute [WG15 1991b].

Standardized Profile

When a profile is approved as a standard, it becomes a *Standardized Profile (SP)*. A National Profile is usually a Standardized Profile because no other group than the national standards body could normally produce one.

International Standardized Profile

An *ISP (International Standardized Profile)* is a *Standardized Profile (SP)* that has been approved at the international level [Digital 1991, 10-8]. ISPs and related issues are defined in *TR10000 (Technical Report 10000)*.

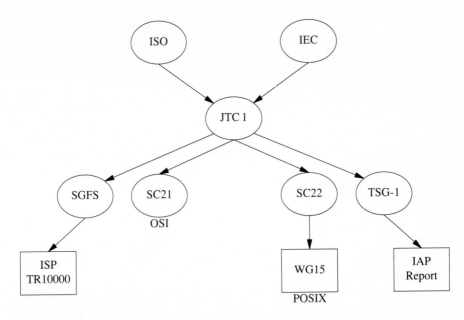

Figure 12.1 International profiles.

12.3   Frameworks

Most early work on profiles and frameworks was done for OSI. Much of that is applicable to OSE, but not without modification. Part of the problem is that OSI was specified at the highest international levels of standardization, whereas much of the OSE work has started at national or even industry levels. This is the source of the problems with the OSI definition of *base standard* as found in TR10000, for example. Requiring international standards or CCITT recommendations was no problem for OSI, since that is what all OSI specifications are. But POSIX mostly originates as IEEE standards, and each part of it takes years to reach international standardization. Meanwhile, many other useful pieces have been specified by industry or user groups, or other national standards bodies. Much work had to be done to adapt the OSI profile nomenclature and taxonomy to OSEs because of these process differences.

Some of the main players in international profiling are sketched in Fig. 12.1. Two of them are closely related to groups we have encountered in previous chapters.

ISO/IEC JTC 1 is the parent of SC22, which is the parent of WG15, the ISO POSIX working group. It is also the parent of SC21, which is the parent of the OSI working groups. It has two stranger children, which have no working groups: SGFS and TSG-1. These are special groups that produced reports focused on very general topics as their main work.

SGFS is the Special Group on Functional Standardization, which is responsible for rules for what goes into an *ISP (International Standardized Profile)*, and produced a report called TR10000 that is a framework and taxonomy for ISPs.

TSG-1 is Technical Study Group One, which produced a report on user requirements for an *IAPs (Interfaces for Application Portability)*.

TR10000, in its original form, is an offshoot of the OSI work, and is largely oriented towards interoperability and conformance testing of network protocols. TSG-1 was motivated by OSE work, and has more goals in addition to those two; it is particularly focused on what users need in standards for application interfaces. TR10000 may be revised or augmented to address OSE issues. Together, the two reports define many of the terms and rules for standardization for OSE profiles.

Work on TSG-1 was influenced by that of the *EWOS Expert Group on the Common Application Environment (EWOS/EG-CAE)*. EWOS/EG-CAE produced a framework and a technical guide for profiles related to OSE.

One of the earliest attempts at a framework was SSI. SSI was a proposal in 1987 for a very large model and related standards that was not approved for formal work, but that either led to or preceded many of the ideas found in TSG-1 and the POSIX Guide. Another early and influential framework was the M.U.S.I.C. *framework* specified by the British *Government Centre for Information Systems (CCTA)* M.U.S.I.C. specifies five broad categories of open system interface standardization. We'll start with M.U.S.I.C. and SSI, and then discuss the rest in approximately chronological order.

M.U.S.I.C.

The *M.U.S.I.C. (Management, User Interface, System Interface, Information, Communications)* model for interface standards was developed by the Government Centre for Information Systems (CCTA) in the United Kingdom. (CCTA was formerly known as the Central Computer and Telecommunications Agency.) This model, provides a framework for talking about a wide range of interface standards. This model also has the advantage that it was not developed by any of the proponents of the major de facto or de jure standards.

Table 12.3 shows the five categories of the M.U.S.I.C. framework, and lists some standards or standards bodies that fit into them [Isaak 1990; Isaak & Hankinson 1990]. The distinction between the I and the C may require clarification: the I corresponds roughly to certain uses of the OSI application and presentation layers, and C is for everything under the whole OSI model.

IEEE P1003.0 considered adopting M.U.S.I.C. [Isaak 1990] for their POSIX Guide [POSIX.0 1991], but evidently decided not to do so.

SSI

The standards discussed in this book are not all of those that exist, and certainly not all of those that might have existed, had history gone a bit differently. For example, there have been several proposals for very comprehensive (one might

Table 12.3 M.U.S.I.C.

Category	Committee	Scope or Project
Management Facilities	P1003.7	System Administration
	P1003.15	Supercomputing Batch
	P1003.6	Security
User Interface	P1003.2	UPE
	P1201.1	Toolkit
	P1201.2	Drivability
	P1201.4	X Window System Libraries
	ISO/SC18	Icons
System and Applications Interface	P1003.1	System Interface
	IS 9945-1	System Interface
	P1003.2	Shell and Tools
	DP 9945-2	Shell and Tools
	PHiGS	Graphics
	GKS	Graphics
Information and Data Format and Interchange	EDI	Electronic Data Interchange
	ODIF	Office Data Interchange Format
	SQL	Database access
Communications	P1224	X.400 API
	P1238	FTAM API
	P1238	Common API
	P1003.8	Transparent File Access
	P1003.12	Protocol Independent Interface
	P1003.13	Namespace and Directory Services
	ISO-OSI	protocol suite
	TCP/IP	protocol suite

say monolithic) standards for large environments. One of the first of these was for a *System Software Interface for Application Programs (SSI).* This was proposed in 1987 to ISO/TC 97 by the Japanese ISO member, *JISC (Japanese Industrial Standards Commission).* It was not focused on any specific historical operating system platform, such as UNIX. It was even broader than operating systems, since it included database management systems and graphic support systems [X3 1987]. The purpose given was "to facilitate portability of application source programs across broad range of computer systems to any system which conforms to this standard, regardless of its architecture with minimum or hopefully no modification" [ISO 1986].

This proposal included the idea of a model of an operating system environment [Isaak 1987]. This idea was later adopted by the IEEE P1003.0 POSIX Guide committee, which uses a model of an *OSE (Open System Environment)* to structure profiles and standards.

The SSI proposal included a proposal to form a subgroup of ISO/TC 97 to write the model and an associated standard. TC97 is the same ISO Technical Committee that later joined with IEC TC 83 to form *ISO/IEC Joint Technical Committee One (ISO/IEC JTC 1)*, which is the parent of the ISO POSIX committee, WG15. JTC 1 is also the parent of TSG-1 and of SGFS, two groups which have been strongly involved in constructing frameworks for environments and profiles.

The proposal itself failed, but many of the ideas in the SSI proposal were adopted (or independently invented; it's hard to tell) by TCOS, WG15, TSG-1, SGFS, or other groups.

The main idea from the SSI proposal that was not developed by other groups was of an operating system interface at a higher level of abstraction than the POSIX System Interface Standard, so as to be independent of the historical UNIX interface (and presumably to be readily implementable on MS-DOS and on new operating systems). This idea was proposed again by Japan in 1991 [JTC 1 1991a] as a *Generic Operating System Interface (GOSI)*. This time, the other main aspects were broken out into separate proposals. These aspects were the model [JTC 1 1991b] and the graphical user interface [JTC 1 1991c].

The GUI proposal outline is similar to a description of what IEEE P1201.1 on Drivability is currently doing: standardizing a programming interface at a higher level than that of any existing GUI. The model proposal accepts the methodology for profiling of TSG-1, but wants a different set of base standards, presumably including GOSI.

The three proposals taken together would, like the SSI proposal, encompass everything POSIX, X/Open, and others have already been doing, but do it differently. However, GOSI also was not approved.

These proposals are evidence that the POSIX way of standardization is not the only possible way, and not necessarily the way some major participants want. Other paths could be charted, with emphases on different historical operating system bases, or on different standardization mechanisms, or on different granularities of standards documents. In fact, several new approaches generally turn up each year. Some of them are abandoned, some become the mainstream, but most are incorporated.

SGFS

The *ISO/IEC JTC 1 Special Group on Functional Standardization (SGFS)* is the group responsible for international standardization of profiles. SGFS has produced a *Technical Report (TR)* on "Framework and taxonomy of International Standardized Profiles," called TR10000. TR10000 is structured in two parts: a framework, and a taxonomy. The framework addresses issues of international standardization, conformance, process and procedures, and maintenance [SGFS

1990]. Its second part is a taxonomy of profiles [SGFS 1991].

TR10000 was written for OSI profiles. Its taxonomy is very specific to OSI and is not very useful for OSE [SGFS 1991]. However, much of its framework is applicable to OSE, especially the definitions and motivations of profiles and related terms that are included [SGFS 1990].

TR10000 permits profiles to subset base standards, which is something that TCOS-SS PSC and SEC have explicitly prohibited in their standards, and have passed a recommendation for such a prohibition up through *JTFS (U.S. JTC TAG for SGFS)*, the U.S. TAG to SGFS.

The definition of base standard in TR10000 has also been controversial. The old definition requires any base standard used in a profile to be an approved International Standard, Technical Report, or CCITT Recommendation. This is quite inconvenient for profiles produced by national groups that want to refer to standards that may become international standards, but have not yet done so. This definition has recently been changed to permit profiles that have not yet become international standards themselves to use base standards that are not of the three types mentioned, as we have already discussed.

EWOS/EG-CAE

The *European Workshop on Open Systems (EWOS)* has long been involved in work related to OSI standardization. More recently, it has become involved in OSE work. The *EWOS Expert Group on the Common Application Environment (EWOS/EG-CAE)* has produced a taxonomy [EWOS 1991a] and a technical guide [EWOS 1991b] for profiles for CAE.

This group is an indirect result of events of 1989. Increasing user demand for a broad spectrum of IT standards caused *XPG3 (X/Open Portability Guide, Issue 3)* to be balloted by the *European Committee for Normalisation (CEN)* as a European standard for CAE. The ballot failed, but made clear the need for CAE profiling. Much of this work was taken up by EWOS, in the EWOS/EG-CAE.

Even though the name of the group includes the acronym "CAE," the actual documents use the acronym "OSE" to align with other bodies working in this field [EWOS 1991a], presumably meaning TCOS and TSG-1, among others. Much of the work of this EWOS Expert Group has been adopted by TSG-1.

TSG-1

The ISO/IEC JTC 1 *Technical Study Group 1 (TSG-1)* has provided a set of user requirements for interfaces for application portability and is thus related to, but different from, SGFS, which standardizes profiles. TSG-1 recommends the use of profiles to promote application portability, both directly, and by finding gaps in existing standards. TSG-1 puts strong emphasis on the user's viewpoint, and recommends continual involvement by users in standardization work. TSG-1 was the first Technical Study Group in standards, and was partly a result of the SSI proposal described in the previous section [TSG-1 1991].

TSG-1 delegates most of its work to groups such as WG15, which produced the IS9945-1/1990 POSIX standard. These working groups have national representation, such as that provided by the U.S. TAG to WG15. There are also national delegate bodies directly to TSG-1, such as the *U.S. TAG to JTC 1 Applications Portability Study Group (JTAP)* JTAP functions similarly to the U.S. TAG to WG15, but is not composed of all the same people, and is functionally distinct.

The TSG-1 Technical Report addresses application portability issues such as

• Definitions

• User requirements

• Portability

• Internationalization

• A framework for application portability

12.4   Profile Issues

Some issues cut across levels of profiles from diverse sources. Many of them were discussed and documented in convenient form by an ad hoc profile coordination meeting of WG15 [WG15 1991a, 8]. Six major issues were identified as important enough to be recommended for consideration in revising the international profiling framework TR10000 [SGFS 1990] to expand it from applying mostly to OSI to applying to OSE.

These six issues were gaps, nesting, subsets, extensions, harmonization, and taxonomies. The same list was recommended by WG15 for consideration by a special meeting of SGFS [Isaak 1991]. The discussion below does not necessarily represent the specific recommendations or conclusions of any of those groups on any of these issues.

Another issue that affects all of the above issues is user requirements: how to find out what they are; and how to put them into profiles. For this reason, the WG15 ad hoc profile group and later WG15 itself encouraged participation by application developers and others in standardization [Isaak 1991].

Gaps

A traditional use of profiles, taxonomies, and frameworks is in finding gaps in base standards. This use needs to be systematized, and priorities for filling the gaps are needed. The existence of these gaps has also been a prime reason for the expansion of OSI workshops such as EWOS and OIW into the OSE arena, as we discussed in Chapter 5, *Industry Organizations and User Groups.*

Nesting

Some profiles specify other profiles. Is this nesting a problem? For use of the profiles? For creation of a comprehensible and reasonably small set of profiles? Can such nesting correspond to a hierarchy of user requirements?

Subsets

Can a profile require only a part of a base standard, leaving out any parts that are not specified in the base standard as options? Doing so may be convenient for profiling some application environments, but can dilute the meaning of the base standard. This concern was particularly important for the POSIX System Interface Standard. A profile might leave out links and multiple processes and use the rest of that standard to specify an environment similar to MS-DOS. But the P1003.1 committee explicitly chose not to do that, so the result would not be POSIX. The TCOS-SS *Profile Steering Committee (PSC)* decided that such subsetting should not be permitted. This emphasises the question of what, exactly, is an option. There are only three named options in POSIX.1. But P1003.3.1 found 93 "options" specified with the word *may*. Can a profile choose a value for any or all of these other options?

There are related questions. Should any needed subsets be referred back to the original base standards committee for possible incorporation as options in later revisions? Can the potential option be used by a profile before it is revised into the base standard? Before the base standard's committee decides to incorporate it? PSC says subsetting by profiles is not permitted, and a proposed option for a subset must be approved by the base standard's committee before a standardized profile is permitted to reference it. A draft profile can reference a draft option before the base standard committee approves it [Oberndorf 1992].

The WG15 ad hoc also encouraged developers of base standards to include an informative annex listing options, parameters, and places where the behavior of an implementation is permitted to vary. This will make it easier for profile developers to determine what is subsetting and what is not.

Extensions

Can a profile specify behavior left implementation defined, unspecified, or undefined in a base standard? PSC says no; instead, an extension must be submitted to the working group that produced the original standard, just as for a subset option.

Harmonization

Profiles must work together. Channels and forums for achieving this are needed. The recent extension of the *OSE Implementation Workshop (OIW)* (see Chapter 5) to include OSE work was partly motivated by this need. A framework adapted to OSE work is needed. A third part to TR10000 is a likely document to hold it.

Taxonomies

There are already several taxonomies for OSE. They need to be harmonized. A forum is needed to discuss this. The recently expanded OIW is a likely forum for this.

RGCPA: Rapporteur Group on Coordination of Profile Activities

The WG15 ad hoc profile coordination group was succeeded by a *Rapporteur Group on Coordination of Profile Activities (RGCPA)* formed by WG15. RGCPA was to produce a *Terms of Reference* from previous work, such as that of the ad hoc group. RGCPA was also supposed to draft an nonnormative annex "Implementation Variations" for IS 9945-1:1990, including "a summary of the implications and consequences of making a particular selection; and possibly guidance regarding which possibilities should be preferred or avoided" [WG15 1991b]. All members of the former WG15 ad hoc profile coordination group were invited to join RGCPA, and WG15 member bodies were to nominate participants and rapporteurs for RGCPA [WG15 1991b]. Similar annexes are required by the TCOS-SS SEC for all future TCOS standards [Johnson 1991].

12.5   Profiling

The process of producing a profile is called profiling. Normally, you will be producing an AEP. To do so, you need to identify an environment that your organization needs to support its applications, and then to specify standards, specifications, options, and parameter values that describe that environment.

First, you need to decide which applications you are trying to support. This usually involves picking a set of applications that is used in common by a department, workgroup, or other division within your organization. Since that group will need to procure or develop software to fit the eventual AEP, it is important to match the AEP to the group, as well as to the applications.

Then, you need to decide on the environment to support the applications. Subsets of the complete set of applications may be used by different subgroups, or on different hardware or software platforms. If so, you may want to specify a separate AEP for each such environment.

Once you know in general the applications and environment you want, you can pick related standards and specifications. For maximum portability or choice of vendors, it is best to choose formal standards, where available. Sometimes only industry or user specifications are available, or are more widely used than related standards. You can pick whichever seems appropriate for your AEP and organization.

Once you know in general the main standards and profiles that you need, you must decide on options and parameter values to support your environment. You can use these choices to decide among several potential standards or profiles, picking the standards or profiles that have the most harmonized options and parameters. Pragmatically, you also want to check to see which options and parameters are actually available in real implementations

Once you have created your profile, and are ready to use it in procurements or development, it is also useful to publish it. This may not only save someone else the trouble of developing a similar profile, but may enourage vendors to produce what you want to use.

Formal standards bodies develop profiles in much the same way. They are more constrained to using formal standards, rather than industry specifications. They are more concerned with harmonization, and perhaps also with conformance testing. And, of course, they work by more formal rules.

While developing a profile, whether by informal or formal processes, you will probably note gaps and places where harmonization could be improved. You should also provide this information to bodies that can do something with it.

More detailed guidelines on profiling may be found in several places [Digital 1991], including the *POSIX Guide*, which has an appendix on profiling for the POSIX OSE [POSIX.0 1991].

References

Digital 1991.   Digital, *Open Systems Handbook: A Guide to Building Open Systems,* Digital Equipment Corporation, Bedford, MA (1991).

EWOS 1991a.   EWOS, *EWOS/TA/91/08, EWOS/EG-CAE/91/31,* EWOS, Brussels (1991).

EWOS 1991b.   EWOS, "EWOS Guide to Profiles for the Open System Environment; Issue 1, Draft 5," EWOS, Brussels (17 April 1991).

Isaak 1987.   Isaak, Jim, "Re: US TAG Ballot on ISO NWI for Operating System Standard," IEEE P1003, Northboro, MA (26 January 1987).

Isaak 1990.   Isaak, Jim, "POSIX Explained," *CommUNIXations* **X**(7), pp. 10–13, UniForum (September 1990).

Isaak 1991.   Isaak, Jim, "WG15 resolutions related to profile work," WG15, Rotterdam (29 May 1991).

Isaak & Hankinson 1990.   Isaak, James, & Hankinson, Allen, "M.U.S.I.C. — A Finely Tuned Framework For Open Systems?," *UNIX Technology Advisor* **2**(1), p. 7, MYOB, Inc. (January 1990).

ISO 1986.   ISO, *Proposal for a NWI on Standardization of System Software Interface for Application Programs,* 23 December 1986.

Johnson 1991.   Johnson, Lowell, *Proposal for Harmonizing Options,* SEC Profile Steering Committee (15 August 1991).

JTC 1 1991a.   JTC 1, *Generic Operating System Interface,* JTC 1 (1991).

JTC 1 1991b.   JTC 1, *Model and Framework of Interfaces for Application Portability,* JTC 1 (1991).

JTC 1 1991c.   JTC 1, *API for Windowing Systems,* JTC 1 (1991).

Oberndorf 1992.   Oberndorf, Tricia, "PSC Policies and Guidelines: Rules and Definitions Regarding the Development of POSIX Standardized Profiles,"

Standing Document (PSC SD-009, Draft 3), Profile Steering Commitee (15 May 1992).

POSIX.0 1991.   POSIX.0, *Draft Guide to the POSIX Open Systems Environment,* IEEE, New York (September 1991). IEEE P1003.0/D13.

SGFS 1990.   SGFS, *Information technology — Framework and taxonomy of International Standardized Profiles — Part 1: Framework,* ISO/IEC JTC 1 SGFS, Geneva (15 May 1990).

SGFS 1991.   SGFS, *Information technology — Framework and taxonomy of International Standardized Profiles — Part 2: Taxonomy,* 28 June 1991.

TSG-1 1991.   TSG-1, "Standards Necessary for Interfaces for Application Portability," ISO/IEC JTC 1 TSG-1, Tokyo (1991).

WG15 1991a.   WG15, "Minutes of WG15 Ad Hoc Coordination Meeting," WG15, Amsterdam (7-8 May 1991).

WG15 1991b.   WG15, "Additional Parts of WG15 Report," WG15, Rotterdam (11 March 1991).

X3 1987.   X3, ASC, *Proposed TC97 NWI on Standardization of System Software Interface for Application Programs,* 14 January 1987.

CHAPTER 13

TCOS Profiles

Although profiles are relatively new to TCOS, there are quite a few of them now. We have already listed them in Chapter 7, *IEEE/CS TCOS Standards*.

The IEEE P1003.0 POSIX Guide is not a profile itself. It contains a reference model and guidelines for profiling. IEEE P1003.18 and P1003.14 specify general environments, and P1003.18 is intended to be used as a platform for building other profiles. The others are AEPs for more specialized environments, or ASEDs for even more specific kinds of applications.

13.1 PSC: Profile Steering Committee

The *IEEE/CS TCOS-SS Profile Steering Commitee (PSC)* was formed in April 1991 to provide guidance to TCOS committees that are writing profiles. The exact form of this guidance has been rather controversial. The latest conclusion seems to be that the rules generated by the PSC in the spring and summer of 1992 are to be applied rather rigorously to profiles as they go to ballot. These rules are mostly about profile harmonization, including base references, profiles, and base options.

The PSC is supposed to set up and maintain relations with related United States profile activities, including JTFS and OIW. It is also supposed to encourage relations with user groups that generate profiles (such as POSC and UAOS) and to set up relations with international activities, through appropriate channels.

We've already mentioned the idea of a *standardized profile,* that is, a profile that has been standardized. TCOS adds a few more requirements for a *POSIX Standardized Profile (POSIX SP)*. A POSIX SP must require conformance to the central base standard, IS 9945-1. Most POSIX SPs are also intended to become *ISPs (International Standardized Profiles)*. The PSC rules define what a POSIX SP is and who can make one.

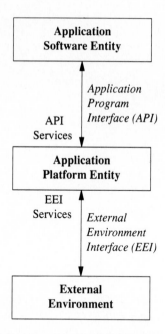

Figure 13.1 POSIX OSE Reference Model.

Figure reproduced from IEEE Draft Standard, P1003.0/D14, Guide to POSIX Based Open System Architecture, *copyright © 1992 by the Institute of Electrical and Electronic Engineers, Inc. with the permission of the IEEE. This is an unapproved draft, subject to change.*

13.2   IEEE P1003.0 POSIX Guide

The IEEE P1003.0 working group is developing a guide document that describes an *OSE (Open System Environment)*. The document details a reference model and provides guidance on how to use POSIX standards and other standards and specifications identified by the group as being necessary or desirable for an OSE [Lewis 1992]. The document is called the *POSIX Guide (IEEE P1003.0)*. The OSE is usually known as the *POSIX OSE (POSIX Open System Environment)*.

The POSIX OSE reference model is shown in Fig. 13.1. The model assumes an application program interacts with an application platform, which interacts with the external environment. These are the three basic entities in the reference model. The first two of these entities are what we have called the application and the implementation in Chapter 3. However, the model carefully uses generic terminology to avoid any implication that the platform or application must be implemented as a single program or machine.

The application program does not interact with the external environment directly, rather only through the application platform. Since POSIX specifies interfaces, the reference model names the two interfaces between the three basic

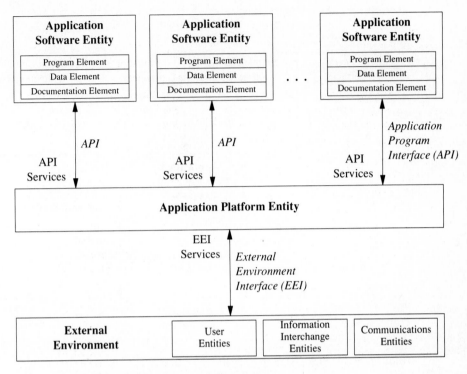

Figure 13.2 POSIX OSE Reference Model — Entities.
Figure reproduced from IEEE Draft Standard, P1003.0/D14, Guide to POSIX Based Open System Architecture, *copyright © 1992 by the Institute of Electrical and Electronic Engineers, Inc. with the permission of the IEEE. This is an unapproved draft, subject to change.*

entities. The *Application Program Interface (API)* is between the program and the platform, and the *External Environment Interface (EEI)* is between the platform and the external environment. The model also names the services provided by the platform: API services and EEI services. A single standard may specify all of these interfaces and services, or different standards may be needed.

The entities in the POSIX OSE are shown in more detail in Fig. 13.2. Many different (or identical) programs may use the same application platform simultaneously. The model uses a generalized *Application Software Entity (ASE)* that may include program, data, and documentation elements. These are the main three elements that standards specify for applications. Different standards may be required for different ASE elements, but a single API standard (or set of standards) should support multiple ASEs.

The external environment may contain several kinds of entities, including users, information interchange entities (such as tape drives), and communications entities (such as networks). Different standards may be required for each type of

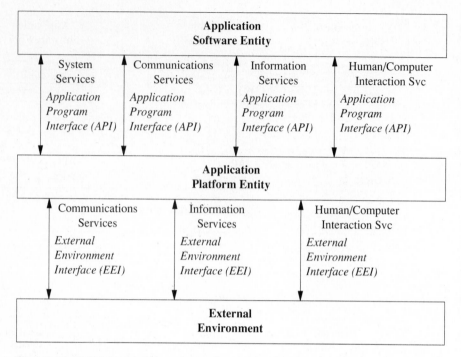

Figure 13.3 POSIX OSE Reference Model — Interfaces.
Figure reproduced from IEEE Draft Standard, P1003.0/D14, Guide to POSIX Based
Open System Architecture, *copyright © 1992 by the Institute of Electrical and Electronic Engineers, Inc. with the permission of the IEEE. This is an unapproved draft, subject to change.*

external environment entity, such as P1201 for users, P1003.1 (Chapter 10) for information exchange, and P1003.12 for network interfaces.

The interfaces in the model are shown in more detail in Fig. 13.3. There may be different EEI for each of the kinds of external environment entities. These different EEI correspond to the different standards that may be needed. There may be different API for each kind of external environment entity, and there may also be API for system services provided by the application platform.

The Guide also includes guidance on writing profiles. A profile must be not only complete, but also coherent. It must specify the interactions of specific standards on a single system [Isaak 1990a]. This involves harmonizing the interfaces involved, such as those shown in Fig. 13.3.

Every TCOS standard must have a section in the POSIX Guide saying how it fits with other TCOS standards. The IEEE P1003.0 committee cannot write all of these; the individual committees are now expected to do so, following the guidelines in the 1003.0 document, and with the assistance of the PSC.

13.3   IEEE P1003.18 PEP

The *PEP (POSIX Environment Platform profile)* is an outgrowth of the IEEE 1003.1 work. Although 1003.1 is descended from the more general */usr/group 1984 Standard,* it defines only a very narrow set of system interface functions, plus a few additional facilities, such as archive and data interchange formats. It does not cover enough area to define the sort of environment UNIX users were used to. A profile was needed to define such an environment. The original proposal for what became P1003.18 was called *TIMS (Traditional Interactive Multiuser System).*

Since the AEP defined by PEP is one from which other AEPs can be derived by selection (for an ASED) or addition (for even more general AEPs), PEP also is a platform profile. It is intended for use in writing other profiles.

PEP is intended to be the first *POSIX SP (POSIX Standardized Profile).* It, and profiles that refer to it, will be reviewed by WG15 for harmonization with international standards and profiles.

The base documents used in PEP are

- ISO/IEC 9945-1

- XPG

- NIST FIPS (e.g., FIPS 151-1)

- Historical implementations

AEP and ADP

PEP permits conforming implementations to cross-compile programs on one system for use on another system. It distinguishes the *ADP (Application Development Platform),* where a program is translated (compiled or interpreted) from the *AEP (Application Execution Platform),* where the program is executed. The latter acronym is unfortunately similar to *AEP (Application Environment Profile),* but is actually unrelated. PEP, AEP, and ADP are shown in Table 13.1.

A program may be compiled on a multiuser system with a large amount of disk space, for execution on a workstation or a single-user PC. The compilation

Table 13.1 PEP: ADP and AEP.

System A	System B	Environment Type
ADP + AEP	none	Self-hosting
ADP	AEP	Cross-compilation
none	AEP	ABI (not conformant)

and execution environments may also be combined in a single system. So the compilation and development systems may vary from a single system, to a system with a coprocessor to aid compilation, to two systems connected by a network, to two systems connected over a dialup connection, to two systems that are not connected at all. In the last case, the compiled program might be transferred on a tape or disk.

PEP does not, however, permit an *ABI (Application Binary Interface)* alone to conform. An ABI would be an AEP without an ADP, as shown in Table 13.1. But there must be an ADP for PEP conformance. This is in keeping with the general POSIX philosophy of providing source code compatibility standards, rather than binary standards.

13.4   IEEE P1003.14 Multiprocessing AEP

The *IEEE P1003.14 (P1003.14 Multiprocessing AEP)* defines a general environment, and is thus somewhat similar to PEP, IEEE P1003.18. But P1003.14 is not intended to be a platform profile for use in development of other profiles. It is intended to support a particular kind of platform, represented by historical multiprocessor computer systems.

13.5   IEEE P1003.13 Realtime AEP

We've already discussed the IEEE P1003.4 realtime draft standard, and IEEE P1003.4a, for Pthreads, in Chapter 7, *IEEE/CS TCOS Standards*. Here we discuss some related AEPs the same committee is developing.

The *IEEE P1003.13 (P1003.13 Realtime AEP)* document is being developed by the IEEE P1003.4 committee. The document will specify three AEP subsets. As shown in Table 13.2, these subsets range from Full Function through Realtime Intermediate to Embedded Control System, and are distinguished primarily by the presence or absence of multiple processes and a filesystem. The Full Function AEP has both; the Embedded Control System AEP has neither; and the Realtime Intermediate AEP has a filesystem but only one process.

Table 13.2 IEEE 1003.13 realtime AEP subsets.

1003.13 AEP Subset	Filesystem	Multiple Processes
Full Function	yes	yes
Realtime Intermediate	yes	no
Embedded Control System	no	no

Only the Embedded Control System subset AEP has so far been drafted. It covers these areas of functionality:

• Extensive I/O

• Control logic

• Signal normalization

• Unique interfaces

• Time constraints

• Cyclic operations

It is for hard realtime. That is, a diskless controller might conform to it. It does not target specific applications such as data acquisition or inventory tracking [Digital 1991].

POSIX realtime interfaces are quite different from those of many existing realtime operating systems. But some users expect that the POSIX profiles interfaces, especially in conjunction with the POSIX realtime profiles, will eventually be accepted and will form the basis of viable products [OSSWG 1991].

13.6   IEEE P1003.10 Supercomputing AEP

The *P1003.10 Supercomputing AEP (IEEE P1003.10)* specifies a general environment for supercomputing applications. These are much like ordinary POSIX applications, but have several distinguishing characteristics, some of which the average POSIX implementation might not provide by default.

A supercomputing application is one or more of the following:

• Large

• Long running

• CPU intensive

• Memory intensive

• I/O intensive

• High bandwidth

It is usually run through a shell script, and may involve networking or graphics.

To provide a general supercomputing environment, P1003.10 must specify support for all of these characteristics. So P1003.10 addresses many areas of standardization.

At the system interface, P1003.10 requires

- 1003.1 extensions: checkpoint and restart, resource limits
- P1003.4 realtime files and asynchronous I/O
- FIPS 151-1 plus _POSIX_CHILD_MAX=25 and _POSIX_OPEN_MAX=64
- 48 or 64 bit off_t (file offset)

P1003.10 requirements in other areas include:

- Shell and utilities: P1003.2 with options and UPE
- Graphics: X11R3, C language Xlib and X Toolkit Intrinsics, bitmaps, also many optional standards.
- Languages: Both C and Fortran required; others optional
- Security: P1003.6 DAC, then MAC
- System administration: P1003.7

In networking, P1003.10 specifies two optional protocol stacks:

1)   TCP/IP with FTP, SMTP

2)   OSI with FTAM, X.400, ISO 802/n, and X.25

Either stack must also include P1003.8 TFA, and RPC.

13.7   IEEE P1003.15 Batch AEP

The *P1003.15 Supercomputing Batch Element AEP (IEEE P1003.15)* is being written by P1003.10. It is an offshoot of the P1003.10 document, much like 1003.2a is an offshoot of 1003.2. Having batch issues in a separate document allows deferring them while P1003.10 completes 1003.10.

Because it deals with such issues as very long running programs, and thus with restoration of environment after service interruption, 1003.15 is related to the IEEE P1003.7 system administration standard.

13.8   IEEE P1003.11 Transaction Processing

The *P1003.11 Transaction Processing AEP (IEEE P1003.11)* is coordinated with OSI DTP, X/Open TP, P1003.1, P1003.4, P1003.8, and ANSI 3T5.5 (RPC). P1003.11 is considering transaction-oriented RPC services. There are several related documents, including the *OSI Distributed Transaction Processing (OSI*

DTP) work [OSI 1989]. The *X/Open Transaction Processing (X/Open TP)* group has published several related specifications [X/Open 1987; X/Open 1990].

13.9   TCOS Profiles and Distributed Computing

Most, if not all, TCOS profiles are for single machine environments. Many are for rather specific *Application Environment Profiles (AEP)*, such as P1003.10 for supercomputing, P1003.15 for supercomputing batch environment, and P1003.11 for transaction processing. Some are more eclectic, such as the P1003.13 Real-time profiles. And some are for rather general environments, such as P1003.14 for multiprocessing and P1003.18 for a traditional timesharing environment. Finally, P1003.0 is the Guide that gives a reference model for a general *Open System Environment (OSE),* with detail on how other profiles should select parts of it.

A distributed computing environment is neither a traditional timesharing environment, nor even an OSE in the sense of 1003.0. Even though several TCOS profiles (e.g. 1003.10) require specific stacks of networking protocols, none of them are concerned with a distributed environment beyond a single client/server pair. ISO and RFC documents describe network protocols, and some aspects of their host interfaces (see Chapter 8). The TCOS Distributed Services standards discuss interfaces to distributed services (see Chapter 7). The POSIX Guide and PEP help show how to fit the pieces together to form an open system, but not how to use open systems to glue together an open system environment.

The one TCOS project that is trying to cover large parts of distributed computing is 1003.7, the draft system administration standard. 1003.7 is concerned with the management of a OSE. This is different from the management of a network, as in SNMP, even though the 1003.7 work draws from the prior art of the SNMP work. These topics are discussed in Chapter 14.

One reason that TCOS has not produced a distributed computing profile may be that a large proportion of the participants in the TCOS process are vendors, rather than users. System interface vendors and application vendors want standards that will permit applications to run on a variety of implementations. Large scale transparent interoperability is mostly beyond the immediate financial interests of such vendors. A simpler reason TCOS avoids distributed computing may be that it is a technical committee on operating system interfaces and open system environments, not on distributed computing in general.

13.10   TCOS Profile History

The use of profiles has increased gradually over the past several years [Isaak 1990b; Isaak 1990c]. The IEEE P1003.0 POSIX Guide project was proposed in 1988, and its first draft was completed in the same year. NIST produced two important profiles in 1988: the NIST APP in March, and GOSIP Version 1 in October. GOSIP Version 2 was available in 1991. The IEEE 1003.0 standard was expected to be approved by early 1993.

Most TCOS committees paid little attention to profiles until around mid-1989. Only in 1990 did it become evident that half a dozen committees were actually writing profiles, without sufficient coordination. A Profile Coordination Committee of IEEE 1003.0 attempted to provide such coordination. By April 1991, it became clear that something more structured would be needed, and the TCOS *Profile Steering Committee (PSC)* was approved by the TCOS SEC.

There are still some obscure areas related to profiles, such as where the boundaries lie between profiles and extensions. For example, the IEEE P1003.15 batch processing AEP contains extensions to IEEE 1003.1, in addition to being a profile that specifies relations with other standards. Exactly how to separate the extensions from the profile, or whether it is necessary to do so, is not clear.

References

Digital 1991.   Digital, *Open Systems Handbook: A Guide to Building Open Systems,* Digital Equipment Corporation, Bedford, MA (1991).

Isaak 1990a.   Isaak, James, "Application Environment Profiles: a Significant Tool for Simplification and Coordination of the Standards Efforts," *IEEE Computer* (February 1990).

Isaak 1990b.   Isaak, James, "POSIX Standards: Fact or Friction?," *UNIX Technology Advisor* **2**(1), pp. 1–6, MYOB, Inc. (January 1990).

Isaak 1990c.   Isaak, Jim, "The history of POSIX: A study in the standards process," *IEEE Computer* **23**(7), pp. 89–92 (July 1990).

Lewis 1992.   Lewis, Kevin, Personal communication (26 March 1992).

OSI 1989.   OSI, *ISO/IEC DIS 10026-1 (model), 10026-2 (service), 10026-3 (protocol),* International Organization for Standardization/International Electrotechnical Commission, Switzerland (September 1989).

OSSWG 1991.   OSSWG, "Delta Document for the Next Generation Computer Resources (NGCR) Operating Systems Interface Standard Baseline," Operating Systems Standards Working Group (OSSWG) Next Generation Computer Resources (NGCR) Program, Naval Ocean Systems Center, San Diego, CA (31 December 1991).

X/Open 1987.   X/Open, "Online Transaction Processing Reference Model," X/Open Transaction Processing (1987).

X/Open 1990.   X/Open, "Preliminary Specification — Distributed Transaction Processing: The A Specification," X/Open Transaction Processing (1990).

CHAPTER 14

Industry Profiles

Several industry groups produce specifications for open systems related to the UNIX operating system or the POSIX system interface standards. Many of these specifications are guides to large environments, most of them for distributed computing. Some of them have specific corresponding software products, but in this book we concentrate on the specifications. We describe what is in them, as well as what you might expect but will not find. And we include much contextual information.

The specification documents of interest in this chapter are variously called guides, roadmaps, definitions, or descriptions. We will call them guides, profiles, or specifications, depending on which aspect we are concentrating on. The things they specify are variously called environments, models, architectures, or systems. We usually call them models, although we often refer to them by whatever term is used in their specifications.

Many of these specifications are actually models for distributed computing. A distributed computing environment is a very general computing environment, incorporating as it does environments on network hosts, network protocols, client/server architecture, network management, and more. As we have mentioned in Chapter 1, *Computing Models*, there is a tendency for later models to borrow from or incorporate the others. These interrelations are described in this chapter, along with overviews of the technical contents of the specifications.

Some of these environment specifications were originally developed before related formal standards, such as POSIX, were finished, and most are broader than POSIX. Few formal standards approach the scope of the X/Open XPG, the OSF AES, or USL's SVID. Even fewer reach the scale of the OSF DCE or UI-ATLAS. The POSIX Guide, IEEE P1003.0, is the closest, since the OSE it describes is essentially the open system element of a distributed computing environment. In each of the descriptions of specifications in this chapter, we describe relations to the POSIX Guide, which we have already described in Chapter 13, *TCOS Profiles*.

We also discuss their positions in comparison to the NIST APP, which is described in Chapter 15, *Procurement Profiles*. And we mention some aspects of the influence of technical aspects of these specifications on standards, but we leave details of their development processes to Chapter 5, *Industry Organizations and User Groups*, where we discuss the organizations themselves.

Some of the documents described in this chapter have corresponding software produced by the same organization. For example, OSF produces both a guide and software, and UI produces input to USL, which produces a guide and software. Sun and SunSoft, and Apollo of HP, produce software in addition to the specifications we discuss. We also discuss BSDI, as an example of a simpler approach to open systems.

Because we discuss two specifications in this chapter does not necessarily mean that the specifications are of the same kind, nor that the organizations that produce them are directly comparable. For example, OSF DCE is a set of software products, with a single (or a few) technology selection(s) in each technological area, whereas UI-ATLAS is a framework of APIs, and the USL technologies endorsed by UI are not supposed to be the only ones to fit the framework.

Both the OSF DME and UI-ATLAS address distributed management environments, but we have separated that topic into this chapter, *Industry Profiles*, in which we also gather network management, and the work of the only TCOS committee that deals with distribution beyond interfaces, the IEEE P1003.7 System Administration committee.

14.1   X/Open Portability Guide

The *XPG (X/Open Portability Guide)* is produced by the *X/Open Company, Ltd (X/Open)*. The XPG specifies a *Common Application Environment (CAE)*. X/Open intends this to be a complete environment for the development and execution of applications. The XPG specifies interfaces in a very broad range of technical areas, including POSIX operating system, X Window user interface, X/Open transport service, ISAM, ANSI SQL, Languages C, Pascal, Fortran, COBOL, and Ada [X/Open 1989]. This was one of the earliest and is one of the most comprehensive industry specifications. It has been very influential both on other industry specifications and on formal standards. For these reasons, the XPG is also one of the most widely known specifications, and does not need detailed treatment here.

14.2   SVID: System V Interface Definition

The *System V Interface Definition (SVID)* describes the environment supported by UNIX System V Release 4 [AT&T 1989]. The SVID has long been a strong influence on POSIX, and UNIX System V Release 4 is conformant with the POSIX System Interface Standard. The SVID was formerly produced by AT&T, but is now owned by *UNIX System Laboratories (USL)*.

14.3   AES: Application Environment Specification

OSF produces both software and guides. Since this is a book about standards and specifications, we discuss OSF's specifications. The OSF *Application Environment Specification (AES)* describes the environment supported by the OSF operating system, *OSF/1,* which is based on Mach [OSF 1992]. OSF/1 is compatible with the programming interfaces of UNIX System V Release 3 (not System V Release 4), 4.3BSD, and the POSIX System Interface Standard.

14.4   DCE: Distributed Computing Environment

OSF has been active in distributed computing. We have already mentioned their *Distributed Computing Environment (OSF DCE)* in Chapter 1 as one of the current industry models for distributed computing. We describe OSF DCE in more detail here [Kumar 1991]. OSF's depiction of the DCE architecture is shown in Fig. 14.1. One of the goals of this DCE is to interoperability not only over LANs but also over WANs and beyond organizational boundaries [OSF 1990].

Figure 14.1 OSF DCE.
Permission to reprint the copyrighted illustration titled: Distributed Computing Environment (DCE) Architecture *which appears in this book has been granted by Open Software Foundation, Inc.*

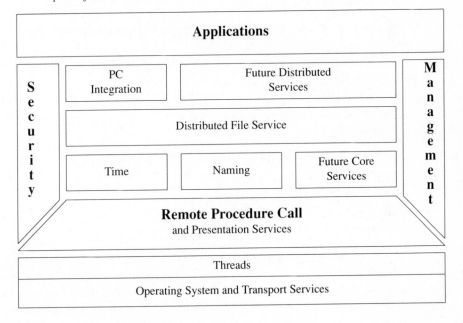

Overview

OSF released a Request for Technology (RFT) on 13 June 1989 for a Distributed Computing Environment (DCE) [OSF 1990, 38–41]. It originally expected to receive responses in five technological areas, but it actually received them in seventeen. Not all of these were addressed directly by OSF, but an attempt was made to construct a framework that could encompass them all. This framework also incorporates elements from two previous distributed computing models: Sun's ONC and Apollo's NCS. Various vendors already working in the area support OSF's DCE, although they may not agree with specific product choices. There is even a reference implementation, by Siemens Nixdorf, of DCE for UNIX System V [OSF 1991a]. This is by Siemens Nixdorf Information Systems, Inc., which is the U.S. subsidiary of Siemens Nixdorf Informationssysteme AG of Germany.

In Chapter 1, *Computing Models*, we mentioned some of the specific elements of OSF DCE, and pictured them in Fig. 1.2. Here, we list the layers and components specified by OSF.

The OSF operating system is called OSF/1, and is based on Mach from CMU. Advantages of Mach included existing ports to many platforms, and support for lightweight processes (threads).

DCE does not emphasize network, internet, or transport protocol layers; practically, however, it is usually used with TCP/IP over the usual network layers, such as Ethernet, although DCE can use X.25. The DCE RPC is used to minimize underlying protocol requirements. Above the transport layer, OSF uses elements of the OSI session, presentation, and application layers.

Infrastructure Components

DCE is built on three components that support and surround all the others:

1. RPC underlies all the distributed services of DCE, which in turn support applications [OSF 1991b].

2. Security affects all levels from RPC up to the application. DCE uses Kerberos as their authentication protocol, and has facilities for user registration and authorization [OSF 1991c].

3. Management affects all levels from RPC up to the application.

Distributed Services

Above RPC are distributed services, within which DCE distinguishes at least three layers.

• Directly above RPC are time and directory services. The time service chosen is *DECdts (Digital's Distributed Time Synchronization Service)*. It can integrate with the Internet *NTP (Network Time Protocol)* for coordination with outside time sources. DCE directory services are built around X.500, adding the *XDS (X/Open Directory Service)* API to it. OSF also adds mechanisms for finding directory cells across multiple organizations. Apparently the Internet *DNS (Domain Name Service)* is used for mapping hostnames to IP addresses [OSF 1991d].

- Above those are distributed file services [OSF 1991e], provided by the *Andrew File System (AFS)*.

- Other distributed services are layered above that include support for diskless network nodes. More distributed services are expected later. Possibilities include accounting and notification services [OSF 1990]. One that has been announced is MS-DOS file and printer support. This is called the *PCI (Personal Computer Integration)* service, and is provided using Sun's PC-NFS, or the HP and Microsoft *LMX (Lan Manager/X) SMB (Server Message Block)* protocol. Both of these are endorsed by X/Open [OSF 1990].

Applications

Finally, there are the applications, most of which are provided by the user or by specific vendors. However, OSF has endorsed the Motif LAFI GUI. Distributed print spooling is a likely future OSF application [OSF 1990].

The OSF DCE RPC is normally used over UDP over IP, but both connectionless and connection-oriented RPC are supported. In fact, isolating services and applications supported by RPC from underlying transport protocols is a major goal of this RPC [OSF 1991f]. Presumably this is at least partly to avoid the political decision of which of TCP/IP or OSI to support.

RPC, Presentation Services, and Programming Tools

Coupled with RPC are presentation services. The specific protocols used are NCS RPC and *NDR (Network Data Representation)*. NDR is programmed with the NCS *NIDL (Network Interface Definition Language)*. The specific version of NCS used was jointly submitted by Digital and HP [OSF 1990]. RPC calls are made more efficient by threads in OSF/1.

OSF DCE's RPC supports internationalization by including support for multibyte character sets [OSF 1991f].

ANDF: Architecture Neutral Distribution Format

We have already discussed the general idea of an *ANDF (Architecture Neutral Distribution Format)* in Chapter 3. Here, we describe the particular ANDF that OSF announced in June 1991 and has been distributing since October 1991 [OSF 1991g]. The general idea is to provide shrink-wrapped software without specifying an ABI.

The basic technique is to use a *ANDF producer* to translate a program into the ANDF format. There is normally one producer per programming language, such as C. A producer is essentially a compiler for a generic platform, which is described by the ANDF specification. The OSF C producer also comes with header files adapted for ANDF, but compatible with POSIX and ANSI C.

The ANDF format is later translated into something a local platform can understand, by an *ANDF installer*. There is normally one installer per platform, where a platform is usually an operating system and hardware architecture combination. OSF claims five reference installers, which can be used by application developers in ensuring that application programs work with ANDF.

Apollo and HP

The *Network Computing System (NCS)* from Apollo Computer has been influential in distributed computing. It is a portable implementation of Apollo's *Network Computing Architecture (NCA)*, which is a specification of an "object-oriented framework for developing distributed applications" [Dineen *et al.* 1987]. NCS runs under implementations of the UNIX system, such as Apollo's DOMAIN/IX. Apollo has since been bought by *HP (Hewlett-Packard)*. NCA was always intended for resource sharing among systems from a variety of vendors in a heterogeneous networked environment.

14.5   UI-ATLAS

UNIX International (UI) provides guidance to USL on the development of the UNIX system [UI 1992]. UI itself does not produce software or specifications for specific software. It does produce high level documents, however, such as its *UI-ATLAS* framework or architecture, and we discuss that here.

UI-ATLAS is an architecture or framework for an open computing environment. The basic idea is to unify the present conflicting approaches to open systems by providing a framework that can incorporate interface specifications that can, in turn, permit multiple implementations. We have already mentioned the UI-ATLAS architecture in Chapter 1 as one of the current industry models for distributed computing. Here we describe it in more detail, starting with the UI diagram of the architecture in Fig. 14.2.

Overview

The UI-ATLAS framework uses standardized APIs, plus reference technologies for incorporating technologies into the system. It does not include specific selections of products for specific technical areas. Although UI endorses reference technologies available from USL, the UI-ATLAS framework is not supposed to be limited to those endorsed products. USL has even called it a procurement specification [USL 1991]. Instead of being a specific software product, UI-ATLAS is intended to encourage competing products so that users will have increased choice among cost-competitive products. And no single company or small group of suppliers is expected alone to deliver all the technology required by UI-ATLAS [UI 1991a].

About twenty vendors endorsed UI-ATLAS at its announcement. Software for UI-ATLAS is becoming available over a schedule from late 1991 through 1994 [UI 1991b].

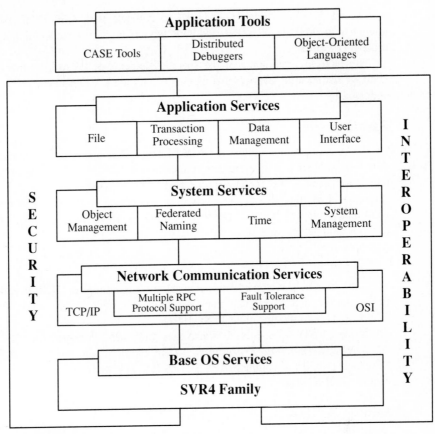

Figure 14.2 UI-ATLAS.
From UNIX International, 1992 UNIX System V Roadmap, *UNIX International,*
Parsippany, NJ, © 1992. Reprinted with permission.

UI-ATLAS has an emphasis on supporting present distributed applications,
but with a migration path to future applications, which it expects to be object oriented [UI 1991c]. It also emphasizes transparency [UI 1991b; UI 1991d]. Interoperability is mentioned frequently, but is taken for granted more than in OSF
DCE. UI seems more concerned with unifying and extending the existing open
systems solutions related to the historical UNIX operating system than in addressing the problem of compatibility with nondistributed mainframe environments,
which appears to be more of a concern to OSF.

UI-ATLAS incorporates aspects of previous architectures, such as Sun's ONC
and OSF DCE. In fact, it explicitly incorporates OSF DCE's "fundamental technologies for interoperability" [UI 1991c]. These apparently include all of OSF
DCE [UI 1991a]. It is not always clear what this means when UI explicitly
endorses a choice that OSF did not, such as NFS, where OSF chose AFS. USL
plans to provide an implementation of OSF DCE for System V Release 4 [USL

1991]. UI does not intend UI-ATLAS to compete with OSF DCE; rather, it intends to incorporate OSF DCE and build beyond it. UI is also planning a testing process [UI 1991a].

We have pictured some of the specific elements of UI-ATLAS in Fig. 1.2. Here we list specific layers and components, and the USL reference technologies endorsed by UI.

Base Operating System

The endorsed operating system is UNIX System V Release 4.1 ES, with enhanced security. Another USL operating system component endorsed by UI is UNIX System V Release 4.0 MP, for multiprocessing. This provides lightweight processes (threads). USL has also recently made an agreement with Chorus systèmes to coordinate with the Chorus distributed operating system. The C++ object oriented programming language is endorsed.

Communication Services

The OSI model is endorsed for networking. USL supplies TCP/IP and, with Retix, an OSI stack. USL also plans to provide gateways and migration tools for TCP/IP to OSI communications [USL 1991].

Since UI-ATLAS uses NFS, it also uses Sun's *RPC (Remote Procedure Call)* and *XDR (External Data Representation)*. In addition, it includes the OSF DCE RPC, and provides a common API [UI 1991a]. Higher layers are kept independent of the RPC in use.

Security Services

Kerberos is used for security, and security features are also provided by each of the lower level technologies, starting from the base operating system [UI 1991a].

Interoperability

Another pervasive feature is interoperability, which also is present in all the other layers. UI particularly wants this interoperability to be noninvasive [UI 1991d]; that is, interoperability should not disturb installed bases of UNIX systems.

System Services

Distributed support service implementations endorsed include NIS from SunSoft for hostname to address translation, and X.500 from USL and RETIX for directory service, with the OSF cell concept. The Internet *DNS (Domain Name Service)* is supported. *Federated Naming* is the term for the UI-ATLAS glue that ties all these directory services together. Time service is also supported. The UI-ATLAS architecture includes management frameworks and endorses software related to them, as we discuss at the end of this chapter.

Application Services

Distributed services in UI-ATLAS include the *Network File System (NFS)* from SunSoft for transparent file access.

PC integration into networks of UNIX machines is explicitly supported. PC-NFS is used for this.

One endorsed application is X.400, in an implementation from USL and RETIX. Another is TUXEDO System/T for distributed online transaction processing. For LAFI GUI, UI-ATLAS supports both Motif and OPEN LOOK, with endorsed technology from USL.

Application Tools

UI-ATLAS includes tools for producing and maintaining distributed applications [UI 1991e].

OLTP: Online Transaction Processing

UI-ATLAS includes distributed *online transaction processing (OLTP)*, using USL's TUXEDO System/T as the endorsed product [UI 1991c].

UI notes that OLTP is the largest segment of the commercial computing industry, with 1991 revenues of about $35 billion. This segment is growing twice as fast as the computer industry at large, and UNIX system OLTP is growing faster than that [UI 1991f]. Obviously, UI and USL are interested in this market.

Sun and SunSoft

Sun Microsystems, Inc. (SMI) produced a Roadmap for *Open Network Computing (ONC)* that has been influential on later architectures [SMI 1990]. Since then, Sun has divided itself into several companies, one of which, SunSoft, is selling a software system, Solaris, which encompasses ONC and other technology.

14.6   BSDI: Berkeley Software Design, Inc.

BSDI (Berkeley Software Design, Inc.) has converted software from UCB *CSRG (Computer Systems Research Group)* into a product for i386 and i486-based machines. The product includes most the code from the latest *BSD (Berkeley Software Distribution)* release, in the line of 4.2BSD and 4.3BSD [Leffler *et al.* 1989]. This release from CSRG, called CSRG Networking-2, is free of any code licensed by AT&T or USL. BSDI has added the pieces needed to run on i386 and i486 architectures.

BSDI provides a running, full function operating system for PCs. It distributes the source code with the system, plus all the manual pages online [Kolstad 1991].

The first BSDI release, called BSD/386, includes

- TCP/IP and OSI networking

- NFS (including optional tcp-nfs)

- X11R5

- Text processing software (groff, TEX, etc.)

- POSIX functionality, and conformance of the kernel and utilities as far as possible with the System Interface Standard current drafts of the Shell and Utilities Standard

- ANSI C and C++

- The traditional Berkeley (McKusick) fast filesystem, plus an in-core filesystem.

This makes BSD/386 a system in a class with those architected according to the OSF DCE or UI-Atlas. It is perhaps not as elaborate, but is less expensive, and a source license is about a thousand dollars.

Final release was expected in June 1992. BSDI also intended to have binary compatibility with System V Release 3.2 by the third quarter of 1992, permitting use of many applications written for other systems.

CSRG is not formally involved with BSDI, but has expressed pleasure at having more BSD-derived systems in use, so that CSRG will get more user input, which is what the BSD systems thrive on [Leffler *et al.* 1989]. The code BSDI has started with is available directly from CSRG:

> While there is contributed 386/486 code, it is not by any means the reference port that some have claimed it to be. CSRG will distribute that code which is sent to them by the time any future release is made. There is no commitment to make any future release. The most recent release is the "Networking-2" release. The 386/486 code does not currently support SCSI devices and will not support SCSI unless someone contributes said support [Kolstad 1991].

14.7 ABI: Application Binary Interfaces

This section is about three *ABI (Application Binary Interface)* consortia.

88open

The *88open Consortium (88open)* was chartered in April 1988 to promote binary compatibility of systems based on the Motorola 88000 series of chips. They call their specifications for this purpose a *Binary Compatibility Standard (BCS)* and an *Object Compatibility Standard (OCS)*. (The acronym BCS is a tradmark of 88open.) The BCS and OCS are essentially two views of an ABI. The BCS specifies traditional operating system facilties, such as system calls and runtime support, and the OCS specifies system commands.

This is similar to the difference in subject matter between IEEE 1003.1 and IEEE 1003.2, respectively, although those are of course source level standards, whereas the BCS and OCS are binary level industry specifications. The combination of the BCS and OCS forms an ABI. There is more emphasis on product independence and use of standards than in some previous industry ABIs that were based on hardware platforms from single vendors.

88open has certified conformance of the APIs of about a dozen vendors of 88000 platforms. The consortium produced a test suite, *ITS/88 (Interoperability Test suite),* for this purpose. 88open distinguishes three levels of platform conformance: base, generate, and object [88open 1992a].

• *Base certification* means the platform can run any application consisting of executable programs and shell scripts that has been certified by 88open for application conformance. A platform with base certification conforms to the BCS and the OCS.

• *Generate certification* includes base certification, and means the platform can not only run certified applications, but can also generate them.

• *Object certification* includes base and generate certification, and means the platform can also produce portable binary programs by linking them with system libraries.

In the terms of the IEEE P1003.1 PEP committee, an platform with 88open base certification is an *AEP (Application Execution Platform),* while a platform with either of the other two kinds of 88open certification is also an *ADP (Application Development Platform).*

88open has produced a test suite for applications, *ACT/88 (Application Compatibility Test suite),* and has used it to verify conformance of several hundred application packages, which are available in shrinkwrapped form.

88open produces a standards guide that we have found useful in writing this book [Dryar *et al.* 1991], and several interesting papers [88open 1992b].

SPARC International

SPARC International is a consortium for an ABI for the SPARC chip. This chip was originated by Sun Microsystems. There is a standard in progress for this ABI: IEEE P1754.

ACE: Advanced Computing Environment

The *Advanced Computing Environment (ACE)* consortium promotes an ABI based on the RISC processor from MIPS [Bernstein 1991]. As we have already mentioned in Chapter 1, *Computing Models,* and shown in Fig 1.3, the ACE model is similar to UI-Atlas and OSF DCE in vertical coverage of technology, but selects in part different specific software. ACE also selects hardware, including the MIPS and Intel CPUs. Current ACE members include Microsoft and Digital.

14.8   Distributed Management

No matter where you go, users and administrators alike complain that there just aren't enough administrators. The cost of UNIX system administration is high. This task usually isn't recognized as important as, for example, product development.

Installations of UNIX machines can cover a large geographical area. Networks are used to connect these machines. Users expect to be able to access more than just the workstation on their desk and the system down the hall. In the standalone environment, a user would have to have authorization configured (or set up) for each machine they wanted to use. But what happens when a user wants to use a group of machines? What if that user needs to be able to use group A machines, but not group B machines? Is it feasible for the system administrator to physically go to each machine to set up the user? The cost of doing this is prohibitive.

The ideal is for the administrator to be able to be physically located anywhere on a network. This ideal environment is shown in Fig. 14.3. There are machines in different geographic locations, but administration can be performed from anywhere. What is required to accomplish this, especially when the machines are purchased from different vendors? The current approach is first to have machines that can communicate with each other. This requires common protocols. The next is to have common tools for the administrator. An interface to some of these tools

Figure 14.3 Heterogeneous systems administration.

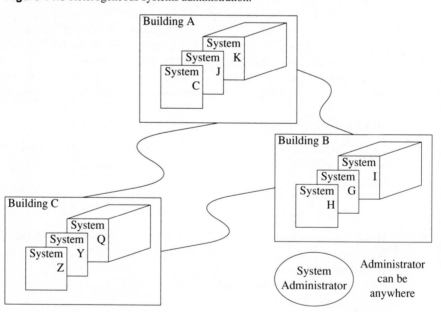

is being defined by the IEEE P1003.7 working group. Some of these common tools and an environment for them to operate within are being defined by OSF, UI, and X/Open.

P1003.7: System Administration

IEEE P1003.7 is defining a standard interface for administration of a standalone system as well as a heterogenous distributed network. This standard should facilitate administering systems from anywhere on the network, as shown in Fig. 14.4. This work will also become IS 9945-3.

In 1988, NIST recognized the need for standard system administration, so it started a draft FIPS. IEEE P1003.7 was started as a reaction to this FIPS, which some felt did not address the real issues of system administration.

Figure 14.4 IEEE 1003.7 common objects.
Figure reproduced from IEEE Draft Standard 1003.7/D8, IEEE Standard for Information Technology — Portable Operating System Interface (POSIX) Part 3: System Administration Interface, *copyright © 1992 by the Institute of Electrical and Electronic Engineers, Inc. with the permission of the IEEE. This is an unapproved draft, subject to change.*

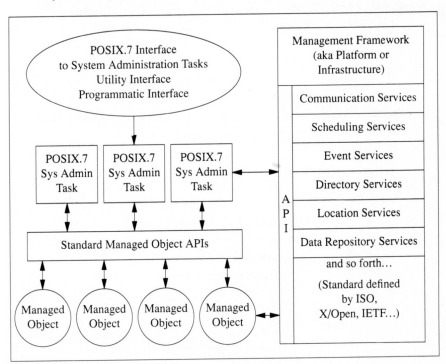

In the beginning, the P1003.7 group tried looking at the system administration problem as a whole. This task proved to be formidable, and progress was very slow. In the summer of 1991, they decided to break the task into areas where there were products available or experience in working with distributed management, so that something could be completed. The first two areas that are being addressed are Software Management and Print Management.

The Software Management facilities will include installation, removal, upgrading, and tracking of software application packages. Print Management is based on the 1991 MIT Palladium Printing Command Language Interface and Program Interface, as well as on the 1991 ISO/IEC JTC 1/SC18 DIS 10175-1 for Document Printing Applications.

The work of P1003.7 interacts with a number of other groups. The batch features being designed by the P1003.15 working group will require administration. The security features developed by the P1003.6 group will also require administration.

P1003.7 will not require a 1003.1 or 1003.2 compliant system. Work by P1003.7 started after ISO/IEC JTC 1 SC22 WG15 requested that the POSIX standards be language independent. Thus P1003.7, unlike other POSIX standards, is not written using C function calls.

XSM: X/Open System Management

X/Open is developing specfications that will provide infrastructure for other activities such as those dealt with by IEEE P1003.7. This *XSM (X/Open System Management)* work is complementary to P1003.7 and should be compatible with OSF and UI/USL. Deliverables as of August 1992 are shown in Table 14.1 [Kirk 1992].

Table 14.1 XSM Deliverables as of August 1992.

Type	Document
SS	Problem Statement
SS	Reference Model
PS	Management Protocols Profile
SS	Guide to Managed Objects
SS	Identification of Management Services
PS	Management protocol API
PS	DMI Contents Package
G	Guide to Translating GDMO to XOM
SS	= Snapshot
PS	= Preliminary Specification
G	= Guide

OSF DME

The OSF *Distributed Management Environment (DME)* provides a "uniform framework for efficient, cost-effective management of open systems" [OSF 1991h]. It is supposed to handle both standalone and distributed systems. It will use de facto and formal standard management standards for network and system management. It is intended to benefit system administrators most directly, then application developers, then end users [OSF 1991i].

Technological areas being considered for the OSF DME include

- Software management, including packaging, distribution, and installation

- License management, including license tracking and revenue protection

- Printing services, emphasizing functionality and manageability; this area was apparently moved into DME from the original DCE plans

- Host management services, such as adding a new user, distributed to a heterogenous environment [OSF 1991j]

All this is to be provided without requiring a centralized clearinghouse, such as a mainframe [OSF 1991i]. The OSF DME is architected to have low level management protocols supporting object services, which then support management services and application services, which jointly support management applications, which finally are accessed by a management user interface. DCE services and development tools transcend all these levels [OSF 1991j].

OSF DME includes software from TIVOLI Systems for managing heterogenous distributed systems. Selecting technology for a DME is proving harder than was selecting that for a DCE, since there is less prior art, and huge gaps that are not covered at all by existing technology.

DOMM: Distributed Object Management Model

UI-ATLAS includes a *DOMM (Distributed Object Management Model)*, for distribution of objects across networks. The framework came from HP and Sun, with a candidate technology implementation from the same source.

UI-ATLAS includes a *SMF (Systems Management Framework)* for managing heterogenous distributed systems. The framework and endorsed implementation are from TIVOLI Systems.

Network Management

Network management is important in networked environments, and a large and increasing proportion of UNIX systems are used in such environments. We have already discussed some history of network management in Chapter 8, *Protocols and Standards*.

The de facto industry standard is the *Simple Network Management Protocol (SNMP)*, which is used with TCP/IP. The *Common Management Information*

Protocol (CMIP) is under development for use with OSI. *CMOT (CMIP over TCP/IP)* is related to CMIP, and is intended for use over TCP/IP. Both SNMP and CMIP (and CMOT) use the idea of a *Management Information Base (MIB)* to describe a set of objects on the network. The information in the MIB is structured according to a *Structure of Management Information (SMI)*. SNMP and CMIP use somewhat different MIB and SMI. The idea of a MIB, an SMI, and of defined operations on the MIB and between the administrator, the MIB, and the affected network components has been influential on the IEEE P1003.7 system administration working group.

An overview of network management may be found in [Quarterman 1990], and the topic is treated extensively in [Rose 1990]. There is an *OMG (Object Management Group)* that deals with network management issues, and a *Network Management Forum (NMF)* that has X/Open, UI, and OSF in it [UI 1991a].

References

88open 1992a.   88open, "Definition of Terms," *88open Report: The Newsletter of the 88open Consortium Ltd.* **3**(1), 88open Consortium, Ltd. (January 1992).

88open 1992b.   88open, "Evolution of Open Systems," 88open Consortium, Ltd., San Jose, CA (January 1992).

AT&T 1989.   AT&T, *System V Interface Definition (SVID), Issue 3,* UNIX Press, Morristown, NJ (1989).

Bernstein 1991.   Bernstein, David, "The SCO Vision for Advanced Computing Environments," *Proceedings of Interop 91* (San Jose, California, 7–11 October 1991), Interop, Inc. (October 1991).

Dineen et al. 1987.   Dineen, Terence H., Leach, Paul J., Mishkin, Nathaniel W., Pato, Joseph N., & Wyant, Geoffrey L., "The Network Computer Architecture and System: An Environment for Developing Distributed Applications," *Proceedings of the Summer 1987 USENIX Conference* (Phoenix, Arizona, 8–12 June 1987), pp. 385–398, USENIX Association (1987).

Dryar et al. 1991.   Dryar, Cindy, Glaze, Kymberly, Kosinski, Peter, Silverman, Andy, & Wade, Erni, *The World of Standards: An Open Systems Reference Guide,* 88open Consortium, Ltd., San Jose, CA (1991).

Kirk 1992.   Kirk, Martin, Personal communication (10 June 1992).

Kolstad 1991.   Kolstad, Rob, "Berkeley Software Design, Inc. (BSDI)," Berkeley Software Design, Inc. (BSDI), Falls Church, VA 22042 USA (December 1991).

Kumar 1991.   Kumar, Ram, "OSF's Distributed Computing Environment," *AIXpert,* pp. 22–29, IBM (Fall 1991).

Leffler et al. 1989.   Leffler, Samuel J., McKusick, Marshall Kirk, Karels, Michael J., & Quarterman, John S., *The Design and Implementation of the 4.3BSD UNIX Operating System,* Addison-Wesley, Reading, MA (1989).

OSF 1990.   OSF, "Distributed Computing Environment: Rationale," Open Software Foundation, Cambridge, MA (14 May 1990).

OSF 1991a.   OSF, "Siemens Nixdorf, OSF announce contract for SVR4 reference port of DCE," Open Software Foundation, Cambridge, MA (October 1991).

OSF 1991b.   OSF, "Remote Procedure Call in a Distributed Computing Environment: A White Paper," Open Software Foundation, Cambridge, MA (August 1991).

OSF 1991c.   OSF, "Security in a Distributed Computing Environment: A White Paper," Open Software Foundation, Cambridge, MA (April 1991).

OSF 1991d.   OSF, "Directory Services for a Distributed Computing Environment: A White Paper," Open Software Foundation, Cambridge, MA (April 1991).

OSF 1991e.   OSF, "File Systems in a Distributed Computing Environment: A White Paper," Open Software Foundation, Cambridge, MA (November 1989).

OSF 1991f.   OSF, "Distributed Computing Environment: Overview," Open Software Foundation, Cambridge, MA (April 1991).

OSF 1991g.   OSF, "OSF Delivers First ANDF Snapshot," Open Software Foundation, Cambridge, MA (21 October 1991).

OSF 1991h.   OSF, "Corporate Background," Open Software Foundation, Cambridge, MA (October 1991).

OSF 1991i.   OSF, "Distributed Management Environment: An Overview," Open Software Foundation, Cambridge, MA (September 1991).

OSF 1991j.   OSF, "Distributed Management Environment: Rationale," Open Software Foundation, Cambridge, MA (September 1991).

OSF 1992.   OSF, *Application Evironment Specification (AES)*, Open Software Foundation, Cambridge, MA (1992).

Quarterman 1990.   Quarterman, John S., *The Matrix: Computer Networks and Conferencing Systems Worldwide*, Digital Press, Bedford, MA (1990).

Rose 1990.   Rose, Marshall, *The Simple Book: An Introduction to Management of TCP/IP-based internets*, Prentice-Hall, Englewood Cliffs, NJ (1990).

SMI 1990.   SMI, "Distributed Computing Road Map: The Future of Open Network Computing," Sun Microsystems, Mountain View, CA (May 1990).

UI 1991a.   UI, "UI-ATLAS Questions and Answers," UNIX International, Parsippany, NJ (September 1991).

UI 1991b.   UI, "UI-ATLAS Availability Schedule," UNIX International, Parsippany, NJ (1991).

UI 1991c.   UI, "UNIX International Announces UI-ATLAS — An Open Framework for Computing Solutions," UNIX International, Boston (16 September 1991).

UI 1991d.   UI, "UI-ATLAS Distributed Computing Architecture: An Introduction," UNIX International, Parsippany, NJ (September 1991).

UI 1991e.   UI, "UI-ATLAS at a Glance," UNIX International, Boston (16 September 1991).

UI 1991f.   UI, "Open System OLTP: Industry Direction for the 1990s," UNIX International, Parsippany, NJ (July 1991).

UI 1992.   UI, "1992 UNIX System V Roadmap," UNIX International, Parsippany, NJ (January 1992).

USL 1991.   USL, "News Release," UNIX System Laboratories, Boston (16 September 1991).

X/Open 1989.   X/Open, *X/Open Portability Guide, Issue 3*, Prentice-Hall, Englewood Cliffs, NJ (1989).

CHAPTER 15

Procurement Profiles

Various organizations produce profiles for use in acquisition and procurement. In this chapter, we describe such profiles produced by NIST (FIPS 151-2, the NIST APP, and GOSIP), IAB (RFCs and Internet Standards for TCP/IP), PSSG of DISA (the old TCP/IP MIL-STD specifications), CCTA (a CAE procurement profile), and others, such as those produced by the CEC, POSC, UAOS, and Bellcore. We note which are governmental standards and which are not.

15.1 NIST Profiles

The *National Institute of Standards and Technology (NIST)* has been active in producing profiles. One of their earliest related projects was NIST FIPS 151-1, which specified options of IEEE Std 1003.1-1988 and was thus an *option set*. NIST has also produced at least one actual profile, the NIST APP, which may be seen as a platform profile, as a kit used to build profiles, or as a catalog.

NIST FIPS 151-2

It is sometimes possible to produce one standard from another by specifying the values of options permitted in the first standard. NIST produced such an *option set* in its FIPS 151 *NIST FIPS 151 (FIPS 151)*, which applied to Draft 10 of IEEE P1003.1 [NIST 1987]. A *FIPS (Federal Information Processing Standard)* is a specification that can be used by government agencies in procurements.

This FIPS was partly motivated by concern on the part of NIST as to the large number of options and other gray areas in the then-current drafts of IEEE 1003.1. The FIPS specified options and parameters wherever choices were left in the P1003.1 draft. Because it applied to only one base standard, this FIPS was really an *option set*, not a true profile. It was, nonetheless, quite effective in persuading IEEE P1003 to have fewer options and parameter choices in the final IEEE 1003.1

standard. Many people claim that this and other NIST FIPS for POSIX specify
things that were not supposed to be specified, however, including facilities that the
POSIX committees carefully described using the words *may* or even *unspecified*.

NIST updated FIPS 151 for the published IEEE Std 1003.1-1988 as *NIST
FIPS 151-1 (FIPS 151-1)*. FIPS 151-1 appeared 31 August 1988 [NIST 1988].
NIST updated this FIPS again, in 1991, to correspond to IEEE Std 1003.1-1990.
The new FIPS is known as NIST FIPS 151-2 [NIST 1991a].

   The actual IEEE 1003.1 standard is just as voluntary as previous P1003.1
drafts had been. IEEE/CS TCOS-SS, like most standards bodies, has no authority
to make any standard mandatory. NIST, however, as the standards agency for the
U.S. government, can make requirements on U.S. government agencies. FIPS
151-2 is a mandatory procurement standard for those agencies. NIST does not
have authority to make it mandatory for anyone else. But because the U.S. government market is such a large share of the total UNIX systems market, FIPS
requirements have been a major influence in making standards compliance important to vendors. FIPS even have effects in other countries, many of which have
their own FIPS or equivalents, many of which are modeled on U.S. FIPS. The
indirect effect is also strong: even foreign vendors want to sell to the U.S. government, because it buys so many machines. Because vendors worldwide want to be
FIPS conformant, the entire worldwide supply of UNIX systems is affected by
U.S. FIPS.

   FIPS 151-2 requires these 1003.1 options:

• Multiple groups; NGROUPS_MAX >= 8

• Job control

• *chown* only with appropriate privileges

   Where 1003.1 allows variant behaviors, FIPS 151-2 specifies exactly one
behavior. For example, the group of a new file is that of the parent directory,
rather than the effective group of the creating process. This is to promote portability and interoperability on government systems.

   NIST is especially concerned about conformance testing, and has a testing
policy for implementations of FIPS 151-2. The FIPS itself requires conformance
to FIPS 160, for ISO 9899, the C Language Standard. It also requires implementations to document all features that FIPS 151-2 refers to but does not require to
be present on all conforming implementations.

NIST APP

About the same time as FIPS 151-1 was published, NIST also produced an *APP
(Application Portability Profile)*. This APP specifies a base *Open System Environment (OSE)* Profile for the U.S. federal government. It thus gives the minimal set
of standards that NIST recommends for use by all federal agencies in their *ADP
(automated data processing)* procurements.

This NIST APP actually appeared as an Appendix to FIPS 151-1, but it is not a normative part of FIPS 151-1. It is not a separate FIPS, either, and NIST does not intend to make it one [Martin 1990a]. Nonetheless, there has been some confusion about the formal status of the APP, and some other documents, possibly including requisitions, have specified conformance to the APP. This is not entirely appropriate, since the APP is not a formal standard of any kind.

NIST does not want to make the APP a FIPS, because NIST would prefer other government agencies to develop their own profiles. Each agency would then have its own AEP tailored to its own needs. This is particularly desirable as the needs of each agency change in different directions and at different rates. Each agency can issue RFPs using its own AEP instead of expecting NIST to tell it what to procure.

The APP selects specifications for the following services:

• Operating system services

• User interface services

• Programming services

• Data management services

• Data interchange services

• Graphics services

• Network services

When FIPS are available, the APP refers to them [Martin 1990b].

GOSIP

The *Government OSI Profile (GOSIP)* described here is the one specified by NIST of the U.S. government. There are others, such as UK GOSIP. U.S. GOSIP Version 1 was approved as a draft in October 1988, as a Full Use version in NIST Special Publication 500-187. The current version is GOSIP Version 2, which is FIPS 146-1 of 3 April 1991.

This document has been the focus of much technical and political activity. FIPS 146-1 says it "shall be used by Federal Government agencies when acquiring computer networking products and services and communications systems or services that provide equivalent functionality to the protocols defined in GOSIP" [NIST 1991b]. The document also includes an interesting definition of an open system: "An open system is a system *capable* of communicating with other open systems by virtue of implementing common international standard protocols.... However, an open system may not be accessible by all other open systems. This isolation may be provided by physical separation or by technical capabilities based upon computer and communications security" [NIST 1991b]. This is consistent with the status of GOSIP as an acquisition and procurement profile. It says what U.S. government agencies have to buy; it does not say what they have to use.

ISO-OSI Model	GOSIP Protocols			
7 *Application* what: ISO: CCITT:	VT (login) ISO 9040	ODA FTAM (files) ISO 9571	MHS (messages) ISO 10021 X.400	Directory (directory) ISO 9594 X.500
	ISO 8850: ACSE			
6 *Presentation*	ISO 8823			
5 *Session*	ISO 8327			
4 *Transport*	ISO 8073: TP4			
3 *Network* internet convergence subnet	CLNS ISO 8473: CLNP (ISO-IP)			
2 *Data Link*	ISO 8802-2 ISO 8802-3 IEEE 802.3 (CSMA/CD)	ISO 8802-4 IEEE 802.4 (token bus)	ISO 8802-5 IEEE 802.5 (token ring)	ISO 7776 X.25 LAPB (HDLC)	ISDN
1 *Physical*	(various)			

Figure 15.1 GOSIP Version 2 primary protocol stack.

The basic GOSIP Version 2 protocol stack is shown in Fig. 15.1. The key protocol is *CLNP (Connectionless Network Protocol),* which is essentially the Internet IP protocol with a larger address space. CLNP is used to support the *CLNS (Connectionless Network Service).* Above that is TP4, which is very like TCP. Above that are the OSI session, presentation, and application layers. *ODA (Office Documentation Architecture)* is an additional application protocol layered on top of *FTAM (File Transfer, Access, and Manipulation)* and *MHS (Message Handling System)* Other GOSIP application protocols include *VT (Virtual Terminal)* and the OSI Directory service, X.500. For each application protocol (except ODA), Fig. 15.1 shows the acronym (e.g., MHS), the general type (messages), the International Standard number (ISO 10021), and (where appropriate) the CCITT recommendation number (X.400).

The protocols shown in the Data Link layer in Fig. 15.1 are often considered in other documents to be in the network layer. Here we follow the layering shown in the GOSIP document itself. Other protocols, may also be used at this layer, such as *FDDI (Fiber Distributed Data Interface).*

ISO-OSI Model	GOSIP Protocols			
7 *Application* what: ISO: CCITT:	VT ·(login) ISO 9040	ODA		
		FTAM (files) ISO 9571	MHS (messages) ISO 10021 X.400	Directory (directory) ISO 9594 X.500
	ISO 8850: ACSE			
6 *Presentation*	ISO 8823			
5 *Session*	ISO 8327			
4 *Transport*	ISO 8073: TP4			
3 *Network* internet convergence subnet	CONS			
	ISO 8878: X.25			
2 *Data Link*	ISO 7776 X.25 LAPB (HDLC)			ISDN
1 *Physical*	(various)			

Figure 15.2 GOSIP Version 2 secondary protocol stack.

GOSIP Version 2 also permits another protocol stack, shown in Fig. 15.2. This other stack substitutes the *CONP (Connection Oriented Network Protocol)* (X.25) for CLNP, to support the *CONS (Connection Oriented Network Service)* in place of CLNS. GOSIP intends CONS and CONP to be used over X.25 and ISDN. The rest of the stack, from the transport layer through the application layer, remains the same. GOSIP permits use of the ISO 8602 connectionless transport protocol (UDP) for applications that need it.

GOSIP also permits use of TP0 for some purposes, such as connecting to public messaging systems. That stack looks like the one shown in Fig. 15.2, except with TP0 in place of TP4. This latter stack with TP0 is essentially the traditional European OSI protocol stack.

GOSIP also specifies assignment of network addresses, requirements for MHS O/R attributes, guidelines for testing products for compliance, and security options.

There are books devoted to the use of GOSIP [NIST 1991c; Lini & Moore 1990], and a plethora of related literature [Nightingale 1991; Cooney 1991; Mills 1991; desJardins 1991].

15.2   IAB: Internet Architecture Board

Internet Architecture Board (IAB) and its associated bodies such as the *Internet Engineering Task Force (IETF),* produce the specifications for the TCP/IP protocols, which are widely used in building distributed computing, and are the basis of the world's largest computer network, the Internet. We have detailed the standardization procedures these bodies use in Chapter 8, *Protocols and Standards.* The IAB, IETF, and related bodies such as the *Internet Society (ISOC)* are described in Chapter 5, *Industry Organizations and User Groups.*

RFCs

The IAB produces a series of documents, each of which is known as an *RFC (Request for Comment).* RFCs are numbered, and may be referred to by their number. The most basic RFCs are listed in Table 15.1. For example, RFC-1360 is the "IAB Official Protocol Standards" document [Postel 1992a]. That document lists the RFCs that specify all the TCP/IP protocols. It is periodically updated in a new RFC with a new number. RFCs for additional applications and for other services are shown in Table 15.2.

STDs

Some RFCs are also Internet Standards, which have passed through the IAB Standards Track by the processes described in Chapter 8. Internet Standards are also numbered in an STD (standards) series. RFC-1360 is also STD-1. Later updates of RFC-1360 will have different RFC numbers, but will still be STD-1. STD-1 is the authoritative source for references on Internet Standards [Postel 1992b]. An STD number generally refers to a protocol, rather than to a specification, so an STD number may apply to several RFCs.

All of the STD numbers that were assigned when the STD series was begun (by grandfathering existing protocols) are listed in Table 15.1, plus those shown in Table 15.2. These tables also show the requirement status of each STD, as Required, Recommended, or Elective. A basic status for each STD is assigned by STD-1. A protocol specification like STD-6 for TCP that is a *Technical Specification (TS)* is given a status by another document, called an *Applicability Statement (AS).*

All STDs are given statusses by STD-1; for example STD-1 makes TCP Recommended. However, another AS may be needed for a given application, and may give another status. For example, a host that supports TCP/IP must conform to STD-2, which could make TCP Required.

Any AS may also amend, extend, or otherwise generally modify a TS, and STD-1, STD-2, and STD-3 do this. It is not enough to look at just the basic specification for a protocol, such as RFC-793 for STD-6 (TCP). An implementer, application programmer, or tester must also examine STD-1, as well as STD-2, STD-3, or any other AS that is relevant to the platform or application.

Table 15.1 Some Internet Standards.

Acronym	Name	MIL-STD (old)	RFC	Status (current)	STD
Model and	IAB Official Protocol Standards	—	1360	Req	1
Taxonomy	Assigned Numbers	—	1060	Req	2
Requirements	Host Requirements	—	1122	Req	3
Documents	— Communications				
	Host Requirements	—	1123	Req	3
	— Applications				
	Gateway Requirements	—	1009	Req	4
Internet Layer					
IP	Internet Protocol	1777	791	Req	5
	IP Subnet Extension	—	950	Req	5
	IP Broadcast Datagrams	—	919	Req	5
	IP Broadcast Datagrams with Subnets	—	922	Req	5
ICMP	Internet Control Message Protocol	—	792	Req	5
IGMP	Internet Group Multicast Protocol	—	1112	Rec	5
Transport Layer					
TCP	Transmission Control Protocol	1778	793	Rec	6
UDP	User Datagram Protocol	—	768	Rec	7
Application Layer					
TELNET	Telnet Protocol and Options	1782	854, 855	Rec	8
TOPT-BIN	Binary Transmission	Option 0	856	Rec	27
TOPT-ECHO	Echo	Option 1	857	Rec	28
TOPT-SUPP	Suppress Go Ahead	Option 3	858	Rec	29
TOPT-STAT	Status	Option 5	859	Rec	30
TOPT-TIM	Timing Mark	Option 6	860	Rec	31
TOPT-EXTOP	Extended-Options-List	Option 255	861	Rec	32
FTP	File Transfer Protocol	1780	959	Rec	9
SMTP	Simple Mail Transfer Protocol	1781	821	Rec	10
MAIL	Format of Electronic Mail Messages	—	822	Rec	11
CONTENT	Content Type Header Field	—	1049	Rec	11

Table 15.2 More Internet Standards.

Acronym	Name	RFC	Status	STD
Application Layer				
NETBIOS	NetBIOS Service Protocols	1001, 1002	Ele	19
ECHO	Echo Protocol	862	Rec	20
DISCARD	Discard Protocol	863	Ele	21
CHARGEN	Character Generator Protocol	864	Ele	22
QUOTE	Quote of the Day Protocol	865	Ele	23
USERS	Active Users Protocol	866	Ele	24
DAYTIME	Daytime Protocol	867	Ele	25
TIME	Time Server Protocol	868	Ele	26
Distributed Services				
NTP	Network Time Protocol	1119	Rec	12
DNS	Domain Name System	1034, 1035	Rec	13
DNS-MX	Mail Routing and the Domain System	974	Rec	14
Network Management				
SNMP	Simple Network Management Protocol	1157	Rec	15
SMI	Structure of Management Information	1155	Rec	16
MIB-II	Management Information Base-II	1213	Rec	17
Routing				
EGP	Exterior Gateway Protocol	904	Rec	18

RFCs, STDs, and MIL-STDs

As we have detailed in Chapter 5, *Industry Organizations and User Groups*, the IAB and IETF are not governmental organizations. In particular, they are not affiliated with the U.S. *Department of Defense (DoD)*.

There is a DoD agency, formerly DCA, now DISA, that has produced its own specifications for some of the TCP/IP RFCs. Those are numbered in a MIL-STD series, for military standards. All of the TCP/IP MIL-STDs are listed in Table 15.1. We also discussed DISA in Chapter 5, and we say more about it in the next section in this chapter.

All of the MIL-STDs have been superseded by RFCs. Those RFCs and many others are also STDs. All the current specifications for TCP/IP are found in RFCs, particularly in the ones that are Internet Standards, or STD documents.

15.3   PSSG: Protocol Standards Steering Group

The *PSSG (Protocol Standards Steering Group)* produced a set of documents called *military standard (MIL-STD)* for some of the major TCP/IP protocols. As we discuss next, these are not the main specifications for those protocols.

The secretariat for PSSG is held by *Defense Information Systems Agency (DISA)*, which was formerly known as the *Defense Communications Agency (DCA)*. DISA continues standards work through its Center for Standards, as we discussed in Chapter 5, *Industry Organizations and User Groups*.

TCP/IP MIL-STD Specifications

As we have discussed above and in Chapter 8, *Protocols and Standards*, the current TCP/IP protocol specifications are part of the *RFC (Request for Comment)* series of documents, and those that are Internet Standards are also in the STD series.

Some Internet protocols are also specified as U.S. *Department of Defense (DoD) Military Standard (MIL-STD)* specifications [Postel 1992a]. All of the TCP/IP MIL-STDs are listed in Table 15.1. They include only the most basic Internet protocols: IP, TCP, FTP, SMTP, and TELNET. They are also out of date, have bugs, and are superseded by the RFCs that are shown in Table 15.1. Nonetheless, they have very useful state diagrams, and are of historical interest.

It is commonly believed that, since the IAB is not an accredited standards body, formal standards bodies such as TCOS cannot reference Internet Standards made by the IAB, but they can reference MIL-STDs, which are U.S. government standards. But this is not true. IEEE rules permit TCOS to reference anything that has been published, even magazines. The IEEE 1003.0 POSIX Guide project has converted its references to MIL-STDs into references to RFCs. And even the DISA PSSG has agreed that references to these MIL-STDs should be accompanied by matching references to the RFCs for accuracy and completeness [Cerf 1992].

15.4   Other Profiles

This section mentions several profiles, or the bodies that produce them. Two of these bodies are governmental, but the documents discussed are not mandatory governmental profiles like GOSIP or U.K. GOSIP.

The other documents discussed are user profiles, that is, profiles produced by industry bodies that use computer software and hardware but do not produce it. These user profiles may have greater leverage with vendors than vendor profiles. The users they represent are the customers who keep the vendors in business.

CCTA Profiles

The *Government Centre for Information Systems (CCTA),* is a division of the U.K. Treasury Ministry. It provides guidance to government departments on the application of POSIX, GOSIP, and the XPG.

Towards Open Systems: A CAE Procurement Profile

This is not a governmental standard of the type of U.K. GOSIP.

CEC: Commission of the European Communities

The *Commission of the European Communities (CEC)* has produced an "Open Systems Services Standards Handbook" through EWOS [CEC 1991].

POSC

The *Petrotechnical Open Software Corporation (POSC)* produces user industry profiles, and has been described in Chapter 5, *Industry Organizations and User Groups.* They have produced an RFC for an AEP for use in oil exploration and production [POSC 1991]. Their series of specifications is listed in Table 15.3.

UAOS

The *User Alliance for Open Systems (UAOS)* has been described in Chapter 5, *Industry Organizations and User Groups.* Their Barriers document has been influential in defining obstacles to the implementation and acceptance of open systems [UAOS 1991].

Bellcore

Bellcore develops software for the U.S. regional telephone operating companies, as well as for other clients and affiliates. Bellcore wants the systems it develops to be portable in source code form across a broad range of hardware platforms. User portability is also a major goal. To promote these goals, Bellcore defines a

---

Table 15.3 POSC specifications.

Specification	Title
POSC 0.0	Base Standards Endorsements
POSC 1.0	Exploration and Production Data Model
POSC 2.0	Application Programming Interface for Data Access
POSC 3.0	User Interface and Style Guide
POSC 4.0	Utilities and Tools

Standard Operating Environment (SOE). The SOE is a profile; perhaps an AEP; perhaps a platform profile; maybe a model. The SOE is specified in a document called a description [Bellcore 1991a]. The security requirements of the SOE are discussed in a technical report [Bellcore 1991b]; another technical report discusses the security requirements of operations systems [Bellcore 1991c].

The main basis for the operating system requirements of the SOE is the XPG, Issue 3. The SOE description also requires facilties from a variety of other sources, including the SVID (Issue 1 and Issue 2), 4.3BSD, and SunOS 4.1. The SOE description is unusual among profiles related to the UNIX system in that it hardly even refers to the POSIX System Interface Standard, or to any part of POSIX, for that matter.

The SOE description ranges across a field, including text processing (troff and relatives), data managment (SQL and ISAM), graphics (GKS and PHIGS), windowing (the X Window System and Motif), security (software and life cycle requirements), data communications (including ASCII, X.25, UUCP, IEEE 802.n, TCP/IP and eventually OSI, 3270 emulation, RPC, NFS, XTI, and STREAMS). Areas of future work include transaction processing and system administration. Product support and fault tolerance are discussed.

References

Bellcore 1991a.   Bellcore, "Description of the Bellcore UNIX Standard Operating Environment (SOE); Issue 1," Bellcore, Morristown, NJ (October 1991).

Bellcore 1991b.   Bellcore, "Bellcore Standard Operating Environment Security Requirements; Issue 2," Bellcore, Morristown, NJ (June 1991).

Bellcore 1991c.   Bellcore, "Bellcore Operations Systems Security Requirements; Issue 1," Bellcore, Morristown, NJ (June 1991).

CEC 1991.   CEC, "Open Systems Services Standards Handbook V5.00," Commission of the European Communities, DG XIII/E.4, Rue de la Loi, 200, B-1049 Brussels, Belgium (December 1991).

Cerf 1992.   Cerf, Vinton G., Personal communication (March 1992).

Cooney 1991.   Cooney, Robert A., "NCTS Washington Presents at Interop," *Proceedings of Interop 91* (San Jose, California, 7–11 October 1991), Interop, Inc. (October 1991).

desJardins 1991.   desJardins, Richard, "The Latest GOSIP: Overview," *Proceedings of Interop 91* (San Jose, California, 7–11 October 1991), Interop, Inc. (October 1991).

Lini & Moore 1990.   Lini, Kenneth F., & Moore, Joyce Y., *GOSIP Made Easy: The Complete Procurement Guide,* Corporation for Open Systems, McLean, VA (1990).

Martin 1990a.   Martin, Roger, Personal communication (30 May 1990).

Martin 1990b.   Martin, Roger, "Overview of the APP," National Computer and Telecommunications Laboratory, National Institute of Standards and Technology, Gaithersburg, MD (1990).

Mills 1991.   Mills, Kevin L., "Deploying GOSIP," *Proceedings of Interop 91* (San Jose, California, 7–11 October 1991), Interop, Inc. (October 1991).

Nightingale 1991.   Nightingale, Stephen, "The U.S. GOSIP Testing Program: The Adventure Continues," *Proceedings of Interop 91* (San Jose, California, 7–11 October 1991), Interop, Inc. (October 1991).

NIST 1987.   NIST, *FIPS 151,* National Computer and Telecommunications Laboratory, National Institute of Standards and Technology, Gaithersburg, MD (1987).

NIST 1988.   NIST, *FIPS 151-1,* National Computer and Telecommunications Laboratory, National Institute of Standards and Technology, Gaithersburg, MD (1988).

NIST 1991a.   NIST, *FIPS 151-2,* National Computer and Telecommunications Laboratory, National Institute of Standards and Technology, Gaithersburg, MD (1991).

NIST 1991b.   NIST, *Government Open Systems Interconnection Profile; Version 2,* National Computer and Telecommunications Laboratory, National Institute of Standards and Technology, Gaithersburg, MD (3 April 1991).

NIST 1991c.   NIST, *Government Open Systems Interconnection User's Guide,* NTIS, Springfield, VA (1991).

POSC 1991.   POSC, "Exploration and Production AEP RFC," Petrotechnical Open Software Corporation, Houston (April 1991).

Postel 1992a.   Postel, Jon ed., "IAB Official Protocol Standards; STD-1/RFC-1360," *Network Working Group Requests for Comments* (STD-1/RFC-1360), Network Information Systems Center, SRI International (September 1992).

Postel 1992b.   Postel, Jon, "Introduction to the STD Notes," *Network Working Group Request for Comments* (RFC1311), Network Information Systems Center, SRI International (March 1992).

UAOS 1991.   UAOS, "Overcoming Barriers to Open Systems Information Technology First Official Report," User Alliance for Open Systems, c/o COS, McLean, VA (27 January 1991).

APPENDIX A

Resources

This appendix lists access information particularly related to open systems, POSIX, or the UNIX operating system. It does not include exhaustive listings of standards bodies. For more extensive listings, see some of the books listed here.

Bodies, standards, and specifications are listed here in roughly the same order as in the body of the book. Formal standards bodies come first, arranged from international to national to regional, as in Chapter 4, *Formal Standards Bodies.* Industry groups and user groups come next, as in Chapter 5, *Industry Organizations and User Groups.* Then there is contact information for working groups, and access information for standards documents and other specifications. Approximately the second half of the appendix consists of information on books, technical reports, periodicals, newsletters, and sources of information over networks.

Because the world of standards is changing at a rapid pace, people, addresses, and prices may change from what is found here. Prices in particular are supplied only as representative, not as definitive, of current prices. The prices should be useful in determining whether an item costs tens, hundreds, or thousands of dollars. Prices also vary by country or even bookstore. The contact information given should be useful in determining prices more accurately. It would be prudent to check before ordering.

A.1 Standards Bodies

This section provides access information for a selection of the international, regional, and national formal standards bodies we discussed in Chapter 4.

International Standards Bodies

International Organization
for Standardization (ISO)
1 Rue de Varembe
Case Postale 56
CH-1211 Geneva 20
Switzerland

+41 22 34 12 40

International Electrotechnical
Commission (IEC)
3 Rue de Varembe
Case Postale 131
CH-1211 Geneva 20
Switzerland

+41 22 34 01 50

International Consultative
Committee on Telegraphy
and Telephony (CCITT)
Place de Nations
CH-1211 Geneva 20
Switzerland

+41 22 99 51 11

National Standards Bodies

Association Francaise pour la Connaisance
et l'Application des Normes (AFNOR)
Secretaire General
Tour Europe - Cedex 7
F-92080 Paris - La Defense
France

+33 1 42 91 55 27
fax: +33 1 42 91 56 56

British Standards
Institution (BSI)
2 Park Street
London W1A 2B5
England

+44 1 629 90 00
fax: +44 1 629 05 06

Deutsches Institut fur Normung (DIN)
Burggrafenstr. 6
D-100 Berlin 30
Germany

+49 30 26 01 302
fax: +49 30 26 01 231

Dansk Standardiseringsraad (DS)
Aurehojvej 12
Postbox 77
DK-2900 Hellerup
Denmark

+45 1 62 32 00
fax: +45 1 62 30 77

IEEE Computer Society Press
10662 Los Vaqueros Circle
PO Box 3014
Los Alamitos, CA 90720-1264
U.S.A.

1-800-CS BOOKS
1-800-272-6657
+1-714-821-8380
fax: +1-714-821-4010

Europe:
IEEE Computer Society
13, Avenue de l'Aquilon
B-1200 Brussels
Belgium

+32 2 770 21 98
fax: +32 2 770 85 05

Asia and Pacific Rim:
IEEE Computer Society
Ooshima Building
2-19-1 Minami-Aoyama
Minato-ku, Tokyo 107
Japan

+81 33 408 3118
fax: +81 33 408 3553

IEEE Standards Department
445 Hoes Lane
P.O. Box 1331
Piscataway, NJ 08855-1331
U.S.A.

+1-201-562-3809
800-678-IEEE

ANSI Sales Department
1430 Broadway
New York, NY 10018
U.S.A.

+1-212-642-4900

Roger Martin
National Institute of
Standards and Technology (NIST)
Systems and Software Technology Division
Technology Building, Room B266
Gaithersburg, MD 20899
U.S.A.

+1-301-975-3290
fax: +1-301-590-0932
rmartin@swe.ncsl.nist.gov

Don Folland
CCTA
Gildengate House
Upper Green Lane
Norwich, NR3 IDW
United Kingdom

+44-603-69-4713
fax: +44-603-69-4817
def@cctal.co.uk

National Voluntary Laboratory
Accreditation Program (NVLAP)
National Institute of
Standards and Technology (NIST)
Bldg 411 Room A124
Gaithersburg, MD 20899
U.S.A.

+1-301-975-4016
fax +1-301-975-3839

National Measurement Accreditation Service (NAMAS)
National Physical Laboratory
Queens Road
Teddington, Middlesex TW11 0LW
United Kingdom

+44 1 943 71 33
fax: +44 943 21 55

Regional Standards Bodies

European Committee for Standardization (CEN)
+32 3 519 68 11

European Committee for Electrotechnical Standardization (CENELEC)
+32 2 519 68 50

Rue Bréderode 2
B-1000 Brussels
Belgium

A.2   Industry Organizations and User Groups

Here are addresses for many of the major industry consortia and user groups that were described in Chapter 5, *Industry Organizations and User Groups* and Chapter 14, *Industry Profiles*.

POSIX Process Participants

BSD. 4.3BSD is described in this book:

> Leffler, Samuel J., McKusick, Marshall Kirk, Karels, Michael J., & Quarterman, John S., *The Design and Implementation of the 4.3BSD UNIX Operating System,* Addison-Wesley, Reading, MA (1989). $40, ISBN 0-201-06196-1.

The Fourth.3 Berkeley Software Distribution (4.3BSD) is documented in its manual, whose volumes are shown in Table A.1.

They are available at the prices shown from

USENIX Association	+1-415-528-8649
P.O. Box 2299	office@usenix.org
Berkeley, CA 94710	uunet!usenix!office
U.S.A.	

Unfortunately, there are some license restrictions. Contact the USENIX office for details. 4.4BSD shipped at the end of 1992.

Table A.1 BSD manual volumes.

Volume	Topics
4.3BSD User's Manual Set	*$25.00*
	User's Reference Manual
	User's Supplementary Documents
	Master Index
4.3BSD Programmer's Manual Set	*$25.00*
	Programmer's Reference Manual
	Programmer's Supplementary Documents, Vol. 1
	Programmer's Supplementary Documents, Vol. 2
4.3BSD System Manager's Manual	*$10.00*

X/Open. The X/Open *Common Application Environment (CAE)* is specified in this series of books:

> X/Open, *X/Open Portability Guide, Issue 3,* Prentice-Hall, Englewood Cliffs, NJ (1989).

There are currently seven volumes in the XPG, as shown in Table A.2.

Mike Lambert   +44 734 508 311
X/Open   mgl@xopen.co.uk
Apex Plaza, Forbury Road   uunet!mcsun!inset!xopen!mgl
Reading, Berkshire RG1 1AX
England

Table A.2 XPG volumes.

Volume	Title	ISBN
1	XSI Commands and Utilities	0-13-685835-X
2	XSI System Interface and Headers	0-13-685843-0
3	XSI Supplementary Definitions	0-13-685850-3
4	Programming Languages	0-13-685868-6
5	Data Management	0-13-685876-7
6	Window Management	0-13-685884-8
7	Networking Services	0-13-685892-9
(all)		0-13-685819-8

Table A.3 SVID volumes.

Volume	Topics	Document Number
I	Base System	020-1566524
	Kernel Extension	
II	Basic Utilities	020-1566532
	Advanced Utilities	
	Administered Systems	
III	Programming Language Specification	020-1566540
	Software Development	
	Terminal Interface	
	Real Time	
	Remote Services	
IV	Window System	020-1566559
	X11 Library Routines	
	NeWS	
V	Security	020-1566567
	Auditing	
	Remote Administration	
(all)		020-1582250

Comments, suggestions, error reports, etc., for XPG Issue 3 may be mailed to:

> xpg3@xopen.co.uk   uunet!mcsun!inset!xopen!xpg3

UI. UNIX System V is described in this book:

> Bach, M. J., *The Design of the UNIX Operating System,* Prentice-Hall, Englewood Cliffs, NJ (1987). ISBN 0-13-201799-7 025

UNIX System V is specified in the *SVID (System V Interface Definition)* The SVID is made up of five volumes, whose contents are shown in Table A.3.
SVID Issue 3 is available from

AT&T Customer Information Center	800-432-6600 (Inside U.S.A.)
Attn: Customer Service Representative	800-255-1242 (Inside Canada)
P.O. Box 19901	+1-317-352-8557 (Elsewhere)
Indianapolis, IN 46219	
U.S.A.	

The document numbers in Table A.3 should be used in placing orders. The cost is 49.50 U.S. dollars for each volume or $222.95 for all four volumes plus state sales tax. Major credit cards are accepted for telephone orders: mail orders should include a check or money order, payable to AT&T.

UNIX International (UI)   +1-201-263-8400
20 Waterview Blvd.   800-UI-UNIX-5
Parsippany, NJ 07054   800-848-6495
U.S.A.

OSF. The OSF *Application Environment Specification (AES)* describes OSF/1:

OSF, *Application Evironment Specification (AES),* Open Software
Foundation, Cambridge, MA (1992). ISBN 0-13-043522-8.

Open Software Foundation (OSF)   +1-617-621-8700
11 Cambridge Center
Cambridge, MA 02142
U.S.A.

Open Software Foundation   Open Software Foundation
Excelsiorlaan, 32   11-10, Kita-Aoyama 2-chome
1930 Zaventem   Minato-ku, Tokyo 107
Belgium   Japan
+32 2 729 7853   +81 33 3479 4740

Industry User Groups

Petrochemical Open Software   +1-713-784-1880
Corporation (POSC)   fax: +1-713-784-9219
10777 Westheimer, Suite 275
Houston, TX 77042
U.S.A

User Alliance for Open Systems (UAOS)
c/o COS
Corporation for Open Systems (COS)   +1-703-883-2796
1750 Old Meadow Road, Suite 400
Mc Lean, VA 22102-4306
U.S.A.

Traditional User Groups

Japan UNIX Society (jus)   +81-03-3356-0156
Marusho bldg.   fax: +81-03-3356-1094
5F 3-12 Yotsuya, Shinjuku-ku   board@jus.or.jp
Tokyo 160
Japan

Table A.4 IAB membership, March 1992.

Office	Person	Affiliation
Chair	Lyman Chapin	BBN
IETF and IESG Chair	Phill Gross	ANS
RFC Editor and IRTF and IRSG Chair	Jonathan Postel	USC-ISI
Executive Director	Robert Braden	USC-ISI
Member	Hans-Werner Braun	SDSC
Member	Vinton Cerf	CNRI
Member	Christian Huitema	INRIA
Member	Stephen Kent	BBN
Member	Anthony Lauck	Digital Equipment Corp.
Member	Barry Leiner	ADS
Member	Daniel Lynch	Interop, Inc.

ADS: Advanced Decision Systems
ANS: Advanced Network and Services
BBN: Bolt Beranek and Newman, Inc.
CNRI: Corporation for the National Research Initiative
INRIA: French National Institute for Research in Informatics and Automation
MIT: Massachusetts Institute of Technology
SDSC: San Diego Supercomputer Center
USC-ISI: University of Southern California, Information Sciences Institute

EurOpen secretariat   +44 763 73039
Owles Hall   fax: +44 763 73255
Buntingford   europen@EU.net
Herts SG9 9PL
England

UniForum Association   USENIX Association
2901 Tasman Drive, Suite 201   2560 Ninth Street Suite 215
Santa Clara, CA 95054   Berkeley, CA 94710
U.S.A.   U.S.A.

+1-408-986-8840   +1-415-528-8649
fax: +1-408-986-1645   fax: +1-415-548-5738
                                office@usenix.org
                                uunet!usenix!office

OSI Industry Promotion Groups

Corporation for Open Systems (COS)   +1-703-883-2796
1750 Old Meadow Road, Suite 400
Mc Lean, VA 22102-4306
U.S.A.

Standards Promotion and   +32 2 219 10 20
Application Group SA (SPAG)
1–2 Avenue des Arts, Bte. 11
B-1040 Brussels
Belgium

TCP/IP Protocol Standardization Bodies

ISOC: Internet Society. ISOC oversees IAB, and IETF, in turn.

Internet Society   isoc@nri.reston.va.us
1895 Preston White Drive, Suite 100
Reston, VA 22091
U.S.A.

IAB: Internet Architecture Board. IAB membership is shown in Table A.5.

IETF: Internet Engineering Task Force. A list of current IESG members and a description of the IETF can be retrieved by anonymous FTP as the file 1ietf-description.txt from the IETF shadow directories, on these hosts:

East Coast (US) Address   nnsc.nsf.net   (128.89.1.178)
West Coast (US) Address   ftp.nisc.sri.com (192.33.33.22)
Europe Address   nic.nordu.net   (192.36.148.17)

ABI Consortia

88Open Consortium Ltd.   +1-408-436-6600
100 Homeland Court, Suite 800   fax: +1-408-436-0725
San Jose, CA 95112
U.S.A.

SPARC International
Menlo Park, CA
U.S.A.
+1-415-321-8692

A.3   Working Groups

Some of the actual working groups that produce standards documents from drafts are listed here. This section is limited to working groups directly related to the POSIX standards.

ISO/IEC JTC1

See the contact information for ISO and IEC.

TCOS

POSIX falls under the Technical Committee on Operating Systems (TCOS) of the IEEE Computer Society. The IEEE Computer Society can be contacted at the following office:

> IEEE Computer Society   +1-202-371-0101
> 1730 Massachusetts Ave. NW   fax: +1-202-728-9614
> Washington, DC 20036-1903
> U.S.A.

For general information about P1003 contact

> James Isaak   +1-603-884-3634
> Chairperson   fax: +1-603-884-3682
> IEEE/CS TCOS Standards Subcommittee   isaak@decvax.dec.com
> Digital Equipment TTB1-5/G06
> 10 Tara Blvd.
> Nashua, NH 03062
> U.S.A.

Current drafts are available from the Computer Society for a charge to cover duplication and shipping. There is a subscription service available for receiving drafts as they become available from the working group. Write to TCOS Standards Subscriptions, c/o Lisa Granoien at the Computer Society address above. The cost for the subscription service is $40.00 US per 500 page unit.

If you want to follow a particular POSIX group you can receive the working group's mailings by writing to:

> TCOS Standards Subscriptions   +1-202-371-0101
> c/o Lisa Granoien   fax: +1 202 728 9614
> IEEE Computer Society
> 1730 Massachusetts Ave. NW
> Washington, DC 20036-1903
> U.S.A.

The list cost is $40.00 US per 500 page unit. Working group minutes, drafts, presentation slides, and pertinent reading materials are included in the mailings. A working group can be followed closely by reading the mailings.

IEEE

IEEE also sells drafts directly. See the contact information for IEEE.

UniForum Technical Committee

The current Chair may be contacted through

> chair@techcomm.uniforum.org

A.4   Standards Documents

Standards documents are mostly available only on paper, but some can be obtained by other means, as well. Here we list formal standards, followed by the *usr/group 1984 Standard*, followed by Internet Standards.

ISO

JTC 1 and CCITT standards documents are available in the United States from

> OMNICON, Inc.   1-800-666-4266
> 115 Park Street S.E.   +1-703-281-1135
> Vienna, VA 22180-4607   fax: +1-703-281-1505
> U.S.A.   telex: 279678 OMNI UR

For access from other countries, see the addresses for IEC and ISO.

IEEE TCOS

IEEE Std 1003.1-1990 Portable Operating System Interface for Computer Environments is available from both the IEEE Service Center and The Computer Society. Prices from the IEEE Service Center are $37.00 for non-members and $18.50 for IEEE, affiliates, and Computer Society members (plus $4.00 tax, shipping, and handling). The price from The Computer Society is $32.00 for non-members and $28.80 for Computer Society members. This document is identical to ISO/IEC IS 9945-1:1990, except for the cover.

Other IEEE standards are available from IEEE, and some of them are also available from the Computer Society. IEEE has a Hypertext version of the 1003.1 standard available, and is working on tools and format descriptions to maintain documents in SGML, using an ISO standard from SC18. IEEE distributes some standards documents on CD/ROM:

> Information Handling Services   +1-303-790-0600
> Inverness Business Park   +1-303-397-2627
> 15 Inverness Way East
> Englewood, CO 80150
> U.S.A.

Draft working documents are obtainable from the IEEE Service Center, but see also the section on TCOS working groups.

IEEE Service Center   +1-201-981-0060
445 Hoes Lane   telex 236-411
PO Box 1331   telecopier +1-212-705-7589
Piscataway, NJ 08855-1331   cable: ITRIPLEE
U.S.A.

ANSI

ANSI documents may be ordered from

Global Engineering Documents   +1-714-261-1455
2805 McGaw   1-800-854-7179
Irvine, CA 92714
U.S.A.

The C Standard ANSI X3.159-1989 is available for $87.50.

ANSI documents are also available directly from ANSI, and ISO/IEC documents may be ordered from ANSI.

NIST FIPS

For copies of FIPS 151-2 contact:

Barbara Blickenstaff   +1-301-975-2816
National Institute of Standards and Technology
Technology Building, Room B64
Gaithersburg, MD 20899
U.S.A.

/usr/group 1984 Standard

The *usr/group 1984 Standard* was the basic document from which P1003.1, X/OPEN, and X3J11 sprang. It may be ordered for $15.00 from UniForum (Uni-Forum was once known as /usr/group).

Internet Standards

We discussed RFCs and STDs (Internet Standards) in Chapter 8, *Protocols and Standards* and Chapter 14, *Industry Profiles*. You can get them on paper, or by electronic mail, or by anonymous FTP.

SRI NISC. SRI's Network Information Service Center provides RFCs and STDs on paper, on CD/ROM, and by electronic mail.

Cerf, Vint, *Internet Technology Handbook,* SRI International, Network Information Systems Center, Menlo Park, CA (November 1991). $785; six individual volumes at $150 each.

SRI, *TCP/IP CD,* SRI International, Network Information Systems
Center, Menlo Park, CA (February 1992). $195 (updated about every
6 months).

Network Information Service Center
SRI International   To: mail-server@nisc.sri.com
Room EJ291   Subject: anything
333 Ravenswood Avenue
Menlo Park, CA 94025   STD 1
U.S.A.   RFC 1311

ISI. ISI has a sophisticated electronic mail server for documents.

```
To: RFC-INFO@ISI.EDU          To: RFC-INFO@ISI.EDU
Subject: anything             Subject: anything


Help: Help                    Retrieve: RFC
                              Doc-ID: RFC1310
```

DDN NIC. The Defense Data Network Network Information Center provides
RFCs by electronic mail and anonymous FTP.
By electronic mail:

```
To: service@nic.ddn.mil
Subject: RFC 1311
```

By anonymous FTP:

```
ftp nic.ddn.mil
Connected to nic.ddn.mil.
Name (nic.ddn.mil:you): anonymous
331 Guest login ok, send "guest" as password.
Password: guest
230 Guest login ok, access restrictions apply.
ftp> cd rfc
250 CWD command successful.
ftp> get rfc-index.txt
200 PORT command successful.
150 Opening ASCII mode data connection for rfc-index.txt
local: rfc-index.txt remote: rfc-index.txt
169451 bytes received in 131.6 seconds (1.3 Kbytes/s)
ftp> quit
221 Goodbye.
```

A.5   Books

There are a few books available in the general area of standards. Each IEEE 1003 standard and the X3.159 C standard contains a Rationale and Notes appendix that explains obscure technical issues. However, these appendices do not adequately explain the context of the interrelations of standards bodies, and do not even attempt to deal with matters like the AFCAC case and its influence.

General Standards Books

Cargill, Carl F., *Information Technology Standardization: Theory, Process, and Organizations,* Digital Press, Bedford, MA (1989). $28.95, ISBN 1-55558-022-X.

This book analyzes the standardization process and presents some of the standards bodies. It does not discuss any of the IEEE POSIX efforts.

IOS, *Information Technology Atlas — Europe,* IOS Press and C.G. Wedgwood & Company, Ltd., Amsterdam (1990). $88.

This is an even more general book that includes information about standards. However, it has very little specific information about POSIX and is strongly oriented towards Europe, with minimal information about North America.

IOS U.S.A.
Attn: Mr. Timothy Donovan
P.O. Box 10558
Burke, VA 22009
U.S.A.

+1-703-323-9116
fax +1-703-250-4705

IOS
Van Diemen Straat #94
Amsterdam, 10013 CN
Netherlands

+31 20 382189

The Omnicom Index of Standards for Distributed Information and Telecommunication Systems, McGraw-Hill Information Services Co., New York (1990). ISBN 0-07-607017-4.

This is a list of standards, grouped by developing organization.

Open Systems Books

Gray, Pamela, *Open Systems: A Business Strategy for the 1990s,* McGraw-Hill, London (1991). $39.95, ISBN 0-07-707244-8.

Digital, *Open Systems Handbook: A Guide to Building Open Systems,* Digital Equipment Corporation, Bedford, MA (1991).

Dryar, Cindy, Glaze, Kymberly, Kosinski, Peter, Silverman, Andy, & Wade, Erni, *The World of Standards: An Open Systems Reference Guide,* 88open Consortium, Ltd., San Jose, CA (1991).

Quarterman, John S., & Wilhelm, Susanne, *UNIX, POSIX, and Open Systems: The Open Standards Puzzle*, Addison-Wesley, Reading, MA (1993).

Susanne Wilhelm	John S. Quarterman
Windsound Consulting	Texas Internet Consulting
406 Lamar Drive	1106 Clayton Lane, Suite 500W
Mukilteo, WA 98275-3810	Austin, TX 78723
U.S.A.	U.S.A.
+1-206-742-5008	+1-512-451-6176
fax: 206-348-8095	fax: +1-512-450-1436
sws@calvin.wa.com	jsq@tic.com

Books about IEEE 1003.1

Zlotnick, Fred, *The POSIX.1 Standard: A Programmer's Guide*, Benjamin Cummings, Redwood City, CA (1991). ISBN 0-8053-9605-5.

Lewine, Donald, *POSIX Programmer's Guide: Writing Portable UNIX Programs*, O'Reilly & Associates, Inc., Sebastopol, CA (1991). $34.95 ISBN 0-937175-73-0.

DMR Group, Inc.

The DMR Group, Inc., of Toronto, together with X/Open and UniForum, publishes a series of books for their program members; membership is $25,000.

DMR, "Open Systems Status Report," DMR Group, Toronto (1990).

DMR, "The Experience with Open Systems: Case Studies," DMR Group, Toronto (1990).

DMR, "The Market," DMR Group, Toronto (October 1990).

DMR, "Standards-based Architecture Planning Guide," DMR Group, Toronto (November 1990).

Executive Co-Director	Executive Co-Director
Strategies for Open Systems	Strategies for Open Systems
DMR Group, Inc.	UniForum
252 Adelaide Street East	
Toronto, Ontario M5A 1N1	
Canada	
+1-416-363-8661	
fax: +1-416-861-0981	

A.6   Technical Reports

Various organizations publish technical reports related to standards. Here we list some from UniForum.

UniForum Reports

UniForum has a series of three publications about POSIX. These are good publications to read for overviews of 1003.1 and 1003.2.

> Jespersen, Hal, "Your Guide to POSIX, Updated," UniForum, Santa Clara, CA (1992). ISBN 0-936593-08-3.

This 20 page report explains what POSIX is.

> Jespersen, Hal, "POSIX Explored: System Interface," UniForum, Santa Clara, CA (1989). ISBN 0-936593-09-1.

This 24 page report discusses technical aspects of IEEE 1003.1, its relations to AT&T System V, BSD, and to other historical implementations, as well as to other standards.

> Jespersen, Hal, "POSIX Update: Shells and Utilities," UniForum, Santa Clara, CA (1992).

This 38 page report describes the IEEE P1003.2 committee. UniForum also produces white papers on specific topic areas, such as these two, on I18N and procurement.

> UniForum, "Standards Update: Internationalization," UniForum, Santa Clara, CA (1992).

> UniForum, "Standards-based Procurement, Using POSIX and XPG," UniForum, Santa Clara, CA (1992).

They are all $10 each, or $5 for members; contact UniForum for more details.

A.7   Periodicals

Many magazines and other periodicals cover standards. Here we list general trade magazines, followed by ones published by professional associations, followed by user group magazines.

Open Systems Today

Occasional opinionated articles on standards appear in *Open Systems Today*, which is a newspaper, published bimonthly, and formerly known as *UNIX Today!*. Subscriptions are given free to those who qualify.

Open Systems Today   +1-516-562-5000
CMP Publications, Inc.   mikea@utoday.com
600 Community Drive
Manhasset, NY 11030
U.S.A.

Sun Expert

Peter Salus writes a standards column in *Sun Expert*. It comes out every month or every other month, and is about three pages long. Recent topics have included national and international standards bodies.

Other articles about standards occasionally appear in this monthly magazine, which usually has about 94 pages, and costs $49.50 annually in the United States, and $70 elsewhere.

Doug Pryor   Peter Salus
Editor   peter@world.std.com
+1-617-739-7002
dpryor@expert.com

SunExpert Magazine   +1-617-739-7001
Computer Publishing Group, Inc.   fax: +1-617-739-7003
1330 Beacon Street   circ@expert.com
Brookline, MA 02146   uunet!expert!circ
U.S.A.

IEEE Computer

IEEE Computer has a standards column of about four pages. *IEEE Computer* is a monthly magazine distributed to the membership of the IEEE Computer Society, and which has about 120 pages per issue. The July 1990 issue has "The history of POSIX: A study in the standards process," by James Isaak.

Norman Schneidewind   +1-408-646-2719/2471
Editor, Standards Column   fax: +1-408-646-3407
IEEE Computer   0442p@cc.nps.navy.mil
Code AS/Ss   N.Schneidewind@compmail.com
Naval Postgraduate School
Monterey, CA 93943
U.S.A.

IEEE Software

IEEE Software carries articles about standards. This magazine is bimonthly by the IEEE Computer Society, and runs to about 132 pages. It is $18 for members of any IEEE group, and $30 for members of other technical organizations.

Carl Chang   University of Illinois
Editor-in-Chief   1120 Science and Engineering Offices
IEEE Software   M/C 154
ckchang@uicbert.eecs.uic.edu   P.O. Box 4348
                                    Chicago, IL 60680
                                    U.S.A.

IEEE Spectrum

Frequent articles about standards appear in *IEEE Spectrum*, which is a monthly magazine of about 84 pages. IEEE members pay for a subscription as part of their dues. Nonmembers can subscribe for $24/year, and libraries and other institutions can get it for $114/year. Contact the IEEE Service Center for details.

Donald Christiansen
Editor
IEEE Spectrum

UniForum Monthly

The UniForum membership magazine *UniForum Monthly* (formerly known as *CommUNIXations*) has regular standards articles by Ralph Barker. The magazine is published monthly, and usually has about 50 pages.

Jordan Gold   jordan@uniforum.org
Director of Publications

EurOpen Newsletter

EurOpen publishes a quarterly membership magazine, *EurOpen Newsletter*, of about 100 pages per issue. It carries the *EurOpen/USENIX ISO Monitor Project Reports* and has occasional other articles about standards.

Tribunix

Tribunix is the bimonthly membership magazine of AFUU, the French Association of Users of UNIX and Open Systems. It usually has about 80 pages, and costs about 3000 French francs. It carries articles about standards from a European and French perspective, particularly about WG15 (ISO POSIX) and the AFUU working groups. Most *Tribunix* articles are in French.

Philippe Dax   +33 1 45 81 76 48
Télécom Paris   dax@enst.fr
46, rue Barrault
75634 Paris Cedex 13
France

Jacqueline Malot   +33 1 46 70 95 90
AFUU   fax: +33 1 46 58 94 20
11, rue Carnot   tribunix@afuu.fr
94270 Le Kremlin Bicetre
France
ISSN: 0298-668X

A.8   Newsletters

Newsletters provide progress reports, analysis, and criticisms of the standards process. Here we list some newsletters published by independent agencies, by standards bodies, and by user groups.

Digital Open System Standards Tracking Report

Digital Equipment Corporation produces a quarterly four page newsletter giving updates on the status of the TCOS and other open systems standards committees. For complimentary subscriptions, or to submit information, contact:

Linda LeBlanc
Editor, Open Systems Standards Tracking Report
+1-603-884-3593
leblanc@decvax.dec.com

Nina Lytton's Open Systems Advisor

The *Open Systems Advisor* contains information about the broad area of open systems. Several articles about standards have appeared. The newsletter is available for $595 for 12 issues a year with discounts for groups or 3 or more. Each issue runs about 20 pages.

Open Systems Advisor   +1-617-859-0859
268 Newbury St.   ninal@utoday.com
Boston, MA 02116
U.S.A.

IEEE/CS Standards Status Report

This magazine-format publication appears about three times a year, and costs $20 per issue, each of which has about 52 pages. It contains details on the officers of all IEEE/CS organizations and committees associated with standards, and is available from the Computer Society.

IEEE/CS TCOS Newsletter

IEEE/CS TCOS has a "regular publication" of about seventeen pages. This newsletter is produced using computer networks, and submissions and other queries should go to its editor.

Terry Slattery   +1-301-278-6808
Editor, *IEEE/CS TCOS newsletter*   tcs@brl.mil
U.S. Army, BRL
SLCBR-SE
Aberdeen Proving Grounds, MD 21005-5066
U.S.A.

IEEE Standards Bearer

IEEE publishes a quarterly newsletter about its standards. It costs $25/year and is usually about a dozen pages long. It covers all IEEE standards, many of which have nothing to do with UNIX. It lets people know about IEEE policy, and changes to it. Judith Gorman is the Editor, and can be reached at the IEEE Standards Office.

La Lettre AFUU

AFUU has a membership newsletter, *La Lettre AFUU* , that often emphasizes standards. It is in French, and is usually two pages. A recent remark in it might be translated as: "Our association commits a more and more significant part of its activities to this context" [of the application of standards]. Contact AFUU for more information.

;login:

The *USENIX Standards Watchdog Reports* and the *EurOpen/USENIX ISO Monitor Project Reports* are published in *;login: The Newsletter of the USENIX Association* , which is a bimonthly membership newsletter that varies in size from a dozen pages to about fifty. To join USENIX and receive *;login:* , contact the USENIX office.

UniNews

The biweekly newsletter *UniNews* is sent to all UniForum members, and is four pages long. It frequently contains news items about standards-related activities.

A.9   Online Information

There are several sources of information about standards activities available over computer networks such as USENET and the Internet.

comp.std.unix

A general place to discuss standards and the standards process is the USENET newsgroup *comp.std.unix*. Everything posted in the newsgroup is also relayed automatically to the electronic mailing list *std–unix@uunet.uu.net*, so that people who do not have access to USENET can participate. Participants include standards committee members and officers, system and application implementors, and users. Discussions range from extremely specific minutae of interpretation or implementation of standards to philosophical discussions of the standards process. The *USENIX Standards Watchdog Reports* and the *EUUG/USENIX ISO Monitor Project Reports* (both described below) are posted to this newsgroup, and frequently spark discussion. Several articles are posted on an average day.

To submit messages for publication, mail them to std–unix@uunet.uu.net or uunet!std–unix, or just post them to the newsgroup comp.std.unix and the USENET software will forward them to the proper address. To subscribe to the USENET newsgroup, use whatever news reading interface you normally use. To subscribe to the mailing list, send mail to std–unix–request@uunet.uu.net or uunet!std–unix–request. Archives of back issues are available: send mail to std–unix–request@uunet.uu.net.

EurOpen/USENIX ISO Monitor Project

The European Forum for Open Systems (EurOpen) and the USENIX Association have, since 1988, co-sponsored a series of reports on the ISO/IEC JTC 1 SC22 WG15 (ISO POSIX) standards committee. The reporter attends WG15 meetings (usually two a year) and related meetings (such as Rapporteur Group meetings), and writes reports on them. These reports contain details of events during the meetings, likely effects on other committees or the industry, and broader speculations. They are usually about half a dozen pages long. They appear in *comp.std.unix*, *std–unix@uunet.uu.net*, *;login: The Newsletter of the USENIX Association*, and the *European Forum for Open Systems Newsletter*, all of which are described in this book. For suggestions as to content, contact USENIX or EurOpen.

Other USENET Newsgroups

Other USENET newsgroups about UNIX-related standards include *comp.std.c*, *comp.std.c++*, *comp.std.internat*, *comp.std.misc*, *comp.org.usrgroup*, as well as *comp.org.ieee*. These are all accessible by the usual USENET transmission and interface methods.

USENIX Standards Watchdog Committee Reports

The USENIX Association formed the USENIX Standards Watchdog Committee to keep its members informed about UNIX-related standards. This is not a standards committee, and its purpose is not to endorse standards. Members of standards working groups volunteer to be on the committee. They submit reports on issues raised in meetings, particularly on decisions that will affect the industry or other committees.

These reports are posted to the USENIX newsgroup *comp.std.unix* and the mailing list *std-unix@uunet.uu.net,* and published in *;login: The Newsletter of the USENIX Association* .

The individual reports average about three pages in length, and there are about a dozen of them each quarter. Each quarterly set of reports also contains an editorial of about a dozen pages by the report editor.

APPENDIX B

Puzzle Challenge

B.1 The Standard Word Search Problem

Your task, should you elect to accept this assignment, will be to locate the open system acronyms hidden in the word search format puzzle; identify the nature of these; and then apply them properly to your business so that you gain the benefits of open systems without falling into the trap of implementation dependency. As you might expect in this topsy-turvy world of standards, you may find the terms forwards, backwards, on the diagonal, or bottom up. Punctuation has not been included, so for example, if X.25 were in the list, the period would not be present.

There are six categories of acronyms listed (that we are willing to acknowledge). Your score is computed as follows:

1 point	for each acronym found and placed in the right category
–1 point	for each one placed in the wrong category
–5 points	for placing the name of a brand name product into either of the categories of standards

You may think this penalty system is a bit harsh. But, consider what happens if you give your applications developers the charter to use a brand name product as if it were a standard; only to find that your applications have reduced portability and less interoperability, and you are faced with the task of rewriting to conform to the standard instead of a specific implementation. It may be that confusion of consortiums and standards bodies will lead to the same effect. If by chance you happen upon any corporation names and place these in the category of being a standards body, you may get what you deserve!

B.3   This Helps a Bit

P	H	I	G	S		D	X	3			B	S	G
E	I	A	R			I	F	I	M	S	S	W	O
I		F	F	D	S	N				Q	I	O	S
S		N		O	S	F			L			D	I
O	G	O	P	S	R		C	A		F	X	N	P
D	K	R	S	I	T	T		A	I		O	I	
C	S	E	P	S			R	D		X	P	W	
E	A	C	I		P	D	O	A		E	X	P	
	T	N			P				N	N	T	C	
		C	O	B	O	L	A	C	S	A	P	I	T
			S	S			S	O	D	S	M	E	
I	D	D	F	C	N	G	A	P	S		N		
X	I	N	U			A		A	M	C	E		
A	N	S	I		I	E	E	E	V		C		
S	G	F	S		C	C	I	T	T				

B.4   The Formal Standards

P	H	I	G	S				X							G
							I					S			O
			F			S						Q			S
				O								L			I
	G		P		S	R						F			P
	K			I			T		A	I					
	S		P					R	D						
		C				P	D	O	A						P
	T									N					C
		C	O	B	O	L	A	C	S	A	P				T
															E
I	D	D	F												

B.5 Standards Bodies and Consortia

					D	X	3		B		
E	I	A			I				S		
I		F			N				I		
S		N		O	S	F					
O		O							X		
		R		T					O		
			S						P		
		I							E		
		N		P					N		
				O		C					
				S			O				
				C	G	A	P	S		N	
		U						A	M	C	E
A	N	S	I		İ	E	E	E		C	
S	G	F	S		C	C	I	T	T		

Glossary

ABI (Application Binary Interface) An interface that permits a compiled program to be moved among hardware platforms.

Access Control List *See* ACL.

accreditation Formal recognition by an accreditation body that a testing laboratory is competent to perform specific test methods in specific fields of testing.

accreditation body An organization that provides unbiased third party evaluation and recognition of the performance of testing laboratories, and perhaps assistance in upgrading that performance. *See also* NVLAP.

Accredited Standards Committee *See* ASC.

Accredited Standards Committee for Information Processing *See* ASC X3.

Accredited Standards Developing Organizations *See* ASDO.

accredited testing laboratory A testing laboratory that has been accredited.

ACL (Access Control List) A security mechanism used with discretionary access control. An access list is associated with each file.

ADP (Application Development Platform) A system that translates (compiles or interprets) programs for an AEP. An ADP has to have language support, but it doesn't have to be able to execute the programs that it translates.

AE (Application Environment) An environment for a class of applications; what an AEP specifies.

AEP (Application Environment Profile) A profile that specifies an environment (a complete and coherent subset of an OSE plus additional options and parameters) to support a specific class of applications. Defined by TSG-1.

AEP (Application Execution Platform) A system that executes programs produced by an ADP; e.g., an embedded realtime system or a turnkey system. An AEP does not have to permit compilation or interpretation of programming languages.

AES (Application Environment Specification)   The description of OSF/1 produced by OSF.

AESC (American Engineering Standards Committee)   The earliest national standards body in the United States; formed in 1918; ancestor of ANSI.

AFNOR (French Association for Normalization)   The formal national standards body for France. It has the secretariats of many ISO groups.

AFS (Andrew File System)   A stateful distributed file system developed by Carnegie Mellon University and now distributed by Transarc, Inc.

amendment   Another name for an extension.

American Engineering Standards Committee   *See* AESC.

American National Standard   *See* ANS.

American National Standards Institute   *See* ANSI.

ANDF (Architecture Neutral Distribution Format)   An application program distribution format intermediate between source code and binary format. *See also* ABI.

Andrew File System   *See* AFS.

ANS (American National Standard)   A standard created by an ASC or ASDO and approved by ANSI.

ANSI (American National Standards Institute)   The formal national standards body for the United States.

ANSI C   X3.159, produced by X3J11; the first standardized form of the C programming language.

anticipatory standard   A standard not based on any existing implementation.

AOW (Asia-Oceania Workshop)   An open public forum for developing International Standard Profiles for OSI.

API (Application Program Interface)   An interface definition that permits writing application programs without internal details of the facility, e.g., ISO 9945-1 for basic system functions.

APP (Application Portability Profile)   A profile intended to promote portability of applications. E.g., NIST APP.

Appeals   A process for alteration of a standard after it has been formally approved.

Applicability Statement   *See* AS.

Application Binary Interface   *See* ABI.

Application Development Platform   *See* ADP.

Application Environment   *See* AE.

Application Environment Profile   *See* AEP.

Application Environment Specification   *See* AES.

Application Execution Platform   *See* AEP.

application portability The ability to move software among computers without rewriting it. This may be provided in at least three ways, as source code portability (with or without conditional compilation or manual changes), pseudocode portability (as in UCSD Pascal), or binary code portability (including ANDF and ABI).

Application Portability Profile *See* APP.

Application Program Interface *See* API.

Application Software Entity *See* ASE.

Application Specific Environment *See* ASE.

Application Specific Environment Description *See* ASED.

appropriate privilege A term substituted for superuser in IEEE 1003.1, so that IEEE 1003.6 could later redefine it.

Approve A penultimate phase of formal standardization, also known as balloting.

Architecture Neutral Distribution Format *See* ANDF.

AS (Applicability Statement) An Internet Standard that specifies a status (Required, Recommended, Elective, Limited Use, or Not Recommended) for an application or class of applications of a TS or a set of TSes; similar to a profile. An AS can also clarify, restrict, subset, or extend a TS.

ASC (Accredited Standards Committee) A standards committee that uses procedures that have been approved by ANSI. X3, X9, and T3 are examples.

ASC X3 (Accredited Standards Committee for Information Processing) The ASC for computers, information processing systems, and office systems. X3 TCs also act as TAGs for ANSI to JTC 1.

ASCII The U.S. seven bit codeset for English. IS 646 is a related European standard.

ASDO (Accredited Standards Developing Organizations) An organization that uses a procedure approved by ANSI to create standards. The IEEE is an example of one.

ASE (Application Software Entity) A generalized entity used by the POSIX Guide. It may include program, data, and documentation elements.

ASE (Application Specific Environment) A complete and coherent AEP subset for a particular application.

ASED (Application Specific Environment Description) A specification of an ASE plus additional options, parameters, formats, resource requirements, etc. for successful operation of the application.

Asia-Oceania Workshop *See* AOW.

assertion A codification of the standard document in the form of logical assertions written in stylized forms that are readily implementable in test suites.

assessors Technical experts used by NVLAP to conduct onsite assessments of testing laboratories.

balloting group A group of people who vote on formal approval of a standard; usually involving more people than participated in the working group for the standard.

Base certification An 88open certification for platform conformance.

base standard A standard that does not require other standards. Formally, an International Standard, Technical Report, or CCITT recommendation used in the specification of a profile.

BCS (Binary Compatibility Standard) The 88open equivalent of an ABI.

Berkeley sockets *See* sockets.

Berkeley Software Distribution *See* BSD.

Binary Compatibility Standard *See* BCS.

Board of Standard Review *See* BSR.

British Standards Institute *See* BSI.

BSD (Berkeley Software Distribution) A major historical version of the UNIX operating system and implementation of POSIX; produced by UCB CSRG.

BSI (British Standards Institute) The formal national standards body for the United Kingdom.

BSR (Board of Standard Review) The board within ANSI that reviews standards to make sure that proper procedures were followed during the creation.

CAE (Common Application Environment) An environment for a wide variety of coordinated interfaces and facilities. Like an OSE, but not specified by a formal standards body. Of particular value in procurements. Used by X/Open and EWOS.

Canadian Standards Association *See* CSA.

Carnegie Mellon University *See* CMU.

CBEMA (Computer Business Equipment Manufacturers Association) A consortium of mostly American hardware manufacturers.

CCITT (International Consultative Committee on Telegraphy and Telephony) An international body that develops recommendations for telecommunications interconnection and interoperability. Its recommendations are often adopted by ISO or ISO/IEC JTC 1 as standards.

CCTA (Government Centre for Information Systems) The part of HM Treasury concerned with information systems in the United Kingdom.

CD (Committee Draft) The first stage of an ISO draft standard.

CEC (Commission of the European Communities) The legislature of the European Community.

CEN (European Committee for Normalisation) A standards body similar to ISO, but for Europe.

CEN/CENELEC (Joint European Standards Institution) An international standards organization in Europe.

CENELEC (European Committee for Electrotechnical Standardization) A standards body similar to IEC, but for Europe.

Central Secretariat An old name for part of the ISO/IEC ITTF.

CEPT (European Conference of Post and Telecommunications Administrations) A European organization superseded by ETSI.

character set A set of graphic characters used in a human language. *See also* codeset.

China, Japan, Korea Joint Research Group *See* CJK JRG.

Chorus A micro-kernel based system related to the UNIX system, produced by Chorus systèmes of Paris, France. Chorus has an agreement with USL for compatibility with UNIX System V.

CJK JRG (China, Japan, Korea Joint Research Group) A group formed to work on a unified codeset to represent the languages of the three countries.

CLNP (Connectionless Network Protocol) An OSI protocol; also known as ISO-IP.

CLNS (Connectionless Network Service) The service provided by CLNP.

CMIP (Common Management Information Protocol) The OSI network management protocol.

CMIP over TCP/IP *See* CMOT.

CMOT (CMIP over TCP/IP) A method of using CMIP with TCP/IP.

CMU (Carnegie Mellon University) The original developer of Mach.

CNRI (Corporation for the National Research Initiative) An initial organizer of ISOC.

coded character set A set of numeric encodings of one or more character sets. *See also* character set.

Commission of the European Communities *See* CEC.

committee A standards committee drafts a standard. This kind of committee is frequently known more technically as a working group.

Committee Draft *See* CD.

Common Application Environment *See* CAE.

Common Management Information Protocol *See* CMIP.

common usage C The form of the C programming language defined in the first edition of *The C Programming Language* by Kernighan and Ritchie.

compliance Tested correspondence of software to a standards document. *See also* conformance.

compromise standard Similar to a minimal standard, but includes features not in all historical implementations and may even have completely new features. POSIX, or at least 1003.1, is an example.

Computer Business Equipment Manufacturers Association *See* CBEMA.

Computer Systems Laboratory *See* CSL.

Computer Systems Research Group   *See* CSRG.

conformance   Formal correspondence of software to a standards document, according to a degree specified in the document, but not necessarily tested. *See also* compliance.

conformance document   Required with a Conforming Implementation of ISO/IEC 9945-1. It is structured like the standard itself, specifies limits and options, specifies implementation defined behavior, may define otherwise undefined or unspecified behavior, and has any other documentation required in the standard.

conforming application   For the System Interface Standard, an application that meets any of the three levels of application conformance specified in the standard.

Conforming Implementation   An implementation of ISO/IEC 9945-1 that supports the execution of all Strictly Conforming POSIX.1 Applications. It has all the interfaces and behavior of IS 9945-1. Any additional functions or facilities must be described in a conformance document, must not change IS 9945-1 behavior, and must not require changes to any Strictly Conforming POSIX.1 Application.

Conforming POSIX.1 Application   An application that is like a Strictly Conforming POSIX.1 Application, but that may also use facilities from standards other than ISO/IEC 9945-1. It must document all standards used, together with options and limit dependencies.

Conforming POSIX.1 Application Using Extensions   An application like a Conforming POSIX.1 Application, except it may also use nonstandard facilities that are consistent with 9945-1. They must be documented.

Connection Oriented Network Protocol   *See* CONP.

Connection Oriented Network Service   *See* CONS.

Connectionless Network Protocol   *See* CLNP.

Connectionless Network Service   *See* CLNS.

CONP (Connection Oriented Network Protocol)   The traditional OSI network protocol, X.25, which provides the CONS.

CONS (Connection Oriented Network Service)   The traditional OSI network service, normally provided by X.25.

consensus   The point when commentators and developers of a standard reach agreement; not the same as majority vote or unanimity.

consistent   An implementation that follows an interface standard, but whose conformance can't be tested because there is no stable test suite, may be said by its vendor to be consistent with the standard.

coordination   Seeking international accord in functional standards; harmonization.

Corporation for Open Systems   *See* COS.

Corporation for the National Research Initiative   *See* CNRI.

COS (Corporation for Open Systems) A user and vendor consortium whose purpose is to help speed the availability of OSI products by defining vendor agreements as to the use of OSI.

Council The ISO Council.

CSA (Canadian Standards Association) The formal national standards body for the Canada.

CSL (Computer Systems Laboratory) The U.S. national test result validation body; part of NIST.

CSRG (Computer Systems Research Group) The group at the University of California, Berkeley that produces BSD. CSRG ceased operations at the end of 1992.

DAC (Discretionary Access Control) TCSEC Level C2 security.

DAD (Driveability Analysis Data) Describes the behavior of a user interface.

Danish Standards Association *See* DS.

Data Representation Interface *See* DRI.

DCA (Defense Communications Agency) The old name for DISA.

DCE (Distributed Computing Environment) A model such as OSF DCE.

de facto standard A widely used specification.

Defense Communications Agency *See* DCA.

Defense Information Systems Agency *See* DISA.

Department of Defense *See* DoD.

Detailed Network Interface *See* DNI.

DIN (German Standards Institute) The formal national standards body for Germany.

DIS (Draft International Standard) The middle stage of an ISO draft standard.

DISA (Defense Information Systems Agency) The U.S. military agency that holds the secretariat for PSSG.

Discretionary Access Control *See* DAC.

distributed computing Requires diversity, manageability, extensibility, and especially transparency.

Distributed Computing Environment *See* DCE.

Distributed Computing Environment *See* OSF DCE.

Distributed Management Environment *See* DME.

Distributed Object Management Model *See* DOMM.

Distributed Services Steering Committee *See* DSSC.

DME (Distributed Management Environment) An OSF specification and product intended to provide a uniform framework for efficient, cost-effective management of open systems.

DNI (Detailed Network Interface)   An API for complicated networking tasks; for direct use with a transport protocol.

DNS (Domain Name Service)   The Internet convention for domain names that can be applied to network nodes. On the Internet, DNS is normally implemented using the Internet Standard Domain Name System.

DoD (Department of Defense)   The United States military agency.

Domain Name Service   *See* DNS.

DOMM (Distributed Object Management Model)   A model for distribution of objects across networks included in UI-ATLAS.

DP (Draft Proposal)   The old term for CD.

Draft   The entry level of formal standardization, after the Propose or Study phases.

Draft International Standard   *See* DIS.

Draft Proposal   *See* DP.

DRI (Data Representation Interface)   A TCOS data representation API for SNI or DRI; like the OSI presentation layer.

Driveability Analysis Data   *See* DAD.

DS (Danish Standards Association)   The formal national standards body for Denmark, which provided a Sample National Profile for IS 9945-1.

DSSC (Distributed Services Steering Committee)   The TCOS-SS SEC steering committee that coordinates committees that are specifying interfaces to network services and protocols, such as P1003.8, P1003.12, P1003.17, P1238, P1238.1, and P1224.

due process   A process of standardization that provides an opportunity for participation from initiation to completion.

ECMA (European Computer Manufacturers Association)   A nonprofit vendor organization that promulgates standards and is also a liaison member of both ISO and IEC.

EDIF (Electronic Design Interchange Format)   A standard for the ASCII file format to be shared between a CAE application and printed circuit board layout applications.

EEI (External Environment Interface)   An interface for information interchange. IEEE 1003.2a UPE, User Portability Extensions, and IEEE 1201, Interfaces for User Portability, are for human to computer EEI. IS 9945-1 Chapter 10, Data Interchange Format, is for information EEI. IEEE 802.3 is for communications EEI.

EIA (Electronic Industries Association)   A consortium, primarily of American vendors, that developed RS-232-C and other ANSI standards.

Electronic Design Interchange Format   *See* EDIF.

Electronic Industries Association   *See* EIA.

ETSI (European Telecommunications Standards Institute) A standards body similar to CCITT, but for Europe.

EUC (Extended UNIX Code) A multibyte coded character code for Japanese.

European Committee for Electrotechnical Standardization *See* CENELEC.

European Committee for Normalisation *See* CEN.

European Computer Manufacturers Association *See* ECMA.

European Conference of Post and Telecommunications Administrations *See* CEPT.

European Forum for Open Systems *See* EurOpen.

European Telecommunications Standards Institute *See* ETSI.

European UNIX system Users Group *See* EUUG.

European Workshop on Open Systems *See* EWOS.

EurOpen (European Forum for Open Systems) An international users group based in Europe.

EUUG (European UNIX system Users Group) The old name for EurOpen.

evaluators Technical experts used by NVLAP to conduct general reviews of testing laboratories.

EWOS (European Workshop on Open Systems) A forum to provide and coordinate European input to international standardization of profiles.

EWOS Expert Group on the Common Application Environment *See* EWOS/EG-CAE.

EWOS/EG-CAE (EWOS Expert Group on the Common Application Environment) An EWOS group that has provided a taxonomy and a technical guide for profiles for CAE or OSE.

Executive Board The ISO Executive Board.

Extended UNIX Code *See* EUC.

extension A standard that adds to or modifies facilities of a base standard such as an API. An extension may be a separate document but the two documents are still a base standard.

External Environment Interface *See* EEI.

FDDI (Fiber Distributed Data Interface) A 100 Mbps fiber optic token ring LAN standard.

feature test macro A name, e.g., _POSIX_OPTION, and language of the form "if _POSIX_OPTION is defined, the implementation shall do one specific thing, otherwise it shall do another specific thing."

Federal Information Processing Standard *See* FIPS.

Fiber Distributed Data Interface *See* FDDI.

File Transfer, Access, and Manipulation *See* FTAM.

FIPS (Federal Information Processing Standard)   A specification produced by NIST for use by U.S. federal government agencies in writing RFPs. FIPS refer to national or international standards where possible and specify the values of all options.

FIPS 151 (NIST FIPS 151)   An option set for Draft 10 of IEEE P1003.1.

FIPS 151-1 (NIST FIPS 151-1)   An option set for the published IEEE Std 1003.1-1988 standard.

FIPS 151-2 (NIST FIPS 151-2)   The updated FIPS from NIST that specifies options for IEEE 1003.1-1990.

formal standard   Another name for a standard; sometimes used to distinguish it from a specification. Same as a de jure standard.

French Association for Normalization   *See* AFNOR.

FTAM (File Transfer, Access, and Manipulation)   The OSI file transfer protocol.

functional standard   Another name for a profile; often used in ISO documents, such as TR10000.

General Assembly   The policy making body within ISO.

General Services Administration Board of Contract Appeals   *See* GSBCA.

Generate certification   An 88open certification for platform conformance; includes base certification.

German Standards Institute   *See* DIN.

GOSIP (Government OSI Profile)   The U.S. government OSI procurement profile specified by NIST; FIPS 146-1.

Government Centre for Information Systems   *See* CCTA.

Government OSI Profile   *See* GOSIP.

Group of Ten   *See* SOS.

GSBCA (General Services Administration Board of Contract Appeals)   The U.S. government agency that tried the AFCAC 251 case where the Air Force attempted to specify SVID and SVVS for procurement.

GUI Wars   The historical discussion about GUI standardization, particularly as it involved Motif and OPENLOOK, eventually resulting in MTE and OTE. *See also* Tar Wars.

guide   A specification of good practices, perhaps in several alternatives, without specific IEEE recommendations.

guide   A model and a specification for an OSE or CAE, together with contextual information.

Han Characters Collection   *See* HCC.

Hangul   The Korean syllabary.

Hanzi   Chinese ideograms. Simplified Hanzi are used on the mainland, and traditional Hanzi are used elsewhere.

harmonization   Seeking international accord in functional standards; coordination.

HCC (Han Characters Collection)   A codeset for all known Hanzi (traditional and simplified), Kanji, and Hangul characters.

header files   *See* parameter files. *See also* headers.

headers   The 1003.1 standard requires these instead of parameter files; they are the same, except they are not required to be implemented as files.

HEMS (High-Level Entity Management System)   A proposal for remote node management on TCP/IP networks.

High-Level Entity Management System   *See* HEMS.

Hiragana   A Japanese syllabary used for foreign words.

historical implementation   An implementation that was used in deriving a standard or specification.

hosted   An implementation of a standard operating system interface on a dissimilar operating system is said to be hosted, or to be an emulation.

IAB (Internet Architecture Board)   The group responsible for design, engineering, and management of the TCP/IP protocols.

IANA (Internet Assigned Numbers Authority)   The authority who assigns protocol, port, and other numbers for TCP/IP protocols.

IBM Conformance Test Suite   *See* IBM CTS.

IBM CTS (IBM Conformance Test Suite)   A tool that measures conformance of a computer system to software standards, developed by IBM and written by Mindcraft.

ICMP (Internet Control Message Protocol)   A protocol that must be used with IP. ICMP provides routing redirection and some flow control.

IEC (International Electrotechnical Commission)   An international standards body for electrical and electrotechnical issues. *See also* JTC 1.

IEC TC47 (IEC Technical Committee 47)   The IEC TC for semiconductor devices that merged with ISO TC97 and IEC TC83 to form JTC 1.

IEC TC83 (IEC Technical Committee 83)   The IEC TC for information technology equipment that merged with ISO TC97 and IEC TC47 to form JTC 1.

IEC Technical Committee 47   *See* IEC TC47.

IEC Technical Committee 83   *See* IEC TC83.

IEEE (Institute of Electrical and Electronics Engineers)   An international professional organization. It creates its own standards and also submits standards to ANSI for approval as ANS.

IEEE Computer Society   *See* IEEE/CS.

IEEE P1003.0   *See* POSIX Guide.

IEEE P1003.10 (P1003.10 Supercomputing AEP)   This profile specifies a general environment for supercomputing applications.

IEEE P1003.11 (P1003.11 Transaction Processing AEP)   The POSIX profile for transaction processing.

IEEE P1003.13 (P1003.13 Realtime AEP)   A three part AEP being developed by the IEEE P1003.4 Realtime committee.

IEEE P1003.14 (P1003.14 Multiprocessing AEP)   This profile defines a platform, like P1003.18 PEP, but is not intended for direct use in other profile development.

IEEE P1003.15 (P1003.15 Supercomputing Batch Element AEP)   A profile being written by P1003.10, for issues specific to batch computing.

IEEE/CS (IEEE Computer Society)   The parent body of TCOS, which is the parent of TCOS-SS, which is the sponsor of the POSIX committees.

IEEE/CS Standards Activities Board   *See* SAB.

IEEE/CS Standards Coordinating Committee   *See* SCC.

IEEE/CS TCOS-SS Profile Steering Commitee   *See* PSC.

IEEE/CS TCOS-SS Sponsor Executive Committee   *See* SEC.

I18N (Internationalization)   The process of making a standard or interface independent of code sets, human languages, or cultural conventions. Such an interface must then allow localization. The acronym I18N is used because there are 18 letters between the I and the N of internationalization.

IESG (Internet Engineering Steering Group)   The steering group for the IETF.

IETF (Internet Engineering Task Force)   The group that creates detailed specifications of TCP/IP protocols for the IAB.

implementation   A software package that conforms to a standard or specification.

Implementation Agreement   An agreement to implement a standard in a certain manner and with specified options.

implementation defined   The implementation shall define and document program and data constructs and behavior.

information portability   The ability to move information among computers (perhaps across a network) without manual intervention.

Information Technology   *See* IT.

Information Technology Steering Committee   *See* ITSTC.

Information Technology Task Force   *See* ITTF.

Institute of Electrical and Electronics Engineers   *See* IEEE.

Institutional Representative   *See* IR.

interculturized   Another word for internationalized. Sometimes preferred because cultural conventions and language can vary within a nation.

International Association of Open Systems Professionals, The *See* UniForum.

International Consultative Committee on Telegraphy and Telephony *See* CCITT.

International Electrotechnical Commission *See* IEC.

International Organization for Standardization *See* ISO.

International Standard *See* IS.

International Standardized Profile *See* ISP.

International Telecommunications Union *See* ITU.

Internationalization *See* I18N.

internationalized A utility that can format its output according to local conventions as defined by users at runtime (a localization).

Internet Architecture Board *See* IAB.

Internet Assigned Numbers Authority *See* IANA.

Internet Control Message Protocol *See* ICMP.

Internet Engineering Steering Group *See* IESG.

Internet Engineering Task Force *See* IETF.

Internet Protocol *See* IP.

Internet Research Task Force *See* IRTF.

Internet Society *See* ISOC.

Internet Standard A specification approved by the IETF, IESG, and IAB, using the Internet Standards Process, and thus accepted for use in the Internet.

interoperability The ability of a system to provide information portability.

Interpretations A process of clarification of a standard after it has been formally approved.

IP (Internet Protocol) The key protocol in the Internet protocol suite, which is also known as the TCP/IP protocols. IP provides a common address space and routing over diverse network or link layer protocols.

IR (Institutional Representative) A representative to a standards body of an organization with an interest in standardization. Unlike most TCOS participants, IRs speak and ballot for their institutions.

IRTF (Internet Research Task Force) A research group for TCP/IP protocols, responsible to the IAB.

IS (International Standard) The final stage of an ISO draft standard.

is Considered by POSIX to be an obsolete equivalent for shall.

ISO (International Organization for Standardization) An international standards body with a wide range of responsibility. *See also* JTC 1.

ISO C ISO 9899:1990, produced by ISO/IEC JTC 1 SC22 WG14. Also known simply as Standard C.

ISO Development Environment *See* ISODE.

ISO TC97 (ISO Technical Committee 97)   The ISO TC for information processing systems that merged with IEC TC47 and TC83 to form JTC 1.

ISO Technical Committee 97   *See* ISO TC97.

ISOC (Internet Society)   An international nonprofit membership organization, formed in January 1992 to promote the use of the Internet for research and scholarly communication and collaboration. In June 1992 it became affiliated with the IAB, and thus with the IETF, the body that produces specifications for TCP/IP Internet Standards.

ISODE (ISO Development Environment)   A software package that emulates TP0 over TCP, thus permitting development of OSI protocols on top of TCP/IP networks.

ISO/IEC Conforming POSIX.1 Application   A Conforming POSIX.1 Application that uses only ISO/IEC standards.

ISO/IEC JTC 1 SC22 WG15 Security Rapporteur Group   *See* SRG.

ISO/IEC JTC 1 Special Group on Functional Standardization   *See* SGFS.

ISP (International Standardized Profile)   A Standardized Profile approved at the international level. Defined by TR10000.

IT (Information Technology)   A general term for technical topics related to computing and data communications.

ITSTC (Information Technology Steering Committee)   A standards group formed by the three European bodies CEN, CENELEC, and ETSI.

ITTF (Information Technology Task Force)   The ISO and IEC group that handles the publication and administrative details of creating standards.

ITU (International Telecommunications Union)   A United Nations treaty agency that is the parent body for CCITT.

Japan UNIX Society   *See* jus.

Japanese Industrial Standards Commission   *See* JISC.

JISC (Japanese Industrial Standards Commission)   The formal national standards body for Japan.

Joint European Standards Institution   *See* CEN/CENELEC.

Joint Technical Committee One   *See* JTC 1.

JTAP (U.S. TAG to JTC 1 Applications Portability Study Group)   U.S. input to TSG-1.

JTC 1 (Joint Technical Committee One)   A joint committee of ISO and IEC that is responsible for information processing standards, and is an ancestor body of WG15, the ISO POSIX committee.

JTFS (U.S. JTC TAG for SGFS)   U.S. TAG to SGFS.

jus (Japan UNIX Society)   A nonprofit organization that promotes sound development of technology, culture, and industry in information technology, especially that involving the UNIX system.

Kanji   Japanese ideograms.

Katakana   A Japanese syllabary used for Japanese words.

Kerberos   The de facto standard for authentication of users over networks; developed by MIT Project Athena.

K&R C   The form of the C programming language defined in the first edition of *The C Programming Language* by Kernighan and Ritchie; also known as common usage C.

language binding   A standard that specifies how a language independent standard is to be used with a specific programming language.

language binding defined   The language binding shall define and document program and data constructs and behavior.

language independence   *See* LI.

language-independent standard   *See* LIS.

legacy system   A system that does not necessarily conform to current standards, but must be taken into account anyway, due to large previous investment according to previous computing models.

LI (language independence)   A base standard not specified in terms of a specific programming language is language independent.

LIS (language-independent standard)   A specification of a base standard that does not depend on a specific programming language.

locale   An execution environment involving a human language and cultural conventions, settable in part or whole by the user at runtime.

localization   *See* L10N.

L10N (localization)   The local set of languages, character sets, and cultural conventions for setting at runtime by the user.

MAC (Mandatory Access Control)   TCSEC Level B1 security, involving security labels.

Mach   A micro-kernel based system related to the UNIX system, that was originally developed by CMU, and now by Transarc, Inc. The basis for OSF/1 of OSF.

Management, User Interface, System Interface, Information, Communications   *See* M.U.S.I.C.

Mandatory Access Control   *See* MAC.

may   An optional feature of an implementation. Most options have feature test macros instead of being specified using this word.

Memoranda of Understanding   Documents produced by OIW, EWOS, and AOW to coordinate their activities.

Message Handling System   *See* MHS.

MHS (Message Handling System)   The OSI mail and message protocol.

MIA (Multivendor Integration Architecture Consortium) A consortium founded in Tokyo that intends to produce an architecture that can be used to build distributed information processing systems with products from multiple vendors.

Military Standards *See* MIL-STDs.

MIL-STDs (Military Standards) A set of U.S. military standards, including some obsolete specifications for the TCP/IP protocols.

minimal standard A standard that avoids controversy and includes only easily agreed-upon features; least common denominator of existing products, e.g., SQL.

Ministry of Posts and Telecommunications *See* MPT.

Modular Toolkit Environment *See* MTE.

Motif A GUI favored by OSF. *See also* MTE.

MPT (Ministry of Posts and Telecommunications) The Japanese body that oversees telecommunications policy in Japan. It is not usually delegated formal responsibility for Japanese standards, but is influential.

MTE (Modular Toolkit Environment) The IEEE P1295.1 standards project related to Motif.

Multivendor Integration Architecture Consortium *See* MIA.

M.U.S.I.C. (Management, User Interface, System Interface, Information, Communications) A model for interface standards developed by CCTA in the United Kingdom.

NAMAS (National Measurement Accreditation Service) The U.K. national accreditation body for testing laboratories.

<National Body> Conforming POSIX.1 Application A Conforming POSIX.1 Application that also uses national standards.

National Bureau of Standards *See* NBS.

National Institute of Standards and Technology *See* NIST.

National Measurement Accreditation Service *See* NAMAS.

National Voluntary Laboratory Accreditation Program *See* NVLAP.

NBS (National Bureau of Standards) The old name for NIST.

NCSC (U.S. National Computer Security Commission) The group that produced TCSEC, the *Orange Book* security criteria.

NCSC specification and evaluation of trusted systems *See* TRUSIX.

NesCom (New Standards Committee) The IEEE Standards Board subcommittee that approves new work, along with the IEEE/CS SAB.

Network File System *See* NFS.

Network Management Forum *See* NMF.

New Proposal *See* NP.

New Standards Committee *See* NesCom.

Next Generation Computer Resources *See* NGCR.

NFS (Network File System) A stateless network file system developed by Sun Microsystems, Inc. and now widely distributed by other vendors.

NGCR (Next Generation Computer Resources) A U.S. Navy program that provides the Navy interface standards for computer resources in order to facilitate procurement of appropriate industry products.

NIST (National Institute of Standards and Technology) A United States federal government agency that produces government standards for procurement called FIPS. Formerly known as NBS.

NIST FIPS 151 *See* FIPS 151.

NIST FIPS 151-1 *See* FIPS 151-1.

NIST FIPS 151-2 *See* FIPS 151-2.

NIST POSIX Conformance Test Suite *See* NIST-PCTS.

NIST-PCTS (NIST POSIX Conformance Test Suite) A test suite for POSIX developed by NIST that tests for conformance to FIPS 151-1, which specifies option values for the IEEE Std 1003.1-1988 POSIX System Interface Standard.

NMF (Network Management Forum) A group that coordinates network management issues. Its members include X/Open, UI, and OSF.

NP (New Proposal) The preliminary stage of ISO standardization; similar to what IEEE/CS and TCOS call a PAR.

Number Czar Another name for IANA.

NVLAP (National Voluntary Laboratory Accreditation Program) The U.S. national accreditation body for testing laboratories; part of NIST.

Object certification An 88open certification for platform conformance; includes base and generate cetification.

Object Management Group *See* OMG.

OIW (OSE Implementation Workshop) A workshop cosponsored by NIST and IEEE/CS that produces implementation agreements among its participants to implement standards in certain manners and with specified options.

OIW *See* OSI Implementor's Workshop.

OMG (Object Management Group) A group that coordinates network management issues.

ONI (OSI Network Interface) A TCOS OSI service API (MHS, MOTIS, FTAM).

Open Software Foundation *See* OSF.

open specification A specification consistent with international standards, updated to conform to new standards, accomodate new technologies, and maintained by a public open consensus process. An open specification is usually also a de facto standard.

open system A system that implements interface specifications (preferably open specifications or standards) that promote application portability, interoperability, and user portability.

Open System Environment *See* OSE.

Open Systems Interconnection *See* OSI.

Open Toolkit Environment *See* OTE.

OPENLOOK A GUI favored by UI. *See also* OTE.

Operating Systems Standards Working Group *See* OSSWG.

option set A set of parameters or options to apply to a certain base standard. FIPS 151-1 is an option set for IEEE 1003.1 for use by U.S. government agencies in RFPs.

Orange Book *See* TCSEC.

OSE (Open System Environment) An environment specified by a set of IT standards and profiles for interfaces, services, and formats for interoperability and portability of applications, data, and people. The profiles should be comprehensive and consistent. Open specifications may be used where there is no standard. IEEE P1003.0 POSIX Guide specifies an OSE.

OSE Implementation Workshop *See* OIW.

OSF (Open Software Foundation) A consortium that produces both specifications, such as the AES, and software products, such as OSF/1. OSF produces the OSF DCE architecture.

OSF DCE (Distributed Computing Environment) The OSF model for distributed computing.

OSF/1 The OSF operating system, based on Mach.

OSI (Open Systems Interconnection) The movement of data and information among systems on a network by means of well-known network protocols, thus providing information portability. Several protocol suites fit this definition, including ISO-OSI and TCP/IP. As defined by ISO, OSI refers to a specific protocol model (with seven layers) and a specific protocol suite (that includes X.25, TP0, and TP4).

OSI Distributed Transaction Processing *See* OSI DTP.

OSI DTP (OSI Distributed Transaction Processing) ISO/IEC DIS 10026-1 (model), 10026-2 (service), 10026-3 (protocol), all September 1989.

OSI Implementor's Workshop (OIW) The old name for the OSE Implementation Workshop.

OSI Network Interface *See* ONI.

OSSWG (Operating Systems Standards Working Group) A U.S. Navy group within NGCR that handles operating system interface standards. OSSWG has been very active in POSIX standardization.

OTE (Open Toolkit Environment) The IEEE P1295.2 standards project related to OPENLOOK.

P1003.10 Supercomputing AEP   *See* IEEE P1003.10.

P1003.11 Transaction Processing AEP   *See* IEEE P1003.11.

P1003.13 Realtime AEP   *See* IEEE P1003.13.

P1003.14 Multiprocessing AEP   *See* IEEE P1003.14.

P1003.15 Supercomputing Batch Element AEP   *See* IEEE P1003.15.

PAR (Project Authorization Request)   The IEEE/CS term (used by TCOS-SS) for a new standards work proposal.

parameter files   Files in historical systems that specify numeric values for parameters, declare library functions, or define data types. *See also* headers.

pax   The P1003.2 user interface to both tar and cpio; also the Latin word for peace. *See also* Tar Wars.

pcode (pseudocode)   A language intermediate between the source code a programmer writes and the binary format a computer executes. Developed in UCSD Pascal to promote application portability.

PCTS (POSIX Conformance Test Suite)   A generic term defined in the IEEE 1003.3 Test Methods Standard, for a test suite that tests conformance of a system to POSIX.

PEP (POSIX Environment Platform profile)   The IEEE P1003.18 offshoot of IEEE P1003.1 that is producing a platform profile for general timesharing systems.

Petrotechnical Open Software Corporation   *See* POSC.

platform profile   A profile for a base environment, such as a time sharing system (P1003.18 PEP or NIST APP), workstation, personal computer, or multiprocessor system (P1003.14). Can be used in writing other profiles.

PMC (Project Management Committee)   A TCOS-SS SEC subcommittee that reviews requests for new projects or committees and reviews progress of existing projects or committees. The PMC can take no action itself, but it can recommend actions to the SEC.

Portable application   In relation to the POSIX System Interface Standard, the same as a conforming application.

portable filename character set   A source of considerable discussion during the standardization of 1003.1. It defines a minimal character set that is independent of any particular codeset, and requires that upper and lower case Latin characters be distinct.

Portable Operating System Interface   *See* POSIX.

POSC (Petrotechnical Open Software Corporation)   A consortium of information technology users that intends to develop a software platform for oil exploration and production.

POSI (Promoting Conference for OSI)   A Japanese OSI promotion group, analagous to COS or SPAG.

POSIX (Portable Operating System Interface)   A set of standards that will define a portable interface to the operating system. The term POSIX is a pun on UNIX and on Portable Operating System Interface.

POSIX Conformance Test Suite   *See* PCTS.

POSIX Environment Platform profile   *See* PEP.

POSIX Guide (IEEE P1003.0)   The document that specifies the POSIX OSE and serves as a reference model for POSIX standards and implementations. Produced by IEEE P1003.0, or POSIX.0.

POSIX Open System Environment   *See* POSIX OSE.

POSIX OSE (POSIX Open System Environment)   The OSE based on ISO 9945 (POSIX) and specified in IEEE 1003.0: POSIX Guide.

POSIX SP (POSIX Standardized Profile)   A standardized profile that requires conformance to IS 9945-1 (POSIX) and is coordinated with IEEE 1003.0.

POSIX Standardized Profile   *See* POSIX SP.

POSIX Standards Style Guide   *See* PSSG.

Professional and Technical UNIX Association, The   *See* USENIX.

profile   A document that indicates several base standards, with parameters, options, classes, or subsets, for building a complete computer system or in accomplishing a specific function. The term is defined by TR10000 (SGFS) and IEEE P1003.0.

Project Authorization Request   *See* PAR.

Project Management Committee   *See* PMC.

Project Proposal   The first step in the formal creation of a standard. Any individual can submit a Project Proposal to an ASC or ASDO to propose the creation of a standard.

Promoting Conference for OSI   *See* POSI.

Propose   A preparatory stage before formal standardization, in which interested parties meet to dicuss the need for a standard.

Protocol Standards Steering Group   *See* PSSG.

PSC (IEEE/CS TCOS-SS Profile Steering Commitee)   A committee to provide guidance for TCOS committees that are writing profiles.

pseudocode   *See* pcode.

PSSG (POSIX Standards Style Guide)   An internal TCOS-SS document about stylistic issues in writing POSIX standards.

PSSG (Protocol Standards Steering Group)   A U.S. military joint group chaired by DISA.

pthreads   POSIX threads, that is, the IEEE P1003.4 specification for lightweight processes.

public domain specification   A term used by OIW that is closely related to open specification and public specification.

public specification   A specification with a publicly available and stable specification. It is not required to have been produced by an open process.

Rapporteur Group on Conformance Testing   *See* RGCT.

Rapporteur Group on Coordination of Profile Activities   *See* RGCPA.

Rapporteur Group for Internationalization   *See* RIN.

recommended practice   A specification of procedures and positions preferred by IEEE.

Regional Workshop Coordinating Committee   *See* RWCC.

Remote File System   *See* RFS.

Remote Procedure Call   *See* RPC.

Request for Comment   *See* RFC.

Request for Proposals   *See* RFP.

Request for Technology   *See* RFT.

Requirements Specification   An Internet Standard AS for a class of protocols for a general purpose. Similar to a platform profile.

Review   Review of a standard for possible reballoting or retirement.

RFC (Request for Comment)   One in a series of Internet documents published online, including protocol specifications, technical reports, and poetry. All Internet Standards are RFCs, but not all RFCs are Internet Standards.

RFC 822   The Internet Standard for the format of electronic mail messages.

RFC 1036   The specification for the format of USENET news articles.

RFP (Request for Proposals)   A request for proposals to supply software or hardware, usually from a government agency.

RFS (Remote File System)   A stateful distributed UNIX file system developed by AT&T.

RFT (Request for Technology)   A term used by OSF; similar to an RFP.

RGCPA (Rapporteur Group on Coordination of Profile Activities)   A WG15 subgroup that produced terms of reference for profile coordination.

RGCT (Rapporteur Group on Conformance Testing)   A WG15 subgroup that helps coordinate conformance testing activities among member bodies.

RIN (Rapporteur Group for Internationalization)   A WG15 subgroup that helps coordinate I18N activities of members.

romaji   The Japanese use of Latin characters for foreign words.

root access   The almost unlimited privileges of the superuser. *See also* appropriate privilege.

RPC (Remote Procedure Call)   An API for remote execution of detailed functions.

RWCC (Regional Workshop Coordinating Committee)   A coordinating committee for OIW, EWOS, and AOW.

SAB (IEEE/CS Standards Activities Board)   The IEEE/CS group that normally approves standards projects after they have been proposed or balloted by their sponsor, such as TCOS-SS.

SC (Subcommittee)   A standards group that handles a specific technical subject for its parent Technical Committee. It may have Working Groups.

SCC (IEEE/CS Standards Coordinating Committee)   A high level standards oversight body within IEEE/CS.

SCCT (Steering Committee on Conformance and Testing)   The TCOS-SS SEC steering committee that coordinates assertions and test methods as specified by TCOS committees.

SCGUI (Steering Committee for Graphical User Interfaces)   The TCOS-SS SEC steering committee that Coordinates work on graphical user interfaces.

SEC (IEEE/CS TCOS-SS Sponsor Executive Committee)   The group that decides which committees and projects TCOS will sponsor. It is composed of committee chairs, officers, and Institutional Representatives.

Secretariat   A sponsoring body for a standard.

Senior Executives for Open Systems   *See* SOS.

Senior Executives for Standards   *See* SOS.

SGFS (ISO/IEC JTC 1 Special Group on Functional Standardization)   The JTC 1 group responsible for international standardization of profiles.

SGMP (Simple Gateway Management Protocol)   A predecessor of SNMP.

shall   A requirement on an implementation, or a requirement on a strictly conforming application.

should   A recommendation for an application, a requirement for a strictly conforming application, or a recommendation for an implementation.

SII (System Internal Interface)   An interface between components within an application platform. It may be standardized or not.

Simple Gateway Management Protocol   *See* SGMP.

Simple Mail Transport Protocol   *See* SMTP.

Simple Network Interface   *See* SNI.

Simple Network Management Protocol   *See* SNMP.

SMF (Systems Management Framework)   A model for managing heterogenous distributed systems included in UI-ATLAS.

SMTP (Simple Mail Transport Protocol)   The Internet Standard TCP/IP mail transport protocol.

SNAcP (subnetwork access protocol)   Used in the subnet sublayer of the OSI network layer.

SNDCP (subnetwork-dependent convergence protocol)   The convergence sublayer of the OSI network layer.

SNI (Simple Network Interface)   An API for simple networking with DNI or ONI.

SNICP (subnetwork-independent convergence protocol)   Used in the internet sublayer of the OSI network layer.

SNMP (Simple Network Management Protocol)   The de facto industry standard for network management; used with TCP/IP.

sockets (Berkeley sockets)   An interface for general networking services, first available in 4.2BSD.

SOE (Standard Operating Environment)   Bellcore's software environment for source code and user portability.

Software Testing International   *See* STI.

SOS (Senior Executives for Open Systems)   Also known as the Group of Ten, or Senior Executives for Standards, these high level executives from large corporations that use computers extensively sent a User Requirements Letter to each corporation's computer vendors in June 1992.

SP (Standardized Profile)   A profile that has been approved as a standard.

SPAG (Standards Promotion and Application Group)   A European OSI promotion group, analogous to COS or POSI.

specification   A document that specifies a certain technological area perhaps with a well-defined scope. A specification may be produced by a vendor, consortium, or user, and is not a formal standard.

SRG (ISO/IEC JTC 1 SC22 WG15 Security Rapporteur Group)   The WG15 forum for coordination for security work.

SSI (System Software Interface for Application Programs)   A historical proposal for a very comprehensive standard for large environments.

standard   A document that specifies a technological area within a well-defined scope; produced by a formal standardization process by a formal standards body, such as ISO, IEC, ANSI, or IEEE.

Standard Operating Environment   *See* SOE.

Standard Test Environment   *See* STE.

Standardized Profile   *See* SP.

Standards Promotion and Application Group   *See* SPAG.

Standards Subcommittee   *See* TCOS-SS.

STE (Standard Test Environment)   An assertion-based test suite from STI.

Steering Committee on Conformance and Testing   *See* SCCT.

Steering Committee for Graphical User Interfaces   *See* SCGUI.

STI (Software Testing International)   The coordinating body for STE.

Strictly Conforming POSIX.1 Application   An application that uses only IS 9945-1 facilities and applicable language standards, and that permits all implementation-defined or unspecified behavior, and all ranges of constants allowed in ISO/IEC 9945-1.

Study   A preparatory stage before formal standards development, in which proposals for formation of a formal standards working group may be made to a sponsoring body.

Subcommittee   *See* SC.

subnetwork access protocol   *See* SNAcP.

subnetwork-dependent convergence protocol   *See* SNDCP.

subnetwork-independent convergence protocol   *See* SNICP.

successful   A word formerly used of a true test.

superuser   The traditional UNIX security level that permits almost everything.

supplement   Another name for an extension.

SVID (System V Interface Definition)   The description of UNIX System V produced by USL.

SVVS (System V Verification Suite)   A test suite for System V developed by AT&T.

System V Interface Definition   *See* SVID.

System V Verification Suite   *See* SVVS.

System Internal Interface   *See* SII.

System Software Interface for Application Programs   *See* SSI.

system under test   A set of hardware, software, and documentation being tested for conformance to a standard.

Systems Management Framework   *See* SMF.

TAG (Technical Advisory Group)   One form of national delegation to an international body such as ISO.

Tar Wars   The historical discussion about standardization of a format for information archiving and interchange, originally involving P1003.1, which could not decide between tar and cpio and included specifications related to both. P1003.2 attempted to avoid the problem by specifying a common user interface, called pax. *See also* GUI Wars.

TC (Technical Committee)   A standards group that handles a general technical area for its parent standards body. It may have Subcommittees and Working Groups.

TCOS (Technical Committee on Operating Systems and Application Environments)   The IEEE Computer Society technical committee that is responsible for operating systems. *See also* TCOS-SS.

TCOS-SS (Standards Subcommittee)   The IEEE Computer Society subcommittee that is the formal sponsor for the POSIX standards projects.

TCP (Transmission Control Protocol)   The Internet transport protocol that provides a reliable duplex byte stream. *See also* UDP.

TCP/IP (Transmission Control Protocol/Internet Protocol)   The most widely implemented and used protocol suite worldwide. IP is the key protocol. TCP is a transport protocol used over IP.

TCSEC (Trusted Computer Security Evaluation Criteria)   The *Orange Book* of NCSC security levels and criteria.

Technical Advisory Group   *See* TAG.

Technical Board   The ISO Technical Board.

Technical Committee   *See* TC.

Technical Committee on Operating Systems and Application Environments   *See* TCOS.

Technical Report   *See* TR.

Technical Report 10000   *See* TR10000.

Technical Specification   *See* TS.

Technical Study Group 1   *See* TSG-1.

Test Environment Toolkit   *See* TET.

test method   A program or other method that performs a test, perhaps implementing an assertion.

test scaffold   A set of programs, libraries, directory structures, and configuration files that are used to run test suites. A test scaffold may be used to run more than one test suite.

test suite   Software that tests conformance to a standard or specification. A test suite may be run by a test scaffold.

testing laboratory   An organization that applies test methods to determine conformance of software to a standard.

TET (Test Environment Toolkit)   An environment for the development and execution of information processing system conformance and system tests, produced by Project Phoenix of OSF, UI, and X/Open.

TFA (Transparent File Access)   A distributed service that makes remote files appear to be local. NFS and AFS are examples of protocols that provide TFA.

thick language binding   A language binding with standardized interfaces for core services and language facilities plus a language independent description of the relevant system services.

thin language binding   A language binding with only standardized interfaces for core services and language facilities.

TIMS (Traditional Interactive Multiuser System)   The old proposed name for PEP, IEEE P1003.18.

TLI (Transport Layer Interface)   An interface for general networking services, derived in part from Berkeley sockets.

TR (Technical Report)   When produced by an ISO or JTC 1 committee such as SGFS, a TR is almost equivalent to an International Standard.

TR10000 (Technical Report 10000)   An ISO/IEC JTC 1 framework for standards and profiles, including issues of international standardization, conformance, process and procedures, maintenance, and taxonomy.

Traditional Interactive Multiuser System   *See* TIMS.

Transmission Control Protocol   *See* TCP.

Transmission Control Protocol/Internet Protocol   *See* TCP/IP.

Transparent File Access   *See* TFA.

Transport Layer Interface   *See* TLI.

true test   A test that returns PASS.

TRUSIX (NCSC specification and evaluation of trusted systems)   A testing organization for the *Orange Book.*

Trusted Computer Security Evaluation Criteria   *See* TCSEC.

TS (Technical Specification)   An Internet Standard for a protocol; similar to a base standard. *See also* AS.

TSG-1 (Technical Study Group 1)   The JTC 1 group responsible for interfaces for application portability.

UAOS (User Alliance for Open Systems)   A group of major North American users that formed to communicate to vendors their requirements for open systems. This group is creating a process to influence the rapid development of open systems by vendors.

UDP (User Datagram Protocol)   The Internet transport protocol that provides unreliable datagrams. *See also* TCP.

UI (UNIX International)   A corporation that provides guidance to USL on the development of the UNIX system. UI produces the UI-ATLAS architecture.

UI-ATLAS   The UI model for an open computing environment.

UNIX International   *See* UI.

UNIX System V   The major historical version of the UNIX operating system and implementation of POSIX, originally produced by AT&T, now by USL, with the guidance of UI.

UNIX System Laboratories   *See* USL.

undefined   An implementation may define a facility, but an application should not use it, unless it is a conforming application using extensions.

UniCode   A codeset that defines character codes to support most languages, in sixteen bits.

UniForum (International Association of Open Systems Professionals, The)   The user group with the most involvement in standards.

Universal Transformation Format 2   *See* UTF2.

unspecified   An application should accept any plausible behavior, and an implementation may specify a behavior. An application that depends on a specific behavior is using extensions.

U.S. JTC TAG for SGFS   *See* JTFS.

U.S. National Computer Security Commission   *See* NCSC.

U.S. TAG to JTC 1 Applications Portability Study Group   *See* JTAP.

USENIX (Professional and Technical UNIX Association, The)   The oldest UNIX system user group.

User Alliance for Open Systems   *See* UAOS.

User Datagram Protocol   *See* UDP.

user group   A non-profit organization related to the UNIX operating system, with individual members, and with education as one of its goals.

USL (UNIX System Laboratories)   The corporation that owns the UNIX trademark, writes the SVID, and produces UNIX System V. *See also* UI.

/usr/group   The old name for UniForum.

UTF2 (Universal Transformation Format 2)   A mechanism favored by ISO/IEC JTC 1 that converts characters into one or more bytes that can pass cleanly through a system. Plan 9 from Bell Labs implements a UniCode interface using UTF2.

Verification Suite for X/Open   *See* VSX.

Virtual Terminal   *See* VT.

VSX (Verification Suite for X/Open)   A test suite for the X/Open Portability Guide, developed by UniSoft.

VT (Virtual Terminal)   The OSI remote login protocol.

weasel wording   Careful choice of words to avoid deciding among two or more choices.

WG (Working Group)   A standards group that drafts a standard for its parent standards body. It may be a subsidiary of a Subcommittee or a Technical Committee.

will   Considered by POSIX to be an obsolete equivalent for shall.

working group   A group that drafts a standard. It may be composed of technical experts (as in IEEE), delegations from national bodies (as in ISO), or such other members as are deemed appropriate by the parent standards body.

Working Group   *See* WG.

X/Open (X/Open Company, Ltd)   A consortium that produces specifications, such as the XPG, and test suites, such as VSX, to resolve incompatibilities among computer systems and software components.

X/Open Company, Ltd   *See* X/Open.

X/Open Portability Guide   *See* XPG.

X/Open System Management   *See* XSM.

X/Open TP (X/Open Transaction Processing) Published "Online Transaction Processing Reference Model," 1987, and "Preliminary Specification — Distributed Transaction Processing: The A Specification," 1990.

X/Open Transaction Processing *See* X/Open TP.

X/Open Transport Interface *See* XTI.

XPG (X/Open Portability Guide) The specification produced by X/Open for a Common Application Environment (CAE).

XSM (X/Open System Management) An X/Open project to develop specifications for infrastructure for other system management activities, such as those of IEEE P1003.7.

XTI (X/Open Transport Interface) An API for general networking services, derived from AT&T TLI.

Index

N